Canine Nutrigenomics

The New Science of Feeding Your Dog for Optimum Health

W. Jean Dodds, DVM
Diana R. Laverdure

Wenatchee, Washington U.S.A.

Canine Nutrigenomics
The New Science of Feeding Your Dog for Optimum Health
W. Jean Dodds, DVM
Diana R. Laverdure, MS (2015)

Dogwise Publishing
A Division of Direct Book Service, Inc.
403 South Mission Street, Wenatchee, Washington 98801
1-509-663-9115, 1-800-776-2665
www.dogwisepublishing.com / info@dogwisepublishing.com

Limits of Liability and Disclaimer of Warranty:
The author and publisher shall not be liable in the event of incidental or consequential damages in connection with, or arising out of, the furnishing, performance, or use of the instructions and suggestions contained in this book. This publication contains the opinions and ideas of its authors. It is intended to provide helpful and informative material on the subjects addressed in the publication. It is sold with the understanding that the authors and publisher are not engaging in rendering veterinary, medical, health or any other kind of personal or professional services in the book. The reader should consult his or her veterinary, medical, health or other competent professional before adopting any of the suggestions in this book or drawing inferences from it. The authors and publisher specifically disclaim all responsibility for any liability, loss or risk, personal or otherwise, which is incurred as a consequence, directly or indirectly, of the use and application of any of the contents of this book.

Library of Congress Cataloging-in-Publication Data
Dodds, W. Jean, author.
  Canine nutrigenomics : the new science of feeding your dog for optimum health / W. Jean Dodds, DVM, Diana R. Laverdure.
     pages cm
  Includes bibliographical references and index.
  ISBN 978-1-61781-154-8
  1. Dogs--Nutrition. 2. Dogs--Food. 3. Dogs--Health. I. Laverdure, Diana, 1965- author. II. Title.
  SF427.4.D62 2014
  636.7--dc23
                           2014036035

ISBN: 978-161781154-8

Printed in the U.S.A.

To all dogs with vibrant health
waiting to be uncovered, and
people who love them.

Let food be thy medicine and medicine be thy food.

-Hippocrates

Table of Contents

Acknowledgments

The authors would like to acknowledge and thank the many people whose support and efforts made this book possible. Our gratitude begins with the dedicated team of scientists of the National Human Genome Research Institute (NHGRI) and throughout the world who collaborated on the Human Genome Project, the international effort to sequence and map the known genes in the human body, known as the genome. Their groundbreaking work has paved the way for new advances in the study of genetic components of diseases, including the important role of environmental factors such as nutrition on gene expression and complex disorders, and has enabled the emerging study of nutrigenomics.

The NHGRI also supported a project to sequence the dog genome, led by Kerstin Lindblad-Toh, Ph.D. of the Broad Institute/MIT Center for Genome Research, enabling our canine companions to benefit from the same advances in genomic technologies as humans. The cat genome has also been sequenced. We are extremely grateful for the work of these pioneering scientists.

We would also like to thank the scientists and researchers who are applying this information of human and companion animal genomics to advancing the fields of individualized medicine and nutrition for people and the animals we love. We have cited hundreds of their studies throughout this book. (Note that even though this book focuses on the dog, important parallel studies are also being applied to the cat.)

Jean and Diana would especially like to acknowledge and thank Drs. Barbara Fougère of Australia and Sue Armstrong of the United Kingdom for their valuable contributions that address the herbs, raw foods and other nutrient needs of animal cancer patients.

Writing a book, especially one of this scope and magnitude, is a team effort, and in our case we are grateful to all those at Dogwise Publishing who have enabled us to bring our vision to life. We would like to thank Charlene Woodward, Nate Woodward, Jon Luke and Lindsay Peternell for understanding the importance of this subject matter and supporting us along the lengthy journey from the book's gestation to completion. We would especially like to thank Larry Woodward, our editor at Dogwise, whose editing prowess enabled us to raise this book to levels far surpassing what we had originally thought possible. That is what great editors do, and that is what Larry did for us.

To our significant others, we thank Jean's husband Charles and Diana's partner Rodney for their support and devotion through more than two years of long nights, rewrites and seemingly endless attention to detail. Thankfully, they are also perfectionists.

Jean would also like to remember her faithful companions over the years, and especially Issho, the angel whose short life on earth taught us so much about caring and how wholesome nutrition helps animals to thrive even in the face of adversity.

Diana would also like to thank her beloved dog, Chase. For more than a dozen years he has been her best friend, confidante and inspiration on her journey to help all dogs be the best they can be. She looks forward to many more wonderful years, and adventures, together.

INTRODUCTION

Obesity. Gastrointestinal disorders. Skin irritations. Chronic yeast infections. Behavioral issues. Arthritis. Autoimmune diseases. Heart disease. Cancer. These are just a few of the common health conditions plaguing our dogs in skyrocketing—and in some cases epidemic—numbers.

These conditions might not appear to share much in common, but they all result from inflammation that originates at the deepest level in your dog's body—his cells. Where does this inflammation come from? Much of it stems from the lifestyles our dogs share with us, their caretakers—and especially from their modern diet. As you will soon see, many of the foods that are marketed to nourish our dogs actually wreak havoc on them from the inside out, resulting in rampant obesity and chronic disease (Dodds, 2014; Dodds, 2014a). But it doesn't have to be this way.

There is scientific information out there to help your dog live a long life bursting with health and free of chronic illness. You just likely haven't heard much about it until now. This information is what *Canine Nutrigenomics: The New Science of Feeding Your Dog for Optimum Health* is all about.

In the following pages, we will reveal the latest scientific findings showing how nutritional ingredients "speak" to your dog's body at the cellular level. We will disclose how many of the foods you (and likely your veterinary professional) consider healthy are really sending *un*healthy messages to your dog's genes. And, we will offer powerful tools to maximize your dog's health by feeding him to promote optimal gene expression, no matter what his current condition (more on gene expression in a minute).

The concept of eating healthy is not new, but it's only over the past decade that scientists have really begun to understand how diet affects us at the deepest level—the level of our cells. The major breakthrough occurred in 2003 with the completion of the

Human Genome Project, a groundbreaking international research program in which scientists sequenced and mapped the location of the known genes in the human body. (Sequencing means determining the exact order of the chemical base units, signified by the letters A, T, G and C that make up a strand of DNA) (NHGRI, 2011). Our DNA contains our genes, which provide the instructions to make proteins that determine everything about us, from our gender and eye color to our ability to fight off disease. An organism's complete set of DNA, including all of its genes, is called its genome. The human genome contains an estimated 20,000 to 25,000 genes, each of which codes for an average of three proteins. We all have trillions of cells, and just about every one of these cells contains a complete copy of our **genome** (NHGRI, 2011; NHGRI, 2012). Understanding the genome is critical to treating, managing and preventing illness, because *virtually every disease has a genetic basis* (NHGRI, 2011).

And humans aren't the only ones to benefit from genomic mapping. Scientists have also sequenced the genomes of many other species, including dogs. (A Boxer named Tasha was the first dog to have her DNA sequenced!) The Dog Genome Project demonstrated that people share an even closer bond with our canine companions than we previously realized—right down to the structure and evolution of our genes (Broad Institute, 2014). There are approximately 21,000 genes in the canine genome (Starr, 2011). In 2013, researchers from the University of Chicago and other international institutions found that *humans and domestic dogs share an extensive parallel genomic evolution, particularly in genes associated with digestion and metabolism, neurological processes and diseases such as cancer.* According to the researchers, these genes have likely evolved in parallel due to the close living environment shared by humans and dogs over many thousands of years, including possibly scavenging for food together (Lee, 2013; Wang et al., 2013). This is really exciting news (but probably not *surprising* to those of us who feel deeply connected to our dogs!) because it means that both species can benefit from much of the same new scientific information regarding the best way to eat for optimum cellular health.

But exactly how does food communicate with our cells and control our genes? Although the body contains trillions of cells that contain complete copies of the genome, not all cells behave the same; rather, they specialize with different identities and functions (The University of Utah, 2014). Some cells become heart cells, while others become bone cells, brain cells, kidney cells, muscle cells, skin cells and so on. What makes cells different? Every gene codes for proteins, but not all genes make proteins in all cells all of the time. Instead, different sets of genes are turned on (active) or off (suppressed) to make proteins in various cells at different times (NHGRI, 2012a; The University of Utah, 2014). The process of turning genes on or off inside a cell is called **gene expression**. The way our genes express determines a great deal about our destiny. But what controls gene expression?

This is where the **epigenome** comes in. The epigenome is a structural layer that surrounds our DNA and the proteins they are attached to. The epigenome initiates chemical reactions within cells that control gene expression, determining which genes are turned on or off and which proteins are produced (NHGRI, 2012a; Sample, 2009; The University of Utah, 2014). By changing a cell's gene expression, the epigenome also changes the cell's destiny, determining whether it will become a brain cell, a heart cell or a skin cell—and whether it will become a healthy cell or a diseased cell (The University of Utah, 2014).

And *this* is where food comes in. We now know that the epigenome is highly responsive to environmental signals—including diet. This brings us to the exciting new scientific field—and the topic of this book—called **nutrigenomics** (nutri-gen-*om*-ics). Nutrigenomics, a combination of the words *nutrition* and *genomics*, is the science of how diet affects the epigenome and thus gene expression, which in turn alters our genetic predisposition toward health or disease (Dodds, 2014; Dodds, 2014a; Elliot and Ong, 2002; Fekete and Brown, 2007; Swanson, Schook and Fahey, 2003).

Just as we inherited our genes from our parents, our epigenome also has a cellular memory that can be passed from one generation to the next (The University of Utah, 2014). This means that a mother and father's lifestyle decisions—including the quality of their diet—will influence the epigenome of their offspring! Unlike the genome, however, we *can* alter our epigenome over time with new environmental signals, such as optimum nutrition. And that is exactly what you will learn to do with your dog's diet!

In the following pages, we'll explore how diet has contributed to many of the chronic illnesses prevalent in the canine population today, and we will provide you with the latest scientific findings on nutritional ingredients that can prevent, manage and even reverse these illnesses. You will also learn how to distinguish between foods that *appear* healthy, but for one reason or another actually send unhealthy signals via the epigenome and should be removed from your dog's diet.

We have also identified certain foods that show so much scientific promise to create cellular health and vitality in dogs that we have deemed them "canine functional superfoods." These foods are listed in Chapter 2 and all mentions of them throughout the book appear in ***bold italic*** type so that you can easily identify them.

You will also learn about a simple, cost-effective testing method to determine whether your dog has an underlying epigenetic food intolerance/sensitivity, so that you can remove any offending ingredient(s) from his diet. This is important because no food, regardless of how healthy it is supposed to be, can send healthy messages to the cells if it causes an undesirable reaction. At the time of this writing, co-author W. Jean Dodds' groundbreaking saliva-based food sensitivity test, NutriScan (which we will discuss at length in Chapter 6), can identify sensitivities to 24 different foods with a simple saliva test that you do at home and mail to the author's Hemolife Diagnostics laboratory. You'll receive the results back within ten days. The implications of such a test for individually tailoring your dog's diet are exciting!

For your convenience, we've broken the book into four sections, as follows:

Part I: *Nutrigenomics: An Overview of the Science-based Approach to Creating Health through Food* (Chapters 1, 2 and 3). These chapters provide a detailed background of nutrigenomics and introduce the concept of functional foods. We'll show you how to tell the "good" from the "bad" and give you many examples of foods you're likely feeding your dog that could be sending unhealthy messages to his cells. In Chapter 3, we'll uncover some astounding revelations about mass-market commercial pet foods that you likely have not read about before.

Part II: *Building the Canine Nutrigenomics Diet: The Basal Diet* (Chapters 4 and 5) shows you how to formulate your dog's nutrigenomics basal diet—the "foundation" on which the rest of the diet will be built. We'll cover basal diet options for puppies, adult dogs, seniors and high-performance dogs (athletes, pregnant bitches and lactating dams). In this section, you'll learn that much of the information about "complete and balanced" diets that you've been "fed" (pun intended!) by the commercial pet food industry (and perhaps even your veterinary professional) is based on an outmoded way of thinking about our dogs' nutritional needs, and you'll be offered an alternative solution based on the principles of nutrigenomics.

Part III: *Functional Food Solutions for Common Canine Health Conditions* (Chapters 6 to 11) delves into some of the most prevalent chronic canine health issues, their underlying causes and nutritional solutions to get your dog back on the road to optimum health. We'll discuss at length conditions such as obesity, food sensitivities/intolerances, arthritis, cancer and many more. If your dog currently suffers from one or more health issues, this is the section you'll find yourself turning to again and again for the ingredients scientifically proven most effective at treating, managing and even reversing these diseases at the cellular level. In this section you'll also learn about NutriScan.

Part IV: *Living the Nutrigenomics Lifestyle* (Chapters 12 to 14) shows you how to apply what you've learned to suit your individual situation and gives important tips for making any category of diet, from kibble to home-cooked, more nutrigenomic-friendly. You'll also learn how to stock your kitchen so that you always have ideal dog-friendly foods on hand, and we'll give you tips to help you remain on track for the duration of your dog's life. For those of you who feed a commercial diet, you'll find important information on how to read pet food labels in Appendix B.

We have also included numerous Case Studies beginning in Chapter 6 describing the remarkable success that can be achieved using a nutrigenomic-based nutritional approach. You will find them under the heading "Success!"

Throughout this book, you'll find the following icon 🦴. This bone represents the concept of "digging deeper" (just like a dog digs deep to bury a cherished bone!). When you see it, along with a short caption next to it, you'll know that you can turn to Appendix A, aptly titled "Digging Deeper," and find more information about the topic. This is our way of giving those of you who want a bit more science on certain topics the opportunity to get it, without bogging the book down with too much technical jargon for those of you who aren't interested.

Takeaway Points at the end of each chapter summarize the key ideas and will likely come in handy to refresh your memory of the chapter's contents. And, you won't want to miss our Resources section at the end of the book, which directs you to online retailers offering the ingredients and products mentioned throughout.

As you become empowered with groundbreaking nutrition knowledge, you might find yourself making shifts in your own diet based on the principles of nutrigenomics. That's great! As we said, humans and dogs share a lot in common genomically, and we can *all* benefit from consuming foods that send healthy signals via our epigenome.

Before we begin, there is one important point we want to make clear. We're thrilled and excited by the amazing nutritional world that's about to open up to both you and your dog, but we don't want you to become intimidated by this information, thinking that you have to implement all of it. This book is not an all or nothing doctrine; please use what works for your schedule, finances and lifestyle. If you want to prepare your dog's meals, that's great and we'll show you how. If you want to continue feeding kibble, you'll be especially interested in Chapter 12, where we'll offer valuable tips to help you purchase a product free of ingredients that can send unhealthy messages to your dog's cells and that is closest in keeping with the principles of nutrigenomics, as well as how a few small changes can "kick up your kibble" and greatly boost its nutritional impact. So, as with anything in life, our advice is to take what works for you and leave the rest. Whatever that is, your dog will thank you for it!

Just one last note. While we refer to dogs in the male gender throughout the book, we mean no offense to the girls. We do this strictly to keep the language of the book simple and streamlined.

We hope that you're excited about becoming a driving force in a movement aimed at reversing some disturbing health trends taking place among companion animals today.

If you're ready to get in on the cutting-edge of canine nutrition and start your dog's journey toward optimal health, then turn the page and let's get started!

Part I

Nutrigenomics: An Overview of the Science-based Approach to Creating Health through Food

Chapter 1

Nutrigenomics: An Overview

"It's all in the genes." How many times have you heard this expression, or a variation of it, uttered by a relative, friend or co-worker, typically meaning that they have little or no control over their own state of health and longevity? "I can't help it if I'm overweight. It's all in my genes." Or, perhaps, "It doesn't matter if I eat this ice cream. My grandparents and parents had diabetes, so I will, too. It's just in our genes." Maybe you have even allowed your own thoughts to wander down this path, where you justified certain poor nutritional decisions by telling yourself that your destiny, for better or worse, is largely pre-determined by your inherited DNA. And while you likely don't take this thought process to quite the same level with your canine companion, there are parallels. Many genetic disorders are accepted in certain breeds, as are a whole host of age-related chronic illnesses. In the waiting room of a veterinarian's office, one of the authors (DRL) once overheard a veterinarian (not hers!) casually inform his client that, "dogs just begin breaking down at age 11." If "breaking down" at a certain age is an inevitable by-product of our dogs' collective genomic heritage, is it worth investing more time and money on their diet? Can nutrition prevent or cure their current chronic illnesses? Can food really mean the difference between a senior dog who is riddled with disease and decay and one who enjoys vibrant health?

The answer is—absolutely!

Our genes make us unique

As you'll recall from the Introduction, humans and dogs have genomes, which is the collection of all the genes in our bodies. The human body contains an estimated 20,000 to 25,000 genes (NHGRI, 2011), while dogs have about 21,000 genes in their genomes (Starr, 2011). Everyone's genome contains two sets of genes—one inherited from each parent. Genes, which are made up of strands of DNA, contain the instructions, or genetic code, for building all of the proteins that make a living organism

(NHGRI, 2012; NHGRI, 2012a; Silverman, 2008; The University of Utah, 2014). But genes do not all behave the same in their protein-making activity. Not all genes make proteins all of the time in all of the cells. They also do not all make the same types and amounts of proteins. Certain genes in cells can be turned on (active), meaning that they produce proteins, while others are turned off (suppressed). This protein-making process is called gene expression, and it determines how cells look, grow and act. As we already discussed, gene expression determines the identity and function of cells (e.g., the difference between a brain cell, a heart cell and a skin cell); it can also determine the difference between a healthy cell and an unhealthy cell (NGHRI, 2012a; The University of Utah, 2014).

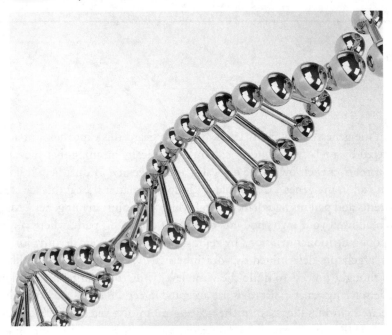

A rendering of DNA (istockphoto.com)

Each of us has a specific genetic code that makes us unique (except for identical twins, who have the same genetic code). Genes determine why you have blue eyes and your brother has brown eyes, and why your dog is a Labrador Retriever and not a Chihuahua. DNA does not change; this underlying genetic code remains the same throughout our lives, no matter what. Regardless of the outside environment, you will always have blue eyes (unless you wear colored contact lenses) and your Labrador will never become a Chihuahua!

Most genes are the same or similar in everyone, but a small number (less than one percent of the total) are slightly different. It is that tiny difference that determines our unique genetic characteristics, called our **genotype** (NHGRI, 2012; Ostrander, 2012; Ostrander & Wayne, 2005; Science Daily, 2007; Stein, 2004).

Our epigenome communicates with our genes and tells them how to behave

As we discussed in the Introduction, we are also born with a second layer of chemical compounds that surrounds our DNA, called the **epigenome** (epigenome means "above the genome"). The epigenome acts as the instruction manual for our genes (NHGRI, 2012a). But unlike our DNA, which is inherited from our parents, the chemical "tags" that make up the epigenome come from a variety of *environmental* sources, both good and bad. These include natural sources such as food and man-made sources such as medicines or pesticides. As the epigenome marks the genome with its chemical tags, it modifies gene expression, instructing genes whether to turn on or off (i.e., produce proteins or not), and which types of proteins to produce (NHGRI, 2012a; The University of Utah, 2014). Chemical tags that originate from unhealthy environmental sources may send unhealthy messages to the genome, producing undesirable modifications in gene expression. In this way, the epigenome serves as a bridge (or perhaps more of a superhighway) between the environment and the genome.

The graphic on the next page illustrates the relationship between genetics and environmental factors that influence the epigenome and play a large role in determining whether genes will express for health or disease. Notice that the dynamic between all of these circles converges in the center, forming a diamond shape: this diamond represents nutrition.

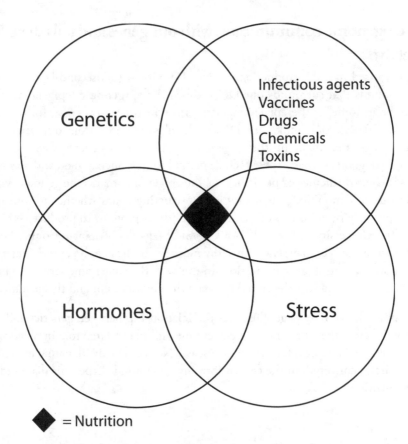

Role of nutrition in etiology of autoimmune diseases
(adapted from: Talal, N. (1998) Transpl Proc 20(4), June)

How does the epigenome turn genes on and off?

The epigenome uses two main signaling tools to mark the genome and turn genes on and off:

- **DNA methylation** is the process by which chemical tags, called methyl groups, are added to one of the four chemical bases that make up a DNA molecule, which directly affects the DNA in the genome. DNA methylation that is functioning improperly can work in such a way as to throw gene expression off balance, which can lead to a variety of serious health consequences, including numerous diseases (Hardy & Tollefsbol, 2011; Hyman, 2011; NHGRI, 2012a; Phillips 2008). For example, cancer cell genomes are often hypomethylated (under-methylated) compared to normal cells, while genes that suppress tumors are often silenced in cancer cells due to hypermethylation (over-methylation) (Phillips, 2008). Later on, we'll give you examples of foods that promote optimum DNA methylation. If your dog has cancer, you'll want to pay special attention to this section in Chapter 9.

> • **Histone modification** indirectly affects the DNA in a genome. Histones are proteins found in cell nuclei that act like spools around which very long molecules of DNA wind, condensing the DNA into neat chromosome packages that enable them to fit inside the nuclei. When epigenetic chemical tags grab onto the tails of histones, they affect how tightly or loosely the DNA is wound. A tight wrapping can hide certain genes and cause them to be turned off, while a loose wrapping can reveal previously hidden genes, causing them to turn on (NHGRI, 2012a).

Just like the genome, the chemical tags that make up the epigenome can also be inherited (NHGRI, 2012a; The University of Utah, 2014). *This means that parents who make unhealthy lifestyle choices—such as poor diet—can pass down epigenetic tags to their children, predisposing them to unhealthy gene expression!*

But, unlike our genetic code, which remains fixed for life, *the epigenome can change according to environmental signals* (NHGRI, 2012a; The University of Utah, 2014). This means that even individuals who are dealt a poor epigenetic hand can alter their fate by making consciously healthy lifestyle choices. As the epigenome transforms according to these positive environmental signals, it will in turn create chemical tags that initiate beneficial gene expression. This is critical because gene expression determines an individual's **phenotype**, which is the sum of the traits we can see or measure, such as height, blood type and behavior—as well as the presence or absence of disease (Dodds, 2014; Dodds, 2014a).

By feeding your dog nutritional ingredients that send desirable signals to his epigenome and promote healthy gene expression, you can manage environmental influences to help him live a life of optimum health, rather than one plagued with chronic illness (Dodds, 2014; Dodds, 2014a; Choi & Friso, 2010; Epigenetics NoE, 2014).

🦴 **A brief history of epigenetics**

🦴 **The epigenome: a tale of two twins**

🦴 **Epigenetics: the difference between queen bees and worker bees**

Remember, the dog bone icon means these subjects are explored in more detail in Appendix A.

Food and inflammation

When lifestyle factors such as poor nutrition send unhealthy messages to the epigenome, it can take years before an outward problem manifests. This means that your dog could appear fine today, but inside his tissues are percolating with inflammation. One day, you might wake up and find that your seemingly healthy dog suddenly can't stop scratching, or that he has gas and diarrhea that won't go away, or that he suffers from recurring yeast infections—or, Heaven forbid, that he has cancer. Or, maybe his temperament has changed, and you simply chalk up his agitated or aggressive behavior as "bad" or "obstinate." But these physiological and behavioral changes are anything but sudden. They are the result of long-term inflammation triggered by a combination of factors that are strongly influenced by environmental assaults on the epigenome. When these assaults become too much for the body to handle, it finally reaches a tipping point, and a disease state appears (Dodds, 2014; Dodds, 2014a).

Most of us think of inflammation as something we can see on the outside of our bodies, such as swelling, bruising or redness. In fact, internal inflammation at the cellular level is a natural part of the body's defense mechanism (Perricone, 2010).

There are two types of cellular inflammation:

Acute cellular inflammation is a temporary state of inflammation that arises for a specific purpose and then goes away once its job is done. Acute inflammation is necessary to attack and kill pathogens such as bacteria, protozoa and other parasites, fungi and even viruses that cause infection (Punchard, Whelan & Adcock, 2004).

Chronic cellular inflammation is a sustained inflammatory condition that leads to a variety of diseases. Chronic inflammation occurs when the tissues or organs receive inflammatory mediator messages that cause them to react as though the pathogen were still present; as a result, they don't complete the inflammatory cycle. Rather than repairing themselves, they throw their infection-fighting response into overdrive and remain in an ongoing state of inflammation that can wax and wane for an entire lifetime (Beynen et al., 2011; Perricone, 2010; Punchard, Whelan & Adcock, 2004). Chronic inflammation creates an environment in the body that leads to obesity and other chronic illness, which we'll discuss throughout the book.

What is inflammation?

Here are just a few examples of the many conditions associated with chronic inflammation:

- Allergies
- Arthritis
- Autoimmune diseases
- Cancer
- Cognitive issues
- Diabetes
- Gastrointestinal disorders
- Heart disease
- Kidney disease

- Liver disease
- Obesity
- Skin and coat disorders
- Urinary tract disorders

Functional foods: the key to your dog's health

We know that diet plays a critical role in determining gene expression (Daniel, 2002), but how can we know *which* foods promote optimum gene expression by sending healthy signals to the cells? Scientists have lately invested a lot of time researching specific nutritional ingredients that alter gene expression in a manner that can help prevent, manage and even reverse a variety of chronic illnesses (Daniel, 2002; Elliot & Ong, 2002; German et al., 2002; Swanson, Shook & Fahey, 2003). These beneficial ingredients are called **functional foods**.

Functional foods are nutritional ingredients, such as certain botanicals, amino acids, vitamins and **phytonutrients** (plant chemicals that have been shown to convey beneficial affects on health) that send signals to the epigenome to trigger healthy gene expression (Essa & Memon, 2013; Kaput & Rodriguez, 2006). You will learn about a variety of functional foods that fight inflammation, promote healthy DNA methylation and treat, manage and prevent disease throughout the book.

To promote optimum gene expression, we must do two things: (1) create a diet based around functional foods that send healthy signals to the cells; and (2) reduce or eliminate foods that promote unhealthy gene expression. But this is not always as obvious as it might seem. A number of factors can complicate whether or not a specific ingredient, or a combination of ingredients, is functional. Even foods that are typically functional can become harmful if laced with added chemicals, hormones or antibiotics that adversely affect the epigenome. You know the old saying, "An apple a day keeps the doctor away?" Well, if that apple has been genetically modified (more on GMOs in Chapter 3) or laced with pesticides, it may send unhealthy signals to the cells, sabotaging its functional effect (Dodds, 2014; Dodds, 2014a).

The fact that every dog is an individual with his own genome also complicates matters *because an ingredient that benefits one dog's genetic code might not benefit a dog with a different genetic code.* That same ingredient could even prove harmful. For example, your dog might thrive on lamb, while your neighbor's dog could have a genetically inherited (or an acquired) intolerance to lamb that causes him to become itchy and bloated if he eats it. NutriScan, which we'll discuss in detail in Chapter 6, can tell you how your dog will react to specific foods so that you can eliminate any reactive ingredients from his diet.

Myth: I feed my dog a commercial prescription diet, so I don't need to worry

Some commercial pet food manufacturers have responded to the latest scientific findings regarding nutrition and gene expression by creating specialized diets that incorporate functional ingredients. The issue is that in order to achieve commercial success, pet food manufacturers must target these diets to large groups of dogs. Common commercial diets are segmented by body type (e.g., small breed, large breed), life stage (e.g., puppies, pregnant or lactating bitches, adults, seniors), activity level (e.g., growth, active, performance) or medical condition (e.g., overweight, kidney disease). While these products might work for some dogs, they are still limited in their effect. There are just too many genetic and environmental variables for a generalized prescription diet to meet every dog's needs.

Another concern is "mystery" ingredients that find their way into mass-market commercial pet foods. For example, if your dog has a food allergy, you might purchase a limited-ingredient, novel protein commercial diet. But consider this: a recent study from Europe looked at 12 limited-ingredient commercial foods intended for use in food elimination trials for dogs with adverse food reactions (Ricci et al., 2013). Eleven novel protein diets and one hydrolyzed diet were checked for contamination by any animal ingredients not identified on the label. *Ten of the 12 foods studied contained ingredients of animal and fish origin that were not listed on the label!*

If your dog doesn't respond favorably to a commercial **limited-antigen diet** (a diet that contains few, or no, ingredients known to cause adverse food reactions), the diet could be contaminated with potential allergens. Yet, you have no way of knowing about those allergens because the sources are not listed on the label.

Because of the mystery surrounding undeclared ingredients in commercial pet foods, the authors of the above study concluded that if a dog is unresponsive to a commercial limited-antigen diet, a homemade diet containing a novel protein should be tried before ruling out an adverse food reaction as the cause of the problem (Ricci et al., 2013).

There are a whole host of issues associated with mass-market commercial dog foods that can counteract their functional effect. We will discuss them in detail in Chapter 3.

Your dog can do better

While nutrigenomics is a new and emerging scientific field, we already know enough about the genome and epigenome to help our dogs benefit from a diet that creates amazing health improvements. As Professor Michael Müller, scientific director of the Netherlands Nutrigenomics Centre at Wageningen University, points out:

> *A statistical genetic risk to a disease or condition does not mean that you will express the disease or condition… It is an important starting point, but then the freedom and responsibility is to choose your way; to choose the right diet and optimized lifestyle for your genetic pre-disposition (Epigenetics Project Blog, 2012).*

Takeaway Points

- The genome is the collection of all the genes in the body. Dogs have about 21,000 genes.

- Genes, which are made up of strands of DNA, contain the instructions, or genetic code, for building all the proteins that make a living organism.

- Gene expression, the process of turning genes on and off, determines how cells look, grow and act.

- All individuals have a specific genetic code, which remains fixed for life.

- The epigenome is a second layer of chemical compounds that surrounds DNA and acts as an instruction manual for genes, modifying gene expression by instructing genes whether to turn on or off (produce proteins or not).

- The epigenome uses two main signaling tools to mark the genome and affect gene expression—DNA methylation and histone modification.

- Just like the genome, the chemical tags that make up the epigenome can also be inherited.

- Unlike genetic code, which remains fixed for life, the epigenome is highly responsive to environmental signals.

- Sending positive environmental signals to the epigenome will in turn create chemical tags that initiate beneficial gene expression.

- Sudden health issues typically take a long time to develop and are triggered by environmental assaults on the epigenome. When these assaults become too much for the body to handle, disease manifests.

- Certain inflammation is normal and serves an important function; however, chronic inflammation is harmful and leads to a host of health problems.

- Epigenetic signaling tools can manage and prevent chronic inflammatory diseases by affecting the expression of pro-inflammatory molecules.

- Functional foods include certain botanicals, amino acids, vitamins and phytochemicals that activate disease-fighting genes and suppress genes that promote disease.

- Many factors can complicate whether or not a food is functional, such as added chemicals, hormones or antibiotics.

- Since each dog has his own genome, a food that benefits one dog might not create the same effect for another—or might even prove harmful.

- NutriScan saliva test for food intolerances can determine how a dog will react to specific foods so that reactive ingredients can be removed from his diet.

- Commercial prescription diets might work for certain subsets of dogs, but they are too generalized to meet the individual needs of every dog.

- Commercial diets can be contaminated with ingredients of animal origin that are not declared on the label.

- There are many other reasons why commercial foods can send unhealthy messages to the cells. The functional effect of a food is only as good as the sum total of its ingredients.

Chapter 2

Functional Nutrition:

What to Feed Your Dog

So far, we've learned that creating optimum health at the cellular level involves two key nutritional steps:

- Step 1: Feeding a diet rich with functional foods that signal the epigenome to initiate healthy gene expression.

- Step 2: Reducing or eliminating foods that send harmful messages to the epigenome and trigger unhealthy gene expression (Fekete & Brown, 2007).

Functional foods, as you'll recall, are nutritional ingredients that switch on a gene's expression to fight disease and switch off the expression to promote disease (Bauer, 2001; Kaput & Rodriguez, 2006).

In this chapter, you'll learn how to identify functional ingredients within the three major categories that comprise your dog's diet:

- Carbohydrates
- Protein
- Fat

We'll also discuss the benefits of incorporating as many organic foods as possible into your dog's diet.

Functional carbohydrates

With all the rage of "low-carb" or "no-carb" diets for both people and dogs, you might be surprised that we're even addressing this food category. It's true that dogs don't have a specific dietary requirement for carbohydrates, but, once again, we're not looking at your dog's diet based on numbers; we want to create an optimized diet that sends healthy messages to his epigenome. It just so happens that carbohydrates are essential to accomplishing this goal because they contain lots of functional nutrients—*if they are the correct type of carbohydrates*. Functional carbohydrates are packed with health-promoting vitamins, minerals and phytonutrients (also called phytochemicals) that promote health at the cellular level.

As we mentioned in Chapter 1, phytonutrients are chemicals that occur naturally in plants ("phyto" means plant in Greek). While phytonutrients are not essential to keep you alive like proteins, fats, vitamins and minerals are, they have been shown to convey important health benefits on those who consume them. **Carotenoids**, which include alpha-carotene and beta-carotene, are probably the most widely known class of phytonutrients. Carotenoids are the red, orange and yellow pigments that give vegetables such as sweet potatoes, carrots and pumpkins their lovely hue. **Flavonoids**, another class of phytonutrients, include anthocyanin pigments that give berries and other dark-colored fruits and vegetables their blue, purple and red tints (Linus Pauling Institute, 2013). Phytonutrients have potent **antioxidant** properties (antioxidants are substances that help protect cells from oxidative damage caused by free radicals) and research shows that they protect against heart disease and cancer and block tumor activity (Drewnowski & Gomez-Carneros, 2000) (much more on this in Chapter 9).

Phytonutrients may work via a variety of mechanisms, including:

- Serving as antioxidants.
- Enhancing immune response.
- Enhancing cell-to-cell communication.
- Altering estrogen metabolism.
- Converting to vitamin A (retinol) (more on this in Chapter 8).
- Causing cancer cells to die (apoptosis) (more on apoptosis in Chapter 9).
- Repairing DNA damage caused by exposure to environmental toxins.
- Detoxifying carcinogens through the activation of the cytocrome P450 and Phase II enzyme systems (USDA, 2005).

But the benefits of fruits and vegetables don't stop there. A groundbreaking 2014 study conducted on mice and published in the journal *Molecular Nutrition and Food Research* identified how components called exosomes secreted by plant and animal cells actually "speak" to each other via a form of interspecies (plant-animal) cellular communication. The investigators showed that exosome-like nanoparticles (EPDENs) derived from edible plants including ginger and carrot modulated the cellular pathways of the mice cells in a manner that created anti-inflammatory and antioxidant effects. This new finding is among the latest in what is sure to be an ongoing emergence of new information regarding the link between nutritional ingredients, the epigenome and gene expression (Ji, 2014; Mu et al., 2014). It's also one more reason to make sure your dog eats his fruits and veggies!

We recommend incorporating the following functional carbohydrates into your dog's diet:

- **Cruciferous vegetables,** such as broccoli, cauliflower, Brussels sprouts, cabbage and bok choy (see Chapter 9 for the benefits of these foods in fighting cancer).

- **Fresh, whole fruits,** such as apples, bananas, *berries* (see Chapter 9), cantaloupe and watermelon. Note that while fruits contain the simple sugars fructose and glucose, *fruits in their whole, unadulterated form* possess functional attributes. Fruit contains lots of healthy fiber, which insulates the sugar. Because it takes the digestive tract longer to break down the fiber, sugar from fruit is absorbed into the bloodstream slowly, avoiding any sharp rises in blood sugar (Egan, 2013). Fiber in fresh fruit also helps promote optimal GI functioning and weight loss. Note that fruit juice, without the benefit of fiber, is a sugary fiasco! Also, *never* give your dog grapes or raisins, which are toxic fruits for dogs.

- **Gluten-free grains,** such as millet, quinoa, sorghum and gluten-free oats.

- **Green leafy vegetables**, such as kale and collard greens (see sidebar).

- **Legumes**, such as kidney beans, pinto beans, black-eyed peas, garbanzo beans (chickpeas), lentils, lima beans and peas.

Leafy greens and oxalates

Oxalates are naturally occurring plant substances present in many fruits, vegetables, nuts and seeds—including green leafy vegetables. Under certain circumstances (such as in the case of "leaky gut syndrome"), excessive amounts of oxalates may be absorbed from the gut into the blood, urine and tissues. When oxalates are excreted via the urine they can bind with calcium, causing calcium-oxalate crystals and potentially forming into kidney stones (Oxalosis and Hyperoxaluria Foundation, 2008).

Many people warn against feeding green leafy vegetables to dogs due to the presence of oxalates. However, few "experts" on this topic mention that many other foods, such as sweet potatoes, certain types of beans (black beans, white beans, great northern beans, navy beans and pink beans), beets, brown rice, buckwheat and peanuts also contain high levels of oxalates, as do corn, wheat and soy (Oxalosis and Hyperoxaluria Foundation, 2008), which as we know are commonly found in commercial pet foods!

Since leafy greens contain so many health benefits for our canine companions, we do not recommend eliminating them all from your dog's diet, unless under the medical advice of your veterinarian. The key is simply to avoid greens with the highest oxalate levels, including spinach, beet greens and Swiss chard, and to opt instead for lower oxalate choices, such as collard greens, watercress, cabbage, bibb lettuce and dino kale. And, of course, feed in moderation. Please visit the Oxalosis and Hyperoxaluria Foundation (www.ohf.org) for a list of oxalate levels in various foods.

> Dogs with diet-related hyperoxaluria, the condition of high levels of oxalates in the urine, can benefit from supplementation with calcium citrate given with meals (and avoiding other mineral supplements). Calcium binds oxalates in food, creating a calcium-oxalate complex that cannot be absorbed in the gut and instead passes without harm via the stool (NYU School of Medicine, n.d.; Puotinen & Straus, 2010).

Modern dogs and high starch diets

We'd like to bring up one more important point before we move on. In January 2013, a group of evolutionary geneticists from Uppsala University in Sweden published a study in the journal *Nature* showing that dog domestication was accompanied by evolutionary selection at three key genes involved in starch (complex carbohydrate) digestion—AMY2B, MGAM and SGLT1. The authors concluded that mutations in these genes enable dogs to thrive on a high-starch diet. The researchers stated: "Our results indicate that novel adaptations allowing the early ancestors of modern dogs to thrive on a diet rich in starch, relative to the carnivorous diet of wolves, constituted a crucial step in the early domestication of dogs" (Axelsson et al., 2013, pp. 360).

Notice that the researchers qualify their statement with, "relative to the carnivorous diet of wolves." A key finding of the study was that dogs have between four and 30 copies of a gene that codes for amylase, the enzyme that breaks down starch, while wolves have only two copies (Axelsson et al., 2013). But the authors fail to give us a reference by telling us how many of these genes a true, undisputed omnivore has. What if that number is 100 or 10,000? This omission certainly makes the significance of their finding ambiguous (Knueven, 2014). The authors also note that humans, who are true omnivores, express amylase in the saliva (the first point of contact for starch digestion), while dogs only express amylase in the pancreas (Axelsson et al., 2013).

Obviously, we do not disagree that dogs can benefit from certain functional complex carbohydrates—in fact, we just finished saying as much. However, there is a big difference between incorporating some functional starches into a dog's diet and drawing the conclusion that dogs "thrive on a diet rich in starch," without even qualifying the type or quality of the starch. Making that stretch is, in our opinion, a mindset that has resulted in the decades-long deterioration in the health of our nation's dogs and landed us right in the middle of a national canine health crisis, where obesity and chronic disease are the norm, not the exception. Given that most modern dogs consume a primarily high-starch diet turned out by the mass-market pet food companies, we think the evidence quite clearly indicates that dogs *do not* thrive on a high-starch diet!

In fact, we will continually reveal throughout this book that high-glycemic starches such as corn and cereal grains used in pet foods are a leading cause of the rampant obesity and chronic disease pervading the canine population. To quote our dear friend and noted holistic veterinarian, Doug Knueven, DVM, "To say that because dogs can digest starch proves that they thrive on a high-starch diet is like asserting that because people can process ethanol and glucose we thrive on a diet rich in rum and cookies!" We couldn't agree more!

Functional proteins

Protein is arguably the most important nutrient in your dog's diet because he cannot survive without it. Protein is responsible for building and repairing muscles and tissues and provides the structure for skin, hair, nails, bones, joints, tendons, ligaments, cartilage and muscle fibers (Case et al., 2011).

Here are a few important functions of protein:

- Antibodies made of proteins help protect the body from foreign "attackers" such as viruses and bacteria, keeping the immune system strong.

- Collagen (a protein) forms most of the body's connective tissue.

- Messenger proteins, including some types of hormones, regulate various systems in the body (e.g., insulin, which is essential to controlling blood glucose levels).

- Protein enzymes carry out almost every one of the thousands of chemical reactions that take place in the cells.

- Proteins help regulate muscle action.

- Protein provides essential amino acids.

- Transportation proteins in the blood carry essential vitamins and nutrients throughout the body (e.g., hemoglobin, which carries oxygen to the tissues).

(Case et al., 2011; National Library of Medicine, 2013; PetMD, 2013)

Given protein's many important jobs, it stands to reason that dogs should eat lots of it to flourish. This is especially true because protein is constantly being turned over, so the body needs a constant supply to replenish it (Case et al., 2011; PetMD, 2013).

High quality protein

But it isn't just the *amount* of protein that's important; it's the *quality*. Much has been written in the past about protein quality. In fact, you can pick up just about any bodybuilding magazine and learn detailed information about protein and the types of foods you should eat for maximum muscle development. That's all very important, but we're going to examine protein quality in a whole new way. Your dog's protein will still need to be high quality in the traditional sense, but from here on in it will also need to be *functional*. In the next chapter, we'll divulge all the factors that can turn an otherwise high quality protein into an unhealthy food that contributes to inflammation and chronic disease, which is the exact opposite of what we're trying to achieve for optimum cellular health and beneficial gene expression.

Amino acids: the building blocks of protein

Proteins are made up of long chains of smaller units called amino acids. One protein molecule can contain hundreds or even thousands of amino acids (Case et al., 2011). Dogs utilize 22 different amino acids, which combine in various sequences to form different proteins. Twelve of these amino acids are called "non-essential" because a dog's body can make them in sufficient amounts to meet their nutritional requirements, so they're not necessary in the diet.

The other ten are called "essential amino acids" because dogs cannot manufacture enough of them in their bodies to maintain health. The essential amino acids must be supplied by the diet (Case et al., 2011).

The ten essential amino acids for dogs:

- Arginine
- Histidine
- Isoleucine
- Leucine
- Lycine
- Methionine
- Phenylalanine
- Threonine
- Tryptophan
- Valine

In addition to supplying the ten essential amino acids, dietary protein is also the body's primary source of nitrogen. The body needs nitrogen to synthesize the non-essential amino acids and other molecules necessary for life, such as various hormones and neurotransmitters (Case et al., 2011).

The body can only synthesize protein if *all* essential amino acids are present in a sufficient amount. If even one essential amino acid is deficient, the entire process of protein synthesis shuts down, regardless of how much of every other amino acid is available. So, the body's dietary requirement isn't for protein per se; *it's for essential amino acids*. As the building blocks of protein, amino acids are the building blocks of life. So, for a protein source to be high quality, it must supply the correct composition of essential amino acids. It must also have a high biological value, meaning that the body can efficiently absorb and utilize the amino acids and nitrogen the protein supplies (Case et al., 2011).

Based on these criteria, the highest quality proteins for dogs come from animal sources. The winners (in alphabetical order) are:

- Dairy
- Eggs
- Fish
- Muscle meats
- Organ meats

But "high quality" takes on new meaning when it is re-defined to include sources that are *functional*. Here's how we define a high quality, functional protein according to the principles of nutrigenomics:

- Bioavailable (easily digested and assimilated).
- Free of contaminants such as chemicals, hormones and antibiotics.
- Does not promote a food intolerance/sensitivity.
- Does not contain compounds that send unhealthy messages to the epigenome, triggering unhealthy gene expression.
- Unadulterated (e.g., non-GMO) and unprocessed or minimally processed.

Based on this definition, we encourage you to rotate among the following functional, high quality protein sources:

- Dairy products made from *goat or sheep sources*, including milk, cheese and yogurt (preferably raw and organic).
- Eggs (preferably free-range and organic).
- Fish that are low in mercury, including sardines, wild-caught Alaskan salmon (avoid farm-raised), Pollack and catfish. Avoid high-mercury fish such as tuna (especially albacore or white tuna), King mackerel, tilefish, shark and swordfish. We also typically do not recommend giving your dog shellfish, such as shrimp, crab, lobster, oyster and clams, since some dogs can experience the same severe allergic reactions as people. (Note that later on in this book, we do recommend several supplements that contain shellfish derivatives due to their therapeutic properties, including glucosamine and green-lipped mussel extract. These are safe for most dogs, but if you have any concern that your dog may be allergic to shellfish, consult with your veterinarian before using these products.)
- Muscle meat and organ meat from novel animal sources, such as bison or buffalo, duck, goat, pork, rabbit, turkey and venison (preferably grass fed and naturally raised without hormones or antibiotics). These sources are less likely to cause food intolerances/sensitivities than more common animal proteins, such as beef, chicken and lamb.

The amount of protein your dog requires depends upon his age, activity level, specific health issues and also the quality of the protein (Kealy, 1999). Remember that the less bioavailable the protein source, the more of it your dog will need in order to assimilate the amino acids. So, if your dog eats a commercial diet chock full of inferior quality, grain-based proteins (more on this in the next chapter), that diet will need to contain a higher percentage of protein than a home-prepared diet relying on fresh, highly bioavailable animal protein sources.

Functional fats and oils

Just as low carb and no carb diets are all the rage, so, too, are low fat diets. But unless your dog has a specific medical condition that warrants fat restriction, such as pancreatitis, don't deny your dog this important source of nutrients. Dietary fat supplies dogs with the most concentrated and digestible form of energy (more than twice the amount of calories per gram than protein or carbs), provides important essential fatty acids such as *omega-3 fatty acids*, plays a necessary role in the absorption of fat-soluble vitamins and promotes a healthy nervous system (Case et al., 2011; PetMD, 2013). Dogs can also consume a higher proportion of their diets as fat because they have a much greater capacity to burn fat for energy than humans do (more on this in Chapter 5 when we discuss canine athletes) (Hill, 1998). Plus, they love the taste!

Fats are broken down into two main categories:

- Saturated fats, which are mostly found in animal foods (e.g., meat, dairy). Saturated fats are solid at room temperature.

- Unsaturated fats, which are mostly found in plant oils. Unsaturated fats are liquid at room temperature. There are two types of unsaturated fat:

  - Monounsaturated fat e.g., olive oil, peanut oil.

  - Polyunsaturated fat e.g., sunflower oil, sesame oil (also known as polyunsaturated fatty acids, or PUFAs). Omega-6 and *omega-3 fatty acids* are also types of PUFAs. You will be hearing much more about the amazing benefits of *omega-3s* throughout the book.

(Web MD, 2014)

We recommend incorporating a variety of functional fats into your dog's diet. Here are some of our favorites:

- Chicken fat or lamb fat (as long as your dog does not have a food intolerance/sensitivity to chicken or lamb).

- Fatty fish that are low in mercury and rich in *omega-3 fatty acids*, such as those listed above.

- Novel meat sources, such as those on page 23 above.

- Oils, such as fish oil (for *omega-3s*), borage oil, *coconut oil,* hemp oil, olive oil, primrose oil, pumpkin seed oil and sunflower oil.

How to purchase oils

When purchasing oils, look for those that are "expeller pressed" to ensure optimum purity. Expeller pressing mechanically crushes the oil from the nut or seed. Otherwise, the oil has likely been extracted using hexane, a petroleum product made from crude oil! According to the U.S. government's Agency for Toxic Substances and Disease Registry (ATSDR) Toxic Substances Portal:

Most of the n-Hexane used in industry is mixed with similar chemicals called solvents. The major use for solvents containing n-Hexane is to extract vegetable oils from crops such as soybeans. These solvents are also used as cleaning agents in the printing, textile, furniture, and shoemaking industries. Certain kinds of special glues used in the roofing and shoe and leather industries also contain n-Hexane. Several consumer products contain n-Hexane, such as gasoline, quick-drying glues used in various hobbies, and rubber cement (ATSDR, 2011).

But don't bother checking for hexane on the ingredient label; it won't be there. Since hexane evaporates during processing, the FDA doesn't require it to be listed on food labels! Expeller pressed oils cost a little more than those using hexane, but we think it is a small price to pay to avoid consuming crude oil!

We urge you to never feed hydrogenated oils (trans fats) to your dog (or to eat it yourself!). Hydrogenated oils, created when liquid oil is converted to a solid, have been implicated in chronic diseases such as heart disease, diabetes and obesity. The most common hydrogenated oils are margarine and vegetable shortening.

Since dietary fat is much more energy dense than carbohydrates and protein, the higher the percentage of it in your dog's diet, the more calories he'll consume. This is an especially important consideration for overweight dogs, which we'll discuss at length in Chapter 7.

> ## Functional canine superfoods
> We love the following functional foods for dogs so much that we deemed them "canine functional superfoods." As we mentioned in the Introduction, these foods are listed in bold, italic type throughout the book for easy reference:
>
> - Berries (e.g., blueberries, cranberries, but not strawberries)
>
> - Coconut oil
>
> - Curcumin
>
> - Honeybee products, *raw* (not suitable for puppies)
>
> - Medicinal mushrooms
>
> - Milk thistle
>
> - Omega-3s
>
> - Pomegranates
>
> - Probiotics
>
> - Spirulina

Organic: A term your dog can sink his teeth into

You'll recall from Chapter 1 that the epigenome is made up of chemical compounds that originate from environmental sources such as food that may contain harmful pesticides and herbicides, many of which have been linked to a variety of adverse health effects ranging from neurological disorders to cancer (more on pesticides and herbicides in the next chapter). Unless you grow your own food, purchasing organically farmed foods is the only way to reduce or eliminate harmful pesticides from your dog's diet. The term "organic" is legally defined and regulated for both human and pet food by the USDA's National Organic Program (NOP), which sets and enforces national standards for organic products.

NOP definition of organic

The USDA regulates the use of the term "organic" on food packaging as follows:

- **100% Organic:** Made with 100% organic ingredients.

- **Organic:** Made with at least 95% organic ingredients.

- **Made With Organic Ingredients:** Made with a minimum of 70% organic ingredients with strict restrictions on the remaining 30%, including no genetically modified organisms (GMOs).

- **Products with less than 70% organic ingredients** may list organically produced ingredients on the side panel of the package, but may not make any organic claims on the front of the package.

(Organic.org, 2013)

Organic foods *do not* contain the following:

- Antibiotics or growth hormones (in food production animals)
- GMOs
- Ionizing radiation
- Pesticides
- Sewage sludge
- Synthetic fertilizers

(EWG, 2014; Organic.org, 2013)

Some people claim that because of toxic runoff, air pollution, acid rain and other factors related to the generally toxic environment in which we live, no food is truly organic. Our belief is that there are things in life we can control and things we cannot. While we can't control the depleted state of our nation's soil or the chemical composition of the rain, we *can* control the ingredients we consume and feed our companion animals, and we choose to promote vibrant health by selecting ingredients that are as pure and functional as possible. People who eat organic products have been shown to have lower pesticide levels in their bodies (Lu et al., 2006; Lu et al., 2008), and we like the sound of that. Other health problems linked to pesticides include brain and nervous system toxicity, cancer and hormone disruption as well as skin, eye and lung irritation (EWG, 2012). If you want to create optimum health at the cellular level, choosing organic whenever possible just makes sense.

Buying organic: building your organic priority list

For many of us, feeding our dogs a primarily organic diet is not feasible because of the higher cost of organic foods. For that reason, we suggest that you do as we do—create an organic priority list. Prioritizing your organic purchases will help you provide your family and animal companions with the safest, purest foods possible, while not blowing your entire budget at the grocery store. For those of you who can afford to buy everything organic, fantastic! But if you're like most of us, you'll want to pick and choose which organic foods you invest in.

The Dirty Dozen Plus™ and the Clean 15™

To help us determine which foods to buy organic, we have turned to The Environmental Working Group (www.ewg.org). The EWG provides research-based information about the toxins in our food supply and environment, so that we can make healthier choices about how we live. Each year, the EWG releases two important lists to help us reduce our exposure to pesticides from fruits and vegetables: the Dirty Dozen Plus™ reveals the 12+ fruits and veggies that contain the most pesticides, while the Clean 15™ tells us the 15 that contain the least (EWG, 2014).

Below are the EWG's two most recent lists (2014) at the time of this writing. Please note that while we have included all the foods in the lists in order to make them complete, we have placed an asterisk (*) next to the foods that you should *not* feed your dog, due to potential toxicity or danger. However, you can feel free to indulge in them yourself!

The Dirty Dozen Plus™ (2014) (buy these foods organic if possible):

- Apples
- Strawberries*
- Grapes* (*never* feed your dog grapes!)
- Celery
- Peaches
- Spinach
- Sweet bell peppers
- Nectarines—imported
- Cucumbers
- Cherry tomatoes
- Snap peas—imported
- Potatoes
- Hot peppers*
- Kale/collard greens

(EWG, 2014)

This year, the EWG's Plus category highlights leafy greens (kale and collard greens) and hot peppers* (do not feed these to your dog). These crops did not meet the EWG's traditional Dirty Dozen™ ranking criteria, however they did frequently contain trace levels of highly hazardous pesticides that are toxic to the nervous system (EWG, 2014).

Note: The EWG found that the average potato contained more pesticides by weight than any other food (EWG, 2014). This is very important, as many people who prepare homemade diets for their dogs use potatoes, and they are commonly substituted for grains in grain-free commercial dog foods. Given this, we strongly advise using organic potatoes in your home-prepared diet or purchasing products listing organic potatoes if you feed your dog a commercial food containing this ingredient.

The Clean 15™ (2014) (these foods are considered safe to purchase conventional):

- Avocados (Note that dogs should never eat the leaves, skin or pit of avocados.)
- Sweet corn
- Pineapples
- Cabbage
- Sweet peas—frozen
- Onions*
- Asparagus
- Mangoes
- Papayas
- Kiwi
- Eggplant
- Grapefruit*
- Cantaloupe
- Cauliflower
- Sweet potatoes

(EWG, 2014)

Be sure to check back with the EWG frequently for the most updated information on pesticides in fruits and vegetables, and as a general resource on how to avoid toxins in your environment.

Honeybee products: functional foods for general health

Honeybees are the only insects to produce food for humans, and considering that the average bee lives only three to six weeks, these plump, gravity-defying winged wonders accomplish *a lot* in their short lives. Bee products contain a wide range of properties that can benefit dogs with various health conditions. Here's a bit more about them:

Raw honey

Honey is a part of the honeybee's beautiful symbiotic relationship with flowers—a relationship that results in **pollination** (fertilization) and plant reproduction, which is vital to all life on earth. Honey is comprised of simple sugars—mostly glucose and fructose—manufactured by honeybees from the nectar of flower blossoms.

But if we know that simple sugars can cause a variety of health problems, then why is honey a canine functional superfood? In fact, why feed it to your dog at all? As with other foods, whether or not honey is function depends upon the *type* you choose.

Note that not all honey is created equal. You can either purchase honey in its raw, un-processed state (which is typically thick and milky in appearance) or you can purchase a pasteurized (heat treated), filtered version. *Pasteurization compromises these beneficial properties.* Processed commercial honey typically looks clear and smooth and may even be so thin that you can pour it. The healthful, nutrition-packed honey that can benefit you and your dog originates from wild, unfiltered, ***raw honey***—*not* from the processed honey so prevalent on supermarket shelves (Mercola, 2009)!

Raw honey contains many beneficial properties, including:

- Alkaline-forming.
- Antimicrobial effect against a number of fungi and bacteria.
- High in antioxidants.
- Packed with natural enzymes and nutrients.
- Powerful antibacterial and antimicrobial properties.

(Mercola, 2006; Mercola, 2009)

Medical studies have identified ***raw honey's*** ability to help heal ulcers, manage diarrhea and soothe sore throats (Mercola, 2006). And, since it becomes alkaline and does not ferment in the digestive system, it is also useful in counteracting indigestion.

Raw honey is also beneficial in treating topical wounds, which results from a chemical reaction that occurs between glucose in the honey and an enzyme added by honeybees called glucose oxidase. When the honey comes in contact with the skin, the right conditions occur that enable the glucose oxidase to break down the glucose into hydrogen peroxide, which is antibacterial. Pasteurized honey, however, is *not* a viable wound care treatment (Mercola, 2009).

Some other common uses for ***raw honey*** include:

- Healing ulcers.
- Managing diarrhea.
- Soothing indigestion.
- Soothing sore throats.
- Treating sunburn and mild burns.

(Mercola, 2006; Mercola, 2009; Wolf, 2009)

Locally grown honey may help prevent seasonal allergies

Both canine and human anecdotal evidence suggests that eating locally grown honey may help prevent seasonal allergies. The theory is that locally grown honey contains local pollen spores picked up by the bees, so consuming it can slowly build immunity to the pollen (Mercola, 2011; Puotinen, 2007).

A study published in 2011 supports the anecdotal evidence. The study followed 44 patients diagnosed with birch pollen allergy. The purpose of the study was to evaluate the effects of pre-season consumption of birch pollen honey on the patients' allergy symptoms and medication use during the birch pollen allergy season. The participants consumed incremental amounts of birch pollen honey from November 2008 to March 2009 and then recorded their daily allergy symptoms and medication use during the birch pollen allergy season, from April 2009 to May 2009. An additional 17 patients serving as the control group took only their usual allergy medication. The results were highly encouraging. During the 2009 birch pollen allergy season, the patients who consumed the birch pollen honey reported:

- A 60% lower total symptom score.
- Twice as many asymptomatic days.
- 70% fewer days with severe symptoms.
- 50% less antihistamine use compared to the control group.

(Mercola, 2011; Saarinen & Haahtela, 2011)

Manuka: the "king" of honey

While all types of *raw honey* are beneficial, the "king" of all honeys—celebrated for its *super* health benefits—is Manuka honey from New Zealand. Made from the nectar of flowers from the medicinal Manuka bush, Manuka honey has been shown in clinical trials to kill more than 250 strains of bacteria, including:

- MRSA (methicillin resistant *Staphylococcus aureus*)
- MSSA (methicillin sensitive *Staphylococcus aureus*)
- VRE (vancomycin-resistant enterococci)
- *Helicobacter pylori* (which can cause stomach ulcers)

(Mercola, 2009)

In addition to the hydrogen peroxide antibacterial activity contained in most honeys, some strains of Manuka honey have additional healing antibacterial properties known as UMF (Unique Manuka Factor), which is indicated by a rating on the jar; the higher the UMF rating, the more potent the honey's antibacterial strength. The lowest recognized UMF is ten. Manuka honey is so effective in fighting infection that in 2007 the FDA approved its use for treating wounds and burns in the Unites States (Mercola, 2009).

Some common-sense cautions about bee products

If your pet is diabetic, consult with your holistic veterinarian or veterinary nutritionist before feeding honey because about 70 to 80% is fructose, which if overfed can contribute to obesity, diabetes and systemic inflammation (Mercola, 2011). Since *raw honey* can potentially become contaminated with a botulism-related toxin, we advise against feeding it to very young dogs (or children under one year) because their immune systems are not yet developed enough to defend themselves. Adult dogs and people are not affected.

Raw honey in moderate amounts is a functional, and delicious, addition to your dog's diet. Try mixing in a tablespoon with some fresh *blueberries* or goat's milk yogurt, or just letting him lick it right off the spoon!

Pollen

Pollen is a fine, golden dust-like substance containing the male reproductive cells of flowering plants. Bees and other insects carry *pollen* from a plant's stamen, the organ where it is produced, to the receptive part of another plant, resulting in fertilization and reproduction.

Pollen is made up of about 40% protein, about half of which is comprised of free-form amino acids that require no digestion and are ready for immediate use by the body. It is also rich in vitamins (especially B-complex and folic acid), enzymes and the bioflavanoid rutin, which contains potent antioxidant and anti-inflammatory properties and strengthens capillaries (Mercola, 2009; Puotinen, 2007).

It takes one bee working eight hours per day for one month to gather just *one teaspoon* of *pollen*—and that same teaspoonful contains more than *2.5 billion grains* of flower *pollen* (Mercola, 2009)!

According to both clinical and experiential studies, bee *pollen*:

- Possesses antibiotic qualities.
- Contributes to healthy intestinal function.
- Benefits the blood by increasing both white and red blood cells.
- Reduces cholesterol and triglycerides.
- Increases HDL ("good" cholesterol) and decreases LDL ("bad" cholesterol).
- Strengthens the immune system by increasing blood lymphocytes, gamma globulins, and proteins.
- Stimulates ovarian function.
- Treats hay fever and seasonal allergies when taken at least six weeks prior to the allergy season and continued throughout the season (similar to the effects of local *raw honey*).
- Increases strength and stamina.
- Stimulates metabolism, increasing caloric burn and weight loss.
- Improves skin.
- Delays tumor development in mice bred to die of tumors.

(Mercola, 2009)

Dose: It's extremely important to begin feeding just *one grain* of *pollen* at a time because dogs, like humans, can exhibit severe allergic reactions that include breathing problems and anaphylactic shock, which can be fatal. Carefully monitor your dog and if he shows no adverse symptoms, give him two grains the next day. Continue adding a grain a day until you reach a maintenance dose of one teaspoon per 30 pounds of body weight per day. Mix with food or blend with honey (Puotinen, 2007).

Be sure not to cook or heat the ***pollen***, as this will destroy the enzymes and decrease its nutritional value. Refrigerate to maintain freshness (Mercola, 2009).

Propolis

Could it be that bees innately understand how to fight infection? If their use of ***propolis*** is any indication, it would seem so. ***Propolis***, which means "defense of the city" and is also known as "bee glue," is the sticky resin found on the buds, bark and leaves of deciduous trees and some vegetables. Bees gather ***propolis*** and put it to a number of creative uses in their hives, including sealing cracks and building panels, disinfecting the hives, protecting the hives from bacteria and viruses and to embalm invaders, such as mice, which are too large for the bees to drive out (Mercola, 2009; Puotinen, 2007; Wolf, 2009).

Propolis contains a number of therapeutic properties, including:

- Analgesic
- Anesthetic
- Antibacterial
- Antibiotic
- Antifungal
- Anti-inflammatory
- Anti-microbial
- Antioxidant
- Antiseptic

(Mercola, 2009; Wolf, 2009)

Propolis contains flavonoids and phenolic acids and their esters, which display numerous effects on bacteria, fungi and viruses. Research indicates that ***propolis*** may be useful for a variety of pathological conditions such as tumors, infections, allergy, diabetes and ulcers, and it has also been shown to lower blood pressure and cholesterol (Castaldo and Capasso, 2002; Sforcin and Bankova, 2011).

Propolis is typically sold as tinctures (liquid extracts) or in capsules. But beware: it tastes terrible, so you might have to get creative in hiding it in your dog's food (Puotinen, 2007)!

Royal jelly

Royal jelly, or "pollen mush," is a thick, milky substance made from a combination of digested *pollen* and *raw honey* and a chemical secreted from the pharyngeal glands in the heads of worker bees. Animal studies have shown that royal jelly possesses a number of benefits, including:

- Anti-inflammatory
- Anti-microbial
- Antioxidant
- Anti-tumor
- Disinfectant

(Ramadan & Al-Ghamdi, 2012)

You can purchase fresh organic *royal jelly* in natural foods markets. Since it's highly perishable, be sure to refrigerate it to preserve its nutritional properties. If your dog dislikes the taste, you can purchase a mixture of royal jelly and honey, or create your own at home (Puotinen, 2007).

Dose: Because it's so potent, suggested doses of royal jelly for people are only one-quarter to one-half teaspoon per day. Be sure to adjust the dose on the label according to your dog's weight. For dogs weighing 60 to 80 pounds, for example, divide the recommended dose in half (Puotinen, 2007).

To make your own royal jelly/honey blend at home, mix two ounces (four table-spoons) organic royal jelly with six ounces (¾ cup) of local *raw honey* and feeding your dog one-half to one teaspoon twice per day, morning and night. Be sure to keep the mixture refrigerated (Puotinen, 2007).

A common-sense precaution: *do not give any bee product to dogs who are allergic to bees or bee products.*

As you'll recall from the beginning of this chapter, feeding your dog for maximum cellular health and beneficial gene expression involves a two-step process:

- Incorporating as many functional foods into his diet as possible.
- Reducing or eliminating potentially harmful (i.e., non-functional) ingredients.

In this chapter, we covered Step 1 and discussed how to increase functional carbohydrates, proteins and fats in your dog's diet. Now, let's move on to the next chapter and learn how to identify and avoid non-functional foods that wreak havoc on your dog's cells. As we'll demonstrate, we believe these foods are responsible for the rampant obesity and skyrocketing chronic illness plaguing our nation's dogs and robbing them of their birthright of vibrant health.

Takeaway Points

- Creating optimum health at the cellular level involves two key nutritional steps: 1) feeding a diet rich with functional foods that signal the epigenome to initiate healthy gene expression; and 2) reducing or eliminating foods that send harmful messages to the epigenome, triggering unhealthy gene expression.

- While not an essential nutrient, functional carbohydrates are packed with vitamins, minerals and phytonutrients (phytochemicals) that promote optimum cellular health.

- Phytonutrients from functional carbohydrates have potent antioxidant properties and have been shown to convey a number of health benefits on those who eat them, including protecting against heart disease, cancer and blocking tumor activity.

- Carotenoids, which include alpha-carotene and beta-carotene, are probably the most widely known class of phytonutrients.

- Phytonutrient-rich functional carbohydrates include cruciferous vegetables; fresh, whole fruits (*never* feed your dog grapes!); gluten-free grains; green leafy vegetables; and legumes.

- Protein is arguably the most important nutrient in a dog's diet because he cannot survive without it.

- To flourish, dogs must eat a plentiful amount of high quality, functional protein.

- Functional protein is: bioavailable (easily digested and assimilated); free of contaminants such as chemicals, hormones and antibiotics; does not promote a food intolerance/sensitivity; does not contain compounds that send unhealthy messages to the epigenome; is unadulterated (e.g., non-GMO); and is unprocessed or minimally processed.

- Functional proteins include: dairy products made from goat or sheep sources (avoid cow's dairy); eggs (preferably free-range and organic); low-mercury fish such as sardines and wild-caught Alaskan salmon (avoid farm-raised); and muscle and organ meat from novel animal sources.

- Functional dietary fats are important to creating optimum health.

- Dietary fat supplies dogs with the most concentrated and digestible form of energy, provides important essential fatty acids such as ***omega-3 fatty acids***, plays a necessary role in the absorption of fat-soluble vitamins and promotes a healthy nervous system.

- Functional fats include chicken fat or lamb fat (as long as your dog does not have a food intolerance/sensitivity to chicken or lamb); fatty fish that are low in mercury and rich in ***omega-3 fatty acids***; novel meat sources; and oils, such as fish oil (for **omega-3s**), borage oil, **coconut oil**, hemp oil, olive oil, primrose oil, pumpkin seed oil and sunflower oil.

- When purchasing oils, look for those that are expeller pressed, which uses a mechanical process to crush the oil from the nut or seed. Otherwise, the oil has likely been extracted using hexane, a petroleum product made from crude oil.

- Since fat is so energy-dense, be aware that the higher the percentage of fat in your dog's diet, the more calories he'll consume. Restrict fat intake in overweight dogs or dogs with medical conditions such as pancreatitis.

- Choose clean, pure, organic foods whenever possible to avoid health problems related to pesticides, GMOs, antibiotics and other man-made hazards that have infiltrated our food system.

- Create an organic priority list based on the Environmental Working Group's (EWG) Dirty Dozen™ and Clean 15™, avoiding all foods on the list that are unsafe for your canine companion.

- *Bee products—raw honey, pollen, propolis* and *royal jelly*—are functional superfoods that contain a wide variety of health benefits for dogs.

- When giving **bee pollen** to your dog, begin with feeding just one grain because dogs, like humans, can exhibit severe and potentially fatal allergic reactions.

- If your dog suffers from a chronic health condition, please don't give up hope. Just because the professionals you are turning to have run out of answers, doesn't mean those answers don't exist. Your dog's cells have a remarkable ability to repair, regenerate and renew, and by using the information in this book, you can help them do just that.

- Our canine functional superfoods are: **berries** (not strawberries); **coconut oil**; **curcumin**; **medicinal mushrooms**; **milk thistle**; **omega-3 fatty acids** (EPA and DHA); **pomegranates**; **probiotics**; **raw honey** products (not suitable for puppies); and **spirulina**.

Chapter 3

How to Identify and Avoid
Non-Functional Foods

Many foods are inherently non-functional for dogs because they are toxic and can cause severe illness or even death. For example, you never want to feed chocolate or grapes to your canine companion. These foods are easy to identify and avoid. But there are also non-functional foods that masquerade as functional. Like the "wolf in sheep's clothing" in the children's tale, these ingredients trick us into trusting they are conveying health on our dogs, when in fact they are creating epigenomic signals that disrupt optimum gene expression. Remember the example of the apple laden with pesticides from Chapter 1? In general, apples are a healthy, functional food, but when bathed in a toxic coating, they can wreak havoc at the cellular level. Deciding which foods you should avoid is not always obvious and involves a number of factors we will cover in this chapter, including:

- Factory farmed foods.
- Foods that contain chemical additives, such as artificial colors and preservatives.
- Foods that contain added hormones and antibiotics.
- Foods that could cause an intolerance/sensitivity to your individual dog.
- Genetically modified foods (GMOs).
- High glycemic carbohydrates.
- Inferior sources of protein for dogs (corn, wheat and soy).
- Poorly packaged foods.
- Toxic foods that should be avoided in all cases.

You will also discover how to how to evaluate mass-market commercial pet foods and their claims. We guarantee that this section will surprise you!

Foods that are *never* functional for dogs

Your dog should never eat these foods. They are toxic and can cause severe illness or even death:

- Alcohol

- Chocolate

- Citrus fruits

- Coffee, tea and cola

- Grapes and raisins

- Mushrooms (except medicinal mushrooms, as discussed later)

- Nutmeg

- Nuts (especially certain kinds, such as macadamia)

- Onions (Garlic is fine in moderation, and many pet foods use it.)

- Peanuts. While peanuts and peanut products are not inherently toxic, they are a common cause of potentially severe allergic reactions in dogs as well as people. Peanuts are also susceptible to aflatoxin contamination—see below.

- Spoiled or moldy foods. Mold toxins and other **aflatoxins** (mycotoxins produced by several species of fungi) are very toxic to pets and can cause severe gastrointestinal damage and even liver failure. We will discuss more about aflatoxins later in the chapter.

- Strawberries

- Xylitol (artificial sweetener)

- Yeast dough (unfermented)

In the previous chapter, you learned how to select functional carbohydrates, proteins and fats for your dog's diet. Now, let's talk about Step 2 in creating a diet based on the principles of nutrigenomics: detecting and ditching non-functional ingredients.

Steer clear of high glycemic (high-GI) carbohydrates

When you hear the word *carbohydrate*, images of bread, pasta, cereal and other processed foods likely pop into your mind. But these foods, often referred to as "junk" carbs, contain sugary, refined ingredients that rank high on the **Glycemic Index (GI)**, an index that rates ingredients by how quickly and how high they cause blood sugar levels to rise after eating them. High-GI carbohydrates trigger the body to produce a chronic inflammatory response, contributing to a variety of health problems including obesity, diabetes, heart disease, arthritis and cancer, which we'll talk about at length in the coming chapters.

Avoid feeding your dog these high glycemic carbs:

- Corn
- Sugar
- Wheat (white or whole wheat)
- White rice (brown rice is fine)

Notice how the above list is comprised of ingredients commonly found in mass-market commercial pet foods. And, to add insult to injury, processing these inferior quality carbohydrates increases their GI ranking! You might also be interested to learn that whole wheat flour and white flour both have the same effect on raising blood sugar levels. So, please don't be fooled by pet food manufacturers that are selling healthy, "whole wheat" products.

Instead of feeding your dog high-GI carbs, opt for the healthy, functional carbohydrates you read about in the previous chapter.

Note: You'll notice that we have excluded white potatoes from this list, even though they rank high on the GI. The reason is because white potatoes, which are soothing to the bowel and liver, can benefit dogs suffering from certain health conditions, such as gastrointestinal issues and liver disease. You will find recipes for these conditions, which use white potatoes, in Chapter 11. However, we do advise not over-feeding white potatoes to an otherwise healthy animal.

Issues with factory farmed meat

In the previous chapter, we talked about protein sources that provide high quality, bio-available amino acids as well as other important nutrients. But are they functional? In their "cleanest" state, the answer is yes; they are definitely functional. But the problem stems from outside influences that alter their original purity and cause them to send unhealthy messages to the cells. Let's take a closer look at what we mean.

Factory farms: what does your dog's meat eat?

One major problem with animal proteins today stems from the ingredients consumed by food production animals. For the most part, their diets do not meet the criteria of functional foods. But when you or your dog consume animal protein, in a way both of you are also eating the food the animal ate, because you are ingesting many of the impurities that have been left behind in the animal's muscles, organs, bones and tissues.

Most of the small, family owned and operated farms prevalent in the early 1900s have been replaced in the past 60 or so years by factory farms—large-scale, corporate-owned operations designed to maximize food production and minimize costs. Rather than grazing on lush green fields, today's factory-raised animals are crammed into tight spaces where they suffer from severe stress and ingest feeds that are specifically formulated to increase growth rates in order to keep up with high consumer demand for meat (Sapkota et al., 2007).

To give you an idea what today's livestock eat, here's a rundown of some ingredients that are approved by the U.S. Food and Drug and Administration (FDA) and the Association of American Feed Control Officials (AAFCO) for use in livestock feed:

- Animal waste, including dried ruminant waste, dried poultry litter and dried swine waste. According to AAFCO, processed animal waste should not contain pathogenic microorganisms, pesticide residues or drug residues that could harm animals or find their way into the food system. However, AAFCO is not a regulatory body, and oversight of these guidelines is left to the federal government or individual states which may or may not enforce them.

- Antibiotics, including tetracyclines, macrolides, streptogramins and fluoroquinolones are used in both animal feed and water to promote growth and improve feed efficiency. According to the FDA, "Drugs may be added to some animal feeds to prevent or treat diseases, or to improve animal growth and productivity." The follow categories of drugs are FDA-approved for use in animal feeds:

  o Anthelmintics to fight parasitic worms.

  o Anti-bloating drugs to prevent swelling of the stomach compartments or intestinal tract of cows caused by excessive gas.

  o Anticoccidials to fight coccidial parasites.

  o Antimicrobials (such as antibacterial drugs) to fight infections.

  o Beta agonists to promote leanness in animals raised for meat.

  o Hormones to suppress estrus (the female heat cycle) in cattle.

  o Sulfonamides to fight certain types of infections.

- Food containing heat-treated rodent, roach or bird excreta.

- Metals, including organoarsenicals (that's arsenic!).

- Plant and animal-based fats, which may contain contaminants such as dioxins and polychlorinated biphenyls (PCBs).

- Plastics, including polyethylene roughage replacement.

- Preservatives including butylated hyroxyanisole (BHA) and sodium bisulfate.

- Rendered animal protein, including animal digest from dead, dying, diseased, or disabled animals including deer and elk.

- Restaurant food waste.

(Sapkota et al., 2007; USFDA, 2009)

If you find this disturbing, you're not alone. But there's more. Several studies have detected some decidedly *non-functional* agents in U.S. animal feeds, including:

- Antibiotic resistant bacteria, including those resistant to vancomycin, genta-micin, streptomycin ampicillin, cephalothin, cefoxitin, amoxicillin/clavulanic acid, sulfamethoxazole, cephalothin and ceftiofur.

- Dioxins, a group of toxic chemicals including PCDDs and PCDFs, and PCBs.

- Food-borne bacterial pathogens, including *Salmonella* spp. and *E. coli.*

- Mycotoxins, toxic secondary metabolites produced by microfungi (molds) that can contaminate crops such as cereal grains during growth, processing or stor-age and can cause disease and death in humans and animals. Mycotoxins of greatest concern are aflatoxins, ochratoxins, trichothecenes, fumonisins, zeara-lenone and ergot alkaloids. Aflatoxins are classified as a Group 1 human car-cinogen by the International Agency for Research on Cancer and zearalenone are recognized as endocrine disruptors.

- Prions, infectious agents composed of tiny proteins that are not detectable by standard microscopy.

(Sapkota et al., 2007)

As you can see, determining whether a food is functional—whether it promotes health at the cellular level—involves much more than "meats" the eye (okay, bad pun). We can put a nice, fresh bowl of spinach in front of you, and you would say that it's healthy. But if we cooked that spinach in water laced with insecticide, you'd certainly change your mind! Likewise, our goal here is to get you to look at your dog's diet in a whole new way and to realize that *every* aspect of a food affects how it regulates gene expression.

At the same time, we understand the realities of the world we live in, and we don't suggest that you move to a farm and raise your own animals to feed your dog. But we do have choices, such as opting for organic foods whenever possible (see previous chapter) and asking some tough questions of commercial pet food manufacturers, which you'll learn about in Chapter 12.

It's not functional if it causes a food intolerance/sensitivity in your dog

Many dogs have food intolerances, also called food sensitivities. We'll talk a lot more about this topic in upcoming chapters and discuss the latest testing options in Chap-ter 6, but for now let's just say that food intolerances/sensitivities are different from food allergies. Food allergies typically involve signs that occur immediately, such as hives or **anaphylactic shock** (when the airwaves close, such as with an allergy to peanut products), while food intolerances/sensitivities build up over months, or even years, of exposure to the **antigen** (offending ingredient). But, even though you might not have to rush your dog to the veterinarian due to a food intolerance/sensitivity, over time it can cause devastating health problems, including "**leaky gut syndrome**" (see sidebar on page 44). Because food intolerances/sensitivities are often confused with other medical conditions, such as a skin allergy, skin infection or gastrointestinal disease, many dogs are undiagnosed, untreated and left to suffer needlessly.

Foods that commonly cause intolerances/sensitivities in dogs are:

- Beef
- Chicken
- Corn
- Cow's milk products (e.g., milk, cheese, yogurt, cottage cheese, etc.)
- Soy
- Wheat and other grains (e.g., barley, rye, spelt and kamut) containing gluten

Obviously, not *all* dogs will react to *all*—or even some—of these ingredients, which is why genotype-based testing such as NutriScan is so important. If, through appropriate testing, you discover that your dog tolerates some or all of these ingredients, there should be no harm in including them in his diet. But if you don't plan to test your dog, it's best to exercise caution and eliminate them.

What exactly is a "novel" protein?

To avoid food intolerances/sensitivities, many of us opt to feed our dogs "novel" animal proteins. Proteins commonly considered novel are:

- Bison
- Buffalo
- Duck
- Fish
- Goat
- Lamb
- Pork
- Turkey
- Venison

But many people don't realize that an animal protein source that's novel for one dog won't necessarily be so for another. *A protein is only novel for your dog if he has never eaten it before.* This is because, unlike a food allergy (which is an immediate reaction), intolerances/sensitivities build up over consistent exposure to an ingredient. For example, kangaroo, emu, and ostrich are novel proteins for most dogs in the United States (at least at the time of this writing); however, these foods are mainstream and not at all novel in countries such as Australia.

Similarly, lamb, turkey and venison were once considered novel proteins in the United States, but now that they are more mainstream in pet food, dogs are beginning to manifest food intolerances/sensitivities to them (Dodds, 2013).

Unfortunately, potentially reactive ingredients such as corn, wheat and soy are common protein sources found in many mass-market, commercial pet foods because they're cheap to produce. Did you know that farms are heavily subsidized to produce certain crops? The U.S. government doled out $292.5 billion in farm subsidies between 1995-2012. Which crops were the most heavily subsidized? Corn was the number one subsidized crop with $84,427,099,356 in subsidies, wheat came in at number two with $35,505,320,839 in subsidies and soy subsidies totaled $27,829,683,988, earning it the number five ranking (EWG, 2012).

Given the massive subsidies and low cost of corn, wheat and soy, it's no surprise that these inferior quality proteins predominate mass-market commercial pet foods. It's also no surprise that more dogs than ever suffer from chronic skin and gastrointestinal issues—the primary signs of food intolerances/sensitivities.

But the menacing powers of corn, wheat and soy go even further than you might imagine. Let's take a closer look at the truth behind three of the most popular ingredients used in commercial pet food.

Cutting back on corn consumption: a smart idea for your dog

In addition to its being one of the top three genetically engineered crops in the country (see below in "Just say no to GMO") as well as one of the leading causes of food intolerances/sensitivities in dogs, corn is a high-glycemic carbohydrate that has been implicated as a major contributor to the nation's obesity epidemic—and companion animals also suffer from its ill effects. Because of huge subsidies, US farmers grow corn at astounding rates, producing a bumper crop of 10.8 billion bushels in 2012 (National Corn Growers Association, 2013; Williams, 2012).

What happens to all this corn? Certainly, it's not all lining the shelves of produce aisles! In fact, it's not even the same type of corn that's found in the produce aisle. The corn that you buy fresh, canned or frozen is called "sweet corn," but it's likely not what you see growing when you drive by a sprawling field in the Corn Belt. That's because most corn grown in the United States is "dent corn," a type that is processed and used for foods such as cornstarch, high fructose corn syrup, corn cereal, corn oil, livestock feed, pet food and even ethanol (National Corn Growers Association, 2013; Williams, 2012).

High fructose corn syrup is an alternative to natural sugar found in an astounding number of human foods that has been linked to health hazards such as obesity, diabetes and heart disease. We strongly urge against purchasing any pet food that contains high fructose corn syrup, and to investigate its use in your own foods as well.

Along with wheat and soy, corn contains high levels of **lectins**, sugar-binding proteins that act as natural insecticides and fungicides to protect plants from predators. Lectins are sticky molecules, enabling them to effectively bind to their sugars. The problem is that this stickiness can also cause lectins to bind onto the lining of the small intestine. This can cause damage to the intestinal lining, including disruption of the intestinal villi, resulting in a decreased ability to absorb nutrients. Lectin can also harm the gut **microflora**, the trillions of beneficial bacteria that live inside the mucosal tissue lining of the gut, resulting in leaky gut syndrome (Sisson, 2013). While many foods contain lectins, not all are harmful.

> ### What is leaky gut syndrome?
> The gut, which is made up of the stomach, small intestines and colon (large intestine), is actually a complex microsystem of microflora (the "good" bacteria we mentioned previously). While bacteria also live in our mouths, on our skin and in our urogenital tract, more than 70% reside in the mucosal tissue lining of the gut, which is known as the gut-associated lymphoid tissue, or GALT. The trillions of beneficial bacteria inside the gut comprise a metabolically active organ—the largest immune organ in the body—and are important for a variety of essential functions, including regulating digestion, producing and metabolizing vitamins and other trace nutrients, and protecting the body from infection.
>
> The lining of the gut also serves as a barrier, preventing unwanted invaders such as food toxins, toxic chemicals, bad bacteria, undigested food particles and fungi from entering our systems (Robinson & Reeves, 2013). Gluten causes the intestines to release a protein called zonulin, which creates openings between the intestinal cells (Hyman, 2012; Hyman, 2013a; Kressler, 2012). These openings cause the lining of the gut to become more permeable, or "leaky."
>
> Once the intestinal barrier has been breached, all sorts of undesirable substances can cross into the bloodstream, including the gluten itself (Robinson & Reeves, 2013). As these particles roam about the body and bind to tissues, the immune system recognizes them as foreign invaders and reacts by attacking them. At the same time, it attacks the healthy tissue, waging an internal autoimmune war that creates inflammation throughout the entire body (Hyman, 2012; Hyman, 2013a; Robinson & Reeves, 2013; Sisson, 2013)

Gluten-free grains and legumes also contain lectins, however these foods are excellent plant-based sources of protein and other nutrients, including functional phytonutrients, fiber and essential vitamins and minerals. Soaking and cooking beans can also help diminish their lectin content. While we recommend not going overboard with these foods, we believe that their nutritional benefits warrant including them as an occasional part of your dog's diet. Just be sure to test them in small amounts first to determine whether they agree with your dog's GI system (flatulence is *not* a good sign!).

Corn also carries the risk of contamination with dangerous mycotoxins, such as aflatoxin. Mycotoxins, as mentioned above, are toxic metabolic by-products produced by fungi that can cause serious illness, and even death, to people and animals that eat foods contaminated with them. In 2007, researchers studying mycotoxin contamination in pet food found that it "poses a serious health threat to pets" (Boermans & Leung, 2007, pp. 95).

Research from the University of Guelph in Canada also found that pet foods containing plant-derived proteins are more likely to contain harmful mycotoxins than foods that rely on animal-based fish and meat proteins. The researcher who led the study suggested that pet owners avoid "cheaper" pet foods that are more likely to contain vegetable cereals and corn or wheat fillers, as well as those with large amounts of rice bran (PetfoodIndustry.com, 2013).

In a separate study, cattle fed primarily corn developed high stomach acidity that appears to breed a deadly strain of *E. coli* bacteria (Voiland, 2007)—definitely *not* in keeping with promoting health at the cellular level.

Finally, unless you purchase an organic product, the corn used is more than likely genetically modified. We'll discuss the potential hazards of GM crops in a minute.

Wheat protein: is it making your dog sick?

If wheat is a grain, why is it used in pet foods as a low-cost source of protein? It's because of gluten, a sticky protein in wheat. Gluten is what holds bread together and makes it rise. Gluten is linked to a whole host of serious health conditions in people and dogs, many of which we'll talk about throughout this book.

Many people have heard of celiac disease, a genetic sensitivity to gluten that can wreak havoc on the body. Irish Setters share a similar genetic intolerance, called wheat-sensitive enteropathy, which can cause gas, bloating, diarrhea and far more severe health problems.

But your dog doesn't have to have wheat-sensitive enteropathy (and you don't have to have celiac disease) to suffer from the harmful effects of gluten. A less obvious, low-grade autoimmune reaction to gluten can trigger a wildfire of chronic inflammation that affects every organ system in the body, including the brain, heart, joints and digestive tract (Hyman, 2013). It can even create an immune response that causes subclinical brain inflammation, resulting in age-related dementia (Perricone, 2010). We'll talk more about the effects of gluten on the brain in Chapter 10.

Gluten has been linked to 55 diseases in people and may also promote negative health effects in dogs, including:

- Adverse behavioral changes
- Autoimmune diseases
- Inflammatory Bowel Disease
- Cancer
- Fatigue
- Obesity
- Neurologic disorders
- Systemic inflammation
- Thyroid dysfunction and thyroiditis

Researchers estimate that millions of people suffer from some form of gluten intolerance and don't even know it (Hyman, 2013; Kressler, 2012). We believe that number could be as high in our canine companions, who are not genetically adapted to eating wheat. If your dog suffers from a chronic malady and no matter what you do, you just can't seem to cure it, try removing all gluten from his diet. You just might be surprised at the remarkable turn-around.

The controversy with soy

Soy is a complex and controversial food. Unlike corn and wheat, many people— vegetarians and vegans especially—turn to soy products such as tofu, tempeh and soymilk as plant-based substitutes for animal protein. For humans, moderate intake of soy can provide taste and versatility to many meat-free dishes. As vegetarians, both authors here often opt for soy in everything from soymilk ice cream to tempeh "meat" loaf to satisfy our culinary cravings.

On the pro-soy side, studies have found that certain **soy isoflavones**, particularly genistein, daidzein and glycitein, can modulate epigenetic mechanisms to protect against various types of cancers, including colorectal and prostate (Jamadar-Shroff, Papich & Suter, 2009; Mount Sinai Medical Center, 2013; University of Illinois, 2013; Yamka et al., 2006; Zhang, Li & Chen, 2013). On the other side, conflicting studies exist as to whether phytoestrogens in soy worsen estrogen-dependent breast cancer. Phytoestrogens have also been implicated in other health problems (see below).

Phytoestrogens in soy activate estrogen-dependent breast cancer genes

After reviewing the research on soy, we believe that the key to enjoying it as part of a healthy, balanced diet hinges on three key factors: consuming it in moderation; avoiding the most highly processed forms; and steering clear of anything made with genetically modified (GM) soybeans (see below). Most natural food stores and major supermarkets offer high quality, minimally processed and organic soy products such as edamame (whole soy beans), tempeh and sprouted tofu. Unfortunately, the same cannot be said for the commercial pet food industry, which uses highly processed soy ingredients likely made with GM soybeans (unless the product uses organic soybeans). Moreover, many dogs fed mass-market, commercial pet foods eat the same bag of kibble day in and day out, throwing any hope of consuming soy in moderation out the window. For these reasons, we believe that for our canine companions, the potential health problems associated with consuming more than a moderate amount of soy outweigh the potential benefits.

Here are a few issues surrounding soy in the canine diet:

Soy is a common reactive antigen for dogs

Soybeans and the many soy derivatives commonly found in dog foods are recognized as some of the most prevalent causes of both acute and sub-acute food allergies, as well as long-term food intolerances/sensitivities. Symptoms of food allergies can include dry, scratchy, red and inflamed skin, hives and rashes, while food intolerances/sensitivities typically manifest as skin disorders (primarily itching) or gastrointestinal tract issues (a leaky gut), which occur over longer periods of exposure to the food antigen. Soy can appear in dog foods in many forms, including soybean meal, soybean germ meal, soy flour, grits, hulls, soy protein concentrate, soy isoflavones, isolated soy protein and textured vegetable protein (TVP) (Fahey, n.d.). If you plan to feed soy-based products to your dog, we strongly suggest that you have him tested via NutriScan for a soy intolerance/sensitivity.

Phytoestrogens in soy can disrupt endocrine function

Isoflavones are a group of phytoestrogens that are present in large concentrations in soy (Allred et al., 2001). Phytoestrogens are chemicals found in plants that act like the hormone estrogen and can either mimic or block estrogen's effect. A 2004 study analyzing 24 commercial dog foods containing soy found that these products contained phytoestrogens in comparable amounts to levels known to create biological effects in other species. Potential hazardous effects of dietary phytoestrogens include infertility, precocious or delayed puberty, immune system abnormalities and decreased hair growth (Cerundolo et al., 2004; Cerundo et al., 2009; Fort et al, 1990). Please note that peas are also phytoestrogens, and that many commercial pet foods now include pea or pea fiber protein.

Soy affects the thyroid gland

As those of you who have read our book *The Canine Thyroid Epidemic* know, soy interferes with the ability of the thyroid gland to make T4 (thyroxine) and (T3) tri-iodothyronine, hormones necessary for normal thyroid function. We'll talk more about soy's effect on thyroid function in Chapter 11.

Soy can cause other problems for dogs

Soy also:

- Can cause serious gastric distress (gas and discomfort).

- Contains antinutrients that inhibit trypsin (a pancreatic enzyme) and other enzymes necessary for protein digestion.

- Contains phytates that block absorption of essential minerals.

(Fallon & Enig, 2000; Yamka et al., 2006)

If your dog's soy comes from commercial pet food, it's likely genetically engineered

Along with corn, soy is one of the top three genetically engineered crops in the U.S. Unless your dog's food is made with organic soy, it's probably made with a genetically modified version, potentially increasing the antigenic characteristics and creating other as yet unstudied health effects.

As we discussed earlier, not all protein is created equal—far from it. Regardless of what mass-market commercial pet food manufacturers want us to believe, processed corn, wheat and soy are not legitimate sources of high quality, bioavailable protein for dogs. On the contrary, these ingredients replace fresh, whole animal-based proteins because they are inexpensive. They can cause food intolerances/sensitivities, inflammation, issues of the skin and gastrointestinal tract and even—as we'll talk about in detail in Chapter 10—decline in brain function. Corn, wheat and soy are definitely *not* functional ingredients for dogs, and we strongly advise that you steer clear of products that contain them.

See the Resources section for manufacturers and online retailers of grain-free foods, treats and supplements.

The devil in the (cow's) milk?

The problem with feeding cow's milk to dogs may reach far beyond a simple dairy intolerance. The real culprit could prove much more mysterious and menacing—a genetically mutated protein in some cows' milk known as A1 beta-casein. Agricultural scientist Keith Woodford, in his 2009 book, *The Devil in the Milk: Illness, Health and the Politics of A1 and A2 Milk*, claims that the dairy industry has spent years concealing the health issues related to A1 milk from the public (Woodford, 2009).

All cows were originally A2 before the genetic mutation of some herds occurred and then spread over thousands of years (Woodford, 2009). Although "A1 cows," as they are known, originated in Europe, today about half of cows in the United States produce A1 beta-casein rather than A2 beta-casein, which is the original and natural version of the protein. Even organic and raw milk contain A1 beta-casein. It has nothing to do with the processing of the milk and everything to do with the genes of the cows.

While the topic of A1 beta-casein is hotly debated, with experts offering vocal opinions on both sides of the controversy, strong anecdotal evidence exists that this aberrant protein could contribute to a host of serious illnesses in people and animals. Woodford uncovered research in more than 100 peer-reviewed scientific papers indicating that A1 beta-casein might be responsible for autoimmune-related diseases ranging from heart disease and Type 1 diabetes to autism (Woodford, 2009).

Woodford says that A1 beta-casein protein digests differently from the original A2 beta-casein, releasing a peptide called beta-casomorphin-7 (BCM7), which he refers to as "the milk devil." BCM7 is an opioid with morphine-like characteristics. The protein is capable of entering the bloodstream from the stomach, where the body tries to reject it. In this process, the body creates an autoimmune response and attacks itself, resulting in a whole host of autoimmune diseases in susceptible individuals (Woodford, 2009).

Woodford cites studies where mice and rats fed A1 beta-casein showed much higher incidences of diabetes than those fed A2 beta-casein. He also cautions of a potential link between A1 milk and autism in children. Woodford points out that many autistic children have leaky gut syndrome, which enables the genetically mutated protein to more easily cross from the digestive tract into the blood, where it can then travel through the blood-brain barrier. He claims that even people who believe they are lactose intolerant often have no problem tolerating A2 milk, which also contains lactose; these lactose intolerant individuals might actually be reacting to the A1 beta-casein (Woodford, 2009).

More clinical evidence needs to be gathered on the effects of A1 milk to substantiate Woodford's claims; however, we feel that he makes a compelling case. The potential issues he warns against, combined with the fact that cow's milk is highly antigenic for dogs, warrants us to exclude it as a functional food for our canine companions.

Fortunately, nutritious, tasty and functional alternatives exist. Goat's milk and sheep's milk both contain A2 protein, and most dogs tolerate them well. You can find goat and sheep's milk products, including a variety of cheeses and yogurts, in your natural food store and even some regular supermarkets.

Food additives: an unwelcome addition to your dog's food

By now, you're getting a good idea of the factors that make an ingredient functional or not. At the basic level, it's pretty simple. Functional foods promote health at the cellular level, while non-functional foods sabotage the cells to create inflammation and disease. The trick comes in training ourselves to assess food in a whole new way and to ignore marketing messages and manufacturers' claims. We also need to look at food products as the sum of their individual ingredients. If a product contains any ingredient that sends unhealthy messages to the cells, that food cannot be functional. In mass-market, commercial dog foods, chemical additives are frequent culprits. These include:

- Artificial colors, flavors and palatability enhancers.

- Chemical preservatives such as antioxidants, antimicrobials and preventatives of food discoloration.

- Emulsifying agents such as stabilizers/thickeners.

- Humectants (substances that help foods retain moisture, such as sorbitol and polydextrose).

(Roudebush, 1993)

Does your dog's food contain any of the following non-functional ingredients?

Artificial colors and color protectants. Synthetic coloring agents, including azo (coal-tar derivatives) and nonazo dyes are used to impart artificial color to pet foods in order to increase consumer appeal (obviously, dogs could care less about the color of their food!). Chemicals including nitrites/nitrates (used to preserve the color of meats) and sulfites (e.g., potassium bisulfate) are used to prevent foods from discoloring. A wide variety of adverse reactions in both humans and pets have been reported from such food additives, including nausea, vomiting, diarrhea, abdominal cramping and pain, headache, provocation of asthma, chronic allergic symptoms, inhalant dermatitis and behavioral disorders (Roudebush, 1993). According to the Royal Society for the Prevention of Cruelty to Animals (RSPCA) in Australia, certain preservatives including potassium bisulfate may cause health issues in pets, including thiamine (vitamin B1) deficiency in dogs and cats, severe neurological problems and even death (Ferrara, 2010; Markovich, Heinze & Freeman, 2013).

Butylated hyroxyanisole (BHA) and butylated hydroxytoluene (BHT). BHA and BHT have been used as fat preservatives in human and animal foods in the U.S. and other countries for more than 30 years. While many countries have banned them from use in human foods, they are still allowed in pet foods. BHA and BHT have been indicated as carcinogenic in animal experiments and are suspected of contributing to cancer and tumor growth.

Ethoxyquin is another preservative that some pet food manufacturers may still be using in small amounts because of its reputation as an excellent, highly stable antioxidant. However, ethoxyquin's safety was called into question in the late 1980s, when it was acknowledged that the only long-term feeding trials in dogs were conducted more than 40 years before and that these trials were medically and scientifically flawed by today's standards. Ethoxyquin is used as a pesticide as well as a food preservative and has been linked clinically with liver and kidney cancer in dogs, as well as with the interruption of fertility and fetal growth. In 1997, the Food and Drug Administration (FDA) described a verifiable connection between ethoxyquin and the buildup of Protoporphyrin IX (a building block of hemoglobin) in the liver of post-partum lactating bitches, as well as elevations in serum liver-related enzymes in some animals. As a result, the FDA's Center for Veterinary Medicine Update of August 14, 1997 requested that the amount of ethoxyquin allowed in pet foods be limited to not more than 75 ppm (USFDA, 1997).

Vitamin K3 (Menadione Sodium Bisulfate) (Also listed as Menadione Dimethyl-Pyrimidinol Bisulfate, Menadione Dimethyl-Pyrimidinol Bisulfite, Menadione Sodium Bisulfate Complex, Menadione Sodium Bisulfite and Menadione Sodium Bisulfite Complex.) Vitamin K3 is a synthetic form of vitamin K (the natural forms are vitamin K1 and vitamin K2) used as an inexpensive vitamin K supplement in commercial pet foods. Menadione has been implicated in a variety of negative effects on the body, including damaging the natural vitamin K cycle (natural vitamin K is essential for blood clotting), cytotoxicity in liver cells, possible mutagenic effects, weakening of the immune system, irritation of skin and mucous membranes, allergic reactions, eczema and toxicity in high doses (The Dog Food Project, 2012).

Just say no to GMO

Genetically engineered or modified (GM) foods, also called GMOs (genetically modified organisms) are increasing in the food supply and causing alarm among consumers and food safety advocates who worry about their implications on public health and safety. What are GMOs and why should you care about whether you and your family (two-legged and four-legged) eat them?

According to the World Health Organization:

> Genetically modified (GM) foods are foods derived from organisms whose genetic material (DNA) has been modified in a way that does not occur naturally, e.g., through the introduction of a gene from a different organism. Currently available GM foods stem mostly from plants, but in the future foods derived from GM microorganisms or GM animals are likely to be introduced on the market. Most existing genetically modified crops have been developed to improve yield, through the introduction of resistance to plant diseases or of increased tolerance of herbicides (World Health Organization, 2013).

Genetically engineered crops are *patented inventions* developed mainly by six chemical companies—Monsanto, Dow, BASF, Bayer, Syngenta and DuPont. Most GM crops were invented so they could be sprayed with more weed-killing herbicides without harming the genetically engineered plant. As a result, GM crops have led to substantial increases in the use of herbicides and insecticides, often in amounts that have never been tested for safety in humans, animals or other plants (EWG, 2013).

Not surprisingly, the top three GM crops grown in the U.S. are corn, soybeans and cotton—two of which, as you already learned, are among the most highly subsidized and are also main ingredients in many mass-market commercial pet foods. Most sweet corn, which is the type of corn found in the produce aisle, is non-GMO. However, nearly all field corn, which is used to make processed foods such as tortillas, chips, corn syrup and animal feed, is made with genetically modified seeds. The same is true of soybeans (EWG, 2013a).

From 1996 to 2011, pesticide use on these crops increased by more than 527 million pounds. Most of this resulted from increased use of the herbicide glyphosate, the key ingredient in Monsanto's Roundup, which is the best selling weed killer in the world. According to the U.S. Geological Survey, glyphosate is now commonly found in air and rain throughout the Midwest during spring and summer, and levels are also increasing in many aquatic ecosystems (EWG, 2013). This means that in addition to all the other problems associated with corn and soy products, unless you buy an organic product, your dog is also munching on genetically altered food laden with heavy-duty pesticides and herbicides.

More on the dangers of glyphosates and GMOs

As of this writing, 62 countries around the world have passed laws requiring labeling of GMO foods, some as far back as 2003; the U.S., however, is not one of them (EWG, 2013).

There is good news on this topic, though. Whole Foods, the nation's leading health food grocery chain, has pledged that by 2018 all GMO products sold in its U.S. and Canadian stores will be clearly labeled (Gallo, 2013). In addition, Target has announced that it will add a new brand to its shelves, called Simply Balanced, and that it will phase out all GMOs by the end of 2014 (Renter, 2013). We are also thrilled that in April 2014, the Vermont legislature became the first state lawmakers to pass a bill requiring labeling of GMO foods; we anticipate the governor will have signed this bill into law by the time you read this book (Gram & Rathke, 2014). We hope that this commitment by major grocery chains—and now state governments—represents the beginning of greater consumer awareness and choice regarding GMOs in our food supply.

Since this book is about creating a diet for your dog based on foods that communicate healthy messages to his cells, we cannot endorse feeding ingredients that have had their DNA genetically modified until such time these foods have been thoroughly tested by independent authorities and proven safe for both humans and animals. We also can't endorse foods containing an herbicide that has been shown to promote the expression of certain cancerous genes, especially when that effect is further increased when the herbicide is combined with soy (see "More on the dangers of glyphosates and GMOs" in Appendix A) (Ji, 2013; Thongprakaisang et al., 2013).

Avoiding GMOs is one more good reason to steer clear of ingredients such as corn and soy in your dog's food.

Pet food packaging and the epigenome

It's not only your dog's food that can affect his epigenome, but also the packaging the food is stored in. That's right. BPA (Bisphenol A), a chemical used to make plastics and resins, is a known endocrine disrupter that continues to infiltrate our food system, despite its documented hazardous effects. BPA is found in many plastic water bottles, as well as the cans that house many foods that people and pets eat on a regular basis. BPA is able to harden plastics, yet still remain flexible enough to avoid breaking—a big plus for plastics manufacturers. In cans, resin liners made of BPA create a barrier that blocks the acids, enzymes, vitamins, minerals and other food components from chemically interacting with the can's metal (Kerns, 2012).

Because BPA leaches into foods and beverages, it can be passed into the system of anyone that eats or drinks the contaminated ingredients. It has been documented that at any given time, BPA can be detected in 95% of the population. Studies show that BPA present in the same levels found in humans is linked to changes in the prostate, breasts, testis, mammary glands, body size, behavior, brain structure and chemistry of laboratory animals (Kerns, 2012).

Despite BPA's potential dangers, on March 30, 2012, the FDA released an announcement stating, "the scientific evidence at this time does not suggest that the very low levels of human exposure to BPA through the diet are unsafe" (USFDA, 2012).

In July 2012, relenting to pressure from—ironically—the American Chemistry Council, the FDA banned the use of BPA in baby bottles and sippy cups, but it is currently still allowed in many other products for human and animal use, including:

- Plastic bottles
- Plastic food containers
- Tin food cans (pet and human)
- Other food packaging

More on BPA

If you are concerned about BPA in your dog's food, we suggest avoiding canned packaging.

Evaluating mass-market commercial pet food

Most of us include at least some commercial food in our dog's diet, and many of us feed commercial food exclusively, so it's important to discuss the functional aspect of protein and other ingredients commonly found in commercial products. This book isn't about tearing apart the commercial pet food industry or telling you not to feed your dog a commercial diet. Many excellent manufacturers, primarily small-to-midsize operations, are sprouting onto the commercial pet food scene offering new products that are more in keeping with the principles of nutrigenomics.

But the commercial pet food industry still has a long way to go. While many mass-market dog foods claim to promote optimum health, they may in fact contain pro-inflammatory ingredients that switch on the genetic expression for many of the chronic diseases prevalent in dogs today, including behavior issues, arthritis, diabetes, cardiovascular disease, obesity and even cancer. You won't discover that by reading the marketing claims on the label, however (USFDA, 2010).

What do common pet food claims really mean?

If you've strolled down a dog food aisle lately, you know that a seemingly endless selection of bags, cans, boxes and tubs claiming to contain healthy ingredients crowd shelves and freezers. But before you grab that package of "natural," "holistic," "premium" or "gourmet" food, let's review what these, and other common claims, really mean.

Is my dog's food functional if it's labeled "complete and balanced?" "Complete and balanced" is probably the most recognized term on dog food labels and signifies that a food meets the nutritional adequacy guidelines for its intended purpose as set by the Association of American Feed Control Officials (AAFCO), the organization responsible for setting nutrient standards and ingredient definitions for animal feeds and pet foods. But many "complete and balanced" foods as defined by AAFCO contain one or more ingredients that can cause genes to express for inflammatory disease. We'll talk a lot more about these ingredients coming up, but for now be aware that just because a food meets AAFCO's nutritional adequacy guidelines doesn't mean it promotes optimum health at a cellular level.

If it's "natural" it must be healthy, right? Rolling green pastures dotted with colorful flowers are "natural." Crisp, fresh mountain air is "natural." Pure white sand between our toes is "natural." However, so are arsenic and lead. We hate to burst your bubble, but when it comes to food, the term "natural" is essentially meaningless. Why? Because it has not been legally defined by the FDA's Center for Veterinary Medicine, which, along with the states, creates and enforces pet food regulations.

AAFCO definition of natural: *A feed or ingredient derived solely from plant, animal or mined sources, either in its unprocessed state or having been subject to physical processing, heat processing, rendering, purification, extraction, hydrolysis, enzymolysis or fermentation, but not having been produced by or subject to a chemically synthetic process and not containing any additives or processing aids that are chemically synthetic except in amounts as might occur unavoidably in good manufacturing practices* (AAFCO, n.d.).

AAFCO, however, has no regulatory authority. The organization provides model pet food regulations that each state can choose to adopt and enforce—or not—at its discretion. Because it's such a vague word, the term "natural" is ripe for misuse by manufacturers that want to create the false image of a healthy product. We've seen natural products packed with processed ingredients, such as refined flour and sugar, which send pro-inflammatory messages to the cells.

The bottom line: a claim of "natural" on your dog's food does not ensure that it is functional, or that it is even any healthier than any other food on the market.

> ### Resource for state pet food labeling regulations
> Want to know your state's pet food labeling regulations? The AAFCO Web site contains a list of state feed control officials to contact for more information. Visit (http://www.aafco.org/Directory/FindMembersbyState.aspx).

The truth about "premium," "gourmet" and "holistic" pet foods

Manufacturers might bend and stretch the claim "natural" sometimes, but certainly terms like "premium," "gourmet" and "holistic" mean something, right? Sorry, but no. These terms also have no legal definition by the FDA and are not even included as part of AAFCO's pet feed definitions. According to the FDA, "Products labeled as premium or gourmet are not required to contain any different or higher quality ingredients, nor are they held up to any higher nutritional standards than are any other complete and balanced products" (USFDA, 2010).

Let's take a look at some of the pro-inflammatory ingredients that might be lurking in your dog's commercial food—even if it's labeled "natural," "premium," "gourmet" or "holistic":

Animal by-products

Animal by-products continue to stir debate among producers and consumers of commercial pet food. Proponents steadfastly believe that animal by-products provide a nutritious and economical form of protein, while others—including yours truly—are very concerned with the nature of their origin.

AAFCO definition of Meat By-Products:

The non-rendered, clean parts, other than meat, derived from slaughtered mammals. They include, but are not limited to, lungs, spleen, kidneys, brain, liver, blood, bone, partially defatted low-temperature fatty tissue, and stomachs and intestines freed of their contents. It does not include hair, horns, teeth and hooves.

AAFCO definition of Poultry By-Product Meal:

Consists of the ground, rendered, clean parts of the carcass of slaughtered poultry, such as necks, feet, undeveloped eggs, intestines, exclusive of feathers, except in such amounts as might occur unavoidably in good processing practices.

Remember that functional proteins are high quality and bioavailable. Dogs don't gain optimum health at the cellular level from eating poor quality protein sources such as animal heads, feet, backs and intestines as their primary protein source.

But that's not the only problem with animal by-products. A huge industry called the rendering industry exists to convert by-products from dead animals into a variety of ingredients used in industrial and consumer goods, from candles to by-product meals used in pet foods.

A 2004 report to Congress titled *Animal Rendering: Economics and Policy* (Becker, 2004) on the rendering industry defines the rendering process as follows:

In most systems, raw materials are ground to a uniform size and placed in continuous cookers or in batch cookers, which evaporate moisture and free fat from protein and bone. A series of conveyers, presses, and a centrifuge continue the process of separating fat from solids. The finished fat (e.g., tallow, lard, yellow grease) goes into separate tanks, and the solid protein (e.g., MBM, bone meal, poultry meal) is pressed into cake for processing into feed. Other rendering systems are used, including those that recover protein solids from slaughterhouse blood or that process used restaurant grease. This restaurant grease generally is recovered (often in 55-gallon drums) for use as yellow grease in non-human food products like animal feeds.

That same report to Congress sheds even more disturbing insight into the rendering process, including the raw materials used to make by-product meals for pet food. Here are some direct excerpts from the report (we've added the bold to highlight some particularly alarming facts):

*Renderers annually convert 47 billion pounds or more of raw animal materials into approximately 18 billion pounds of products. Sources for these materials include meat slaughtering and processing plants (the primary one); dead animals from farms, ranches, feedlots, marketing barns, **animal shelters**, and other facilities; and fats, grease, and other food waste from restaurants and stores.*

***Renderers convert dead animals and animal parts that otherwise would require disposal into a variety of materials,** including edible and inedible tallow and lard and **proteins such as meat and bone meal (MBM). These materials in turn are exported or sold to domestic manufacturers** of a wide range of industrial and consumer goods such as livestock feed and **pet food**, soaps, pharmaceuticals, lubricants, plastics, personal care products, and even crayons.*

*Poultry operations and **pet food manufacturers accounted for 66% of the domestic MBM market of nearly 5.7 billion pounds in 2000**, while hog and cattle operations took most of the rest.*

*Independent operations handle the other 30%-35% of rendered material. These plants (estimated by NRA [National Renderers Association]) at 165 in the United States and Canada) usually collect material from other sites using specially designed trucks. They pick up and process fat and bone trimmings, inedible meat scraps, blood, feathers, and dead animals from meat and poultry slaughterhouses and processors (usually smaller ones without their own rendering operations), farms, ranches, feedlots, animal shelters, restaurants, butchers, and markets. **As a result, the majority of independents are likely to be handling mixed species. Almost all of the resulting ingredients are destined for nonhuman consumption (e.g., animal feeds, industrial products).***

While animal by-products used for human consumption (think bologna, sausage, hot dogs and organ meats) are regulated by the United States Department of Agriculture's (USDA) Food Safety and Inspection Service (FSIS), those intended for animal feed and pet food are not. The report states, "The U.S. Food and Drug Administration

(FDA) regulates animal feed ingredients, but its continuous presence in rendering plants, or in feed mills that buy rendered ingredients, is not a legal requirement" (Becker, 2004).

Animal by-products, fluoride and osteosarcoma

As if these unsavory images of animal by-products and by-product meals aren't reason enough to ditch them from your dog's diet, we uncovered even more disturbing information. In an independent laboratory test of 10 major national brands of dog food, *eight* of the foods were found to contain fluoride in amounts up to 2.5 times higher than the Environmental Protection Agency's (EPA) maximum legal dose allowed in drinking water. The eight dog foods also contained significantly more fluoride than levels implicated by a 2006 Harvard study to cause osteosarcoma in young boys. *In all eight cases, bone meal and animal byproducts were the likely sources of the excess fluoride* (EWG, 2009).

This connection makes perfect sense. When livestock drink fluoridated water or eat plants grown in high-fluoride soil, the fluoride accumulates in the animal's bones. When the bones are then rendered into meal (see above), concentrated and potentially dangerous levels of fluoride are added to the food. Dogs who eat a high-fluoride food day in and day out may be exposed to unsafe levels (EWG, 2009).

Ingredients in the eight high-fluoride brands included chicken by-product meal, poultry by-product meal, chicken meal, beef meal and bone meal. A small amount of fluoride in dog food also originates from fluoridated tap water used during manufacturing (EWG, 2009).

We'll talk more about the potential link between fluoride in dog food and canine osteosarcoma in Chapter 9.

By-products and by-product meals can be listed on pet food labels in one of two ways:

- By named species, which identifies the specific animal source (e.g., chicken by-product meal, turkey by-product meal, beef by-product meal).

- Generically, which does not identify which animal(s) make up the by-product or by-product meal (e.g., meat meal, animal by-product meal, meat and bone meal).

For all of the reasons listed above, we strongly advise against feeding your dog any food containing by-products or by-product meals. And, please, *never* feed by-products or by-product meals of generic, un-named origin. You simply cannot know what types of animals were used in these products.

Take the test: Is this "healthy" dog food functional?

Let's take a look at a real ingredients list from the label of a popular mass-market commercial dog food. This food is labeled "complete and balanced for all life stages" as defined by AAFCO:

> *Ground yellow corn, chicken by-product meal, corn gluten meal, whole wheat flour, animal fat preserved with mixed-tocopherols (form of vitamin E), rice flour, beef, soy flour, water, meat and bone meal, propylene glycol, sugar, tricalcium phosphate, phosphoric acid, salt, animal digest, potassium chloride, sorbic acid (a preservative), dried peas, dried carrots, calcium propionate (a preservative), choline chloride, L-Lysine monohydrochloride, vitamin E supplement, zinc sulfate, Red 40, ferrous sulfate, manganese sulfate, niacin, Yellow 6, Yellow 5, Vitamin A supplement, Blue 2, calcium carbonate, copper sulfate, Vitamin B-12 supplement, brewers dried yeast, calcium pantothenate, thiamine mononitrate, garlic oil, pyridoxine hydrochloride, riboflavin supplement, Vitamin D-3 supplement, menadione sodium bisulfite complex (source of Vitamin K activity), calcium iodate, folic acid, biotin, sodium selenite.*

What's wrong with this food? Let's take a closer look at the top ingredients in order of their weight:

- Ground yellow corn: sugary carbohydrate; inferior quality protein; major cause of food intolerances; replaces high quality animal-based protein; high in harmful lectins; genetically modified unless organic.

- Chicken by-product meal: we've already covered the unsavory aspects of by-product meals at length.

- Corn gluten meal: sugary carbohydrate; inferior quality protein; robs the food of higher quality animal-based proteins; high in harmful lectins; genetically modified unless organic.

- Whole wheat flour: inferior quality protein; replaces high quality animal proteins; contains gluten and lectins; major cause of food intolerances.

- Animal fat: according to AAFCO, animal fat is "obtained from the tissues of mammals and/or poultry in the commercial processes of rendering or extracting." This is a rendered product from an unnamed "mammal"!

- Rice flour: high glycemic.

- Beef: major cause of food intolerances; likely tainted with undesirable residues of livestock feed.

- Soy flour: major cause of food intolerances; causes flatulence; contains harmful lectins; endocrine disruptor; goitrogenic; phytoestrogens activate the expression of estrogen-target genes; genetically modified unless organic.

- Meat and bone meal: mystery meat from unnamed animal source; implicated to contain high levels of fluoride; unsavory rendering process; many other issues previous listed.

- Propylene glycol: a small organic alcohol commonly used as a skin conditioning agent in cosmetics; classified as expected to be toxic or harmful to non-reproductive organs; classified as a skin irritant; associated with irritant and allergic contact dermatitis as well as hives in humans (EWG, 2013b).

- Sugar: high-glycemic carbohydrate; pro-inflammatory; empty calories; promotes obesity.

- Animal digest: according to AAFCO, this is "material which results from chemical and/or enzymatic hydrolysis of clean and un-decomposed animal tissue." The source of the "animal" used is unnamed, meaning it can be made from most any unsavory source.

This food also contains chemical preservatives, harmful vitamin K3 (menadione) and *several* artificial coloring agents (Blue 2, Red 40, Yellow 5 and Yellow 6).

Unbelievably, the manufacturer advertises this product as "nutritious." Why? The only reason we can think of is because it meets AAFCO's nutritional guidelines for "complete and balanced for all life stages." It certainly doesn't promote optimum health at the cellular level!

Just imagine the impact this food has on a dog's epigenome. No wonder so many people who strive to provide their canine companions with healthy and wholesome foods end up scratching their heads every time their dog exhibits the signs of a new illness that seems to pop up out of nowhere.

In Part I, you learned the background of nutrigenomics and the important role nutritional ingredients play in cellular health and gene expression. You also learned the two-step process to building a diet based on the principles of nutrigenomics:

- Step 1: Include as many functional foods in your dog's diet as possible.

- Step 2: Eliminate as many non-functional foods from your dog's diet as possible.

We also discussed in detail how to differentiate between functional ingredients and non-functional ingredients, and factors that can contaminate otherwise functional foods. Now, let's move on to Part II, where you'll build an optimum diet for your dog based on the principles of nutrigenomics, regardless of his age, lifestyle or current state of health.

Takeaway Points

- Foods that are toxic for dogs, such as chocolate and grapes, are never functional and should always be avoided (see page 38 for complete list).

- A variety of factors can turn an inherently functional food into a non-functional food, including chemical additives, GMOs and even the food's packaging.

- Unlike the functional carbohydrates discussed in Chapter 2, processed, sugary, high-glycemic "junk" carbs (e.g., corn, white potatoes, sugar, wheat and white rice) are non-functional ingredients that can trigger the body to produce an inflammatory response and contribute to a variety of chronic diseases.

- Factory farming has turned many inherently functional protein sources into non-functional foods through a variety of contamination factors affecting food production animals.

- No food is functional if it causes a food intolerance/sensitivity in your dog. Foods that most commonly cause intolerances/sensitivities in dogs are beef, chicken, corn, cow's milk products, soy, wheat and other grains containing gluten.

- Not all novel proteins are novel for every dog. For a protein to be novel, the dog must never before have eaten it.

- Corn, wheat and soy are common protein sources found in many mass-market, commercial pet foods because they're cheap to produce. Unfortunately, these inferior quality proteins can create a host of health problems for dogs who eat them, including leaky gut syndrome, obesity, neurologic disorders, skin issues, systemic inflammation and thyroid disruption.

- Much of today's cow's milk contains A1 beta-casein, an aberrant protein that has been linked to a host of autoimmune diseases. Cow's milk is also highly antigenic for dogs. We advise feeding your dog only goat and sheep's milk dairy products.

- Many mass-market, commercial pet foods contain non-functional food additives such as artificial colors, flavors and palatability enhancers; chemical preservatives; emulsifying agents; stabilizers/thickeners; and humectants that can send unhealthy signals to the cells.

- Genetically engineered crops are *patented inventions* developed mainly by six chemical companies. Most GM crops were invented so they could be sprayed with more weed-killing herbicides without harming the genetically engineered plant. As a result, GM crops have led to substantial increases in the use of herbicides and insecticides, often in amounts that have never been tested for safety in humans, animals or other plants.

- The top three GM crops grown in the U.S. are corn, soybeans and cotton.

- We advise against feed GM foods until these foods have been thoroughly tested by *independent* authorities and proven safe for both humans and animals.

- Beware of packaging containing BPA (Bisphenol A), a chemical used to make plastics and resin liners for cans. A known endocrine disruptor, BPA can leech into foods and beverages and pass into the systems of anyone eating or drinking the contaminated ingredients.

- Many producers of mass-market, commercial pet foods market their products with claims such as "natural," "holistic," "premium" or "gourmet." However, these terms hold little meaning and do not ensure that the food is functional.

- We strongly advise steering clear of foods containing animal by-products and by-product meals. These foods do not provide high quality, bioavailable protein, may originate from unsavory sources and can lead to dangerous levels of fluoride in your dog's system.

Part II

Building the Canine Nutrigenomics Diet: The Basal Diet

Chapter 4

The Basal Diet: The Foundation

of Optimal Health

We're going to begin building your dog's optimum diet with what we call the "basal" diet. The basal diet is the nutritious base to which you can add other functional ingredients according to your dog's individual needs, including specific health issues he might currently have (*much* more on health conditions in later chapters). Think of the basal diet as you would the foundation of a building. A strong foundation can support a soaring, beautiful skyscraper, while a weak foundation will crumble even under the weight of a rickety old shed. In other words, you can give your dog many of the wonderful functional ingredients we'll discuss later on, but if you toss them on top of a non-functional basal diet, he won't benefit from optimum gene expression and cellular health.

Once again, we're going to ask you to take a fresh (pun intended) approach to how you view a healthy, nutritious canine diet—especially if you've been following the advice purported by many veterinary professionals and mass-market commercial pet food companies to stick with one "balanced" product for your dog's entire adult life. While this advice might benefit the pet food companies selling these foods, just imagine if you were forced to eat one meal, day in and day out, for your entire life. Obviously, you would quickly become bored. And people wonder why their dogs suddenly become "finicky" eaters!

Building a balanced diet

Beyond the disappointment and despair dogs must feel when they eagerly approach their bowl and—*gulp!*—there's that *same* pile of food again, is the fact that sticking to one "balanced" diet day after day is just plain *unbalanced* thinking from a nutritional perspective. It assumes that your dog is a static being whose physiological needs remain unchanged for years, only varying by life stage (i.e., puppy, adult and senior). And manufacturers of "all life stages" foods even claim they've got that covered!

Common sense should tell us that this line of thinking is quite unsound (Hofve, 2013; Straus, 2007).

Imagine if you took your toddler to the pediatrician and she plunked a bag of "kiddie food" in front of you and said, "This bag of dry pellets contains all the vitamins, minerals and nutrients that little Billy will need for his entire life. And, whatever you do, don't give Billy any 'table foods,' such as fresh carrots, broccoli or apples, because that will throw off the entire balance of the diet and could severely jeopardize his health." Hopefully, you'd race out the door and immediately search for a new doctor (Hofve, 2013; Straus, 2007)!

So, then, why do we accept this line of thinking when it comes to our dogs? Why do people live in fear of deviating from one "complete and balanced" (and boring) diet or shy away from feeding their dogs a healthy variety of fresh, wholesome foods?

Just like a person, a dog's physiology is constantly responding to environmental influences, such as weather and seasonal changes, as well as internal factors such as fatigue, stress and hormonal fluctuations. It's unreasonable to think that a single diet can provide the proper nutrition to meet all of a dog's changing needs—not only year-to-year, but day-to-day.

Many "experts" behave as if we have reached our pinnacle of knowledge on dog food nutrition. These experts chastise and frighten caring dog guardians into believing that varying from currently accepted recommendations will spell certain disaster for their beloved canine companions—and that they will have only themselves to blame. But, as we demonstrate throughout this book, new research is emerging all the time, and strictly following guidelines that were established based on old and outdated information simply does not do our dogs justice (Straus, 2007).

Moreover, we demonstrated in the previous chapter that even "complete and balanced" commercial dog foods can contain ingredients not declared on the label, so consumers have no way of knowing the exact nutrient levels of these foods. Commercial foods also commonly rely on the barest amount of inferior quality proteins, by-products, grains and synthetic vitamins to create balance—not to mention all the other unsavory ingredients they can contain. Is that the type of nutrition you would want to feed your child? Of course not. Now, let's also demand better for our *four-legged* children!

So, how can you best meet your dog's ever changing nutritional needs? *By feeding him a variety of nutrient-dense whole foods that promote optimum gene expression and nutritional balance over time.*

The Three Keys

The ideal canine diet contains three key elements, which we call the Three Keys:

Variety: To obtain nutritional balance, you *must* include all necessary food groups, including red meat, poultry (including fat), fish, eggs, organ meats (e.g., liver from beef, chicken, lamb, pork or bison), dairy (sheep and goat), fruits and vegetables (Straus, 2013).

Nutrient-dense: Select fresh, wholesome foods packed with antioxidants, phyto-nutrients, essential fatty acids and high quality amino acids we discuss throughout this book.

Whole foods: This means *real* food, including fresh meats, fish, eggs, dairy, fruits and vegetables—*not* rendered by-products and synthetic chemicals!

Unfortunately, when most home-prepared canine diets are analyzed for nutritional content, they come up short—sometimes very short—in certain nutrients, which is also counterproductive to creating optimum health (Stockman et al., 2013). The fact is that dogs do have certain unique nutritional requirements that differ from our own, which many people fail to take into account when formulating homemade canine diets. For example, dogs require far more calcium per pound of body weight than people do (Straus, 2013). However, we believe that the majority of nutritional deficiencies arise from a failure to follow one of the three dietary keys listed above (with the exception of calcium deficiencies).

For example, you might think that rotating a couple of different protein sources, such as pork and lamb, provides sufficient nutritional variety. In reality, though, you're omitting other important sources—such as fish and organ meats—that deliver different amino acid profiles and essential nutrients. For example, liver provides protein along with fat, vitamin A, copper, iron, niacin, phosphorus, zinc and B vitamins, while fish is an important source of the essential **omega-3 fatty acids** EPA and DHA (VetInfo, 2012).

Rotating foods from the necessary food groups listed above also helps ensure you don't overfeed from any one group. In our liver example, feeding a small amount a couple of times a week is fine, but overdoing it can result in an overdose of vitamin A, which can cause bone deformity, bone spurs on the dog's legs or spine that cause him to limp, digestive upsets, muscle weakness, stiffness or weight loss (VetInfo, 2012). If your dog eats too much of a specific food, especially protein sources, he's also more likely to develop an intolerance/sensitivity to that ingredient (Refer to the section on novel proteins from the previous chapter).

So, yes, feeding a properly balanced diet is of course essential to your dog's health, but such a diet need not originate from a bag or can, or from the "nutrition prescription pad" of a board-certified veterinary nutritionist, who will likely rely on the following: a small amount of one type of lean meat for protein (likely chicken, which is problematic for many dogs); a *lot* of high-GI carbohydrates (such as white rice); a non-functional vegetable oil (such as corn or canola) to provide calories and fat; and an all-purpose synthetic multi-vitamin/mineral mix to balance the diet (Straus, 2013). Such a diet *does not* promote optimum gene expression.

You can create a nutritious, balanced diet that sends healthy messages to your dog's cells by following our Three Keys (variety, nutrient-dense, whole foods), incorporating a variety of functional carbohydrates, proteins and fats discussed in Chapter 2 and supplementing with a few nutrients that are likely to come up short otherwise—preferably in whole food form.

Nutritional supplementation for home-prepared diets

The following nutrients are commonly deficient in *home-prepared diets* (but not "complete and balanced" commercial foods) and require supplementation. Remember that, regardless of the quality of your homemade diet, you *must* supplement with calcium to meet your dog's needs; the exception being if he eats (not just gnaws on, but actually ingests) raw meaty bones (Straus, 2013).

Note: These nutrient recommendations are for adult dogs in a maintenance stage. If your dog is a puppy or senior, please consult with your veterinarian for dosing recommendations.

Calcium

Calcium is the most abundant mineral found in animals. About 99% of the body's calcium is found in the skeleton and teeth, with the blood and soft tissue containing the other one percent. Dogs need a lot of calcium, and most home-prepared diets come up short in this department because meat, veggies and grains are all deficient for a dog's needs. *Therefore, calcium supplementation is necessary.* Calcium deficiency in adult animals causes osteomalacia, resulting in weak bones that are easily broken. Studies also show that calcium influx into the cell's cytoplasm can alter gene expression that affects the brain (Institute of Neuroscience, 2011). Excellent sources of calcium include dairy products (preferably goat and sheep's milk), bananas, dark leafy greens, sea vegetables (nori, kombu, wakami), cooked beans and bone (Case et al., 2011; McDonald et al., 2011).

Dose: 1,000 mg calcium per 1,000 kcal/ME (metabolizable energy) daily (NRC, 2006). We recommend calcium citrate, which is easier to digest than calcium carbonate.

Perhaps the easiest and most cost-effective way to add extra calcium to your dog's diet is to make your own calcium supplement using ground up eggshell (1/2 teaspoon provides about 1,000 mg calcium). Simply rinse the shells and allow them to dry completely, then grind them to a fine powder using a clean coffee grinder. They'll last indefinitely if kept dry (Straus, 2011). We recommend storing them in a clean, dry air-tight bottle, such as an empty supplement bottle.

We also recommend a whole food calcium supplement made from dehydrated seaweed meal from the company Animal Essentials. See our sample one-day adult maintenance diet recipe and the Resources section for purchasing information.

Bone meal powder supplements are also available, however these can be contaminated with heavy metals, such as lead and aluminum. Bone meal may also contain high levels of fluoride, which, as we discuss in Chapters 3 and 9, may contribute to osteoasarcoma in dogs. For those reasons, we do not recommend bone meal as a source of calcium for dogs.

Note: Since calcium is already added to commercial pet foods, additional supplementation is not necessary, and could even cause problems because calcium binds to many other minerals and can cause a deficiency. However, supplementing with calcium is necessary in commercial raw diets that do not include raw meaty bones. If your dog eats at least 20% raw meaty bones, you don't need to supplement with added calcium (Straus, 2011).

How to determine supplement dosing for your dog

Throughout the book, you'll notice that we often list nutrient doses in terms of units (e.g., mg) per "1,000 kcal/ME daily." We do this because it is a common method used in the book *Nutrient Requirements of Dogs and Cats*, published by the National Research Council (NRC), a branch of the National Academy of Sciences. While this method might sound complicated, it's really not once you know the simple three-step formula for converting the dose to fit your dog's daily caloric intake. Here's how:

Step 1: Take the dose as it's listed per 1,000 kcal/ME daily.

Step 2: Multiply that number by the number of kcals your dog eats each day.

Step 3: Divide the new number by 1,000.

The key is not to let the "kcal" part throw you off. One kcal (kilocalorie; the unit of energy measurement used in animal nutrition) equals one Calorie (the energy measurement unit used in human nutrition). This is especially handy to know if you feed your dog a home-prepared diet.

Here's how to determine the daily vitamin E requirement for a 30-pound dog who eats 920 kcal/(Calories) per day:

Step 1: Take 7.5 mg (the original vitamin E dose per 1,000 kcal/ME daily)

Step 2: 7.5 mg x 920 kcal/(Calories) = 6,900

Step 3: 6,900 ÷ 1,000 = *6.9 mg vitamin E daily*

Linoleic acid

Linoleic acid is the most important Omega 6 fatty acid for dogs, since it is used to produce other Omega 6 fatty acids. Linoleic acid is also especially important for the health of a dog's skin and coat, as it allows the skin to become permeable to water. It is primarily found in poultry fat and plant oils, including evening primrose, hempseed, olive, safflower, sunflower and walnut oil. For reasons we've already covered, we do not recommend soybean or corn oil.

Dose: 2,800 mg per 1,000 kcal/ME daily.

Omega-3 essential fatty acids

By the time you're finished reading this book, you'll know *a lot* about the amazing benefits of **omega-3s**. We'll be talking in detail about this canine functional superfood in upcoming chapters, specifically with regard to its benefits for a variety of health conditions. Let's take a look at what **omega-3 fatty acids** consist of and the best ways to supplement your dog's diet with this canine functional superfood.

Omega-3 fatty acids are a type of polyunsaturated fatty acid (PUFA), a dietary fat that is liquid at room temperature (unlike saturated fats such as butter, which are solid at room temperature). There are three types of PUFAs:

- **Omega-3 fatty acids**, which can originate from both plant-based and marine sources, as follows:
  - Alpha-linolenic acid (ALA) is a plant-based **omega-3** found in seeds such as chia and flaxseeds, as well as in nuts such as walnuts and many vegetable oils.
  - Eicosapentaenoic acid (EPA) and Docosahexaenoic acid (DHA) are both found in fish oil and other marine sources, as well as some plant-based sources. *EPA and DHA are the preferred form of **omega-3 fatty acids** for dogs.* We'll discuss why in a minute.
- Omega-6 fatty acids, which include linolenic acid (LA) and arachidonic acid (AA). Omega-6s are found in seeds and nuts and the oils that are made from them.
- Omega-9 fatty acids, which we will not discuss because they are not required in the diet.

Omega-3 and omega-6 fatty acids are essential fatty acids (EFAs) because the body cannot readily produce them, so they must come from dietary sources. Omega-9 fatty acids can be manufactured in the body and so are not considered essential.

Both **omega-3** and omega-6 fatty acids are important for health, however there is an important distinction. **Omega-3 fatty acids** regulate cellular metabolic functions and gene expression in a manner that *reduces inflammation* (Deckelbaum et al., 2006), while omega 6-fatty acids, particularly arachidonic acid (AA), can *promote inflammation* when consumed in excessive amounts (Deckelbaum et al., 2006; Laflamme, 2004; Waldron, 2004).

The problem is that the Standard American Diet (SAD)—or, more appropriately in the case of our canine companions, the Standard American Dog Diet (SADD)—contains a significant imbalance in the ratio of omega-6 fatty acids to **omega-3 fatty** *acids*, with both people and dogs consuming far too much omega-6s and far too little *omega-3s*.

As we noted above, EPA and DHA from fish oil and other marine sources are far better sources of *omega-3s* for dogs than plant-based ALA. This is so for two main reasons:

- Studies clearly show that EPA and DHA are more effective at modulating cellular metabolic functions and gene expression than plant-based ALA (Deckelbaum et al., 2006).

- Although dietary ALA can be metabolized into EPA and DHA in the body, dogs do not efficiently make this conversion. Therefore, they should consume EPA and DHA directly to gain maximum benefit.

We recommend incorporating foods rich in EPA and DHA into your dog's diet. Here are our favorites:

- Anchovies
- Fish oil
- Halibut
- Herring
- Mackerel
- Salmon (select only wild-caught)
- Sardines

Dogs can also benefit from a high-quality EPA/DHA supplement from fish oil or other marine source. Just bear in mind that the more *omega-3s* your dog receives from fresh food sources, the less you will need to supplement.

Dose: 100 to 150 mg of EPA and DHA combined *per 10 pounds of body weight* daily (Straus, 2013).

We cannot stress enough the importance of purchasing a pure, human-grade fish oil supplement from a reputable manufacturer. Unfortunately, much of the fish in our food supply is contaminated with heavy metals and other industrial pollutants, and you definitely don't want to supplement your dog's diet with these toxins that can infiltrate his epigenome! Products made from smaller fish, such as sardines and anchovies, are preferable, since these fish don't accumulate dangerous levels of toxins like their larger, carnivorous relatives (e.g., tuna and swordfish). You can find recommended sources for fish oil in the Resources section.

While fish oil contains an immense amount of beneficial anti-inflammatory properties, it can also increase oxidation in the body, as well as deplete vitamin E levels over time. Vitamin E, a powerful antioxidant, can help counteract these effects and should be used when supplementing with fish oil. Read on for more information on vitamin E, including dosing.

Also, please do not give your dog supplements made from fish liver oil, such as cod liver oil, as these can result in toxic levels of vitamins A and D.

Selenium

Selenium is a trace mineral with many important roles, including defending the body against oxidative damage and boosting immune response. Selenium also potentially increases the effectiveness of vitamin E. Many countries, including the United States, contain soils deficient in selenium and crops grown on these soils will contain relatively low levels. Selenium is important in maintaining the health of the thyroid and a link has recently been shown between selenium deficiency and hypothyroidism. Selenium as it relates to hypothyroidism is often difficult to spot because blood, but not tissue, levels of thyroid hormones rise in cases of selenium deficiency. This means that although a selenium deficient dog may display clinical signs of hypothyroidism, his blood thyroid levels will appear normal. Bear in mind, however, that selenium is also the most toxic mineral, and it is only required in very low doses. Fish, meat and eggs are good sources of selenium (Straus, 2013).

Dose: 87.5 µg (mcg) per 1,000 kcal/ME daily (NRC, 2006).

Vitamin B-6 (pyridoxine)

Vitamin B-6 is essential for a healthy nervous system, protein metabolism, the formation and function of red blood cells and healthy cognitive and immune function. Vitamin B-6 has also been shown to up or down-regulate the expression of certain genes, including genes that control the production of **glucocorticoid** (steroid) hormones and the synthesis of **albumin**, a protein produced in the liver and found in blood plasma. Albumin serves many important functions, including transporting hormones, fatty acids, calcium, medications and other important molecules through the blood (egg whites are a good source of albumin). Signs of vitamin B-6 deficiency include anemia, seizures, skin disorders, arthritis, fatigue, kidney stones and kidney damage. Since all B vitamins are water-soluble, excess amounts are eliminated from the body via the urine rather than stored in the tissues, as with fat-soluble vitamins. Cooking and processing destroys much of the vitamin B-6 present in raw foods. Sources of vitamin B-6 include whole grains, legumes (feed in moderation due to lectins), green leafy vegetables (e.g., kale, collard greens, Brussels sprouts, broccoli and chard), bananas, meat, poultry and fish.

Dose: 375 µg (mcg) per 1,000 kcal/ME daily (NRC, 2006).

Vitamin D

Vitamin D is a fat-soluble vitamin that is well known for its role in maintaining sufficient levels of calcium and phosphorous in the body. But the role of vitamin D extends much further. The metabolic product of vitamin D synthesis, calcitriol, is actually a steroidal hormone that binds to and influences thousands of different genes. Almost every type of cell—from the brain to the bones—contains receptors that respond to calcitriol. Calcitriol up-regulates the body's ability to fight infections and chronic inflammation, and the body's organs use it to repair cellular damage, including damage from cancer cells (Mercola, 2010) (more on vitamin D and cancer in Chapter 9).

Most people get plenty of vitamin D from sun exposure (assuming they don't continuously wear sunscreen), but it's not so easy for dogs because our canine companions cannot efficiently convert the sun's ultraviolet rays into vitamin D. This means that dogs must get their vitamin D from dietary sources or supplementation (Case et al., 2011).

Not many foods naturally contain vitamin D (most are fortified). The best sources are the flesh of fatty fish, such as salmon, tuna and swordfish (NIH, 2011), however we strongly advise against feeding tuna and swordfish due to their high mercury content, and recommend only wild-caught salmon (as opposed to farm-raised, which is the factory farming equivalent for fish) Sardines and egg yolks also contain small amounts and are good options (NIH, 2011).

There are two forms of vitamin D to D2 (ergocalciferol) and D3 (cholecalciferol). Vitamin D3 is more nutritionally important to dogs than D2, as they utilize cholecalciferol more efficiently. Please be sure to purchase a product containing natural vitamin D3 (cholecalciferol), not synthetic vitamin D2 (Mercola, 2010).

Equally important is making sure not to over-supplement with vitamin D. Since vitamin D is fat-soluble, excess levels are stored in the liver and can lead to toxicity, which is potentially life threatening. Symptoms of toxicity in dogs can include excessive drooling, vomiting (sometimes with blood), loss of appetite, increased thirst and urination, weakness, depression, abdominal pain, dark tarry feces, weight loss, constipation, muscle tremors, and seizures (Becker, 2014). Excessive amounts of vitamin D can also cause **hypercalcemia**, or excessive levels of blood calcium, which can result in conditions ranging from bladder stones to coma (in severe cases) (MedlinePlus, 2013; PetMD, 2013). Please consult with your veterinarian regarding the proper vitamin D levels for your dog.

Dose: 136 IUs per 1,000 kcal/ME daily. This is equivalent to 3.4 µg (mcg) of cholecalciferol per 1,000 kcal/ME daily (NRC, 2006).

Vitamin E

Vitamin E is a fat-soluble antioxidant vitamin most recognized for its role in neutralizing harmful **free radicals** (unstable and chemically incomplete atoms) that, left unchecked, can cause cellular oxidation and damage. Via its antioxidant role, vitamin E aids in the prevention of cancer and diseases of the circulatory system, including **arteriosclerosis** (mineral deposits in the walls of arteries) as well as slowing the aging process. Vitamin E has also been shown to significantly impact the expression of T-cells, which are associated with aging: vitamin E improves T-cell function in the old (Han et al., 2006).

Vitamin E also boosts immune function, oxygenates the blood, improves the function of internal organs, prevents hormones from oxidation, reduces inflammation and helps fight infection. It has also been used to treat or modulate skin disorders and immune-mediated diseases in dogs. Animals who are deficient in vitamin E may display brown bowel syndrome, a condition in which their bowels ulcerate and hemorrhage and the tissue degenerates. Good sources of vitamin E include cold pressed vegetable oils, nuts, seeds, green leafy vegetables, eggs, most fish and meats such as beef, duck, turkey leg and chicken breast.

Dose: 7.5 mg of alpha-tocopherol per 1,000 kcal/ME daily (NRC, 2006).

Zinc

Zinc is a trace mineral critical to the function of the entire immune system and plays a key role in more than 300 enzymatic and metabolic processes, including cell replication and the production of thyroid hormones. It is also vital to the health of the skin. Zinc deficiency commonly results in a condition known as zinc responsive dermatosis, which is especially prevalent among Huskies, Malamutes and Samoyeds—breeds that have a genetic predisposition to poor zinc absorption. Symptoms of zinc responsive dermatosis include: hair loss; dull and dry hair coat; scaly, crusty skin around the legs, head, and face (especially on the nose and circling the eyes, ears, chin, and mouth); poor wound healing; and thick and crusty foot pads. Zinc deficiency can also affect reproduction. Red meat and liver are excellent sources of zinc. Egg yolks are also a good source (Straus, 2013).

Dose: 15 mg per 1,000 kcal/ME daily (NRC, 2006).

You can give your dog a high quality, whole food human or canine multi-vitamin to fill any nutritional gaps, but always be sure to include a separate source of calcium supplementation, as a multi-vitamin will fall short in this nutrient. Be careful when purchasing supplements, since many brands contain known antigens, such as wheat or corn that can trigger food intolerances/sensitivities. Also steer clear of products containing artificial colors, flavors, fillers, sugars or other unwanted ingredients, as these will counteract their functional effect.

Some reputable manufacturers also produce high quality freeze-dried pre-mixes, which are made with a combination of vegetables and nutrients that, when rehydrated with your own animal protein and fat source (i.e., oil) create a nutritionally balanced meal. This is an excellent option if you want to prepare a fresh, wholesome meal, but don't have the time to purchase and cook your own vegetables.

See the Resources section for purchasing information.

Sample one-day maintenance diet for an adult dog

The following is a sample one-day diet for a 30-pound adult dog in a maintenance stage (based on 765 kcal/Calories per day). This diet includes breakfast, dinner and supplementation:

Breakfast

- Instant oatmeal (preferably gluten free)—1 individual packet
- *Blueberries* (frozen work perfectly)—1/2 cup
- Virgin *coconut oil*—1 teaspoon
- *Raw honey*—1 teaspoon

Pour oatmeal from packet into bowl. Stir in boiled water. Immediately stir in the frozen *blueberries*, then the *coconut oil* and *raw honey*. The hot water warms the *blueberries* instantly! Make sure the oatmeal is warm, but not too hot. Serve to your dog and watch him lick the bowl clean!

Dinner

- Brown rice (can use instant), cooked—1/2 cup
- Turkey, ground crumbles, fat-free, pan-broiled—6 ounces
- Chicken (or turkey) liver, simmered and chopped—1/2 ounce
- Broccoli florets, cooked and chopped (preferably steamed; can use frozen)—1/2 cup
- Carrot (if serving raw, finely chop)—half of a medium-sized
- Goat cheese—1 ounce

Cook the brown rice according to the package directions. Brown the turkey and liver in a little bit of olive oil. Steam the broccoli and carrot (or finely chop raw carrot). Combine the ingredients in your dog's bowl. Add one dose of supplements (see below). Mix in the goat cheese or sprinkle on top. Serve to your happy dog!

Supplements to balance diet*

- Nordic Naturals Omega-3 Pet—1 soft gel daily
- Vetri-Science Canine Plus (multi-vitamin)—2 tablets daily
- Animal Essentials Seaweed Calcium—as directed on package
- Innate Response Balanced Minerals (*note*: this is a human supplement)—3 tablets daily

*When giving more than one supplement dose per day, split doses between morning and evening. These supplements provide the vitamins and minerals that are often missing in home prepared diets, as discussed above.

See Resources section for manufacturers and online retailers of these products.

Note that this diet represents just a one-day sample. Be sure to follow our Three Keys discussed above and refer to the specific functional carbohydrates, proteins and fats discussed in Chapter 2 to create a delicious and varied diet that both tantalizes your dog's taste buds and provides optimum cellular health and balance over time.

Now, let's take a look at the special functional nutritional needs of puppies and senior dogs.

Special considerations for puppies

Imagine developing from birth to maturity in a few short months (after all, it takes humans more than a decade)! Puppies develop most rapidly during the first six months, which is known as the "pediatric life stage." During this time, puppies:

- Grow mature bones, tissues, muscles and internal organs.
- Form new nervous system connections.
- Further develop brain and cognitive functions.
- Build a strong immune system.

Puppies require the same nutrients as mature dogs, however they require *different amounts* of these nutrients to support optimum growth—for example, about twice the protein and 2.25 times the number of calories (adjusted for size) as their older adult counterparts (Wannemacher & McCoy, 1966). While the best way to control the quality of your puppy's food is to prepare it yourself, formulating a homemade diet for a puppy is much trickier than for an adult dog because his nutritional needs can literally change weekly as he sprouts into adulthood. An excess or deficiency in any key nutrient can spell disaster for a puppy's growth and development and jeopardize his lifelong health.

Calcium and phosphorus are key examples. These are the most abundant minerals in the body and the primary components of bone and teeth. Puppies require the correct amount and balance of these minerals to promote proper musculoskeletal development. However, both a deficiency and excess of calcium and phosphorus are dangerous. Deficiency can lead to weak bones and fractures, while excess can cause Developmental Orthopedic Disease (DOD). This is especially true for large breed puppies that must grow at a slow, steady rate to avoid serious orthopedic problems.

To ensure that your pup receives the correct amount and balance of nutrients, as well as a diet that promotes optimum health at the cellular level, we advise working with a veterinarian experienced in functional nutrition, such as the author, WJD or a functional canine nutritionist trained at a reputable university, such as the author, DRL. Be sure to check education and training credentials, as anyone can deem herself a "canine nutritionist" or a "pet nutritionist."

If you are caring for a puppy who has been orphaned, or whose mother cannot supply enough milk to meet his developmental needs, you can feed a protein milk substitute such as Esbilac or Puppylac (see below for an emergency recipe). However, puppies who do not nurse will not receive essential **colostrum** (the first milk produced by their mothers), which contains antibodies to protect newborns against infectious diseases until they are able to form their own. These puppies will require fresh-frozen canine plasma as an alternate source of antibodies within the first 24 to 48 hours after birth, which must be given *before* they receive a protein milk substitute. If a protein milk substitute is given before the plasma, vital antibodies in the plasma will not be absorbed through the puppy's intestinal lining and the pups will be unprotected from infectious diseases until the time they receive their puppy vaccinations, which will not occur for several weeks. During this interval, they will remain vulnerable to a variety of potentially life-threatening diseases.

Emergency Puppy Milk Replacer (Adapted from Drs. Foster & Smith, www.pet-education.com):

- 1 cup whole milk (preferably sheep or goat)
- 1 pinch table grade salt
- 3 egg yolks—no whites
- 1 tablespoon olive oil
- ¼ teaspoon liquid vitamins

In addition to functional meats, fish, eggs and dairy as discussed above, puppies thrive on vegetables like green beans, broccoli and carrots as well as fruits such as bananas and melons. These make wonderful, healthy treats packed with lots of nutrition. Try freezing some fruits and veggies and giving them to your teething puppy. The cold will soothe his sore gums while giving him something to chew on other than your shoes and furniture!

Additional functional nutrients beneficial to puppies include:

- ***Omega-3 fatty acids***: vital to a puppy's physical and cognitive development. Adding fish oil to your puppy's diet increases his learning ability, psychomotor skills, memory, immunologic and retinal functions (Zicker et al., 2012).
- Beta-glucans: found in the cell walls of yeast, fungi and certain plants such as oats and barley, beta-glucans are polysaccharide sugars that have powerful beneficial effects on the immune system after vaccination (Haladová et al., 2009; Haladová et al., 2011; Stuyven et al., 2010).

Special considerations for senior dogs

Senior dogs are on the opposite end of the activity spectrum as puppies. As with adults, senior dogs are in a maintenance phase; however, they are generally less active and have slower metabolisms. To avoid excess weight gain, special care should be taken to adjust their energy intake according to their activity level. Of course, each senior dog is unique, but in general, a dog's energy needs decline as he ages. Dogs older than eight years have been found to consume about 18% fewer calories than same-breed dogs younger than six years (Case et al., 2011; Segal, 2007; Sheffy, 1985).

Protein and senior dogs

There is a lot of misinformation floating around regarding optimum protein intake for senior dogs (Case et al., 2011; Wannemacher & McCoy, 1966). Many people believe that protein overworks older kidneys and that protein should automatically be decreased in an older dog's diet. This is false. Dietary protein does not stress or harm the kidneys of otherwise healthy senior dogs. On the contrary, healthy older dogs require slightly *more* protein. Protein minimizes loss of lean body mass that accompanies the aging process. Protein reserves are also important because the body mobilizes protein as a natural part of its response to stress, including disease, infection and injury; therefore, loss of protein reserves inhibits an animal's ability to respond to stress. In direct opposition to common recommendations, senior dogs actually *benefit* from moderate to high levels of high quality, readily bioavailable dietary protein (Case et al., 2011).

Functional foods for senior dogs

Older dogs have a decreased ability to fight disease, creating the potential for health problems ranging from infections to cancer. For example, genetic differences have been identified that determine which geriatric dogs will get kidney disease and which ones will remain healthy (Frantz et al., 2008). These conditions are perilous enough to a younger body, but can spell debilitation or death to an older animal. Providing your senior dog with specific functional nutrients can help enhance and balance his immune systems' function.

We recommend the following foods for seniors:

- Apples: protect the heart, block diarrhea, improve lung capacity, cushion joints.
- Bananas: protect the heart, strengthen bones, control blood pressure, block diarrhea.
- Beans: lower cholesterol, combat cancer, stabilize blood sugar (feed in moderation due to lectins).
- Beets: combat cancer, strengthen bones, protect the heart.
- *Berries*: combat cancer, protect the heart, stabilize blood sugar, boost memory (do no feed strawberries to your dog).
- *Coconut oil*: supplies medium-chain triglycerides, supports healthy brain aging.

- Cranberries: antioxidant, lower urine pH, coat the bladder lining.

- *Curcumin*: powerful antioxidant, antimicrobial and **antineoplastic** (prevents or halts tumor development).

- Fish (low mercury, such as sardines) and fish oil: excellent source of *omega-3 fatty acids*, anti-inflammatory, protect the heart, combat cancer, support healthy immune system and much more (see following chapters).

- Plant-based oils (listed above): help the joints, skin, kidneys and brain. (Avoid oils that can promote inflammation such as corn, safflower and canola oils.)

- *Pomegranates*: antioxidant, help buffer against cell damage, help cardiac oxygenation.

- *Raw honey* (*not* pasteurized): aids digestion, increases energy (not for puppies under one year).

- Sweet potatoes: combat cancer, strengthen bones, improve eyesight.

- Yogurt (from goat or sheep's milk): strengthens bones, supports the immune system, supplies *probiotics*, aids digestion.

In the next chapter, we'll discuss the functional nutritional needs of high-performance dogs.

Takeaway Points

- The basal diet is the sturdy foundation that will support the rest of your dog's optimum diet based on the principles of nutrigenomics.

- Advice to stick with one "complete and balanced" diet for your dog's life assumes that he is a static being whose physiological needs remain unchanged for years. This line of thinking is nutritionally unsound, not to mention boring for your dog!

- Just like a person, a dog's physiology constantly responds to environmental influences and internal factors. A single diet cannot provide the proper nutrition to meet all of a dog's changing nutritional needs.

- To best meet your dog's changing nutritional needs, feed him a variety of nutrient-dense whole foods that promote optimum gene expression and nutritional balance over time.

- The ideal canine diet contains The Three Keys: variety, nutrient-dense, whole foods.

- You can create a nutritious, balanced diet that sends healthy messages to your dog's cells by following these Three Keys, incorporating a variety of functional carbohydrates, proteins and fats discussed in Chapter 2 and supplementing with a few nutrients that are likely to come up short otherwise—preferably in whole food form.

- Home-prepared diets always require separate calcium supplementation, regardless of the diet's quality.

- Other commonly deficient nutrients that require supplementation include: linoleic acid; *omega-3 fatty* acids EPA and DHA; selenium; vitamin B-6 (pyridoxine); vitamin D; vitamin E; and zinc.

- Puppies require the same nutrients as mature dogs, however they require *different amounts* of these nutrients to support optimum growth.

- Both a deficiency and excess of calcium and phosphorus are dangerous for puppies. Deficiency can lead to weak bones and fractures, while excess can cause Developmental Orthopedic Disease (DOD), especially in large breed puppies that must grow at a slow, steady rate to avoid serious orthopedic problems.

- To ensure that your pup receives the correct amount and balance of nutrients, as well as a diet that promotes optimum health at the cellular level, we advise working with a veterinarian experienced in functional canine nutrition, such as the author, WJD or a credentialed functional canine nutrition expert trained at a reputable university, such as the author, DRL.

- *Omega-3 fatty acids* and beta-glucans provide important benefits for growing puppies.

- Contrary to popular belief, healthy senior dogs require *more*, not less, protein than younger dogs.

- Functional foods specifically beneficial to senior dogs include: apples, bananas, beans, beets, ***berries***, ***coconut oil***, cranberries, ***curcumin*** (turmeric), low-mercury fish and fish oil that are high in ***omega-3 fatty acids***, certain plant-based oils (not corn or canola oil), pomegranates, ***raw honey*** (not for puppies under one year), sweet potatoes and yogurt (from goat or sheep's milk).

Chapter 5

The Basal Diet and High-
Performance Dogs

From a nutritional perspective, high-performance dogs include canine athletes, pregnant bitches and lactating dams. Men reading this book (especially the sports fanatics among you!) might wonder why pregnant and lactating dogs rank along with athletes as high performance. As we'll elaborate on later in this chapter, pregnancy and lactation place extreme nutritional demands on a bitch's body—more than at any other time in her life. A pregnant or lactating dog must supply all the nutrients for herself as well as her litter of pups—whether those pups are receiving these nutrients through the mother's placental wall during pregnancy or via her milk during nursing. So, yes, pregnancy and lactation are even more nutritionally taxing than catching a Frisbee or running agility!

Let's take a close look at each category of high-performance dog and discuss how to apply the principles of functional nutrition for optimum health and performance.

Canine athletes

Canine athletes require a nutrient-dense diet to support the additional stress placed on their active bodies. For starters, since physical activity increases metabolism, additional energy (calories) is critical to fuel the active dog's lifestyle and enable him to perform at his peak (Gillette, 1999). But before you start feeding your dog like a "jock," be sure to objectively assess his activity level. Is he an agility, search-and-rescue, herding or farm dog, a rigorous jogger or hiker? While your canine companion might enjoy the occasional romp on the beach or brisk weekend hike, that doesn't qualify him as an athlete. If you overestimate your dog's energy needs, you'll feed him too many calories and he'll end up overweight and unhealthy.

Once you've determined that your dog really is an "athlete," the next step is to determine the type of activities he participates in—those that require short bursts of high-intensity energy or endurance sports that require longer-range stamina. This is important because the body uses three different systems to metabolize energy, and the type of activity your dog performs will determine which energy system his body will use. This, in turn, will determine whether his calories (i.e., "fuel") should come primarily from fats or carbohydrates (Gillette, 1999).

The three energy systems are:

- **Adenosine triphosphate–creatine phosphate (ATP-CP) system** (also called the phosphagen system or one enzyme system): This system uses adenosine tri-phosphate (ATP) and creatine phosphate (CP), which are stored in the muscles, to supply just enough energy for a brief, high-intensity activity such as a single vertical jump. It fuels the body for only about five to 20 seconds (Gillette, 1999; Heffernan, 2012).

- **Glycolytic energy system**: This system takes over when the ATP-CP system stops and supplies energy for up to about two minutes. It uses the process of glycolysis to convert glucose from carbohydrates into ATP (energy) and is important for strength and power activities (Gillette, 1999; Heffernan, 2012).

- **Oxidative energy system**: This system is the most complex and takes over where glycolysis leaves off, providing the sustained energy required for endurance activities. The oxidative system is an aerobic system, meaning that it uses oxygen to convert substrates into energy. The oxidative system provides the long, slow energy burn dogs need to delay fatigue, increase stamina and fuel endurance activities (Gillette, 1999; Heffernan, 2102; Hill, 1998).

If your dog participates in endurance sports, his basal diet should contain a high percentage of fat because he's drawing from the oxidative energy system. Dogs in general have a greater capacity to burn fat for energy than people do, both at rest and during exercise (Hill, 1998). In fact, research shows that even without extra conditioning, dogs on high-fat diets have more energy to burn than dogs fed a normal-fat diet. When sedentary dogs are conditioned in addition to eating a high-fat diet, their ability to burn energy increases even more (Coffman, n.d.). Of course, we recommend providing your dog with age and health-appropriate exercise opportunities to avoid weight gain. Besides, exercising with your dog, even if it's a walk around your neighborhood, offers excellent socialization and mental stimulation for him, as well as deepening the bond the two of you share.

So, while it's not unusual for human athletes to "carb load" before a marathon run, this philosophy does not work for dogs (Coffman, n.d.). Dogs also generate less body heat when burning fat, enabling them to remain cooler, which is especially important in warmer climates (Gillette, 1999). And, since fats contain more than twice the kcal (Calories) per gram of food than carbohydrates or protein (8.5 kcal per gram compared to 3.5 kcal for carbs and protein), dogs can eat a smaller portion of a high-fat diet and still obtain the energy they need (Coffman, n.d.). Sled dogs, the ultimate endurance dogs, thrive on a high fat diet (>50% of the energy) (Hill, 1998). You will need to figure out where your dog falls on the "endurance scale" to determine his optimum fat requirements.

Endurance activities also increase a dog's need for high quality animal protein, which provides the amino acids necessary to repair and rebuild muscle tissue and is also necessary to prevent anemia that can result from training (known as "sports anemia") (Gillette, 1999; Hill, 1998). In one study, sled dogs fed a diet containing 28% protein showed a decline in hematocrit (packed red blood cells), but those fed a diet containing 32% or greater of protein did not (Hill, 1998).

If your dog participates in activities that require shorter bursts of energy, his dietary needs will differ because he'll be using the ATP-CP system and the glycolytic system. Dogs in this category are not in motion long enough for their bodies to access the longer-duration oxidative energy system. These athletes require a basal diet that emphasizes a high percentage of carbohydrates, which fuels glycolysis, along with protein (Gillette, 1999). Bear in mind, however, that if your dog repeats these short bursts of activity, his body will eventually begin using the oxidative system and he'll require the addition of more fat to delay fatigue during later competitions (Gillette, 1999).

Note: Don't expect immediate results when you change your dog's diet; it can take between four to six weeks for his body to adapt, especially when switching to a higher-fat diet (Gillette, 2009).

Another factor to consider is that environmental conditions such as temperature, humidity and even wind conditions affect the amount of energy a dog burns during exercise. Be sure to account for these variables and adjust your dog's caloric intake accordingly. If your dog trains outside during the winter, for example, you'll need to increase his energy to compensate for the extra calories he'll burn trying to stay warm.

Added nutrients and supplements for athletic dogs

The following nutrients will help support your canine athlete's performance and stamina:

- Antioxidants, such as carotenoids, Co-Q10, **berries** and **pomegranate** to combat oxidative stress produced during workouts.

- Bioactive nutrients, such as purslane, king of bitters, flame of the forest, **milk thistle** (*Silybum marianum*), purple coneflower (*Echinacea angustifolia*), **curcumin**, Siberian gingseng, valerian root and chamomile.

- Lutein (2-2.5 mg per pound) to protect and stabilize the cell membrane, regulating the immune response.

- **Omega-3s** to combat inflammation.

- Niacin for red blood cell production and to help with carbohydrate metabolism.

- Taurine (250 to 1000 mg twice daily) to assist immune function and protect the heart.

- Thiamin to help minimize the effects of stress.

- Vitamin A for ligament and tendon health.

- Vitamin B12 to help with protein synthesis and formation of red blood cells and hemoglobin.

- Vitamin C to facilitate lactic acid depletion caused by muscle exertion (also antioxidant) (dose: additional 250 to 1000 mg of Ester C daily, based on the dog's weight and degree of exertion).

- Vitamin D to maintain a proper calcium:phosphorous balance.

- Vitamin E to support endurance and agility (also antioxidant) (additional 100 to 600 IU daily, depending upon the dog's weight and degree of exertion).

- Vitamin K to maintain proper blood conditions (*not* imitation vitamin K3!).

(Gillette, 1999; Piercy et al., 2001; Wills & Simpson, 1994)

Water: the ultimate nutrient

Dehydration, which results from an excessive loss of water in the body, is a dangerous condition that requires immediate medical attention because dogs don't sweat through their skin as people do. Active dogs—especially those that perform in hot climates or during summer months—are particularly vulnerable. Drinking water will cool your dog's body from the inside and help prevent him from overheating. Try flavoring your dog's water with a little broth or freezing broth in ice cube trays to encourage drinking.

Pregnant bitches

Gestation (pregnancy) in dogs lasts between 56 to 66 days and averages 63 days. Since puppies in the womb don't grow much during the first four to five weeks of pregnancy, pregnant bitches don't require extra energy or nutrients during this time and should continue to consume the same amount of their regular high quality maintenance diet. In fact, overfeeding a pregnant dog during the first four to five weeks can result in undesirable weight gain and lead to complications during delivery. A pregnant dog might also lose her appetite around the third week of gestation, which is normal and typically doesn't indicate a problem. However, if she continues to refuse food after a few days, consult your veterinarian (Case et al., 2011).

The critical growth period for puppies in the womb occurs after week five until parturition (delivery); during this time, the puppies will require additional nutrition to ensure optimal pre-natal development. Gradually increase the pregnant dog's food consumption during the last three to four weeks of pregnancy, so that by the time of whelping she has gained 15 to 25% of her normal body weight. Depending upon her size and the size of her litter, she'll need to eat about 25 to 50% more than her maintenance diet to achieve this weight increase (Case et al., 2011).

As long as you feed your pregnant dog a diet properly balanced for gestation, additional calcium supplementation is usually not required, and may even prove harmful.

Although little research has been conducted in dogs, studies of dairy cattle indicate that consuming a high-calcium diet during pregnancy can increase the incidence of **eclampsia** (also known as "milk fever," post-partum hypocalcemia, puerperal tetany or parturient paresis), a condition exhibited during lactation. Milk fever occurs when the body cannot adequately mobilize calcium reserves from the bones to replace the calcium that has been diverted to milk production. The resulting low blood calcium levels can result in weakness, loss of appetite, **tetany** (muscle spasms and cramps), convulsive seizures and heart failure (Case et al., 2011). Small breed bitches with large litters are most often affected, typically at peak lactation (two to three weeks after whelping). Over-supplementation of vitamin A should also be avoided, as it can increase the likelihood of cleft palates (Blasa, Booles & Burger, 1989; Merck Veterinary Manual, 2011; Segal, 2007). In smaller breeds, folic acid deficiency has been linked to the formation of cleft palates, although proof of the association is unclear.

Omega-3 fatty acid (EPA and DHA) supplements from fish oil and other marine sources are especially important for both pregnant and lactating dogs because the physiological stress of these conditions reduces the status of these nutrients. The greater the number of puppies in the litter, the more the nutrient status is reduced (Case et al., 2011).

A lactation diet (see section below) is a good choice to feed your pregnant bitch during the last three to four weeks of gestation; it will provide the additional energy, fats, carbohydrates, proteins and nutrients your dog will need to sustain a healthy pregnancy as well as ensuring she is nutritionally prepared to produce lots of high quality milk for her puppies.

Lactating dams

Lactation places enormous physical demands on the **dam** (mother), since the nutrition she consumes must contain enough energy and nutrients to meet her own needs, as well as enable her to produce milk of sufficient quantity and quality to meet the needs of her growing puppies. In fact, lactation places more nutritional demands on a dog than at any other time in her adult life, and in some instances even exceeds the nutrition required by growing puppies. Since the number of suckling puppies determines a lactating dog's milk production, the more puppies a dam is nursing, the greater her nutrient requirements (as we discuss below) (Facetti & Delaney, 2012; Hand et al., 2000; Hand et al., 2010; McNamara, 2006).

Puppies typically wean naturally from their mothers at about eight weeks. Feeding an inadequate diet to a lactating dog will result in health problems such as weight loss, anemia and/or diarrhea. A diet supplying only marginal nutrition may also cause her to overeat in order to meet her nutritional needs, which will overwhelm her GI tract, resulting in diarrhea. Diarrhea is potentially dangerous for a lactating bitch because it can cause dehydration, drain her of essential fluids and impair her ability to produce enough milk. **Agalactia** (absence of milk) or **mastitis**, an infection of the mammary glands, may also occur.

Energy

The most important factor regarding the metabolic and nutrient demands of a lactating dam is her energy requirement; no other stage of growth or production requires as much energy. A lactating bitch can easily require four times the amount of calories as the same size dog in a maintenance stage. It's no wonder, considering that she produces as much milk as a dairy cow, averaging more than 8% of her body weight in milk per day! When formulating a lactation diet, it's extremely important that the energy density of the food is sufficient. If the food doesn't contain adequate calories by volume, the dog won't be able to eat enough to meet her energy requirements and a variety of problems will occur, including undesirable weight loss and the inability to produce sufficient milk to feed her litter. The more puppies being nursed, the more energy a lactating dog requires, with energy requirements greatest during peak lactation (weeks three to four) (Case et al., 2011; Facetti & Delaney, 2012; Hand et al., 2000; Hand et al., 2010; Schenck, 2010). We'll discuss how you can pump up the energy content of her diet below, when we discuss fat.

Also be sure that the lactating dog's diet is highly palatable (so that she *wants* to eat) and highly digestible (to ensure that she's able to absorb a maximal amount of nutrients from it).

Water

Did you know that milk is 78% water? Lactating dams need a plentiful supply of water to produce enough milk to meet the needs of their young. Offer your lactating dam fresh, clean water at all times so she can drink freely as desired (Case et al., 2011; Facetti & Delaney, 2012; Hand et al., 2000; Hand et al., 2010).

Protein

Protein is particularly important during lactation, since a dam's milk has more than twice the protein of cow's milk and even more protein than goat's milk. This makes sense when we think about how quickly puppies grow (much faster than calves!). Protein requirements for lactating dams rise even more than energy requirements. Lactating bitches typically require nearly double the amount of essential amino acids than an equivalent size dog in maintenance and, in the case of the amino acids leucine and valine, nearly triple. Therefore, high quality protein must comprise a large portion of the total energy in the lactating dam's diet (Facetti & Delaney, 2012; Hand et al., 2000; Hand et al., 2010; NRC/NAS, 2006).

Fat

A high fat diet is essential to provide the enormous amount of calories lactating dams require for adequate milk production. Remember that fat is the most energy dense ingredient, delivering more than twice as many calories in the same amount of food as carbohydrates and proteins. A lactating bitch can easily require five times as much fat as the same size dog in maintenance (NRC/NAS, 2006).

In addition to providing important health benefits for lactating dams, supplementation with **omega-3s** from fish oil or other marine sources can increase the fatty acid content of the mother's milk, enabling EPA and DHA to be passed along to the nursing puppies (Case et al., 2011). You'll recall from the previous chapter that puppies require **omega-3s** for normal physical and cognitive development.

Carbohydrates

Dogs do require glucose, but as we previously mentioned, they don't have an actual requirement for dietary carbohydrates. As long as dogs consume an ample amount of protein, they can synthesize glucose in the liver and kidneys. Studies on bitches in gestation and lactation, however, have produced conflicting results, stirring a debate within the canine nutrition community as to whether dietary carbohydrates are necessary during these more stressful times. For example, lactating bitches do require extra glucose to synthesize lactose, the sugar in dam's milk (Case et al., 2011). We advise taking a safe approach and including 10 to 20% of your lactating dog's daily calories from carbohydrates (Schenck, 2010). Be sure to feed only good carbohydrates as we discuss throughout this book.

Foods for lactating bitches

The following foods provide excellent sources of nutrients for lactating bitches:

- Eggs (preferably organic, free-range) supply high quality protein and nutrients.
- Liver, such as chicken liver, contributes vitamins A and D and other important nutrients.
- Low-mercury fish and fish oil supply *omega-3 fatty acids* and other important nutrients.
- Novel animal proteins (e.g., bison, venison and rabbit) supply high quality protein and nutrients.
- Oatmeal (gluten-free) provides a healthy source of carbohydrates that benefits the GI tract.
- Plant based oils, such as borage oil, *coconut oil*, hemp oil, olive oil, primrose oil, pumpkin seed oil and sunflower oil supply healthy calories and essential fatty acids.
- Kelp provides iodine.

(Lauten and Lascola, 2011)

If your dog is overweight or suffers from one or more chronic health conditions, you'll want to immediately turn to Part III. In that section, we'll cover the most common health problem afflicting today's dogs, from food intolerances/sensitivities and obesity to arthritis, cancer and just about every chronic disease in between. In this section, you'll discover how chronic inflammation is a thief robbing your dog of vibrant health, and you'll learn how you can take advantage of the latest advances in nutrigenomics research to treat, prevent and even stop chronic disease in its tracks at the cellular level.

Takeaway Points

- From a nutritional perspective, high-performance dogs include canine athletes, pregnant bitches and lactating dams.

- Canine athletes require a nutrient-dense diet to support the additional stress placed on their active bodies, including extra calories. Be sure to accurately assess your dog's activity level or you will overestimate his energy needs and he'll wind up overweight and unhealthy.

- The body uses three different systems to metabolize energy, and the type of activity your dog performs will determine which energy system his body will use. This, in turn, will determine whether his calories (i.e., "fuel") should come primarily from fats or carbohydrates.

- The three energy systems are: adenosine triphosphate–creatine phosphate (ATP-CP) system (also called the phosphagen system or one enzyme system), which fuels the body for only about five to 20 seconds; the glycolytic energy system, which takes over when the ATP-CP system stops and supplies energy for up to about two minutes; and the oxidative energy system, which is the most complex and takes over where glycolysis leaves off, providing the sustained energy required for endurance activities.

- The following nutrients will help support your canine athlete's performance and stamina: antioxidants, such as carotenoids, Co-Q10, **berries** and **pomegranate**; bioactive nutrients, such as purslane, king of bitters, flame of the forest, **milk thistle** (*Silybum marianum*), purple coneflower (*Echinacea angustifolia*), **curcumin**, Siberian gingseng, valerian root and chamomile; lutein; **omega-3s**; niacin; taurine; thiamin; vitamin A; vitamin B12; vitamin C; vitamin D; vitamin E; and vitamin K to maintain proper blood conditions (*not* imitation vitamin K3).

- It's essential that canine athletes drink enough water to avoid dehydration.

- During the first four to five weeks of pregnancy, pregnant bitches should continue to consume the same amount of their regular high quality maintenance diet. Overfeeding a pregnant dog during the first four to five weeks can result in undesirable weight gain and lead to complications during delivery.

- The critical growth period for puppies in the womb occurs after week five of pregnancy until parturition (delivery). Gradually increase your pregnant dog's food consumption during the last three to four weeks of pregnancy, so that by the time of whelping she has gained 15 to 25% of her normal body weight.

- As long as you feed your pregnant dog a diet properly balanced for gestation, additional calcium supplementation is usually not required, and may even prove harmful. Over-supplementation of vitamin A should also be avoided, as it can increase the likelihood of cleft palates.

- *Omega-3 fatty acid* (EPA and DHA) supplements from fish oil and other marine sources are important for both pregnant and lactating dogs.

- A lactation diet is a good choice to feed pregnant bitches during the last three to four weeks of gestation.

- Lactation places more nutritional demands on a dog than at any other time in her adult life, and in some instances even exceeds the nutrition required by growing puppies. The more puppies a dam is nursing, the greater her nutrient requirements.

- Feeding an inadequate diet to a lactating dam will result in health problems such as weight loss, anemia and/or diarrhea. Diarrhea can cause dehydration, drain her of essential fluids and impair her ability to produce enough milk. Agalactia (absence of milk) or mastitis, an infection of the mammary glands, may also occur.

- No other stage of growth or production requires as much energy as lactation. A lactating bitch can easily require four times the amount of calories as the same size dog in a maintenance stage.

- The more puppies being nursed, the more energy the lactating dog will need, with energy requirements greatest during peak lactation (weeks three to four).

- The lactating dam's diet should be highly palatable (so that she *wants* to eat) and highly digestible (to ensure that she's able to absorb a maximal amount of nutrients from it).

- Milk is 78% water. Lactating dogs require a plentiful supply of clean, fresh water to produce enough milk to meet the needs of their young.

- High quality protein must comprise a large portion of the total energy in the lactating bitch's diet.

- A lactating bitch can easily require five times as much fat as the same size dog in maintenance.

- The following foods provide excellent sources of nutrients for lactating bitches: eggs; liver; low-mercury fish and fish oil; novel animal proteins; oatmeal (gluten-free); kelp; and healthy plant-based oils.

Part III

Functional Food Solutions for Common Canine Health Conditions

Chapter 6

Food Intolerances/Sensitivities and NutriScan Diagnostic Testing

As you discovered in the Introduction, many of the chronic diseases afflicting today's dogs share a lot more in common than you might have previously imagined—they result from chronic inflammation. Foods that create intolerances/sensitivities are major inflammatory culprits. When a dog eats a reactive ingredient, his immune system produces antibodies to fight aff the antigens. Left unresolved, the inflammation caused by these ingredients can create a domino effect, leading to other, more serious diseases. To create optimum health in your dog at the cellular level, it's essential to identify and eliminate any foods from his diet that can create an intolerance/sensitivity and result in inflammation. While the technology to measure and test for exactly what is going on in any given individual is still evolving, amazing strides have been made, including NutriScan, Hemopet's non-profit saliva-based diagnostic system for food intolerance/sensitivity. Let's begin Part 3 with a discussion of these technologies—past, present and future.

Food allergies versus food intolerances/sensitivities

Unfortunately, many people—even veterinary professionals—use the terms food "allergy" and food "intolerance/sensitivity" interchangeably, when in fact they are quite different and have very different implications for your dog's health. Until trusted veterinary experts stop confusing these terms, companion animals will not receive the correct diagnosis and will continue to suffer.

True food allergies are actually quite rare (Challacombe, 1987; Day, 2005; Foster et al., 2003; Kiyono et al., 2001; Kraft, Rothbert & Kramer, 1967). As WJD estimates from professional experience, food sensitivities are at least 10 to 15 times more common than food allergies. So, if your dog scratches incessantly or has chronic GI problems, he probably suffers from an intolerance/sensitivity to one or more ingredients in his diet—*not* from an acute food allergy.

Food allergies reflect a more immediate immunological response (Buchanan & Frick, 2002; Day, 2005; Jeffers, Shanley & Meyer, 1991), such as anaphylactic shock caused by an allergy to peanuts. As soon as susceptible individuals come in contact with the allergen—peanuts—their airways close and they cannot breathe. This response is virtually instantaneous. The antigen (in this case, peanuts) triggers an immediate, and sometimes life-threatening, immunological and physiological reaction. Rashes, hives and swollen eyes are examples of less severe, but also serious, allergic responses. These are all called Type I hypersensitivity reactions. They show up in the *blood* as antibodies to two of the body's immune proteins, immunoglobulins E (IgE) and G (IgG) (Foster et al., 2003). The only way to avoid suffering the effects of a food allergy is to refrain from consuming the offending food.

Contrarily, food intolerances/sensitivities are typically *chronic* conditions that build up over time—perhaps even after months or years of exposure to the offending ingredient(s)—and often do not involve an immunological response. Food intolerances/sensitivities are caused by Types II and III hypersensitivity reactions, which show up in *saliva* or *feces* as antibodies to immunoglobulins A (IgA) and M (IgM) (Lee & Wong, 2009; Miller et al., 2010; Rinkinen et al., 2003; Robinson & Reeves, 2013).

Although they are generally not life threatening, food intolerances/sensitivities can affect many different aspects of a dog's physical and emotional well being. Common signs include:

- GI tract issues similar to IBD.
- Chronic itching.
- Chronic burping and gas rumblings (borborigmi).
- Chronic skin, ear and foot infections (especially with the presence of yeast).

(Dodds, 2014)

The only "cure" for a food intolerance/sensitivity is to identify the cause and then remove the offending ingredients(s) from your dog's diet.

Since food intolerances/sensitivities typically build up over time, connecting your dog's symptoms with a particular food just by observation can be difficult. This is especially true because your dog might actually have been eating the offending food for months or even years before outward skin or GI symptoms appear. As you'll recall from Chapter 3, the more of a particular food a dog consumes, and the more often he consumes it, the more likely he is to develop an intolerance/sensitivity to it over time. This is why when we hear people say things such as, "Chicken can't be causing my dog's itchy skin (or whatever other issue he might have) because he's been eating it for years," they don't realize that constantly consuming a particular food for a long time is *exactly why* it could be causing the problem!

Let's look at the most commonly available forms of food intolerance/sensitivity testing, starting with the oldest and most cumbersome and working our way up to the newest and most accurate.

Food elimination trials: the jigsaw puzzle of food intolerance/sensitivity testing

If your dog suffers from signs of a food intolerance/sensitivity, your veterinarian might suggest that you conduct your own food elimination trial. This involves feeding your dog a diet that consists of one novel protein and one carbohydrate source at a time, typically for a period of eight to 12 weeks, to determine if he shows signs of a reaction. Bear in mind, however, that food elimination trials pose several challenges. This is especially true when dealing with mass-market, commercially prepared foods, which, as we already pointed out, can contain ingredients not listed on the label (Ricci et al., 2013).

Consider kibble. One bag of kibble can easily contain several listed or unlisted protein and carbohydrate sources (Ricci et al., 2013). For instance, while chicken may serve as the primary protein, the product may also contain beef, fish, etc. The same is true for carbohydrates, which may consist of a combination of corn, wheat, soy or other potentially reactive ingredients—all housed in one little nugget. While wet foods tend to contain fewer ingredients, they may also combine more than one source of protein and carbohydrate. For this reason, we recommend against trying to determine if your dog is sensitive to a commercially produced dry or wet food. There are simply just too many variables in place, and you could drive yourself crazy in the process! So, when conducting a food elimination trial, we, along with other experts, advise you stick to your own home-prepared diet, where *you* control every ingredient (Ricci et al., 2013).

Veterinarians usually recommend beginning your food elimination trial with a diet of lamb and potatoes. But what if lamb and/or potatoes are the problem? You could cause more harm than good by feeding him these ingredients. Let's say that after 72 hours on the lamb and potato diet, his symptoms don't subside. At that point, you can persevere and try another combination of one novel protein and one carbohydrate until the symptoms do appear to subside.

But even then you're not done because you still can't be sure exactly which ingredient—the protein or the carbohydrate—is causing the problem. So, you must now reintroduce one protein and one carbohydrate back into your dog's diet each week. When the itchy skin symptoms return, you should know which food is the offender, right? Not necessarily. Clinical signs of food intolerances/sensitivities can take up to five weeks to appear. So let's say that after your dog's symptoms subside, you reintroduce beef into his diet in week five and then reintroduce chicken in week six, and at the end of week six your dog begins to itch again. Is he reacting to the beef or the chicken? It's impossible to tell. It could even be another protein from a few weeks prior!

Confused? You should be. At the end of the day, food elimination trials contain too many variables. They can also be quite expensive, with lots of wasted food, trips to the veterinarian and medications to control your dog's symptoms while you attempt to determine the problem.

Skin patch and prick testing

"Skin Patch and Prick Testing" has long been considered the gold standard for identifying the cause of food intolerances/sensitivities and allergies in people, so it's not surprising that these methods have also become popular for dogs. However, there are drawbacks, including:

- Testing must be performed at the veterinarian's office.
- Testing takes approximately two hours to perform.
- You must withhold food and water for four to five hours in advance.
- Your dog must be sedated.
- The area being tested must be shaved.
- The procedure is invasive.
- Antihistamines are required after the procedure.
- Steroid treatment might be required.
- It's expensive (approximately $500 for 20 antigens).

The most notable problems with these methods, though, are that they do not test for long-term food intolerances/sensitivities—only acute or immediate reactions (i.e., food allergies)—and even then they are unpredictable in accurately identifying the true source of the reaction(s).

Veterinarians and dog parents need to focus on identifying and managing long-term food-related health issues; otherwise, our beloved dogs will continue to suffer.

NutriScan: the most accurate and predictive test to identify canine food intolerances/sensitivities

NutriScan, offered exclusively by author WJD's Hemolife testing laboratory, is the new gold standard for identifying the cause of food intolerances/sensitivities in dogs. NutriScan is not only the most scientifically accurate method; it is also the most convenient and cost-effective for you, as well as the least invasive and most comfortable for your dog. NutriScan identifies the reactive food(s) in 10 days, enabling you to quickly remove the ingredient(s) from your dog's diet (Dodds, 2014).

Nutriscan measures IgA and IgM antibodies in a dog's *saliva*. By detecting high IgA and IgM antibody levels, NutriScan identifies changes in the dog's gene expression when faced with the reactive food, enabling the test to clearly identify the specific ingredient(s) causing the problem. NutriScan can also differentiate between a food intolerance/sensitivity and a food allergy because food allergies are typically mediated by different antibodies (IgE and IgG) than food intolerances/sensitivities (Dodds, 2014).

Why is NutriScan revolutionary?

Let's take a closer look at how NutriScan has revolutionized canine food intolerance testing.

NutriScan can help dogs that appear healthy as well as dogs that are suspected to suffer from food reactivity. Saliva testing can reveal the presence of a food intolerance/sensitivity before your dog shows any outward signs, such as itchy skin or GI issues. This is possible because antibodies to food ingredients appear in saliva *before* a clinical or bowel biopsy diagnosis of inflammatory bowel disease or leaky gut syndrome is typically made (Lee & Wong, 2009; Miller et al., 2010; Vojdani, 2009). This means that NutriScan can *predict* a developing food reaction before it manifests.

NutriScan can now identify intolerances/sensitivities to 24 different foods. As of this writing, NutriScan includes two different panels, each testing 12 food antigens:

> **Panel 1**: beef, chicken, corn, cow's milk, duck, lamb, pork, soy, turkey, venison, wheat and white fish.

> **Panel 2**: barley, hen's egg, lentils, millet, oatmeal, peanut (peanut butter), potato, quinoa, rabbit, rice, salmon and sweet potato.

You can order both panels simultaneously or sequentially. (Patented NutriScan testing for cats is also currently available.)

The panels include the so-called six primary food antigens, including the glutens present in the most commonly fed pet foods and treats, as well as an additional 18 antigens. If a dog (or cat) suffers from a food sensitivity/intolerance, one of these antigens is most likely the culprit.

NutriScan is simple to perform right in your own home. The test requires only two ml of saliva to be collected from your dog's mouth (wet about 1/3 the length of the kit's dental cotton rope with saliva), so it can be run in duplicate. Obtaining the saliva takes just a few easy steps: (Note: Your dog should have fasted for at least three hours before you collect the saliva.)

1. Lift your dog's upper lip.

2. Place the cotton rope in your dog's mouth at corner of the mouth.

3. Leave the free end of rope hanging out of the mouth, but hold on to it.

4. If you need to promote salivation, wave a treat over your dog's nose (but do not feed it).

5. Keep the rope in your dog's mouth for two minutes.

Once you collect the saliva with the cotton rope, simply cut off the wet part of the rope and insert it into the shipping tube, seal the tube and place it into the mailer, along with the completed test request form. The sample can be mailed to Hemolife via FedEx, UPS, Postal Service or other carrier. No refrigeration is necessary, and it is stable for up to 30 days. Hemolife will send the results within 10 days to you (and your veterinarian, if requested).

NutriScan identifies the specific foods to avoid feeding your dog. If your dog tests positive for any of the food extracts in the panel, simply avoid exposing him to any foods, treats, supplements, grooming supplies or drug vehicles (substances such as pill pockets used to administer drugs) that contain these ingredients.

To date, Nutriscan represents the most scientifically advanced diagnostic phase of assessing functional nutrition for individual dogs. The presence (indicated by an intermediate, medium or strong reaction) or absence (indicated by a negative or weak reaction) of salivary antibodies in response to specific food extracts is an indication of the dog's changes in gene expression when faced with these foods. NutriScan therefore depends upon the nutritional influences and factors that can alter gene expression (Fekete & Brown, 2007; Swanson, Schook & Fahey, 2003).

Sample NutriScan Diagnostic Report

A sample NutriScan report beginning on the next page was generated by Hemolife based on Panel 1 (12 foods) and Panel 2 (12 foods). Stronger reaction columns are shown in varying shades of gray. You can see that this dog exhibited his strongest food intolerance reactions (a medium reaction) to corn and venison. Intermediate reactions were also exhibited to several foods, including chicken, milk, soy, turkey, wheat, whitefish and oatmeal, and it was advised that these foods be avoided. The dog showed no significant intolerance to the remaining foods tested.

Test Requested	Result	Remark	General Range	Units
Beef Salivary IgA	10.000	Weak Reaction	< 10	U/mL
Beef Salivary IgM	9.750	Negative Reaction	< 10	U/mL
Chicken Salivary IgA	12.070	Intermediate reaction; best to avoid	< 10	U/mL
Chicken Salivary IgM	12.326	Intermediate reaction; best to avoid	< 10	U/mL
Corn Salivary IgA	**13.649**	**Medium Reaction, avoid**	< 10	U/mL
Corn Salivary IgM	12.42	Intermediate reaction; best to avoid	< 10	U/mL
Duck Salivary IgA	9.382	Negative Reaction	< 10	U/mL
Duck Salivary IgM	10.782	Weak Reaction	< 10	U/mL
Lamb Salivary IgA	10.293	Weak Reaction	< 10	U/mL
Lamb Salivary IgM	9.858	Negative Reaction	< 10	U/mL
Milk Salivary IgA	12.326	Intermediate reaction; best to avoid	< 10	U/mL
Milk Salivary IgM	11.393	Weak Reaction	< 10	U/mL
Pork Salivary IgA	8.300	Negative Reaction	< 10	U/mL
Pork Salivary IgM	10.650	Weak Reaction	< 10	U/mL
Soy Salivary IgA	12.074	Intermediate reaction; best to avoid	< 10	U/mL
Soy Salivary IgM	11.168	Weak Reaction	< 10	U/mL
Turkey Salivary IgA	12.784	Intermediate reaction; best to avoid	< 10	U/mL
Turkey Salivary IgM	12.080	Intermediate reaction; best to avoid	< 10	U/mL
Venison Salivary IgA	**14.866**	**Medium Reaction, avoid**	< 10	U/mL
Venison Salivary IgM	12.273	Intermediate reaction; best to avoid	< 10	U/mL
Wheat Salivary IgA	12.272	Intermediate reaction; best to avoid	< 10	U/mL
Wheat Salivary IgM	11.381	Weak Reaction	< 10	U/mL
White Fish Salivary IgA	12.300	Intermediate reaction; best to avoid	< 10	U/mL
White Fish Salivary IgM	12.020	Intermediate reaction; best to avoid	< 10	U/mL

Test Requested	Result	Remark	General Range	Units
Barley Salivary IgM	10.800	Intermediate reaction; best to avoid	< 10	U/mL
Barley Salivary IgA	9.950	Weak Reaction	< 10	U/mL
Egg Salivary IgA	7.560	Negative Reaction	< 10	U/mL
Egg Salivary IgM	7.840	Negative Reaction	< 10	U/mL
Lentil Salivary IgA	11.292	Weak Reaction	< 10	U/mL
Lentil Salivary IgM	**13.148**	**Medium Reaction, avoid**	< 10	U/mL
Millet Salivary IgM	10.275	Weak Reaction	< 10	U/mL
Millet Salivary IgA	8.494	Negative Reaction	< 10	U/mL
Oatmeal Salivary IgA	10.550	Weak Reaction	< 10	U/mL
Oatmeal Salivary IgM	12.400	Intermediate reaction; best to avoid	< 10	U/mL
Peanut Salivary IgA	9.294	Negative Reaction	< 10	U/mL
Peanut Salivary IgM	10.068	Weak Reaction	< 10	U/mL
Potato Salivary IgA	10.382	Weak Reaction	< 10	U/mL
Potato Salivary IgM	10.323	Weak Reaction	< 10	U/mL
Quinoa Salivary IgA	9.622	Negative Reaction	< 10	U/mL
Quinoa Salivary IgM	10.416	Weak Reaction	< 10	U/mL
Rabbit Salivary IgA	9.305	Negative Reaction	< 10	U/mL
Rabbit Salivary IgM	9.500	Negative Reaction	< 10	U/mL
Rice Salivary IgA	9.050	Negative Reaction	< 10	U/mL
Rice Salivary IgM	10.200	Weak Reaction	< 10	U/mL
Salmon Salivary IgA	9.813	Negative Reaction	< 10	U/mL
Salmon Salivary IgM	9.688	Negative Reaction	< 10	U/mL
Sweet Potato Salivary IgA	10.708	Weak Reaction	< 10	U/mL
Sweet Potato Salivary IgM	11.386	Weak Reaction	< 10	U/mL

Sample NutriScan Diagnostic Report

Analysis

Along with the chart, you will receive a report from HemoLife with recommendations and interpretations:

Dear Colleague:

Food reactivity at a significant level is present for **Corn (including Corn Starch and Fructose), Lentil** and **Venison**. Several other foods had intermediate reactions, which means that these foods are also best avoided.

Jean

NutriScan Interpretation

Pet should avoid food or treats containing ingredient(s) showing intermediate, medium, or strong reactions. Recommend rechecking salivary food sensitivity or intolerance levels, preferably in about six months if intolerances are identified and the diet changed accordingly, or every 12 to 18 months otherwise.

Degree of reactivity

- **<10 U/mL** indicates a normal food antigen tolerance level = **negative result**
- **10-11.4 U/mL** indicates a **weak reaction; clinical significance unclear**
- **11.5-11.9 U/mL** indicates an **borderline reaction**
- **12-12.9 U/mL** indicates an **intermediate reaction**
- **13-14.9 U/mL** indicates a **medium reaction**
- **>/= 15 U/mL** indicates a **strong reaction**

Differences between antibodies to IgA and IgM:

Antibodies to IgA measure the secretory immunity from body secretions (tears, saliva, feces, urogenital tract). They act as a mechanical barrier or the first line of defense to help protect the bowel from invasion by foreign substances, infectious agents, chemicals, and certain foods that it cannot or poorly tolerate.

Antibodies to IgM measure the body's primary immune response to a recent exposure within the last 6 months or so (e.g., to a certain food ingredient).

End of report.

Saliva testing versus serum (blood) testing

Many people have questions concerning the difference between salivary food intolerance/sensitivity testing and serum, or blood, testing. It's easy to assume that a blood test is more reliable and accurate than a saliva test. After all, when we visit our doctor for a check-up, she routinely draws blood and sends it to a diagnostic lab to determine whether we harbor any hidden health issues. In many cases, the blood is considered to be the window to our health; however, in the case of long-term food reactions, saliva testing is more effective (Robinson & Reeves, 2012).

You now know that the gut contains the largest immune organ in the body, and that leaky gut syndrome arises when the cellular lining of the gut becomes compromised. Remember that with a leaky gut, large food particles can be absorbed into the bloodstream, where the body identifies them as antigens. The body's immune system kicks into action, producing protein antibodies to protect it against what was once a harmless food ingredient. The antibodies produced are immunoglobulin A (IgA) and immunoglobulin G (IgG), which circulate in the bloodstream where they can also travel to tissues and cause damage.

Blood tests measure levels of IgA and IgG antibodies. Normal levels indicate a healthy gut with a healthy mucosal barrier, whereas elevated antibody levels indicate increased permeability of the intestinal lining, or a leaky gut. As we've said, food intolerances/sensitivities are present in the body long before outward signs appear, and these problems typically begin with a compromised gut environment.

So, if the blood can measure elevated levels of IgA and IgG antibodies before outward signs appear, why not use blood tests to check for underlying food intolerances/sensitivities? The reason is because saliva testing is even better.

IgA and IgM antibodies produced in saliva (and feces) are detectable *months* before IgA and IgG antibodies appear in the blood and several months before lesions occur on the surface of the GI tract (these lesions enable veterinarians to clinically diagnosis inflammatory bowel disease [IBD] or leaky gut syndrome). *So, the saliva testing system can detect the progressive, pathological process of gut destruction and permeability much sooner than it can be detected via either blood testing or clinical diagnosis.*

Saliva collection is also noninvasive, painless, relatively inexpensive and convenient for the patient. When comparing saliva and serum methods for food sensitivity testing in humans, published studies have shown that a saliva sample provides more accurate and clinically relevant results than a serum sample.

Success!

Getting healthy by getting rid of grains

Meg, a nine-and-a-half-year-old spayed female Scottish Terrier, was generally healthy, except for a long-standing severe food intolerance/sensitivity. Within 30 minutes of eating an offending food ingredient, Meg would begin scratching intensely and rubbing her face on the carpet or furniture. She also had a "weepy" eye discharge and seemed to experience difficulty breathing. Meg's veterinarian placed her on a commercial limited-ingredient, hypoallergenic prescription diet, which lessened the itching and face rubbing. However, a routine annual lab workup found that her alkaline phosphatase (ALP) enzyme and cholesterol levels began to climb from 580 and 320, respectively (normal reference ranges 5-131 IU/L and 92-324 mg/dL) in fall 2007 to 1,852, 1,576, and 1,595 IU/L and 415, 349 and 343, respectively in 2010 and 2011. The rest of her laboratory tests, including thyroid function, remained within normal limits. During this time, Meg did not exhibit any clinical symptoms of liver dysfunction or adrenal hyperactivity (Cushing's disease), although she was somewhat lethargic and lacked the sparkly eyes and exuberance of her prior years.

Upon referral to WJD for her annual health checkup, the diet was changed to avoid any grains, including the cornstarch derivative in her prescription diet. WJD recommended placing Meg on a premium freeze-dried raw diet with venison as the novel animal protein source. Meg, however, preferred the chicken version of this food! This caused some minor face rubbing at first, but it rapidly subsided. (Interestingly, many holistic veterinarians notice that feeding the fresh, raw version of a commonly reactive food such as chicken does not produce the problems that occur when feeding a highly processed, adulterated version of the same food.) At her checkup less than six weeks later, Meg was once more bright eyed and sprightly. In addition, her alkaline phosphatase level had dropped to 296 IU/L and her cholesterol was 170 mg/dL. Meg was a new dog!

This case demonstrates the dramatic effects of switching to a more individualized, compatible diet, along with the benefits of feeding raw, unprocessed foods instead of highly processed ingredients (Cave and Marks, 2004; Vojdani, 2009).

Looking to the future: DNA microarray technology

DNA microarrays represent the future of gene expression study and will open the door for new levels of individualized medicine and functional nutrition for both people and animals. But unless you're a cellular biologist, geneticist or chemist who spends your days in a laboratory staring at glass slides and Petri dishes, you probably aren't interested in the technical details of microarray technology. So, we'll just give you the highlights:

- Previously, scientists could study the expression of only one or a few genes at a time. DNA microarray technology enables scientists to study the expression of an entire human or animal genome (every known gene in the body) at one time.

- Microarray technology looks at cells and tells us which genes are turned on within those cells, and to what degree. This is done by measuring production of messenger RNA (mRNA) in the cell.

- DNA microarrays can be used to study virtually any type of disease. For example, researchers can learn the patterns of gene expression taking place in specific types of tumor cells, such as lymphoma or leukemia cells, and compare that to the gene expression of healthy cells. This will tell them what makes the unhealthy cells different.

- By identifying commonalities in gene expression patterns among individuals who share certain conditions, such as those with a particular type of cancer, researchers can develop treatments specifically targeted for those individuals.

- Microarray technology can also enable the targeting of functional foods based on genomic expression.

More about DNA microarrays courtesy of the National Human Genome Research Institute

How can microarray technology potentially benefit our canine companions?

Suppose that you're the proud parent of a black Toy Poodle and your dog is diagnosed with chronic kidney disease. Now, let's say that by using DNA microarray technology, scientists have discovered that small, dark-haired dogs with chronic kidney disease express certain common genes, while large, light-haired dogs with chronic kidney disease express different genes. Without this knowledge, your veterinarian will treat your small, black Toy Poodle in the same or similar manner as a large, light-haired Golden Retriever. But just imagine the confusion when the treatment that works successfully for the Golden Retriever doesn't help your Poodle at all! Your veterinarian will have to go back to the drawing board and try different medications until she hits upon the correct one for your individual dog.

Imagine how your veterinarian's treatment success rate will skyrocket if she can predict ahead of time which medication will likely work best for your black Toy Poodle. The tedious trial-and-error process can be avoided and your dog can immediately begin the road to recovery—not to mention avoiding the potential negative side effects associated with taking unnecessary drugs (and the expense to you).

The same principle holds true for creating individualized nutrition protocols for people and animals. Imagine that, due to an identified common gene expression pattern, you know that Toy Poodles commonly suffer from an intolerance/sensitivity to wheat, but not corn. Standard Poodles, however, are the opposite; they react to corn, but not to wheat. Just imagine the time and money you can save—not to mention helping your dog avoid all kinds of food-related health problems. The same holds true when selecting functional foods. If you know that your dog is likely to respond favorably to *curcumin*, but not to rosemary, you'll save a lot of money on spices!

How exactly does DNA microarray testing provide us with all this amazing information?

Scientists begin with a reference set of genomic data obtained from healthy animals with different genotypes, combined with a target set of genomic data obtained from animals affected with different physiological conditions (unhealthy animals) and different genotypes. These data sets are then compared to a nutrient data set, which provides information related to the effects of various nutritional compounds on the expression of the genes in the healthy and unhealthy animals. From this comparison, the most appropriate diet formulation is determined for use in cleansing and healing the unhealthy animals. The individual dog's genotype, or genetic makeup, is an essential part of determining which nutrient(s) are biologically active, or functional, for that individual.

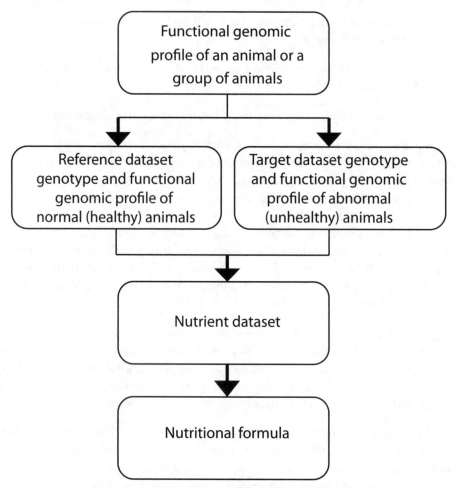

Flow diagram of genomic profiling to select a nutrient formula
(courtesy of Prof. Bruno Stefanon, with permission).

DNA microarray testing is currently used as a clinical research tool, but it's not yet widely available in the mainstream. Once off-the-shelf test kits become more accessible and the price of the technology decreases, we can expect that both human and veterinary diagnostic labs (including WJD's Hemolife diagnostic lab) will routinely offer this service.

Takeaway Points

- Many of the chronic diseases afflicting today's dogs result from chronic inflammation.

- Foods that cause sensitivities/intolerances are major inflammatory culprits. Left unresolved, the inflammation caused by these foods can create a domino effect, leading to other, more serious diseases.

- Identifying and removing potentially inflammatory foods from your dog's diet is essential to creating optimum health at the cellular level.

- Food intolerances/sensitivities are different from—and much more common than—food allergies.

- Food allergies reflect a more immediate immunological response to the antigen, such as anaphylactic shock caused by an allergy to peanuts, while food intolerances/sensitivities are typically chronic conditions that build up over time—perhaps even after months or years of exposure to the offending food(s)—and often do not involve an immunological response.

- The only cure for a food intolerance/sensitivity is to identify the cause and then remove the offending ingredients(s) from your dog's diet.

- Food elimination trials are the oldest, most cumbersome and least accurate method of food intolerance/sensitivity testing.

- There are too many variables and unknown factors to try to conduct a food elimination trial with a commercial diet. If you do attempt this method, stick to your own home-prepared diet, where you control every ingredient.

- Even with a homemade diet, we advise against using a food elimination trial to figure out the cause of your dog's food intolerance/sensitivity. There are just too many factors that make this method inaccurate, confusing and expensive.

- "Skin Patch and Prick Testing" has long been considered the gold standard for identifying the cause of food intolerances/sensitivities and allergies in people, so it's not surprising that these methods have also become popular for dogs. However, there are drawbacks.

- The most notable problems with these methods are that they do not test for long-term food intolerances/sensitivities—only acute or immediate reactions (i.e., food allergies)—and even then they are unpredictable in accurately identifying the true source of the reaction(s).

- Veterinarians and dog parents need to focus on identifying and managing long-term food-related health issues; otherwise, our beloved dogs will continue to suffer.

- NutriScan, offered exclusively by author WJD's Hemolife testing laboratory, is a revolutionary new method for identifying the cause of food intolerances/sensitivities in dogs. NutriScan is not only the most scientifically accurate method;

it is also the most cost-effective, least invasive and most comfortable for your dog. NutriScan identifies the reactive food(s) in less than two weeks, enabling you to quickly remove it (or them, if there are more than one) from your dog's diet.

- Nutriscan measures IgA and IgM antibodies in a dog's saliva. By detecting high IgA and IgM antibody levels, NutriScan is able to identify changes in the dog's gene expression when faced with the reactive food, enabling the test to clearly identify the specific ingredient(s) causing the problem. NutriScan can also differentiate between a food intolerance/sensitivity and a food allergy.

- Benefits of NutriScan include: can predict a developing food reaction before the dog shows any outward signs; can identify reactions to 24 different foods; is simple to perform at home; results are available within 10 days; identifies which specific foods to avoid feeding your dog.

- Saliva testing is proven more effective than serum (blood) testing for identifying food intolerances/sensitivities.

- IgA and IgM antibodies produced in saliva (and feces) are detectable months before IgA and IgG antibodies can be seen in the blood and several months before lesions occur on the surface of the GI tract.

- Saliva collection is noninvasive, painless, relatively inexpensive and convenient for the patient.

- DNA microarrays represent the future of gene expression study and will open the door for new levels of individualized medicine and functional nutrition for people and animals. The technology is not yet widely available in the mainstream, however.

Chapter 7

A Nutrigenomics Approach
to Weight Control

Obesity is the leading health threat to companion dogs (and cats) and the number one preventable medical condition treated by veterinarians (APOP, 2013; Byers et al., 2011). No matter what else you do for your dog, he won't experience optimum health if he's overweight or obese.

Unfortunately, the obesity rate among companion animals is rising dramatically. In its 2012 National Pet Obesity Awareness Day Survey, the Association for Pet Obesity Prevention (APOP) revealed that 52.5% of dogs and 58.3% of cats are overweight or obese, according to the veterinarians who treat them. This means that approximately 36.7 million dogs and 43.2 million cats are at increased risk of suffering from weight-related disorders, including diabetes, osteoarthritis, hypertension and many cancers (APOP, 2013).

Banfield Pet Hospital's *State of Pet Health Report 2012* provides startling insight into the link between obesity and illness. The report, which analyzed data from more than two million dogs and 430,000 cats, found that:

- 42% of dogs with diabetes are overweight (and 40% of cats).
- 40% of dogs with arthritis are overweight (and 37% of cats).
- More than 40% of dogs with high blood pressure are overweight.
- 61% of hypothyroid dogs are overweight.

(Banfield Pet Hospital, 2012)

Overweight dogs are at increased risk for many diseases, including:

- Cardiorespiratory diseases, including airway obstruction syndrome (seen in the brachycephalic dog breeds) and laryngeal paralysis.

- Endocrine disorders, including hyperadrenocorticism (Cushing's disease) and hypothyroidism.

- Functional alterations, such as decreased respiratory capacity, exercise intolerance, heat intolerance/stroke and decreased immune functions.

- Metabolic abnormalities, such as hyperlipidemia/dyslipidemia (high or abnormal blood lipid levels).

- Neoplasia (abnormal growth or division of cells as seen in cancer), including transitional cell carcinoma (tumor of the bladder).

- Orthopedic disorders, such as osteoarthritis, anterior cruciate ligament rupture and intervertebral disk disease.

- Urogenital system conditions, including transitional cell carcinoma bladder tumor.

(Byers et al., 2011; German, 2006)

Studies also show that overweight and obese dogs live an average of *two years less* than their ideal-weight counterparts (Kealy et al., 2002). On the flip side, calorie restriction has been shown to *increase* lifespan by increasing the amounts of dietary activators of **sirtuins** (proteins that regulate metabolism and lifespan), such as resveratrol and other polyphenols (green and black tea, grape seed extract) fed to dogs (Allard et al., 2009; Lawler et al., 2005; Lawler et al., 2007; Yamka, Frantz & Friesen, 2007).

On an even more disheartening note, Banfield's separate survey of pet caretakers found that 76% of dog guardians and 69% of cat guardians believed their pet were at a healthy weight, when in fact they were not (Banfield Pet Hospital, 2012; Howard, 2012). To save our companion animals from falling victim to obesity-related illnesses, and an untimely death, we first need to recognize the issue and then take steps to correct it.

Scientists look to genes for the answer to obesity

Scientists have recently begun searching for a genomic link to obesity—and they have found it.

In 2007, researchers identified the first "obesity" gene variants in what is termed the "fat mass and obesity-associated" gene (HSPH, 2013; Sjøgren, 2013). People who have one of these gene variants are 20% to 30% more likely to become obese than people who do not (HSPH, 2013). Two newer studies have also identified several gene variants that correlate to obesity in both children and adults (Dotinga, 2013). These findings support the theory that a predisposition to obesity is likely not caused by a single gene, but by *multiple* genes (polygenic) (HSPH, 2013; Norris, 2013; Swanson, 2007).

Certain breeds of dogs have been identified as genetically predisposed to obesity, including:

- Basset Hounds
- Beagles
- Boxers
- Cairn Terriers
- Cavalier King Charles Spaniels
- Cocker Spaniels
- Dachshunds
- Doberman Pinschers
- Golden Retrievers
- Labrador Retrievers
- Scottish Terriers
- Shetland Sheepdogs
- West Highland White Terriers

(Byers et al., 2011)

In contrast, sighthounds appear to be less susceptible (Byers et al., 2011) and in the APOP study, German Shepherds had the lowest incidence of obesity (APOP, 2013).

But while researchers continue to identify genetic predispositions to obesity in humans and dogs, what still remains is to find out *how* these genes work to affect body weight over long periods (Swanson, 2007; Yamka et al., 2007). Research has shown that while certain genetic variants increase the risk of obesity *in some people*, others who have the same variants remain lean throughout their lives (Dotinga, 2013). Similarly, there are certainly lean and overweight/obese versions of all the dog breeds listed above!

Could the answer lie outside rather than inside?

If many lean individuals carry the same obesity gene variants as many overweight individuals, it stands to reason that there is something else going on. The determining factor for becoming obese may well be determined by *outside* factors such as environment and lifestyle.

A 2011 peer-reviewed meta-analysis of data from more than 200,000 people who carry a specific gene predisposing them to obesity found that physical activity reduced the likelihood of gaining weight. The researchers found that physically active adults who carried the obesity gene were nearly *one-third* less likely to become overweight or obese than those who didn't exercise (Kilpeläinen, 2011).

Clearly, genetic predisposition does *not* destine an individual to obesity. As we've discussed all along, even though we can't alter our DNA, we *can* alter many of the environmental and lifestyle factors that determine how our genes express (Lavebratt et al., 2012; Veerman, 2011).

> ### Spaying/neutering linked to obesity
> A recent study found that dogs who had undergone gonadectomy (spaying and neutering) were significantly more likely to become overweight in the two years following the procedures, compared with sexually intact dogs. There was no difference between males and females, and the increased risk was not influenced by the dogs' ages at the time of the procedures (Lefebvre et al., 2013).

Like dog parent, like dog

Over the last half-century, we have seen an unsettling parallel between the spike in human obesity and obesity in companion animals. We strongly believe this parallel relates to similar environmental and lifestyle changes, including:

- Decrease in physical activity.

- Progression away from fresh, wholesome foods to highly processed foods packed with ingredients that send unhealthy messages to the genes (as previously discussed at length).

- Proliferation of readily available, energy-dense convenience foods.

Thanks to genomic mapping, scientists can now screen for "obesity genes" in humans and many animals, including dogs. But, as you just learned, screening for obesity does not solve the problem of obesity for several reasons:

- Genetic screening for obesity does not take into account environmental and behavioral contributions.

- Individuals who know they are genetically predisposed to obesity might actually feel discouraged to exercise and eat healthy.

- It fails to take into account the larger societal influences at play.

- It has a low predictive power to determine whether an individual will actually become obese.

(Veerman, 2011)

Can obesity regulate gene expression?

We know that there are "obesity genes" that can switch on an individual's predisposition to being overweight, but let's consider this scenario in reverse. *Can being obese affect gene expression and in turn result in disease?* The answer is "yes," according to several studies (Demerath et al., 2013; Endocrine Today, 2011; Fiore, 2013; Franks & Ling, 2010; Medical College of Georgia, 2013).

Studies linking obesity and gene expression

These studies clearly show that poor diet doesn't just lead to health problems by creating fat in our bodies; it actually changes the expression of obesity-related genes. Feeding your dog foods that suppress his genomic expression for obesity may therefore not only result in a loss of weight, but also in the reduced risk of a whole host of obesity-related diseases, which we'll talk a lot more about in the next few chapters.

Once the body becomes "programmed" for fat, it's like a never-ending cycle because fat cells lead to more fat cells. The more fat cells there are in the body, the more these cells secrete a type of pro-inflammatory cell messenger called **cytokines** and the more chronic, systemic inflammation that is created. Essentially, obesity is a state of chronic inflammation, which leads to chronic inflammatory diseases (Byers et al., 2011; Eisele et al., 2005; Perricone, 2010).

Food sensitivities: a hidden cause of weight gain

As we previously discussed, food intolerances/sensitivities are a major cause of cellular inflammation. During this process, the gut lining becomes inflamed. This inflammation in turn creates small fissures between the cells, allowing foreign invaders, such as bacteria and partially digested food molecules, to cross from the gastrointestinal tract into the bloodstream, creating a further reaction by the immune system to defeat the "enemy." This war inside the immune system causes mayhem, and before you know it, system-wide inflammation occurs (Hyman, 2012; Hyman, 2013).

Eating reactive foods can lead to obesity because food intolerances/sensitivities lead to inflammation, and obesity is an inflammatory condition.

This might not be such a big deal if your dog only eats an offending food every once in a while. But what if he eats it every day—for example, in his commercial dog food—and every day his immune system must wage a battle against the antigen? Just imagine the inflammation occurring inside his poor body! Left undiagnosed, this process can go on for months or even years while the inflammation brews, predisposing your dog to weight gain and other chronic diseases (Hyman, 2012; Hyman, 2013). This is why we strongly advise using NutriScan saliva-based food intolerance/sensitivity testing to identify potential antigens specific to your individual dog. His body cannot express true cellular health if it is a smoldering volcano of inflammation, and he'll have a much more difficult time shedding excess weight.

Is my dog fat?

By now you know that while your pudgy dog may look cute, that extra fat he's carrying is sabotaging his long-term health and vitality at the cellular level. So, it's time to get serious and help your canine curb the battle of the bulge. He'll not only feel better, he'll live a happier, healthier and longer life (Byers et al., 2011; Byers et al., 2011a; Roudebush, Schoenherr & Delany, 2008; Yamka, Frantz & Friesen, 2007).

Since dog (and cat) parents often have a skewed image of their companion's weight, we advise taking a more objective approach and using measurement standards that don't lie (unlike our adoring eyes). Of course, a good old-fashioned scale is one such method, if your dog is small enough. However, even the scale doesn't check for body fat composition, which is important.

We prefer a simple method called the Body Condition Score (BCS), and we suggest you perform one on your dog at least every four—and preferable every two—weeks. To perform a BCS, simply observe your dog from the side and from above and palpate (gently press) his shoulder blades, spinal column, ribs, hips and the underside of his belly to feel the amount of overlying fat. BCS is based on either a 5-point or a 9-point scale, where the middle number of the chart (3 out of 5 or 5 out of 9) reflects optimal body condition associated with 15% to 25% body fat. Lower numbers reflect degrees of "under-condition," or less than optimum body fat. Higher numbers are associated with degrees of "over-condition," or too much body fat. A score of 5 out of 5 or 9 out of 9 indicates more than 35% body fat—an obese dog (Bartges, 2013).

Here's how to check your dog's BCS:

1. With your dog standing on all fours, palpate his shoulder blades, spinal column, ribs, hips and underside of his belly. You should be able to feel them through a thin layer of fat, but they should not protrude. This equals a BCS of 3 on the 5-point scale.

2. View your dog from the top when he's standing on all fours. He should resemble an oblong hourglass—wider at the ribs, narrower at the waist and wider at the hips. If you look down and see two straight lines, your dog is carrying too much fat.

The most obvious signs your dog is overweight are:

- A large body relative to the legs.
- Excess fat around the neck and underside of the belly.
- Round appearance, especially when viewed from above.

(Bartges, 2013)

Other signs include:

- Decreased activity level.
- Difficulty rising or climbing stairs.
- Excessive panting during activity.

(Bartges, 2013)

Your veterinarian should also perform a BCS evaluation as part of your dog's wellness exams.

How much should I feed my dog for weight loss?

Before placing your dog on a diet, be sure your veterinarian examines him for an underlying medical condition that could be causing his weight gain, such as hypothyroidism (as we discussed in *The Canine Thyroid Epidemic*) or Cushing's disease. Failing to do this can result in unsuccessful weight loss for your dog and a lot of frustration for you. Once your dog has received health clearance, your veterinarian will determine his ideal weight and will serve as an important resource for periodic health checks, weigh-ins and motivational support along the way.

The next step is to calculate the amount of daily kcals (calories) your dog needs to eat each day to safely achieve his goal weight. If he has a lot of weight to lose, you might begin by identifying an interim goal weight rather than aiming straight for his ideal weight (Ward, 2007). Your veterinarian or nutritionist should also advise you on any appropriate supplementation needed to ensure your dog receives ample nutrients while on his diet.

For most dogs, a weight loss of 3% to 5% of body weight per month is considered safe (Ward, 2007). This can be achieved by feeding your dog 100% of his **Resting Energy Requirements (RER)**. Your dog's RER represents the daily amount of kcals his body needs to perform no other activities except resting and performing basic metabolic functions, such as digestion, respiration and heart function (metabolism is responsible for about 50% of the average adult dog's daily energy requirements).

The following formula is used to calculate RER in animals weighing between 2 to 45 kg (5 to 99 pounds):

Step 1
Determine his **ideal** weight in kilograms (kg):

- Ideal weight in pounds (as determined by your veterinarian or canine nutrition expert) divided by 2.2 gives you weight in kilograms (kg).

- Example: If your dog's ideal weight (remember that this is not his current weight, it is his goal weight) is 20 pounds, divide 20 by 2.2. His ideal weight in kilograms is 9 kg.

Step 2
Determine his Resting Energy Requirements (RER) based on this ideal weight:

- RER in kcal/day = 30(ideal body weight in kilograms) + 70.

- 30(9) + 70 = 340 kcal/day = RER.

Most dogs should lose weight eating 100% of their RER calories per day. However, if your dog does not respond, your veterinarian or nutritionist will adjust his diet accordingly (Ward, 2007).

The following table saves you from making the calculations by providing RER calories based on weight range:

RER calories based on weight in pounds (Source: Ward, 2007)

Ideal weight (lbs)	Calories to feed (kcal) at 100% RER per day	Ideal weight (lbs)	Calories to feed (kcal) at 100% RER per day
10	210	55	820
15	270	60	890
20	340	65	950
25	410	70	1020
30	480	75	1090
35	550	80	1160
40	615	85	1230
45	680	90	1300
50	750	100	1430

Note: This table is a general guideline only and is not meant as a substitute for your veterinarian's specific recommendations.

Remember that your dog's RER is his daily energy requirement *while at rest*, and it is a suitable amount to feed for safe weight loss. Once he reaches his ideal weight, however, you'll want to feed him enough to *maintain* that weight. This is known as his **Maintenance Energy Requirement (MER)**. Your dog's MER is based on certain factors indicated in the table below. Simply identify the corresponding factor and multiply you dog's RER (which you already figured out) by the appropriate number.

Table to calculate canine Maintenance Energy Requirements

Activity	Daily Energy Requirements
Weight loss	1.0 x RER
Neutered adult, normal activity	1.6 x RER
Intact adult normal activity	1.8 x RER
Light work or play	2.0 x RER
Moderate work or play	3.0 x RER
Heavy work or play (e.g., agility dog)	4 to 8 x RER
Pregnant dog (first 42 days)	1.8 x RER
Pregnant dog (last 21 days)	3.0 x RER
Lactating dam	4 to 8 x RER
Puppy, weaning to 4 months	3.0 x RER
Puppy, 4 months to adult size	2.0 x RER
Geriatric dog	1.4 x RER

If the 20-pound (9 kg) dog in the example above is a neutered adult of normal activity, simply multiply his RER of 340 kcal/day x 1.6 to achieve his daily MER of 544 kcal/day.

Bear in mind, though, that just as no diet is "one size fits all" (which has been the whole point of this book!), neither is one daily caloric intake number. Dogs are much more individualized than people when it comes to their daily MER. Chances are you have similar caloric requirements as other people of your height and gender (unless you're a competitive athlete). Dogs, however, have many factors that can affect their MER, including breed, age, health status, lifestyle and even the thickness of their coats. Knowing the numbers is simply another tool (albeit an important one) in ensuring that you're feeding your canine companion for optimum weight and health.

Beware of feeding manufacturer's "recommended" amounts

If you feed your dog a commercial diet and think you don't need to worry about calculating his MER because you follow the manufacturer's recommended amount, think again. Manufacturers' feeding recommendations are often highly flawed. For starters, they don't take your dog's specific age, health, lifestyle, activity level or any other individual factors into account. They also tend to *over*estimate the amount of daily calories your dog needs to consume, which can result in a fat dog. You'll be far better off using the formulas we've provided to calculate your dog's daily MER, then adjusting the amount up or down based on a weekly or bi-weekly review of his body composition score (BCS).

Not all calories are created equal

Cutting calories is of course essential to weight loss, but it's also important to remember that not all calories are created equal. Since inflammation generates obesity, be sure to follow our two-step process to help your dog conquer the battle of the bulge and achieve optimum health:

> **Step 1**: Feed lots of fat-fighting, anti-inflammatory functional foods (see below).

> **Step 2**: Remove pro-inflammatory ingredients such as those containing artificial colors, flavors and preservatives, added antibiotics and hormones, sugar, high levels of pesticides and GMO foods, as well as high-glycemic (high-GI) carbohydrates.

Go for "good" carbs

Refer to Chapters 2 and 3 for a refresher on the difference between good carbs and high-GI carbs. The key point to remember is that good carbs originate from whole, fresh foods such as fruits, vegetables, beans and unrefined, gluten-free grains. Unhealthy carbs, on the other hand, come from high-GI, processed foods such as bread, pasta and cereal—and, or course, many of the refined grains found in mass-market commercial pet foods!

Short and long-term studies in humans and animals show that high-GI diets are counterproductive to weight control and actually *promote* body fat storage (Brand-Miller et al., 2002). Sugary and starchy foods are also pro-inflammatory (Hyman, 2013), which can certainly sabotage your dog's weight loss.

Fat-fighting functional foods

Once you've removed as many pro-inflammatory ingredients from your dog's diet as possible, it's time to add in fat-fighting functional foods (Roudebush, Schoenherr & Delany, 2008; Yamka, Frantz & Friesen, 2007). Here are some of the most important:

High quality, bioavailable novel protein. Protein is a critical part of a weight-loss regimen. We've talked at length about the importance of protein in tissue building and repair, which is essential to maintaining lean body mass during weight loss. Ideal weight loss regimens are high in protein with moderate fat and restricted in carbohydrates.

Coconut oil (virgin, expeller-pressed, preferably organic). You'll learn a lot about this canine superfood in the following chapters, especially regarding its important role in brain health (Chapter 10). For years, *coconut oil* was shunned as an unhealthy saturated fat. But that couldn't be further from the truth. *Coconut oil* is a medium-chain saturated fat (MCFA), also known as a medium-chain triglyceride (MCT), and is packed with health benefits ranging from immune-boosting to heart-protective properties. *Coconut oil* also digests differently than other fats, creating a higher thermogenic (heat producing) effect that boosts metabolic rate, which helps to melt the pounds away (Perricone, 2010). And dogs love the taste!

Omega-3 fatty acids are another powerful canine functional superfood we'll talk a lot about in upcoming chapters. *Omega-3s* exert a strong anti-inflammatory effect and therefore play an important role in weight loss, since as we just discussed, obesity is an inflammatory condition. *Omega-3s* also activate a type of protein that turns on fat-burning genes (Perricone, 2010).

L-Carnitine is an amino acid that is synthesized in the liver and kidneys from lysine and methionine. When taken as a dietary supplement, L-carnitine has been shown to improve nitrogen retention, which increases lean mass and reduces fat mass. Studies show that L-carnitine reduces lean tissue loss when incorporated into companion animal weight loss regimens at a dose of 50–300 ppm (German, 2006).

White kidney bean extract (*Phaseolus vulgaris*) is an extract derived from the white kidney bean. In human studies, *Phaseolus vulgaris* has been shown to act as a starch blocker that works by blocking the activity of alpha amylase, a digestive enzyme found in saliva that breaks down starch. Overweight people who took a *Phaseolus vulgaris* extract daily and ate a normal diet (2,000 to 2,200 calories) lost significant body fat without compromising lean body mass (Cellano et al., 2007). While dogs produce amylase in the pancreas, but not in the saliva, the author WJD has noted significant clinical effectiveness in patients supplemented with *Phaseolus vulgaris*. As we've said before, the science of nutrigenomics is still in its early stages, and not everything we notice as experientially beneficial has yet been clinically studied in dogs. But it works!

Note: *Never* feed your dog raw kidney beans, as they are potentially toxic. To ensure safety, only purchase white kidney bean extract from a reputable source that uses a standardized extract processed with heat to inactivate the hemagglutinating (HA) activity (clumping of red blood cells) and trypsin inhibiting activity (TIA) of the beans (Cellano et al., 2007). (See Resources for purchasing information.)

Dose: (give 10 minutes before each meal): 500 mg extract daily (small dogs), 1000 mg extract (medium to large dogs) and 1500 mg extract (large to giant breed dogs).

Antiangiogenic foods

Angiogenesis is the process of creating new blood vessels from existing vessels (Mercola, 2012). You'll learn about angiogenesis in detail when we talk about functional foods for canine cancer patients in Chapter 9, so for now we'll just say that fat tissue (like cancer cells) are dependent on angiogenesis. **Antiangiogenic foods** (foods that prevent angiogenesis) can actually *shrink* fat cells by cutting off their blood supply (Li, 2010).

Can't I just feed a prescription weight loss food?

The answer is that, yes, of course you *can* feed your dog a prescription weight loss food—and if you ask your veterinarian, that's probably the advice you'll get. However, we don't believe these foods are the best choices because they typically:

- Are high in carbohydrates (and not the good kind).

- Contain pro-inflammatory ingredients that are contrary to the principles of nutrigenomics (see below).

- Don't contain enough high quality, bioavailable animal protein.

Here are some of the ingredients we found in one of the most popular commercial prescription weight loss foods for dogs:

- Corn gluten meal

- Soybean oil

- Whole grain corn

- Whole grain wheat

We've already discussed the negative effects these ingredients exert on your dog's cells and gene expression, and there are too many issues to repeat here! For example, the only animal-based protein in one popular canine weight loss food is chicken meal; there is not even one fresh meat source. Remember what we said earlier about high-GI carbohydrate sources, including wheat and corn: they actually *promote* storage of body fat and sabotage weight loss while creating pro-inflammatory spikes in blood sugar and insulin. And these ingredients are highly processed, intensifying their effects!

We would much rather see you work with a qualified veterinarian or canine nutrition-ist to create a weight loss plan that relies on fresh, wholesome foods that promote healthy gene expression, maintenance of lean body mass and overall optimum health.

Success!

Dumpling no longer looks like a dumpling
Dumpling, a middle-aged, yellow spayed female Labrador Retriever continued to gain weight despite the fact that she was on a calorie-restricted diet. This phenomenon is not uncommon in Labradors in mid-life, especially spayed females. Other than the climbing weight issue, Dumpling was otherwise healthy. But once she reached 90 pounds, her obesity started to interfere with her ability to exercise, which compound-ed her weight problem. Dumpling's veterinarian recommended a thorough laboratory workup, which included a complete thyroid profile. All results returned well within normal limits for her age and breed type.

In desperation, Dumpling's guardian consulted the author WJD, who formulated a special homemade weight-loss diet. The goal was to restrict Dumpling's caloric intake in step-wise fashion by about 5% every three weeks, until she lost 20 pounds! Her new diet was fed twice daily and consisted of boneless chicken breast or ground turkey, green beans, spinach, zucchini, yellow squash, hard-boiled egg, a small amount of steamed brown rice, rolled oats (preferably gluten free) and wheat bran (which is not a gluten), plus a pet multivitamin, olive oil and bone meal mix (for calcium). White kidney bean extract (*Phaseolus vulgaris*) was also used. (Note: This diet can be made up ahead of time and stored frozen in meal-sized portions, however the supplements should be added at feeding time to preserve their beneficial effects.) Dumpling was also allowed raw, frozen or lightly steamed green beans for snacks. After four months, Dumpling reduced to a svelte—and much more active—68 pounds!

Lean dogs have "happier" cells

Remember that a lean body supports epigenetic tags that signal optimum gene expression and promote vibrant health. So, help your dog shed those pounds, reduce weight-related inflammation, ditch chronic disease and enjoy a body teeming with healthy, happy cells!

If your dog suffers from a health condition other than obesity, you'll likely find it covered somewhere in the remainder of this section. Read on for details and the latest nutritional tips, tricks and changes to prevent, manage or even reverse these conditions at the cellular level. Remember that cells continually regenerate. Today's "sick" dog can transform into tomorrow's vibrantly healthy dog—with a lot of help from his epigenome!

Takeaway Points

- Pet obesity is a national epidemic. A 2012 survey conducted by the Association for Pet Obesity Prevention (APOP) revealed that 52.5% of dogs and 58.3% of cats are overweight or obese.

- Overweight dogs are at increased risk for numerous diseases and live an average of two years less than their ideal weight counterparts.

- Scientists have identified "obesity gene" variants in people, however many lean individuals carry these obesity genes and never become overweight. This means that the determining factor for becoming obese may be an individual's lifestyle.

- One meta-analysis of data from more than 200,000 people who carry a specific gene predisposing them to obesity found that physically active adults who carried the obesity gene were nearly one-third less likely to become overweight or obese than those who didn't exercise. Genetic predisposition does not mean that obesity is our destiny, or our dog's destiny.

- Over the last half-century, we have seen an unsettling parallel between the spike in human obesity and obesity in companion animals. We strongly believe this parallel relates to similar environmental and lifestyle changes that have occurred.

- Studies show that obesity can affect gene expression, resulting in a host of chronic diseases.

- Once the body becomes "programmed" for fat, it's like a never-ending cycle because fat cells lead to more fat cells.

- Essentially, obesity is a state of chronic inflammation, which leads to a host of chronic inflammatory diseases.

- Acute inflammation is normal and serves a purpose. Chronic inflammation, however, leads to a variety of diseases.

- Food intolerances/sensitivities can lead to weight gain because food sensitivities lead to inflammation, and obesity is an inflammatory condition.

- To ensure your dog is carrying an ideal amount of fat, perform a Body Condition Score evaluation every two-four weeks.

- Before placing your dog on a diet, be sure to have him screened by a veterinarian for any possible underlying health conditions that could be causing his weight gain.

- Since inflammation generates obesity, a key step in helping your dog lose weight is to feed him lots of fat-fighting anti-inflammatory foods, while also removing pro-inflammatory foods.

- Fat-fighting functional foods include high quality, bioavailable novel proteins, virgin *coconut oil*, *omega-3 fatty acids*, L-carnitine, white kidney bean extract and antiangiogenic foods.

- Commercial weight-loss foods are not the best choice in your dog's battle against the bulge. These products are typically high in unhealthy carbohydrates, contain pro-inflammatory ingredients and don't contain enough high quality animal protein. Opt instead for fresh, wholesome ingredients that promote healthy gene expression, maintenance of lean body mass and overall optimum health.

- Shedding extra pounds will help your dog reduce weight-related inflammation, ditch chronic disease and enjoy a body teeming with healthy, happy cells.

Chapter 8

A Nutrigenomics Approach

to Arthritis

If your arthritic dog is overweight, please refer back to Chapter 7 and start him on the road to his ideal body condition. Arthritis is a classic inflammatory condition and fat, as you'll remember, creates inflammation. Besides, extra weight means extra stress on your dog's stiff, achy joints. You'll also want to address any potential food intolerances/sensitivities that you suspect your dog might have. Again, antigenic foods create inflammation. See Chapter 6 for a refresher on food intolerance/sensitivity testing and consider utilizing NutriScan to identify foods that are problematic for your specific dog.

Ready for the latest methods to combat your dog's arthritis without the use of potentially harmful drugs? Read on.

What is arthritis?

Arthritis is the most prevalent joint disease in dogs, affecting as many as 20% of adult dogs (Laflamme, 2012). From 2007 to 2011, reports of arthritis increased 38% in dogs and 67% in cats. Every dog is at risk, especially as he ages; in 2011, 13% of geriatric dogs were diagnosed with arthritis (Banfield Pet Hospital, 2012; Howard, 2012).

Arthritis refers to many related conditions involving inflammation of one or more joints. Osteoarthritis (OA), or degenerative joint disease (DJD), is the most commonly diagnosed form of canine arthritis and one of the most frequent causes of lameness in dogs. OA is characterized by: deterioration of joint cartilage, called **articular cartilage**; formation of bony growths or spurs on the joints, called **osteophytes**; changes in the **subchondral bone** (the bone below the articular cartilage); and joint inflammation. These changes occur following alterations in both the biomechanical and biochemical properties of the joint (Logar et al., 2007; Sanchez & Balligand, 2005; Zhang et al., 2012).

Arthritis causes pain, stiffness, limited mobility and—in more severe and chronic cases—debilitation. An arthritic dog might show difficulty or hesitancy rising, jumping, running or walking. It's easy to confuse the signs of arthritis with the normal "slowing down" due to age, so if you notice any change in your dog's behavior or activity level, please take him to your veterinarian for a thorough exam.

Certain large breeds such as Labrador Retrievers, German Shepherds and Mastiffs may be at higher risk of developing OA because these breeds tend to suffer from inherited or congenital defects such as hip dysplasia, elbow dysplasia or a luxating patella. Larger breeds also endure more weight bearing on their joints, so they generally suffer more arthritis than small and toy breeds.

OA: It's in the genes

Historically, doctors have viewed and treated arthritis as a structural disease that involves the breakdown of cartilage and its subsequent effect on the joints, but that view is changing. Thanks to new tools to measure gene expression, including reverse transcription-polymerase chain reaction (RT-PCR), differential display and DNA microarray analysis (which we discussed in Chapter 6), we can now ask the question, "Which came first, the structural changes or the changes in gene expression that led to the structural changes?" (Middleton & Hannah, 2004).

Researchers have identified many inflammatory cell markers that are turned on in dogs with OA. These markers correlate to inflammation within the cells that make up articular cartilage, which are called **articular chondrocytes**. A deeper understanding of how OA occurs at the cellular level opens the door to an entirely new treatment approach, including the use of functional nutrients that target specific genes involved in the disease (Middleton & Hannah, 2004).

Details on the science behind gene expression and arthritis

The OA-obesity link: It's more than just weight

Not surprisingly, obese dogs are at higher risk of developing arthritis because they carry a disproportionate amount of weight for the size of their frames, which places excessive stress on their joints. In fact, about 40% of arthritic dogs are overweight, and these dogs also display more severe symptoms than their leaner counterparts (Howard, 2012).

But the relationship between OA and obesity extends far beyond the wear and tear related to carrying additional weight; there is also a systemic inflammatory connection. In Chapter 7, you learned that adipose (fat) tissue secretes pro-inflammatory cytokines. Researchers have now confirmed that these cytokines increase inflammation in the articular cartilage. Excess adipose tissue not only increases the risk of OA—it also increases the symptoms (Koonce & Braverman, 2013; Laflamme, 2004; Pollack, 2013). In a moment, we'll talk about a powerful functional ingredient in the war against pro-inflammatory cytokines.

Obesity also promotes oxidative stress, which occurs when there is an imbalance in the body of pro-oxidants and anti-oxidants: arthritis is associated with increased oxidative stress. Research shows that when dogs with OA lose weight, they experience a decrease in pain and lameness and an increase in joint mobility (Laflamme, 2004; Laflamme, 2012).

Getting your arthritic dog to optimum weight is an important step in helping manage his arthritis. Not only will a trimmer dog bear less of a weight burden on his musculo-skeletal system, he'll also decrease the systemic inflammation and oxidation associated with OA.

Is OA a cartilage disease or a bone disease?

Osteoarthritis has typically been considered a cartilage disease, but emerging evidence suggests that it might also be a *bone* disease. As we just mentioned, OA is accompanied by changes in subchondral bone, including **sclerosis** (abnormal bone density) and the formation of osteophytes and cysts. Researchers have discovered that bone-forming cells called **osteoblasts** that are in the area near **sclerotic subchondral bone** (subchondral bone with abnormal bone density) appear different than nearby cells in the non-sclerotic area. The expression of some genes associated with sclerotic osteoblasts was significantly up regulated, while other genes were down regulated. This means that *healthy bone cells look and function differently than arthritic bone cells*. It also means that arthritic bone cells can serve as the potential target for specific nutritional and medicinal OA therapies (Logar et al., 2007; Sanchez et al., 2008).

Functional foods for OA

The conventional veterinary community typically relies on non-steroidal anti-inflammatory drugs (NSAIDs), commercial prescription diets and Adequan® injections to treat OA in dogs, while some also recommend glucosamine/chondroitin (see below). Ironically, most commercial prescription OA diets contain grains, gluten and/or white potato—all of which can *promote* inflammation. These diets can also contain a pro-inflammatory ratio of omega-6 to omega-3 fatty acids (see below). NSAIDs, when used long-term, can cause damage or injury to tissues of the liver, kidneys and bone marrow (Dodds & Lassin, 2013).

Fortunately, there are many safe, functional nutritional ingredients that can effectively decrease inflammation, detoxify toxins that promote an inflammatory response and repair/improve cartilage and bone health (Dodds & Lassin, 2013). Let's take a look at those we consider to be among the best.

Avocado-soybean unsaponifiables (ASU)

"Unsaponifiable lipids" are the parts of fats that cannot be used to make soaps. Avocado-soybean unsaponifiables (ASUs) have been studied for their benefits to treat OA and have been shown to produce an anti-inflammatory, antioxidant and tissue building effect on articular chondrocytes (Laflamme, 2012; Lippiello, 2008).

One study of 16 dogs with induced anterior cruciate ligament rupture showed that treatment with ASU can reduce the development of early osteoarthritic cartilage and subchondral bone lesions. The dogs were given ASU at a daily dose of 10 mg/kg body weight, which is approximately double the dosage recommended for humans with OA (Boileau et al., 2009; Laflamme, 2012). Elk or deer velvet antler (EVA, DVA) powder

Elk or deer velvet antler (EVA, DVA) powder

EVA and DVA are nutritional supplements that have been used in Traditional Chinese Medicine for thousands of years and are known to help alleviate arthritic symptoms by rebuilding cartilage, improving joint fluid, increasing tissue and cellular healing times and improving circulation. EVA and DVA are made from the inner core of the antler in the velvet stage of growth. These products contain many beneficial ingredients, including a **peptide** (short chain of amino acids) called "pilose antler peptide," which is known for its anti-inflammatory properties, as well as chondroitin sulfate (see below), which reduces the inflammation, deterioration of cartilage and pain associated with OA (Laflamme, 2012; Moreau, 2004).

EVA and DVA also contain: collagen; lipids; minerals/trace elements (calcium, phosphorus, sulphur, magnesium, potassium, sodium, manganese, zinc, copper, iron, selenium, cobalt); growth factors; glucosamine; **glycosaminoglycans**, or GAGs (a major component of joint cartilage, joint fluid and other soft connective tissue); phospholipids; prostaglandins; and hyaluronic acid. In addition, IGF 1 (Insulin growth factor) and IGF 2 are both found naturally in deer and elk velvet. IGF 1 influences cellular growth that involves every cell in the body, including muscle, cartilage, bone and many other organs. IGF 2 works with IGF 1 to promote cellular growth and organ development.

A 2004 double-blind, placebo-controlled study of 38 client-owned dogs with OA showed that EVA powder effectively alleviated the dogs' conditions (Moreau, 2004). While we have included EVA and DVA powder due to their research-based efficacy in alleviating OA in dogs, we do not personally use or recommend these products due to ethical issues related to their derivation.

Dose: 14 to 21 g EVA or DVA powder/kg body weight per day (Laflamme, 2012) or according to the manufacturer's recommended dosage.

Topical ginger root application relieves symptoms of OA

In a 24-week pilot study, researchers from Edith Cowan University in Australia found that ginger root applied topically either via a compress or transdermal patch (a patent-pending product from New Zealand) significantly improved clinical signs of OA in people diagnosed with moderate to severe OA. Twenty adults aged 35 to 90 were randomly divided into two groups; one group applied a ginger compress and the other group applied a transdermal patch, daily. After just one week, patients in both groups reported a 48% decrease in pain, a 49% decrease in fatigue, a 31% increase in mobility and a 40% increase in well being. The researchers concluded that topical ginger treatment has the potential to relieve symptoms and improve overall health in people with OA (Adams, 2013; Therkleson, 2013).

Glucosamine and chondroitin sulfate

A moment ago we mentioned glycosaminoglycans, or "GAGs" (also known as muco-polysaccharides). Basically, GAGs are long chains of sugar molecules. Glucosamine, which is a glycoprotein, is necessary to synthesize GAGs, while chondroitin sulfate is a GAG. GAGs provide structural support in many areas throughout the body, including in tendons, ligaments and cartilage. They are also found in **synovial fluid** (the fluid that lubricates the joints).

Glucosamine and chondroitin sulfate help dogs with OA in a variety of ways, including:

- Work similar to NSAIDs to decrease production of pro-inflammatory compounds.
- Reduce pain and inflammation.
- Stimulate cells found in cartilage (chondrocytes).
- Serve as the building blocks of new joint cartilage.
- May promote proper joint structure and function by increasing the synthesis of proteoglycans, hyaluronic acid (joint lubricant) and collagen.

(Laflamme, 2012; VCA Animal Hospitals, n.d.)

Studies in humans have shown that taking glucosamine and chondroitin sulfate may even reduce the need for surgery. Don't expect to see results quickly, however. These supplements must be taken for several weeks or longer before a change is noticed, and should be continued indefinitely due to their ability to protect and rebuild cartilage (Huskisson, 2008).

Glucosamine supplements are typically made from chitin, the hard outer shells of shellfish, such as shrimp and crab. Be sure to tell your veterinarian if your dog is allergic to shellfish. Since shellfish allergies are believed to result from the meat of the shellfish, some researchers believe that there is no risk of shellfish allergy related to taking glucosamine supplements. However, it's better to be safe than sorry. Chondroitin is usually made from shark cartilage or bovine trachea.

Chondroitin sulfate works in conjunction with glucosamine to reduce inflammation, slow the deterioration of cartilage and decrease signs of pain in dogs with OA. Although conflicting research exists as to whether glucosamine works better when taken with chondroitin sulfate, studies on dogs indicate a clinical benefit of combining the two (Laflamme, 2012).

Glucosamine daily dosages: 250 to 500 mg for small dogs, 500 to 1000 mg daily for medium to large dogs and 1000 to 2000 mg daily for large and giant breed dogs.

Chondroitin sulfate daily dosages: 200 to 400 mg for small dogs, 400 to 800 mg for medium to large dogs and 800 to 1600 mg daily for large dogs and giant breed dogs.

Green lipped mussel (GLM) extract

A popular cultivated species in New Zealand, the "green lipped" mussel is named, quite appropriately, after the green lip around the edge of the mussel's shell. Green lipped mussel (GLM) powder contains important nutrients for dogs with OA, including GAGs (chondroitin sulfate), the amino acid glutamine, *omega-3 fatty acids* DHA and EPA, minerals (e.g., zinc, copper, manganese) and antioxidant vitamins E and C (Rialland et al., 2013). GLM extract is clinically proven to ease the signs of dogs with OA. Here are two examples:

A 2006, double-blind, placebo-controlled study involving 81 dogs with mild-to-moderate degenerative joint disease found that the dogs significantly benefited from long-term (eight weeks or longer) supplementation with a tablet containing 125 mg GLM extract (The tablet also contained 52.86 mg brewer's yeast, 191.50 mg lactose and 10.64 mg of a tableting aid made of magnesium stearate, acacia and aerosil) (Pollard et al., 2006).

A 2013 study published in the *Canadian Journal of Veterinary Research* reported that a diet enriched with GLM extract significantly improved the gait of 23 companion dogs clinically afflicted with OA, compared with a regular control diet. Dogs fed the GLM-enriched diet also absorbed high levels of EPA and DHA *omega-3 fatty acids* into their blood. The researchers concluded that GLM extract showed a strong ability to benefit dogs with OA, and that it likely works by providing anti-inflammatory effects, translating to better comfort for the dog and probable benefit to the joint structures (Rialland et al., 2013).

Dose: 20 to 49 mg/kg body weight per day (Laflamme, 2012).

Omega-3 fatty acids

Osteoarthritis results in a self-perpetuating inflammatory cycle because **inflammatory mediators** (substances that bring about an inflammatory response) stimulate the production of more inflammatory mediators (Middleton & Hannah, 2004). NSAIDs are often prescribed to break this cycle by inhibiting these inflammatory mediators, most notably the COX-2 enzyme (Laflamme, 2012). However, NSAIDs can cause side effects ranging from vomiting, loss of appetite, depression, lethargy and diarrhea to more serious issues, such as gastrointestinal bleeding, ulcers, perforations, kidney damage and liver problems (Bren, 2006).

EPA and DHA from fish and other marine sources also down-regulate COX-2 expression, making these powerhouse *omega-3 fatty acids* a safe and effective alternative to long-term NSAID use (Laflamme, 2004; Laflamme, 2012; Middleton & Hannah, 2004).

Benefits of EPA and DHA for arthritis include:

- Decrease lameness.
- Improve weight-bearing ability.

- Significantly improve ability to rise, play and walk.
- Reduce the need for NSAIDs.

(Fritsch et al., 2010; Roush et al., 2010; Roush et al., 2010a; Waldron, 2004)

A 2012 study published in the *Journal of Animal Physiology and Animal Nutrition* supports these benefits. The trial involving 30 companion dogs with OA found that a diet enriched with **omega-3 fatty acids** from rainbow trout significantly improvement the dogs' locomotor disability as well as their ability to perform daily activities. In fact, the improvement was comparable to that observed in osteoarthritic dogs taking NSAIDs (Moreau et al., 2012).

Summary of a study supporting the importance of diets containing a high *omega-3* to omega-6 fatty acid ratio for dogs with OA

See Chapter 4 for dosing.

SAMe

SAMe is produced by the body from the amino acid methionine and adenosyl-triphosphate (ATP). Since it isn't found in food, supplementing with SAMe is sometimes advisable.

Clinical trials of people with OA in the knee, hip or spine found that supplementation with SAMe was as effective as NSAIDs, including ibuprofen and naproxen, in several areas, including:

- Decreasing pain.
- Reducing swelling.
- Reducing morning stiffness.
- Improving range of motion.
- Increasing walking pace.

(UMMC, 2011)

SAMe may also promote cartilage repair (UMMC, 2011).

You'll learn more about SAMe and its role in treating cancer and Canine Cognitive Dysfunction Syndrome coming up in Chapters 9 and 10.

Spirulina

Spirulina is a class of ancient, microscopic blue-green algae that grows in warm, fresh water and takes its name from the spiral shape of its strands. *Spirulina* gets its deep green color from chlorophyll and its blue color from **phycocyanin** (C-PC), a compound with strong antioxidant, anti-inflammatory, anti-arthritic, anti-cancer (see Chapter 9) and **hepato** (liver)-protective properties (see Chapter 11) (Messonnier, 2006; Reddy et al., 2000; Romay et al., 2003; UMMC, 2011a; Wolf, 2009).

Like EPA and DHA, C-PC suppresses the COX-2 enzyme, decreasing pain and inflammation of OA without the negative side effects of NSAIDs. C-PC was even shown to be a more potent inhibitor of COX-2 activity than a class of NSAID drugs introduced by two major pharmaceutical companies (Reddy et al., 2000).

Spirulina is also rich in many important nutrients, including B-complex vitamins and vitamin E, a wide array of minerals, chlorophyll, phytonutrients, carotenoids, gamma linolenic acid and superoxide dismutase (a potent free radical scavenger) (Bensimoun, 2013; UMMC, 2011a; Wolf, 2009).

Depending on the variety, *spirulina* contains 65% to 71% protein, which is more protein by weight than any other food. Just one ounce of *spirulina* contains about 16 grams of protein! Moreover, the protein is four times more absorbable per gram than the same amount of beef protein (Bensimoun, 2013; Wolf, 2009). It's especially important that dogs suffering from OA consume an adequate amount of protein since, as you'll recall, protein provides the structure of bones, joints, tendons, ligaments, cartilage, muscle fibers and collagen.

Dose: We suggest 1/4 teaspoon per cup of food daily.

Vitamins C, E and pro-vitamin A carotenoids (antioxidants)

An increase in oxidative stress as well as a *decrease* in antioxidant capacity has been shown to intensify the severity of arthritic lesions (Laflamme, 2012). So, even though clinical trials in humans have produced conflicting results on the role of antioxidants in managing OA, we believe that experiential studies indicate their value.

Supplementation with vitamin C (ascorbic acid) is especially controversial in dogs because, unlike humans, a dog's body can manufacture its own; however, studies over the past two decades have shown that dogs *do* benefit from the addition of vitamin C beyond what their bodies can make. The extra antioxidant power helps them cope with stresses associated with their modern lifestyles, including environmental pollution and sub-optimal diets. Bear in mind that high doses of ascorbic acid can upset the stomach and cause loose stools, though, so use caution and increase the dosage slowly (Sanghi et al., 2009; Straus, 2007). You can also opt for mineral ascorbates, such as calcium ascorbate or sodium ascorbate, which are buffered and less acidic. However, since the mineral portion of the supplement is also absorbed, you need to take that dose into account. For example, 1,000 mg of sodium ascorbate typically contains 111 mg sodium (Linus Pauling Institute, 2013). You don't want to give a dog on a low-sodium diet a high dose of sodium ascorbate, as this could raise his sodium intake through the roof!

Dosage: Begin with a daily dose of vitamin C (we prefer the Ester C® form) as follows: 250 to 500 mg daily for small dogs, divided twice daily and given with food; 500 to 1000 mg daily for medium to large dogs (divided twice daily and given with food); and 1000 to 2000 mg for large and giant breed dogs (divided twice daily and given with food).

You might also be surprised to see carotenoids (e.g., beta-carotene) on the list of antioxidant vitamins. While carotenoids are not vitamins *per se*, these antioxidants are known as "pro-vitamin A" because they are converted to the active form of vitamin A (retinol) in the body. As you'll recall from our earlier discussions, beta-carotene and other carotenoids are found in colorful fruits and vegetables, such as carrots, pumpkins, squash and beets (Evert, 2013). Bear in mind, though, that retinol is not an antioxidant and, as we mentioned earlier, high doses of vitamin A can be toxic.

More functional ingredients for OA

- *Curcumin*: a potent antioxidant with strong anti-inflammatory properties.
- Grape seed extract: a powerful polyphenol and antioxidant. It also has anti-carcinogenic and strong anti-inflammatory properties (Shanmuganayagam et al., 2002).
- Green (or black) tea leaf extract: has potent antioxidant and anti-inflammatory properties, which come from the tannins and polyphenols in teas (Gosslau et al., 2011).
- MSM (MethylSulfonylMethane): acts as a natural anti-inflammatory for joints.
- Thymus glandular: enhances, improves and maintains a strong immune system.
- DLPA (D,L Phenylalanine): an essential amino acid and endorphin stimulant to help control chronic bone and muscle pain.
- Traumeel® and Zeel® (by the company Heel): a popular homeopathic remedy for aches & pains.

(Dodds & Lassin, 2013)

The following herbs also contain powerful anti-inflammatory properties:
- Andrographis paniculata (King of bitters)
- Boswellia
- Hawthorn
- Licorice
- Nettle leaf
- Willow bark (a relative of aspirin; do not combine with NSAIDs)
- Yucca root

(Beynen & Legerstee, 2010; Puotinen, 2010)

As you'll discover in the next chapter, understanding how to dispense herbs is both a science and an art. Taking too many herbs, low quality herbs or inaccurately combining herbs may not only detract from their beneficial effects, but can actually cause harm. For these reasons, we advise either purchasing pre-formulated herbs from a reputable manufacturer (see Resources section) or from your holistic veterinarian.

Also, please be sure to always advise your dog's veterinarian of all herbal formulas he's taking, since, as you'll note above with regards to willow bark, some herbs should not be combined with certain prescription and/or non-prescription medications.

A heat map illustrating the "molecular dietary signature" for dogs treated 28 days with herbals to control the genes expressing for arthritis can be found at www.nutriscan.org. The heat map shows how genes are expressed (up-regulated and turned on in red or down-regulated and turned off in green) in unhealthy dogs of two genotypes (G1 and G2) that were severely affected with arthritis. The data compare the results both before and after administration of the botanical herbs *Andrographis paniculata* (King of bitters) and Curcuma longa (turmeric) for 28 days. The arthritic dogs had mostly red (positive) gene expression in the four left-hand columns before the herbal treatments, and then were "cleansed" with mostly green (negative) and a few red (positive) genes expressed in the four center and four right-hand columns after just 28 days of taking these two herbal compounds. Remarkable!

Success!

A natural approach to treating lameness

Jiggy, a neutered four-year-old male Great Dane, was admitted to his local veterinarian for shifting leg and worsening lameness of both forelimbs. Because of his discomfort, he was unable to exercise and his weight ballooned to over 175 pounds. Jiggy also had a history of gastric torsion and bloat, which was addressed surgically. His stomach was "tacked" to the abdominal wall in an effort to prevent further torsion episodes.

A special functional diet based on nutrigenomic principles and containing nutraceutical plant extracts (bioactive botanicals/herbs) was prescribed. The gluten-free, functional diet consisted of phytotherapy (plant extracts used medicinally) in the form of *Andrographis paniculata* (King of bitters) and **curcumin**, as well as the addition of glucosamine and chondroitin sulphate and **omega-3 fatty acids**. After just 28 days on this botanically enhanced basal diet, Jiggy was free of pain and discomfort. His gait was normal and, much to the delight of his guardians, he was able to resume exercise.

Takeaway Points

- Arthritis is a classic inflammatory disease. It refers to many related conditions involving inflammation of one or more joints.

- Arthritis is the most prevalent joint disease in dogs, affecting as many as 20% of adult dogs.

- Osteoarthritis (OA), or degenerative joints disease (DJD), is the most commonly diagnosed form of canine arthritis and one of the most frequent causes of lameness in dogs.

- Certain large breeds such as Labrador retrievers, German Shepherds and Mastiffs may be at higher risk of developing OA because these breeds tend to suffer from inherited or congenital defects such as hip dysplasia, elbow dysplasia or luxating patella. Larger breeds also endure more weight bearing on their joints, so they generally suffer more arthritis than the smaller and toy breeds.

- Doctors have typically viewed OA as a structural disease that involves the breakdown of cartilage and its subsequent effect on the joints, but we now know that changes in gene expression might precede and lead to these structural changes.

- There is a systemic inflammatory connection between obesity and arthritis. Obesity promotes inflammation and oxidative stress, both of which are associated with OA.

- Researchers have discovered that healthy bone cells look and function differently than arthritic bone cells. Arthritic bone cells can serve as the potential target for nutritional and medicinal OA therapies.

- The conventional veterinary community typically relies on non-steroidal anti-inflammatory drugs (NSAIDs), prescription diets and Adequan® injections to treat OA, all of which have their health risks.

- *Omega-3 fatty acids* are an important functional ingredient for dogs with OA as well as any other inflammatory condition. EPA and DHA from marine sources such as fish oil are a safe, effective alternative to NSAIDs. Studies show that EPA and DHA more effectively modulate both cellular metabolic functions and gene expression than plant-based ALA.

- Other functional ingredients to help dogs with OA include: elk or deer velvet antler (EVA, DVA) powder; green lipped mussel extract; glucosamines and chondroitin; vitamins A, C and E; SAMe; *spirulina*; unsaponifiable lipids; certain herbs; *curcumin*; grape seed extract; green (or black) tea leaf extract; MSM; D,L phenylalanine and the homeopathic remedies Traumeel® and Zeel® by the company Heel.

Chapter 9

A Nutrigenomics Approach

to Cancer

Cancer: it's a word every dog parent fears hearing from the veterinarian, but cancer among companion animals is a fact of life. Cancer is responsible for as many as half the canine (and feline) deaths in the United States and is the leading cause of death in dogs older than two years (Heinze, Gomez & Freeman, 2012; Tremayne, 2010). When a beloved dog is diagnosed with cancer, it's natural to feel confused, frightened and overwhelmed. We hope the information in this chapter will empower you to make changes that can positively impact your companion's outcome and quality of life. And while we in no way discourage you from seeking traditional veterinary cancer treatment, this information provides powerful nutritional tools that can play an important role in an integrated approach to prevention and healing. If your veterinarian attempts to dissuade you from incorporating functional food therapy into your dog's cancer regimen, we encourage you to partner with a more open-minded healthcare professional who understands the latest scientific findings on this topic. As you'll recall from the Introduction, researchers recently discovered a parallel evolution in the human and canine genomes, and genes related to cancer are among the most pronounced examples. Thanks to this genomic similarity, both dogs and people can benefit from the latest cancer research.

Epigenetics and cancer: evidence too strong to ignore

If you think certain people or animals are destined to get cancer as an unfortunate by-product of their inherited DNA, think again. Researchers estimate that only 5% to 10% of all cancer cases originate from genetic predisposition, while *90% to 95% are the result of lifestyle and environmental factors*, such as exposure to pollution and toxins, obesity, lack of physical activity, infection, stress and diet. These factors create epigenetic changes that can turn off genes that suppress tumors and/or turn on **oncogenes**, a type of abnormal gene that predispose cells to develop into cancers (Broad Institute, 2013).

Many studies show that certain nutritional ingredients have epigenetic targets in cancer cells. These ingredients can both defend against the development of many types of cancerous tumors as well as impact their progression. Astoundingly, scientists have concluded that *30% to 40% of all cancers can be prevented simply by implementing dietary changes* (Anand et al., 2008; Divisi et al., 2006; Donaldson, 2004; Hardy & Tollefsbol, 2011; Ziech et al., 2010).

But before you begin *adding* ingredients to your dog's cancer-protective diet, let's first think about what you need to *eliminate*. Please remove foods that contain any of the harmful ingredients previously discussed. This is important because these ingredients can counterbalance the benefits of the functional foods you'll soon incorporate into your dog's diet.

Obesity and cancer: one more reason to keep your dog trim

By now, you've read over and over in this book about the health dangers of obesity, and for good reason. A dog that is overweight or obese is a dog that is at risk for a host of serious, chronic diseases, and cancer is no exception. In fact, there are strong correlations between overeating and cancer (Donaldson, 2004).

Normal cells maintain a proper balance of **cell proliferation** (the rate at which they grow and divide), **differentiation** (the type of cells they become) and **apoptosis** (cell death). Obesity can alter the metabolism of several hormones involved in maintaining this balance, which in turn can lead to cancer. In addition, certain pro-inflammatory cytokines produced by fat cells activate a type of transcription factor (NK-fB) that plays an important role in carcinogenesis and other inflammatory diseases, including asthma, arthritis, cardiovascular disease and inflammatory bowel disease. Obesity-related **hyperglycemia** (high blood sugar) has also been shown to activate NK-fB (Anand et al., 2008; Gilmore, n.d.; Nahleh, Bhatti & Mal, 2011).

New studies have also discovered a link between gene expression in adipose (fat) tissue and insulin resistance (Wein, 2012). Insulin resistance is associated with Type 2 diabetes, which is a major risk factor for cancer (see below).

The following types of cancers have been linked to obesity in people:

- Breast
- Cervical
- Colon
- Endometrial
- Esophageal
- Gastric
- Gall bladder
- Liver

- Multiple myeloma

- Non-Hodgkin's lymphoma

- Ovarian

- Pancreatic

- Rectal

- Renal

- Uterine

(Anand et al., 2008)

The bottom line is that there is a well-established link between obesity and inflammatory diseases, including cancer. If your dog is overweight, please refer to Chapter 7 for guidance on how to help him safely remove those excess pounds. You'll also want to pay special attention to the list of fat-fighting antiangiogenic foods coming up shortly.

Cancer and high-glycemic foods: a recipe for disaster

High-GI foods promote obesity, which plays a role in carcinogenesis. High-GI carbohydrates also promote **hyperinsulinemia** (excess insulin production), which is associated with Type 2 diabetes. In multiple studies, diabetes has been linked with increased risk of several types of cancers, including a three-times higher risk of colon-rectal cancer. Be sure to remove all refined sugars, refined flour products and other unhealthy carbohydrates we previously discussed from your dog's cancer-protective diet (Anand et al., 2008; Divisi, 2006; Donaldson, 2004; Nahleh, Bhatti & Mal, 2011).

Get rid of gluten

We've already talked at length about the link between gluten, leaky gut syndrome and inflammation. You'll remember that gluten causes the intestines to release a protein called zonulin, which creates openings between the intestinal cells, causing the lining of the gut to become more permeable, or "leaky," and allowing unwanted particles to pass from the intestines into the bloodstream (Hyman, 2012; Hyman, 2013; Kressler, 2012). The body recognizes these particles as dangerous foreign invaders, calling upon all of its "troops" (immune-fighting cells) to attack them. At the same time, these cells mistakenly attack the body's own tissue, triggering a system-wide bonfire of inflammation associated with dozens of diseases, including cancer. If your dog has cancer, he certainly doesn't need to eat an ingredient known to promote cancer-causing inflammation.

Fluoride and canine osteosarcoma: nothing to smile about

Osteosarcoma is the most common malignant bone tumor in dogs (and young growing boys); it strikes more than 8,000 dogs a year in the United States, afflicting primarily large dogs with rapidly developing bones. About 900 cases per year are reported in people, which means that dogs are nearly 10 times more likely to suffer from this type of cancer (EWG, 2009).

What's even more shocking is that this deadly bone cancer may originate right under your dog's nose—literally, in his food and water (EWG, 2009; EWG, 2009a; EWG, 2009b).

As we discussed in Chapter 3, an independent laboratory test of dry dog foods commissioned by the Environmental Working Group (EWG) found that eight out of 10 major national brands sold for puppies and adults contained fluoride in amounts between 1.6 and 2.5 times higher than the Environmental Protection Agency's maximum legal dose in drinking water. The amounts detected were also higher than those linked to bone cancer in young boys (EWG, 2009; EWG, 2009b).

Once ingested, fluoride accumulates in the bones. The eight brands all included some form of bone meal, meat meal or meat byproduct meal, which were implicated as the sources of the fluoride contamination. Fluoridated tap water was also used to prepare the foods, increasing the level even further (EWG, 2009; EWG, 2009b).

Based on the EWG's study, a 10-pound puppy that eats about a cup of dry dog food a day would consume 0.25 milligrams of fluoride per kilogram of body weight per day—five times the level deemed safe by the Agency for Toxic Substances and Disease Registry (ATSDR) of the U.S. Department of Health and Human Services (EWG, 2009b).

Fluoride likely contributes to osteosarcoma in two main ways:

- It accumulates in the bones after eating or drinking.
- It stimulates **mitosis** (cell division), causing rapid proliferation of **osteoblasts** (cells that form new bone).

(EWG, 2009a)

Since many puppies and adult dogs tend to eat the same food day after day, this repetitive exposure to high levels of fluoride can certainly be considered a risk factor for osteosarcoma. The dangers may be particularly high in large breed puppies that are rapidly forming new bone (EWG, 2009; EWG, 2009a).

If your dog has cancer, we strongly advise eliminating all foods containing bone meal or animal by-products, as well as switching to low-fluoride or fluoride-free bottled water.

Environmental toxins: it's a risky world out there

Since non-food related environmental factors also play an important role in influencing the epigenome, detoxifying your dog's surroundings is an essential part of any anti-cancer protocol. Here are some common sources of hazardous substances that may be lurking in and around your home:

- Lawn and garden products, such as chemical fertilizers, pesticides, herbicides, swimming pool products, etc. (Glickman et al., 2004).

- Household products, such as chemical cleaning products, laundry detergent, bleach, dishwashing detergent, air fresheners, carpet cleaners, etc.

- Construction materials, such as drywall, asbestos, insulation, paints, varnishes, adhesives, etc.

- Automotive products, such as antifreeze, break fluid, lubricants, sealants, etc.

- Batteries, especially battery fluids.

- Personal care products, such as antiperspirants, shampoos, sunscreens, hair sprays, perfume, cologne, etc.

- Pet care products, such as insect repellents, cat litter, flea and tick collars and shampoos, etc. (Raghaven et al., 2004).

PBDEs (polybrominated diphenyl ethers)

PBDEs are flame-retardant chemicals that have been used in clothing, furniture and electronics since the 1970s. They're especially prevalent in foam products, such as mattresses, pillows, upholstered products and carpet padding, as well as in electronics, such as cell phones, computers, printers, scanners, copiers, hair dryers, toner cartridges, TVs, TV remote controls and video equipment (Becker, 2013). PBDEs can leak into the environment and are known disruptors of endocrine function, especially the thyroid gland. There is also evidence linking them to developmental problems, and possibly even cancer, in animals. Foam products sold in 2005 or later should be free of PBDEs, but they are still found in some new TVs and computer monitors (EWG, 2007).

Residues from PBDEs have been found in the serum, foods and house dust of cats and dogs (Becker, 2013; Venier & Hites, 2011). The PBDE levels in cats were 20 to 100 times those seen in humans, while the levels in dogs were five to ten times higher (The levels were lower in dogs is because dogs can metabolize these chemicals faster than cats, and are thought to have an enzyme that helps break them down) (Becker, 2013; Venier & Hites, 2011).

As we discussed in the section on organic foods, the Environmental Working Group (www.ewg.org) provides a wealth of information for people who want to reduce or eliminate toxic products from their environment, including PBDEs and household chemicals. EWG will provide you with the information you need to select the healthiest products for every aspect of your environment, from cosmetics and colognes to infant formula and kids' bath products. EWG's Guide to Healthy Cleaning even provides safety ratings for 2,000 household cleaning products, so you can make informed choices as to which brands will best support your health and the health of your family, both two-legged and four-legged.

Second-hand smoke

If you're a smoker, you might not think about the dangers of second-hand smoke to your companion animals, but research studies show that dogs exposed to large amounts of second-hand smoke have substantial changes to their lung tissue over time. Changes range from **fibrosis** (scarring of the lung tissue) to pre-cancerous and even cancerous lesions. If you must smoke, please consider doing it outside (Wilson-Robles, 2013).

Topical chemical flea and tick preventives

Of course, we don't want our dogs to suffer the agony and potential diseases associated with fleas, ticks and other insects, nor do we want these potentially harmful pests in our homes. But many of the products used to eradicate these bugs, including monthly spot-on flea and tick treatments that come in a tube or vial and are squeezed between the shoulder blades, contain toxic chemicals that pose both immediate and chronic health risks to dogs—including the risk of death (Raghaven et al., 2004).

As far back as 1989, a study by the Purdue University School of Veterinary Medicine Department of Pathobiology, published in the *Journal of Toxicology and Environmental Health*, found that dogs who received one to two topical pesticide applications per year experienced a 60% increased risk of bladder cancer. Dogs that were given more than two applications per year were 3.5 times more likely to develop bladder cancer. The risk was increased even more in overweight or obese dogs (Glickman et al., 1989; Glickman et al., 2004; Raghaven et al., 2004).

Products containing organophosphates, carbamates and pyrethrins/pyrethroids pose particularly severe health risks and should not be used on dogs with cancer—or any dogs, in our opinion.

Most flea and tick problems can be avoided without the use of toxic chemicals that are absorbed through your dog's skin. To get rid of pests, try the following:

- Bathe your dog frequently to control minor infestations.
- Comb your dog with a special fine-tooth flea comb and check him for ticks after outdoor romps.
- Frequently wash your dog's bedding in hot water.
- Keep your grass raked and cut short in areas your dog frequents.
- Use natural flea and tick repellants that contain essential oils rather than toxic chemicals.
- Vacuum and wash your floors regularly.

If you must use a spot-on flea and tick treatment, please be sure it is under the guidance and supervision of your veterinarian; avoid purchasing over-the-counter products in supermarkets or pet supply stores, as these often contain the most potentially hazardous ingredients (Raghaven et al., 2004).

Hold that needle: risks of vaccination to immune-compromised dogs

A **vaccine** is a biological preparation of either modified live or killed pathogens (viruses, bacteria or parasites) that is introduced into the body in order to promote immunity to a particular disease (Dodds, 2001; Tizard & Ni, 1998; Twark & Dodds, 2000).

Vaccines have achieved many important benefits for companion animals, including:

- Saved more animals' lives than any other medical advance.
- Significantly reduced canine distemper, hepatitis and parvovirus.
- Significantly reduced feline panleukopenia.
- Eliminated rabies in Europe.

However, after spending many years monitoring the results of **vaccinosis** (reactions and side effects of vaccines), those in the animal healthcare field now have a duty to re-examine and improve the current vaccine protocols for the health and safety of their patients. This is especially true for animals with compromised immune systems, since vaccines represent one more stressor that could prove to be the "tipping point" between health and disease. Side effects from dog vaccinations can occur anywhere from instantly up to several weeks or months later. Vaccines can even cause susceptibility to chronic diseases that appear much later in a dog's life (Dodds, 2001).

Mild reactions **associated with vaccines include:**

- Fever
- Malaise
- Urticaria [hives]
- Facial swelling
- Anorexia
- Vomiting
- Stiffness
- Sore joints
- Abdominal tenderness

Severe and fatal **adverse reactions include:**

- Susceptibility to infections.
- Neurological disorders and encephalitis.
- Aberrant behaviour, including unprovoked aggression.
- Collapse with **autoagglutinated** (clumped) red blood cells and **icterus** (jaundice); **autoimmune hemolytic anemia (AIHA)** or the synonym **immune-mediated haemolytic anemia (IMHA)**, when red blood cells are damaged and destroyed; or **petechiae** (pin-point) and **ecchymotic** (splotchy) hemorrhages

from **immune-mediated thrombocytopenia (ITP)**, when the blood platelets are destroyed. Hepatic enzymes may be markedly elevated, and liver or kidney failure may occur by itself or accompany bone marrow suppression.

The two types of vaccines

There are two general types of vaccines—**MLV** (modified live virus) and killed. As the name suggests, MLV vaccines use a modified, but weakened, form of the live virus. When the virus is injected into the body, it multiplies many-fold and stimulates the immune system's production of antibodies, creating an immune response that protects the body against future exposure to the disease. **Killed vaccines** use an inactivated "dead" form of the virus, along with an **adjuvant** (a substance added to a vaccine to enhance its effectiveness without itself causing an immune response). Both MLV and killed vaccines pose greater risks to dogs with impaired immune systems.

Although all dogs are susceptible to vaccine-related side effects, certain breeds are more pre-disposed to vaccinosis. These include:

- Akita
- American Cocker Spaniel
- German Shepherd
- Golden Retriever
- Irish Setter
- Great Dane
- Kerry Blue Terrier
- Dachshunds (all varieties, but especially the long-haired)
- Poodles (all varieties, but especially the Standard Poodle)
- Old English Sheepdog
- Scottish Terrier
- Shetland Sheepdog
- Shih Tzu
- Vizsla
- Weimaraner

Breeds with white or predominantly white coats, as well as those with coat color dilution such as fawn (Isabella) or blue Dobermans, the merle coat color, blue Yorkshire Terriers, grey Collies, harlequin Great Danes, and Australian Shepherds also have increased risk (Dodds, 2001).

If your dog suffers from cancer, we strongly advise against any future vaccines (assuming he has already completed his full puppy series), since this will only place further stress on his already compromised immune system. If you want to make sure your dog is protected from certain diseases, your veterinarian can perform a **titer test**, a simple blood test to check his immunity (Tizard & Ni, 1998; Twark & Dodds, 2000). The only vaccine required by law is rabies, but in situations involving serious illness, your veterinarian can write you a medical waiver. Just understand that if your dog should bite somebody, he will be considered unvaccinated under the law.

Now that we've covered some important non-nutritional environmental factors that affect the epigenome, let's move ahead and talk about functional foods for your dog's cancer-protective diet. It makes sense to begin this discussion with two important discoveries regarding how cancer cells form, grow and multiply—DNA methylation and angiogenesis:

DNA methylation: an important epigenetic cancer marker

We introduced the concept of DNA methylation in Chapter 1 and pointed out that if the process of DNA methylation malfunctions, changes occur in the epigenome that can lead to diseases such as cancer. In fact, tumor cells often contain abnormally methylated DNA (Davis & Uthus, 2004; Hardy & Tollefsbol, 2011).

Abnormal DNA methylation can cause activation of oncogenes (abnormal genes that predispose cells into turning cancerous) and/or it can inactivate genes that suppress tumors. Research shows that when tumors are being formed, at least half of all genes involved in tumor suppression are inactivated through epigenetic mechanisms (Hardy & Tollefsbol, 2011).

The good news is that there are specific bioactive dietary ingredients that promote optimum DNA methylation and help defend against cancer (Esteller, 2008; Hardy & Tollefsbol, 2011). Here are some of the most notable:

- *Curcumin*: A polyphenol compound found in the spice turmeric (see below).

- **Folate**: A B vitamin that controls the repair and methylation of DNA. Folate deficiencies lead to DNA hypomethylation (low methylation), which is associated with tumor development. Many types of cancer, including brain, breast, cervix, colorectal, ovary and lung, have been linked to folate deficiencies. The richest sources of folic acid are leafy greens such as bok choy, escarole, kale, watercress, dandelion, mustard and collard greens. Beans and whole grains are also sources (Hardy & Tollefsbol, 2011; Hyman, 2011).

- **Isothiocyanates** are phytochemicals that exert an anti-cancer effect on the epigenome by inhibiting cancer cell proliferation and inducing apoptosis (cell death). Isothiocyanates are found in cruciferous vegetables such as broccoli, Brussels sprouts, cabbage, cauliflower, collards, kale, radish, turnip and watercress (Hardy & Tollefsbol, 2011).

- **SAMe** is the sole methyl donor in numerous cellular methylation reactions and is vital to cellular metabolism and function. SAMe is not found in food and must be taken via supplementation (Bottiglieri, 2002).

- **Vitamin B-12** (cobalamin) acts as a methyl donor and plays a role in making DNA. Foods rich in vitamin B-12 include fish (opt for low-mercury, wild-caught fish), meat (opt for antibiotic-free, novel proteins), milk (opt for sheep or goat), poultry and eggs (opt for organic, pasture-raised) (WebMD, 2012).

Angiogenesis: eating to starve cancer cells

We mentioned briefly in Chapter 7 that angiogenesis is the process through which new blood vessels form from pre-existing vessels (Mercola, 2012). Creating new blood vessels serves important functions; two examples are during pregnancy to form the placenta or under a scab to facilitate wound healing. In these instances, the body releases special proteins that stimulate angiogenesis. But once these newly formed vessels have done their job (i.e., the baby is born or the wound heals), the body returns them to their previous level by releasing substances that *inhibit* angiogenesis, called **antiangiogenic** substances.

Scientists have discovered that when the process of angiogenesis is out of balance, creating either too few or too many blood vessels, a variety of diseases can occur. For example, if your body can't produce enough blood vessels when you've been cut, the wound won't heal properly. Too few blood vessels can also lead to poor circulation and diseases such as coronary artery disease and stroke. Too *many* blood vessels, on the other hand, cause a different type of problem, leading to diseases such as obesity, arthritis and cancer. *Angiogenesis, or the growth of too many blood vessels, is related to every type of cancer* (Li, 2010).

Just as a person cannot grow and flourish without oxygen and nutrition, neither can cancer cells. So, where do they get their nutrition? It is delivered by the blood vessels formed during angiogenesis. Without these new blood vessels, cancerous tumors would not be able to grow beyond the size of the tip of a ballpoint pen! This means that *by blocking angiogenesis, we can literally "starve" tumor cells of the nutrients they need to grow and turn dangerous* (Li, 2010).

The problem is that cancer cells can actually release factors that *turn on* angiogenesis, providing themselves with the nutrition they need to thrive. The blood vessels formed during angiogenesis also create a "superhighway" for the cancer cells to enter into the bloodstream, enabling them to metastasize (Li, 2010).

The promising news is that certain drugs and dietary ingredients are *antiangiogenic*, meaning that they block angiogenesis and cut off the supply of nutrients to the cancer cells. Antiangiogenic therapies have been used to treat various types of cancers, including mast cell tumors, in more than 600 dogs, with an overall 60% response rate (Li, 2010).

Interestingly, researchers have found that nutritional ingredients were in many cases as successful as—or even more successful than—drugs to reduce angiogenesis (Li, 2010).

Here are a few "dog approved" antiangiogenic foods to add to your canine companion's anti-cancer diet:

- Apples
- Artichokes
- *Berries* (blackberries, blueberries, raspberries)
- Bok choy
- Cherries
- *Curcumin* (turmeric)
- Ginseng
- Kale
- Lavender
- *Maitake mushrooms* (see below for more on medicinal mushrooms)
- Olive oil
- Parsley
- Pumpkin
- Sea cucumber

(Li, 2010)

Other antiangiogenic foods exist that are not safe for dogs (e.g., grapes, nutmeg and dark chocolate) and so we have not included them here; but you can certainly feel free to take advantage of their cancer-protective effects!

And since fat tissue is dependent upon angiogenesis, feeding antiangiogenic foods will also help keep your dog at a healthy weight—which is essential to fighting cancer and all disease (Li, 2010).

Functional nutrients offer powerful anti-cancer protection

We consider the following functional foods to be the most promising for your dog's cancer-protective diet. Some have already been mentioned above and appear throughout the book for their role in preventing, managing and reversing a variety of chronic health conditions.

Berries

Berries are an important antiangiogenic food. They are rich in anthocyanins, which have been shown to interfere with various stages of carcinogenesis by reducing cancer cell proliferation and inhibiting tumor formation (Lila, 2004). Anthocyanins also have anti-inflammatory properties and have been clinically proven to:

- Improve memory by increasing neuronal signaling in the brain.
- Display cardio-protective benefits.
- Improve signs of metabolic syndrome, a group of factors that increase the risk of cardiovascular disease and diabetes.

(Basu et al., 2010; Krikorian, Shidler & Nash, 2010)

Our favorite dog-friendly *berries* are:

Blueberries. In addition to anthocyanins, *blueberries* contain a phytochemical compound called pterostilbene. A derivative of resveratrol (found in grapes, which dogs cannot eat!), pterostilbene is a powerful, dog-approved antioxidant that has been shown to contain potent cancer-fighting properties in animal studies and is especially toxic to breast cancer cells. A study in mice given whole *blueberry* powder demonstrated that consuming *blueberries* altered the expression of genes involved in inflammation, cancer and metastasis, concluding that *blueberries* contain anti-tumor and anti-metastasis activity. The human equivalent of the amount of *blueberries* fed to the mice was 10.6 oz (300 g) of fresh *blueberries* per day (Adams et al., 2011; Pons, 2006).

Cranberries. Many people are aware that *cranberries* promote healthy urinary tract function and help fight urinary tract disease, but did you know that they also contain anti-cancer properties? Recently, cranberries have been shown to inhibit the growth of breast, esophageal and colon cancer cells (Howell, 2012; Neto; 2011).

Note that we do not recommend strawberries for dogs due to potential allergic reactions.

Cruciferous vegetables

Cruciferous vegetables contain potent cancer-protective and cancer-fighting activities. Certain compounds in cruciferous vegetables have demonstrated the ability to stop the growth of cancer cells for tumors in the breast, uterine lining (endometrium), lung, colon, liver and cervix, according to the American Institute for Cancer Research. Cruciferous vegetables include broccoli, cauliflower, Brussels sprouts, cabbage and bok choy (Magee, 2007).

Sulforaphane, one of the many phytochemicals found in cruciferous vegetables, has been shown in laboratory tests to stimulate enzymes in the body that detoxify carcinogens before they have the chance to damage cells. Broccoli sprouts have a very high concentration of sulforaphane. In fact, just one sprout contains as much sulforophane as an entire full-grown broccoli plant! Two other compounds found in cruciferous vegetables—indole 3-carbinol (I3C) and crambene— are also suspected of activating detoxification enzymes (Donaldson, 2004; Magee, 2007).

Shawn Messonnier, DVM, discusses the many anti-cancer benefits of I3C, including:

- Protects against hormone-related cancers.
- Blocks receptors on cells that allow estrogen to enter.
- Converts dangerous estrogens into safer estrogens.
- Restores function of the p21 tumor suppressor gene.
- Induces apoptosis of cancer cells.

(Messonnier, 2006)

Supplementation with I3C is very safe for dogs (Messonnier, 2006).

Cruciferous vegetables are also rich in antioxidants, which may help protect against cancer by reducing oxidative stress caused by an excess of free radicals. One study of humans funded by the National Cancer Institute showed that eating one to two cups of cruciferous vegetables a day reduced oxidative stress by 22% after just three weeks. By contrast, taking a multivitamin with fiber for three weeks produced only a 0.2% drop in oxidative stress (Magee, 2007).

Try lightly steaming your dog's cruciferous vegetables to enhance their digestibility without overcooking them. If you prefer to serve them raw, be sure to first puree them in a food processor or blender to break down their cellulose for easier digestion. Purchasing pre-chopped or frozen vegetables creates added convenience.

Note: Avoid feeding cruciferous vegetables to your hypothyroid dog, as goitrogens in the vegetables can worsen this condition (see Chapter 11).

Anti-cancer broth for delicate dog tummies

If your dog's stomach is too sensitive to eat his veggies "straight up," you can create a nutrient-rich broth for him. Using a big pot on the stovetop, slowly cook a variety of cruciferous vegetables in an appropriate amount of water as you would to make a soup. Steep them at a low temperature for several hours, and then drain out the veggies. The remaining broth will contain the important nutrients, yet will be gentler on your dog's delicate stomach. Offer the broth warm or at room temperature.

Curcumin

Curcumin is a phytochemical that gives the Indian spice turmeric its deep yellow color. It is has been used for centuries in Ayurvedic medicine, and over the past several years *curcumin* has been widely studied in Western medicine and found to contain many beneficial properties, including potent anti-cancer properties (Hardy & Tollefsbol, 2011).

Cancer is a complex disease that uses *multiple* targets and pathways in order to "outwit" the defenses of its host (person or animal), but cancer therapies often address only one pathway. *Curcumin*, however, is able to affect multiple pathways, including down-regulating pro-inflammatory cytokines, enzymes, growth factors and transcription factors that lead to carcinogenesis and tumor growth (Lawenda, 2013; Robinson, 2008; Wilken et al., 2011). *Curcumin* has also been found to alter DNA methylation in colorectal cancer cells (Link et al., 2013).

Curcumin's anti-cancer properties include:

- Alters DNA methylation.
- Antiangiogenic properties.
- Anti-inflammatory properties.
- Antioxidant properties.
- Antitumor properties.
- Boosts the immune system.
- Decreases cell growth.
- Decreases metastasis.
- Induces cancer cell apoptosis.
- Inhibits cancer cell division and growth.
- Inhibits enzymes that aid in the spread of cancer.

(Hardy & Tollefsbol, 2011; Lawenda, 2013; Link et al., 2013; Wilken et al., 2011)

In humans, *curcumin* induces apoptosis in several types of cancer cells, including breast, lung, prostate, colon, melanoma, kidney, hepatocellular, ovarian and leukemia (Robinson, 2008).

In human clinical trials, *curcumin* has been given in doses up to 10 grams per day with no toxicity. Be aware, however, that it may cause an upset stomach, flatulence and yellowing of the stool, so use caution if your dog suffers from a gastrointestinal disorder or nausea due to chemotherapy. *Curcumin* may also increase the risk of bleeding when given in combination with some medications such as NSAIDs, blood thinners and antiplatelet drugs or when given with certain foods such as botanicals, Gingko biloba, garlic and saw palmetto. Consult with your veterinarian if your dog is on chemotherapy, as *curcumin* can decrease the effectiveness of certain chemotherapy drugs (Lawenda, 2013; Robinson, 2008).

Two challenges occur with *curcumin*: it is poorly absorbed across the GI tract and it is rapidly cleared from the blood. To overcome these hurdles, we advise giving your dog a high quality *curcumin* supplement in conjunction with a fatty food such as olive oil or fish oil, which can increase its absorption.

Dose: To ensure a steady supply of *curcumin* in the bloodstream, divide the dosage and space evenly three times throughout the day. While the exact dosing has not been determined in dogs, studies have used *curcumin* in doses ranging from 500 to 3,600 mg per day.

Green leafy and yellow-orange vegetables

As you'll recall, green leafy and yellow-orange vegetables contain beneficial phyto-chemicals, including carotenoids (e.g., alpha-carotene, beta-carotene, beta-cryptoxan-thin, lutein, zeaxanthin, and lycopene), and flavanoids (e.g., quercetin). While phyto-chemicals are not **essential nutrients** (nutrients that are essential to maintaining life, such as vitamins and minerals), they contain important bioactive compounds that are important to health, including antioxidant and anti-cancer activities.

For example, quercetin down-regulates the mutant p53 gene, which promotes cell division and cancer. It also suppresses expression of the RAS gene which, when hyper-activated, can become cancer-causing oncogenes (Armstrong, 2013).

Results of a 2005 study of 92 Scottish Terriers suggests that consuming certain veg-etables might prevent or slow the development of **transitional cell carcinoma (TCC)** (bladder cancer) in this breed. The study compared the 92 Scottish Terriers older than six years who suffered from TCC with 83 Scottish Terriers who had no recent history of urinary tract disease. The dogs' caretakers completed a questionnaire regarding their dog's diet and intake of vitamin supplements during the previous year (Raghavan, Knapp, Bonney et al., 2005).

More than 95% of dogs in both groups ate a diet of dry commercial dog food, how-ever some also consumed fresh vegetables. After adjusting for the dogs' ages, weights, neuter status and coat colors, the dogs who consumed vegetables at least three times per week had a 70% overall reduction in the risk of developing TCC. The most fre-quently consumed vegetables were in the yellow-orange group, with carrots fed most often. For individual vegetable types, *the risk of developing TCC was reduced 90% with consumption of any green leafy vegetables and 70% with any yellow-orange vegetables.* These findings are believed to relate to the presence of pro-vitamin A carotenoids in the vegetables, which apparently also convey a protective effect against develop-ing bladder cancer in humans and in chemically-induced bladder tumors in rodents (Raghavan, Knapp, Bonney et al., 2005).

Foods rich in carotenoids include carrots, collard greens, dandelion greens, mustard greens, turnip greens, squashes, pumpkin, yams, sweet potatoes and kale. Steam or ground the vegetables to break down the cell wall and increase the bioavailability of the carotenoids (Drake, 2009).

As you can see, green leafy vegetables contain bioactive compounds that deliver im-portant health benefits—including anti-cancer benefits—to dogs. In our opinion, these vegetables are too important to ignore, is spite of fears regarding oxalates. The key is choosing your dog's veggies wisely and feeding in moderation. Please refer back to Chapter 2 for a refresher on this topic.

Herbs

Dr. Barbara Fougère of Australia is a holistic veterinarian and respected authority on bioactive compounds used for treating diseased animals. According to Dr. Fougère, certain herbs may be used for anti-tumor activity as well as for complementing conventional cancer treatments, including: aiding recuperation after chemotherapy, radiation or surgery; providing an adjunct or alternative to conventional treatment (with appropriate cautions); assisting with cancer prevention; and supporting various systems affected by cancer. According to Dr. Fougère, herbal medicines combined in moderate, nontoxic doses and targeting specific mechanisms may have an additive or synergistic effect to traditional therapy (Fougère, 2012).

Here are some important herbs with anti-cancer properties:

Ginger. A study testing the benefits of an ethanol extract of ginger showed that the extract produced gene expression changes resulting in apoptosis of breast cancer cells; the extract up-regulated the expression of genes involved in apoptosis and down-regulated the expression of genes that inhibit apoptosis. In addition to suppressing the progression of breast cancer cells, the researchers discovered that the ginger extract down-regulated the expression of hTERT, a gene involved in the immortalization of most cancer cells, leading the authors to conclude that ginger might prove beneficial as a complementary agent in cancer prevention (Ayman, 2012).

Milk thistle is a beautiful purple flowering herb plant native to the Mediterranean region. Its medicinally active ingredient is called silymarin, which is actually the collective name for three flavonoids—silibinin, silidianin, and silicristin—extracted from the plant's seeds (Ehrlich, 2011). Recent research shows a great deal of promise for *milk thistle's* ability to protect against a variety of cancers.

In 2011, researchers found that silibinin stopped the spread of lung cancer in mice by blocking the expression of COX-2 and iNOS enzymes involved in tumor growth, as well as blocking the migration of existing lung cancer cells. When the researchers compared the effects of silibinin to multi-million dollar drugs currently undergoing clinical trials for lung cancer treatment, they found that silibinin was as effective at targeting lung cancer as the drugs (Tyagi et al., 2011; University of Colorado Denver, 2011).

More recently, silibinin has been shown to prevent skin cancer caused by exposure to the sun's damaging UV rays in two different ways—by either repairing the damaged cells or by killing them. In the case of cellular damage caused by UVB rays, silibinin increases expression of a protein (interleukin-12) that works to quickly repair the cells, returning them to normal. In the case of damage caused by UVA radiation (which accounts for about 95% of the sun's radiation that reaches Earth), silibinin rapidly kills the mutated cells. In both cases, skin cancer is prevented because the damaged cells are either repaired or killed (Narayanapillai et al., 2013; University of Colorado Denver, 2013).

We'll talk about more benefits of **milk thistle** for cognitive health in Chapter 10 and liver health in Chapter 11.

Herbal remedies continue to show tremendous promise in the prevention and treatment of cancer, but as we said in the previous chapter, dispensing them safely and effectively is a science as well as an art. If you plan to use herbal formulas as part of your dog's cancer-protective diet, we strongly advise working with a holistic veterinarian who understands their mechanisms and interactions (Fougère, 2012; Wynn and Fougère, 2006).

Some things to consider when working with herbs and supplements:

- More is not always better. The key is adding the correct supplements to the diet, not just piling one on top of another.

- Interactions may occur. Most supplements are safe, however there is the potential for certain ingredients to negatively interact with certain types of cancers (Fougère, 2012). For example, the amino acid glutamine can potentially worsen a brain tumor and should not be used for dogs with this type of cancer (Messonnier, 2006).

- Not all products are reliable. Since supplements are not regulated by the FDA, the quality can vary widely. Many supplements have been found to contain far less of the active ingredients than claimed on the label. Danger of contamination from lead, mercury and other toxins in certain products—most notably herbal products from China—also exists (Tremayne, 2010). Whenever possible, purchase supplements from your holistic veterinarian or opt for products carrying the National Animal Supplement Council (NASC) label, a non-profit trade organization whose members pledge to comply with good manufacturing practices for product safety and quality assurance. Visit http://www.nasc.cc for a list of NASC members.

Medicinal mushrooms

The knowledge that mushrooms contain health-promoting properties is far from new. The ancient Romans called them "the foods of the gods," while throughout Asia various species of mushrooms have been used medicinally for thousands of years. The Chinese—apparently understanding what has taken Western medicine millennia longer to recognize—referred to mushrooms as "the elixir of life" (Smith, Rowan & Sullivan, 2002).

Today, practitioners of traditional Chinese medicine use **_medicinal mushroom_** extracts for a variety of functions, from treating microbial infections, diabetes and cardiovascular disease to promoting liver health (Smith, Rowan & Sullivan, 2002).

At least 270 species of mushrooms are known to contain therapeutic properties, including:

- _Cordyceps spp._
- _Coriolus (Trametes) versicolor_
- _Lentinus edodes (Shiitake)_
- _Hericium_
- _Grifola_
- _Flammulina_
- _Pleurotus_
- _Tremella_
- _Ganoderma lucidum (Reishi)_

(Brown & Reetz, 2012; Oates, 2009; Smith, Rowan & Sullivan, 2002)

Based on the _Dictionary of the Fungi_, scientists are currently aware of 14,000 species of mushrooms—a number thought to represent only about 10% of the estimated 150,000 species believed to be sprouting up all over the planet (Wasser, 2011). **_Medicinal mushrooms_** were historically cultivated from forests where they grew naturally on trees and forest litter; today, however, almost all widely used **_medicinal mushrooms_** are artificially cultivated (Smith, Rowan & Sullivan, 2002).

Medicinal mushrooms are thought to contain 126 different medicinal properties, including:

- Antibacterial
- Antidiabetic
- Antifungal
- Antihypercholesterolemia
- Antiparasitic
- Antioxidant
- Antitumor
- Antiviral
- Cardiovascular
- Detoxification
- Hepatoprotective
- Immunomodulating

- Radical scavenging

(Brown & Reetz, 2012; Smith, Rowan & Sullivan, 2002; Wasser, 2010)

Dr. Fougère recommends a variety of ***medicinal mushrooms*** and herbs for dogs with cancer, including:

- *Cordyceps sinensis* (***medicinal mushroom***; see below)

- Echinacea

- Astragalus

- Withania

- Siberian ginseng

- Essiac

- Cats claw

- Pau d'Arco

- Shitake and Reiishi mushrooms

(Fougère, 2012)

Polysaccharides and polysaccharide–protein (PSP) complexes in mushrooms display potent anticancer and immune-stimulating properties (Brown & Reetz, 2012; Smith, Rowan & Sullivan, 2002; Wasser, 2010). Mushroom polysaccharides have been shown to prevent **oncogenesis** (the process by which normal cells turn into cancer cells), display antitumor activity and prevent the metastasis of tumors. The polysaccharides communicate with the immune system to either up-regulate or down-regulate the immune response, depending on the condition of the individual. They activate a variety of immune cells vital to health, including dendritic cells, natural killer cells (which target viruses and tumor cells), T cells, macrophages, monocytes and neutrophils (Brown & Reetz, 2012; Smith, Rowan & Sullivan, 2002; Wasser, 2010).

Recently, researchers at the University of Pennsylvania School of Veterinary Medicine used a polysaccharopeptide (PSP) compound extracted from the *Coriolus versicolor* mushroom, commonly known as the Yunhzi mushroom, to treat dogs with **hemangiosarcoma**, an aggressive, invasive cancer that originates in the blood vessels and spreads to other parts of the body, most commonly the spleen. The dogs achieved the longest survival times ever reported for dogs with this disease (Brown & Reetz, 2012).

Fifteen companion dogs diagnosed with hemangiosarcoma of the spleen participated in the trial. After surgical removal of their spleens, the dogs received a daily dose of the PSP compound I'm-Yunity® (see Resources). No other treatment was given. The median survival time of dogs on the highest dose (100 mg/kg/day) of I'm-Yunity was 199 days, compared to previous reports of 86 days. Some of the dogs lived longer than a year (Brown & Reetz, 2012).

We recommend I'm-Yunity due to its proven efficacy in the hemangiosarcoma clinical trial and because it undergoes rigorous quality testing, which is not true of all products on the market (Brown, 2013). If you opt to purchase another brand, be aware that in the United States, *medicinal mushrooms* are classified as dietary supplements and as such do not require clinical studies to validate their efficacy. Also, since the standardization of *medicinal mushroom* dietary supplements varies greatly, commercial production can be unreliable and so it can be difficult to know what you're getting. Our advice is to call the manufacturer and ask the following:

- Has your product undergone a clinical trial to prove its safety and efficacy (such as I'm-Yunity)?

- What are your standards and protocols for verifying the components of your product?

- How did you determine the dosage for your product? Is this dosage safe for all life stages, including pregnancy?

- What testing does your product undergo to guarantee its quality?

Note: Never let your dog eat wild mushrooms, as some mushrooms are poisonous. Offer only *medicinal mushroom* products manufactured by a high quality, trusted source.

Omega-3 fatty acids

Studies show that *omega-3s* can inhibit the formation of tumors and prevent cancer from metastasizing (Messonnier, 2006). One of the ways they accomplish this is by inducing apoptosis of cancer cells. *Omega-3s* induce cancer cell apoptosis through a wide variety of molecular mechanisms and with many different types of cancers (Serini et al., 2012), making them a critical part of any anti-cancer diet. Remember to choose a pure, human-grade *omega-3* supplement containing EPA and DHA from mercury-free fish oil or other marine source (see Resources). Refer to Chapter 4 for details and dosing.

Probiotics

Hippocrates, the father of medicine, is quoted as saying, "bad digestion is at the root of all evil" and "death sits in the bowels." Nearly 2,500 years later, scientists are discovering that Hippocrates was right. *You simply cannot have a "sick" gut and express vibrant health.*

You'll remember from earlier that there are trillions of "good" bacteria that live in the mucosal tissue lining of the gut, compromising the largest immune organ in the body. But the gut also contains pathogenic "bad" bacteria. Many environmental factors can disrupt the gut environment, throwing the balance between good and bad bacteria out of whack. These include:

- Antibiotics

- Introducing new foods too fast

- Poor diet
- Stress
- Vaccination

Probiotics offer a powerful defense against these and other factors that can compromise gut health (Weese & Arroyo, 2003).

The word *probiotic* means "for life." *Probiotics* are beneficial microorganisms, or "good" bacteria that, when taken orally, provide beneficial effects to humans and animals, including preventing the overgrowth of bad bacteria in the gut, improving gastrointestinal health, preventing onset of allergies and reducing risk of recurring urinary tract infections (FAO/WHO, 2001; Weese & Arroyo, 2003). Recent research also indicates that *probiotics* may offer anti-cancer benefits (Mason, 2013).

In 2013, researchers from UCLA's Jonsson Comprehensive Cancer Center discovered that specific types of bad bacteria that live in the gut are major contributors to lymphoma, a cancer of the white blood cells. Intestinal bacteria have previously been linked to certain types of epithelial cancers, such as those affecting the coverings of the stomach, liver and colon. The researchers also discovered that certain types of good bacteria have a protective affect against **genotoxicity** (gene damage) that causes lymphoma (Mason, 2013).

To effectively exert benefits, *probiotics* must meet strict standards, including:

- Live, viable bacteria: The product is not a *probiotic* unless the bacteria are live.

- Multiple bacterial strains: Different strains of bacteria exert different biological activities. Look for a product containing at least 10 different strains.

- High potency: When it comes to *probiotics*, the more potent the better. While some products contain one billion beneficial bacteria per serving, we advise purchasing a product containing at least 30 billion or more beneficial bacteria per serving.

- Purity: *Probiotics* are designed to increase gut health. The last thing you want is a product that contains artificial colors, flavors, preservatives, sugar, salt, corn, wheat, soy or other undesirable ingredients.

- Formulated for dogs. Animals' intestinal tracts contain species-specific microflora, so a *probiotic* product designed for humans isn't necessarily beneficial for your companion animal (Weese & Arroyo, 2003).

Pomegranates

Pomegranates contain the most potent antioxidant activity of all commonly consumed fruits. One of the world's oldest known fruits, pomegranates originated in Persia. Their use dates back to ancient Hindi Ayurvedic medicine, where the rind of the fruit and bark of the pomegranate tree were used as a traditional remedy against diarrhea, dysentery and intestinal parasites. Many studies have shown that pomegranates are one of the most powerfully nutrient-dense foods to support overall health, providing beneficial effects on cardiovascular, nervous and skeletal health in humans and animals. **Punicalagins**, highly bioavailable polyphenol compounds found in several plant species, but most predominant in pomegranates, have been identified as the primary active compound responsible for this wonder-fruit's potent antioxidant and health benefits (Tyagi, Singh, Bhardwaj et al., 2012).

Pomegranates also contain powerful anti-tumor activity and anti-cancer effects. Studies indicate that pomegranates inhibit breast cancer, prostate cancer, colon cancer and leukemia and prevent vascular changes that promote tumor growth in laboratory animals (Tyagi, Singh, Bhardwaj et al., 2012).

Spirulina

Phycocyanin (C-PC) possesses potent anti-oxidant and anti-cancer properties (Gantar et al., 2012; Messonnier, 2006; Romay et al., 2003). In the previous chapter, we discussed the ability of phycocyanin to selectively inhibit the pro-inflammatory COX-2 pathway. This is extremely important as it relates to cancer, since COX-2 activity increases in malignant tissue, including colorectal, human gastric and breast tumors (Reddy et al., 2000).

Dosage: We suggest 1/4 teaspoon per cup of food daily.

❧ **A few brief examples of human and animal studies supporting the anti-cancer benefits of spirulina**

Vitamin D

Numerous studies show that vitamin D deficiency plays a key role in cancer development and that vitamin D can actually kill cancer cells in humans and mice (Mercola, 2010).

Here are some of the ways vitamin D protects against cancer:

- Regulates genetic expression.
- Enters cancer cells and triggers apoptosis.
- Causes cells to become differentiated.
- Blocks angiogenesis.

(Mercola, 2010; Mercola, 2012)

Please check with your veterinarian before supplementing with vitamin D. In people with lymphoma, vitamin D has been shown to potentially increase calcium levels, which could lead to kidney stones and other problems (MedlinePlus, 2013). We also discussed the possibility of potentially life-threatening vitamin D toxicity in Chapter 4, so be sure that your dog does not receive excessive levels.

Using raw foods to help fight cancer

The following information regarding raw foods and cancer is provided courtesy of Dr. Sue E. Armstrong, an internationally respected holistic veterinary cancer specialist:

The processing of food, including cooking, alters the food's digestibility and changes the bioavailability of some of the essential nutrients. There can also be hidden ingredients such as artificial colors and preservatives (described earlier) as well as inferior quality ingredients that come under headings of, for example, "meat and meat derivatives" (Armstrong, 2013).

For dogs with good vitality and where the immune system is still functioning well, careful conversion to a raw food diet can be ideal. However, the quality of the ingredients is of paramount importance (e.g., human grade meat only), as is careful attention to the diet's nutritional balance. It is easy to get a raw food diet wrong—too much bone, not enough variety of nutrients, inappropriate vegetables. There are some good commercial companies that produce prepared balanced raw food diets with fully ground bone incorporated into the mix: these are not only easier than preparing the diet yourself, but will also avoid getting the nutritional balance wrong if you are not used to feeding raw (Armstrong, 2013).

When changing diets, always transition your dog to the new diet gradually over a period of 10 to 14 days, substituting more of the new raw diet for the old diet each day. Digestive enzymes and probiotics should be given to help support the dog's digestive system through the transition period (Armstrong, 2013).

A dog who is not **cachexic** (wasting away or emaciated) should eat 2% to 3% of his body weight per day (e.g., a 20 pound dog should eat approximately seven ounces of food per day). Note: This is seven ounces of food by *weight*, not volume.

This following diet is just one example of a suitable raw food diet for cancer patients. Other proteins (e.g., fish, eggs) and different vegetables can be substituted to suit your dog's individual taste preferences and circumstances. Again, please be aware that the quality of the ingredients is of the utmost importance; poor quality raw food is just as dangerous, if not more so, than poor quality kibble.

Once your dog's digestive system has become adapted to digesting ground bone, you can introduce whole bone (e.g., turkey neck, chicken carcass). Take care to oversee your dog until you are sure that he has learned how to properly crush and tear bone, as this skill can take a while to master for dogs who have had kibble all their lives (Armstrong, 2013).

Sample diet for a 65-pound dog (adjust amounts according to your dog's size) (Note: These measurements are by *weight*, not volume):

- Skinned chicken and ground bone (10.5 oz)
- Lamb, ground bone and liver (6.5 oz)

- Cottage Cheese (1 oz)

- Liver (calf or lamb) (6 oz a week)

- Butternut squash/apples/pears/carrots/spinach/*blueberries*. Root vegetables and tougher leafy vegetables should be chopped and lightly steamed or liquidized. Vary the vegetables used over a two-week period, trying to achieve a rainbow spectrum of fruits and vegetables to ensure a wide range of vitamins and minerals.

- Sea kelp/*spirulina*/alfalfa (1/ 4 to 1/ 2 teaspoon)

- *Omega-3 essential fatty acids*: fish oil/krill oil (5000 mg daily) (NOT to be used if your dog has any tumor with a bleeding tendency, such as hemangiosarcoma)

- Oyster shell calcium (750 mg tablet)

- L- Arginine (700 mg)

- Bio-available full spectrum vitamin/mineral supplement two to three times a week (natural food should provide most of these, but the addition of a high quality supplement a few times a week can help ensure that there are none lacking).

If your dog is cachexic, the proportion of carbohydrate will need to be increased, and this is where the addition of rice, oats or pasta may have a place in the diet to give a readily usable energy source. A warm, cooked diet is also preferred at this stage, as it requires less energy for an already depleted animal to digest. You can use the meat and vegetables above to produce this diet as a cooked version, however *bone must never be cooked*, and additional roughage will need to be added to aid digestion (Armstrong, 2013).

When going raw might not be a good idea

If your dog is older and has always eaten kibble, adapting to a raw diet can sometimes be hard on the system, especially when his system is already under pressure coping with cancer. There are some commercial processed foods now available that are produced specifically for dogs with cancer (mostly based on low carbohydrate, high protein and fat with added specific amino acids) and those that are classed as "biologically appropriate," which in general are grain-free, high protein foods. Always read labels carefully and if you choose to use kibble, the better choices are a cancer-specific diet or a biologically appropriate food, preferably with named organic ingredients. Home cooked cancer diets are a good option, particularly for the very old dog or the end stage cancer case where conversion to a raw food natural diet might be too much for a debilitated system (Armstrong, 2013).

Raw food/cancer case studies by Dr. Sue Armstrong

Marley

Marley, an eight-year-old male neutered Boxer, presented with a history of a deep-ening disease state. He had previously been treated for mast cell tumors (some of which remained), hemangioma, plasmacyctoma and histiocytoma and now had been diagnosed with a high-grade **thyroid adenocarcinoma** (cancer of the thyroid gland), which had been surgically excised and secondary tumors were found present in the lungs. Marley also had a heart murmur, deep **pyoderma** (infection and inflammation of the skin), patchy **alopecia** (hair loss), a pendulous abdomen (a possible side effect of the long term steroids he had been on), **nasal hyperkeratosis** (thickening and cracking of the nose) and regurgitation problems. To add to all of this, Marley was profoundly depressed and slow in all his actions. His blood results showed an inflam-matory picture with a moderate hepatopathy (his liver was under pressure, but this can also reflect prolonged use of steroids). He presented on high dose steroids and a tyrosine kinase inhibitor. With such a history, Marley's guardians were concerned about his quality of life for the time he had remaining.

Marley's diet at the time of presentation was a high carb, low protein kibble, so he was transitioned to a biologically appropriate home cooked diet over a two-week pe-riod, with added digestive enzymes to aid his digestion during the transition. It was decided that raw food might be too much for his depleted system to process, however subsequently he was converted to raw food fed in three smaller meals per day. Marley was also given *Coriolus versicolor* (a Chinese *medicinal mushroom*), Transfer Factor, **curcumin**, fish oil (*omega-3s*) and silymarin (*milk thistle*). He was also given sulphur as a homeopathic constitutional remedy. He remained on the tyrosine kinase inhibi-tor, but was slowly weaned off the steroids.

As of this writing, Marley is bright and happy, back enjoying his walks—and he bounces into the consulting room like a Boxer should! His skin and coat have im-proved considerably, as has his nose. To date, the cancer has shown no signs of pro-gression and his blood picture has improved well. Most importantly, Marley is back enjoying his life and his guardians report that, "He has never been so full of energy! Even as a puppy he was slow, but not so now!"

Jock

Jock, a nine-year-old intact (entire) male Labrador retriever, presented with a large aggressive hemangiosarcoma of the ventral neck (confirmed by biopsy), which is an unusual place to find such a tumor. He also had crusting and **ptosis** (drooping) of the eyes, severe generalized arthritis and his blood showed a moderate **hepatopathy** (ab-normal liver), **cholestasis** (a condition where bile flow is slowed down) and anemia. Tumors of the type he presented with commonly bleed, and this was the suspected cause of the type of anemia Jock was showing. He was slow and irritable, disliking be-ing examined or messed with—even by his guardian—and his appetite was dropping rapidly. He was being fed canned commercial dog food and a kibble with table scraps and milk at the time of presentation, which was simply not nourishing for him. There was also a major concern about his level of pain and how to manage the arthritic pain without further compromising his liver or worsening the bleeding from the tumor. The bleeding tendency was also a major consideration when deciding upon the supplements that might help support him.

Turmeric (**curcumin**) was not given, as it contains compounds that can prevent blood clotting. Jock was slowly transitioned over a two-week period onto a home cooked, high protein, low carbohydrate diet with vegetables, fruit and additional raw liver minced into the diet daily, taking care not to induce a loose stool. This diet was fed three times a day so as not to overload his compromised liver. His appetite returned in less than a week, as did his energy. He was given *Coriolus versicolor*, L-Arginine, and s-adenosyl methionine (SAMe). He was also given tramadol hydrochloride as pain relief and was treated homeopathically.

Jock lived for six more months, which might not sound like much, however, the six months he lived were of really good quality. Friends who had seen him just prior to presentation and then met him out and about after his regimen was changed often did not recognize that it could have been the same dog. Jock had regained his joy of life and went from being totally depressed and irritable to returning to the funny, mischievous dog he used to be. The tumor did not go away (and it was the tumor that eventually ended his life), but both he and his guardians had precious time together, allowing them to come to terms with what was happening and make the right decision at the right time for both them and Jock.

Your dog is counting on you

When formulating a cancer-protective diet for your dog, please remember that the Internet is full of Web sites offering information about miracle supplements and cures for cancer. It is very easy to fall into the trap that "natural is safe" and that giving all the supplements available to treat cancer is the answer (Armstrong, 2013). However, please remember that there is a lot of misleading, and just plain incorrect, information floating around out there—and that following it can be dangerous to your dog's health.

The information we have provided in this chapter is based on scientific evidence, not folklore or guesswork. If your dog is battling cancer, we hope that you will find this cutting-edge knowledge helpful in getting him back on the road to optimum health.

If you plan to use supplements, we urge you to seek out a holistic veterinarian trained in treating canine cancer. Cancer is a very complex disease, and conventional veterinarians may not be familiar with many of the supplements available or know how they act within the body (Armstrong, 2013). Combining the information in this chapter with the guidance and care of a qualified holistic veterinarian could very well be the most life-saving step you could take for your beloved dog. We wish you both many healthy, happy years together!

Takeaway Points

- Cancer is responsible for as many as half the canine and feline deaths in the United States and is the leading cause of death in dogs older than two years.

- Researchers estimate that only 5% to 10% of all cancer cases originate from genetic predisposition, while 90% to 95% are the result of lifestyle and environmental factors.

- Scientists have concluded that 30% to 40% of all cancers can be prevented by implementing dietary changes.

- Be sure to remove foods containing any harmful ingredients from your dog's diet, since these can counterbalance the benefits of the functional foods you'll be adding in.

- There is a well-established link between obesity and inflammatory diseases, including cancer. If your dog is overweight, please refer to Chapter 5 for information on how to help him shed those excess pounds.

- Be sure to remove all high-GI carbohydrates from your dog's cancer-protective diet. These "junk carbs" promote obesity, which plays a role in carcinogenesis, and also promote hyperinsulinemia associated with Type 2 diabetes. Diabetes has been linked with increased risk of several cancers.

- Gluten, which can cause leaky gut syndrome and cancer-causing inflammation, should be eliminated from your dog's cancer-protective diet.

- Fluoride found in bone meal, meat meal or meat byproduct meal could be contributing to skyrocketing cases of canine osteosarcoma, especially for dogs who eat the same fluoride-containing kibble day-in and day-out. Be sure to remove all foods containing bone meal or animal by-products from your dog's diet, and switch to low-fluoride or fluoride-free bottled water.

- Detoxifying your dog's environment is an important part of any anti-cancer protocol. Environmental hazards include toxins in and around the home, second-hand smoke, topical chemical flea and tick preventives and over-vaccination.

- Nutrients that promote optimum DNA methylation, including *curcumin*, folate and vitamin B-12, are important anti-cancer ingredients.

- Angiogenesis is the process by which new blood vessels form from pre-existing vessels.

- When the process of angiogenesis is out of balance, creating either too few or too many blood vessels, a variety of diseases result. Angiogenesis is related to every type of cancer.

- By blocking angiogenesis, we can starve tumor cells of the nutrients they need to grow and turn dangerous.

- Certain drugs and dietary ingredients are *antiangiogenic*, meaning that they block angiogenesis and cut off the supply of nutrients to the cancer cells. Anti-angiogenic therapies have been used to treat various types of cancers, including mast cell tumors, in more than 600 dogs, with an overall 60% response rate.

- Researchers have found that nutritional ingredients were in many cases as successful as—or even more successful than—drugs to reduce angiogenesis.

- Powerful functional foods for cancer protection include: **berries**; **pomegranates**; cruciferous vegetables; **curcumin**; green leafy and yellow-orange vegetables; certain herbs such as ginger and **milk thistle**; **medicinal mushroom**s; **omega-3 fatty acids**; **probiotics**; **spirulina**; and vitamin D.

- Please check with your veterinarian before supplementing with vitamin D if your dog has lymphoma. In people, vitamin D has been shown to potentially increase calcium levels, which could lead to kidney stones and other problems.

- A carefully formulated raw food diet can be a good option for certain dogs with cancer, as it provides nutrients that are less adulterated and more bioavailable. However, it might be wise to avoid going raw if your dog is older, as a complete change in diet can add additional stress to his system.

Chapter 10

A Nutrigenomics Approach to Canine Behavior and Cognitive Aging

---

Dogs have been "man's (and woman's) best friend" for thousands of years. In fact, dogs are thought to be the first animal species domesticated by humans, about 15,000 years ago. While they were likely first selectively bred to perform specific jobs, such as hunting, shepherding and guarding, it's thought that for about the last 2,000 years dogs have primarily served as companions (Durham University, 2012). As anyone who has been "owned" by a dog knows, the human-canine bond runs deep (as deep as our genes, as we have pointed out!), and for the most part the relationship is mutually beneficial and rewarding. But tinkering with the genome of any species has its price. Dogs, after all, are a species of canid—social predators that include wolves, foxes, coyotes and jackals (Jensen ed., 2009).

Considering that dogs "speak" a different language than humans, they have adapted amazingly to domestic life. Cross-breeding of dogs over thousands of years has produced more than 400 domestic breeds that today bear little genetic and behavioral resemblance to their wild ancestors (Durham University, 2012). But even though our dogs often seem to understand us better than our closest human friends, they are still not "furry people," and they sometimes exhibit problem behaviors—including aggression, disobedience, destructive behavior, excessive barking, running away and house soiling—considered disruptive by their human caretakers. Sadly, millions of dogs a year are relinquished to shelters, with an estimated three to six million euthanized due to "behavior problems." Even those that manage to avoid euthanization often face a grim future; once a dog has been labeled with behavioral issues, it is difficult for him to overcome the stigma. Approximately 20% of adopted shelter dogs are returned, and many are euthanized (Bosch et. al, 2007).

Unfortunately, when a dog "misbehaves," nutrition is rarely considered as a possible contributing factor. But, with what we now know about the ability of food to communicate with the genome, we need to take a closer look at how this relationship affects a dog's *behavioral health* as well as his physiological health. While little clinical research has been conducted in this area, evidence shows that dietary components *can* modulate the behavior of both humans and animals (Bosch et. al, 2007). This chapter is dedicated to exploring those components.

If your dog exhibits sudden behavioral changes, please be sure to have him examined by his veterinarian to rule out an underlying medical condition. Canine Cognitive Dysfunction (CCD), for example, can lead to anxiety, lack of sociability, house soiling and many other behavioral changes, while hypothyroidism, which we'll cover in the next chapter (and wrote about in *The Canine Thyroid Epidemic*), is associated with abnormal behaviors such as anxiety, phobias, irritability and attention-deficit disorder. Since thyroid disorder is closely tied to behavioral changes, we also recommend a full thyroid panel to rule out this cause. We also advise examining non-diet related environmental influences, such as your dog's dynamic within the "pack" (i.e., family unit), his background (e.g., whether he was previously abused or abandoned) and potential chemical toxins, such as those we discussed earlier. If, for example, you recently brought a new puppy into your home and your adult dog is acting out, chances are it's not due to his diet!

Now, let's discuss dietary influences on your dog's behavior and steps you can take to maximize his cognitive function.

High-glycemic carbs sabotage brain health

You now know that high-GI carbs contribute to numerous chronic illnesses in dogs, but did you realize that they could also negatively affect behavior? Have you ever experienced a child who becomes wildly hyperactive shortly after consuming a sugary food or drink, and then "crashes" into a state of sluggishness a couple of hours later? We agree with Colleen Paige, who in *The Good Behavior Book for Dogs* states that high-GI foods such as corn and wheat create similar mood swings in dogs as they do in people. After ingesting these foods, dogs experience a "sugar high" (e.g., hyperactivity and lack of focus) that owners often mistake as "ill-mannered" and "uncooperative" behavior, but which are actually food-related. This "high" is followed by a "low," which Paige says can cause dogs to become "sleepy, lethargic, moody and irritable" (Paige, 2007, pp. 20).

Impaired glucose metabolism caused by sugary foods may also promote brain starvation, leading to memory problems such as Alzheimer's disease, which is very similar to CCD in dogs. Diabetic people have four times the risk of developing Alzheimer's, while those with pre-diabetes have triple the risk (Mercola, 2012).

High-glycemic foods can also lead to hunger-related behavioral problems. Simple carbohydrates digest and absorb quickly (hence the rapid rise and fall in blood sugar concentrations), leaving dogs feeling hungry again quicker (Boler, 2011; Paige, 2007).

This effect can lead to undesirable begging behaviors or even munching on inappropriate "foods" such as shoes and furniture.

Curbing behavioral problems is just one more reason to skip high-glycemic carbs and instead feed your dog a more satiating diet containing wholesome, functional carbohydrates.

Tryptophan and tyrosine help regulate mood

Tryptophan and tyrosine are amino acids that act as precursors, or building blocks, to **neurotransmitters**, chemical messengers in the brain that transmit signals between **neurons** (nerve cells). Neurotransmitters play an important role in regulating everything from heartbeat and digestion to mood and behavior.

Every wonder why you feel calm and tired after eating a big Thanksgiving meal? Other than the fact that your stomach is full, it's likely because turkey contains tryptophan, a large neutral amino acid (LNAA). Tryptophan is the precursor to serotonin, a neurotransmitter that promotes a sense of relaxation and well being. When tryptophan crosses the blood-brain barrier, it can double serotonin synthesis in the brain. Serotonin affects many parts of the brain, including those involved in controlling appetite, pain, general mood and behavior (Bosch et al., 2007).

Insufficient levels of dietary tryptophan have been associated with aggressive behavior, depression and elevated stress hormone levels such as cortisol in laboratory animals, dogs, livestock and people (Aldrich, 2012; DeNapoli et al., 2000). Studies have also shown that adding tryptophan could play a role in canine socialization, as well as reduce fear and aggression (DeNapoli et al., 2000; Dodman et al., 1996).

Tryptophan is found in just about every food that contains protein, but in lower concentrations than other LNAAs. Since tryptophan "competes" with these other LNAAs, high-protein foods actually decrease the amount of free tryptophan that is available to cross the blood-brain barrier. Increasing the ratio of tryptophan to other LNAAs can increase the amount of serotonin in the brain (Boler, 2011; Bosch et al., 2007).

However, we *do not* advocate a low-protein diet unless your dog has a medical condition that requires it, such as advanced kidney disease. Instead, we advise supplementing with a moderate amount of tryptophan, either via a prescription from your veterinarian, such as NutriCalm, or in the form of a high quality over-the-counter supplement (See Resources).

Tyrosine is the amino acid precursor to dopamine, noradrenaline and adrenaline and has been shown to improve the stress response in rats. Like tryptophan, tyrosine is also found in high-protein foods, but in much higher concentrations. Since LNAAs compete for entry into the brain, consuming high-protein foods will typically raise brain concentrations of tyrosine but decrease levels of tryptophan (Bosch et al., 2007).

Nutritional support for the aging canine brain

It's heartbreaking to watch a beloved dog mentally decline as he ages. Yet, just as many people fall victim to the degenerative effects of Alzheimer's disease, senior dogs can suffer from an equally devastating decline in cognitive function, called Canine Cognitive Dysfunction (CCD) or Cognitive Dysfunction Syndrome (CDS). According to a 2008 study, there are more than 52 million dogs older than age seven in the United States (Head, Rofina & Zicker, 2008). As dogs age, they display many of the same declines in cognitive ability as elderly people. Senior and geriatric dogs often display impaired learning and memory, disorientation, a reduced ability to interact socially, house soiling, destructive behaviors, lethargy and disturbances in sleep patterns (Cotman et al., 2002; Head, Rofina & Zicker, 2008; Manteca, 2011).

The good news is that great strides are being made into the causes of age-related cognitive decline and natural treatments using nutraceuticals and functional foods (Bensimoun, 2013). **Free radicals**, molecules that cause oxidation of cells, have been identified as a major cause of aging (Manteca, 2011). If you're unsure of exactly what oxidation is, think of the rust on an older car or the brown spots on your peeled apple. Both of these arise from the interaction of the substance—in this case the car or the apple—with oxygen molecules in the environment.

Oxidation also occurs in the body's tissues and is a leading cause of age-related signs, ranging from a reduction in muscle mass and wrinkled skin to reduced memory capacity. Whereas younger dogs' bodies can counteract oxidation, seniors are not as capable of protecting themselves from free radical damage. As a result, elderly dogs show signs of increased oxidative stress. Moreover, the brain is extremely vulnerable to oxidation (Manteca, 2011). Left unprotected, oxidation in the brain can cause damage and even death of neurons, resulting in a decline in cognitive function (Head, Rofina & Zicker, 2008).

A diet rich in antioxidants can help counteract the effects of free radicals on the brain. In 2002, scientist Carl Cotman from the University of California's Institute of Brain Aging and Dementia and his colleagues tested the theory that oxidative damage sets off a chain of events that decrease cognitive function. Cotman and his colleagues fed aged Beagles a diet rich in antioxidants; after six months, the dogs showed considerable improvement in cognitive function (Cotman et al., 2002).

Other studies also support the beneficial effects of an antioxidant-rich diet on the cognitive ability of senior dogs. One group of researchers concluded that:

> *The most important aspect of this work is the discovery that cognitive performance can be improved by dietary manipulation. Furthermore, the effects of the dietary manipulation were relatively rapid. Antioxidants may thus potentially act to prevent the development of these age-associated behaviors, and possibly even neuropathologic change, by counteracting oxidative stress (Head, Rofina & Zicker, 2008, pp. 173).*

Which ingredients are proven to ramp up cognitive activity in aging dogs? Cotman and his colleagues fed their dogs the following:

- Vitamins E and C (antioxidants) along with a mixture of fruits and vegetables to reduce free radical damage.
- Alpha-lipoic acid and L-carnitine (mitochondrial cofactors), which improve the function of aged **mitochondria** (specialized parts of cells that produce most of a cell's energy).

(Cotman et al., 2002)

Other important nutrients also show the ability to improve cognitive function in senior dogs. Here are some of the most studied:

- *Milk thistle*
- Phosphatidylserine (a phospholipid)
- SAMe (s-adenosylmethionine)
- Medium chain triglycerides (MCTs) found in *coconut oil*
- DHA and EPA omega-3 fatty acids

(Milgram et al, 2002; Landsberg, DePorter & Araujo, 2011; Bensimoun, 2013)

Let's look closer at each of these brain-boosting functional ingredients:

Coconut oil (medium chain triglycerides)

Coconut oil possesses many therapeutic qualities, but perhaps the most amazing is its scientifically proven ability to improve brain function in older dogs and people. As the body's supercomputer, the brain requires a lot of energy, most of which is satisfied when the body breaks down glucose from food. However, as we age, we metabolize glucose less efficiently, leaving a gap in the brain's energy requirement. When this occurs, alternative sources of fuel become important to fill this gap and provide much-needed energy to the brain. This is where medium chain triglycerides (MCTs), such as those contained in *coconut oil,* can help save the day:

- Unlike regular fats (which the body metabolizes slowly), MCTs break down and absorb rapidly into the bloodstream, providing a quick source of non-carbohydrate energy.
- MCTs readily cross the blood-brain barrier, supplying up to 20% of a normal brain's energy requirement.
- MCTs are important for ketone production, which serve as an additional source of "brain food."
- MCTs help the body use *omega-3 fatty acids* more efficiently and increase *omega-3* concentrations in the brain (a good reason to give your dog both *omega-3s* and *coconut oil*).

(Aldrich, 2009; Laflamme, 2012; Wolf, 2009)

One study showed that when 24 Beagles who were between the ages of 7.5 and 11.6 years old at the start of the trial were fed a diet supplemented with 5.5% medium chain triglycerides, their cognitive ability improved significantly. The dogs showed improvement in learning-related tasks after only about two weeks of consuming the supplemented diet, and within one month their learning ability improved significantly. The authors concluded that supplementation with MCTs can improve age-related cognitive decline by providing an alternative source of brain energy (Pan et al., 2010).

In addition to its brain-boosting qualities, **coconut oil** is purported to provide a host of other benefits, including:

- Contains antiviral, antimicrobial and antifungal properties.
- Helps with weight loss (MCTs increase metabolism, so they send signals of satiety and cannot be stored as fat) (See Chapter 7).
- Improves digestion and absorption of fat-soluble vitamins.
- Benefits the skin and coat.
- Provides a rapid form of non-carbohydrate energy.

(Aldrich, 2009; Wolf, 2009)

The **coconut oil** you select should be unrefined (virgin) and expeller pressed or cold pressed. Again, processed, heat-treated foods lose their natural life-giving nutritional force. If possible, choose organic brands to avoid potential contamination from pesticides. **Coconut oil** does not need to be stored in the refrigerator, but since it is light sensitive (like all oils), it's best to keep it in a dark cupboard. Dark glass containers are excellent storage choices, as they protect the oil from light while also ensuring that no BPAs leech into the product.

There are many ways to incorporate **coconut oil** into your dog's diet. Try mixing a tablespoon into some goat or sheep's milk yogurt or adding a dollop on top of some fresh organic **blueberries**. You can even scoop it straight from the container and let him lick the spoon. Dogs love the taste!

Studies show that **coconut oil** fed as 10% or less of your dog's diet poses no digestive or other health issues (Aldrich, 2009).

Omega-3 fatty acids

By now you've probably noticed a trend that many functional nutritional ingredients don't just benefit one part of the body; they promote health across a wide range of systems. This of course makes sense because the body is not made up of isolated parts (as many Western medical specialists would like us to believe); it contains an intricately related set of systems that all perform a complex, wonderfully intertwined dance. **Coconut oil, omega-3 fatty acids** and many of the other functional ingredients discussed in this book target the body holistically, producing a wide range of benefits from head to toe—or, in the case of dogs, from nose to tail.

You've already learned how the ***omega-3 fatty acids*** DHA and EPA fight obesity, decrease inflammation, combat arthritis and cancer and promote overall health, so it should come as no surprise that DHA and EPA also benefit brain health—especially since the brain is made up of as much as 60% fat (Mercola, 2012).

About 20% of the brain's **cerebral cortex** (the outermost layered structure of neural tissue) is made up of DHA, which also provides structural support to **neurons** (the cells that make up the central nervous system). Studies in people show that supplementation with DHA is beneficial in supporting cognitive health in aging brains and that inadequate levels can cause neurons to become stiff, hindering proper neurotransmission both within cells and between cells (Mercola, 2012; Yurko-Mauro, 2010).

In elderly people, low levels of plasma DHA are associated with cognitive decline in both healthy individuals as well as those suffering from Alzheimer's disease, while higher DHA levels are associated with a decreased risk of Alzheimer's. In one study, patients who supplemented with DHA at 900 mg/day for 24 weeks showed improved learning and memory function associated with age-related cognitive decline. This means that supplementing with DHA does not only work to prevent age-related cognitive decline; it can also *reverse* the symptoms (Mercola, 2012; Yurko-Mauro, 2010).

In addition to Alzheimer's disease, low levels of DHA in people are associated with:

- Bipolar/manic-depressive disorder
- Depression
- Memory loss
- Schizophrenia

(Mercola, 2012)

A study of 48 Beagle puppies showed that dietary fortification of fish oil rich in DHA following weaning resulted in improved cognitive learning, memory, psychomotor, immunologic and retinal functions during the developmental stage. The high-DHA food also contained higher concentrations of the antioxidant vitamin E, taurine, choline, and l-carnitine, which may also have played a positive role on the puppies' development (Zicker et al., 2012).

EPA, along with DHA, can also benefit mood. As anyone who has cared for an elderly relative or friend knows, depression is a common side effect of age-related cognitive decline: EPA from marine sources such as fish oil can decrease cytokines associated with depression (Mercola, 2012).

See Chapter 4 for dosing details.

Milk thistle

You'll recall from the last chapter that silibinin extracted from the seeds of the ***milk thistle*** plant shows tremendous promise as a therapeutic agent to treat cancer, but its benefits don't stop there. Silibinin also prevents impairment of both short-term memory and recognition memory in mice injected with a highly toxic peptide fragment called Aβ25–35, which exerts neurotoxic properties. Aβ25–35 induces cognitive dysfunction, causing learning and memory impairment; it is also detected in the brains of patients with Alzheimer's disease. Silibinin works as an antioxidant, protecting the **hippocampus** (the part of the brain associated with memory) against oxidative damage caused by this powerful neurotoxin (Lu et al., 2009).

Another study on mice showed that supplementation of silymarin for six months markedly protected against Aβ-induced neurotoxicity and improved behavioral abnormalities, including decreasing anxiety. The researchers went so far as to conclude that silymarin shows promise for actually *preventing* Alzheimer's disease (Murata et al., 2010).

Phosphatidylserine

Phosphatidylserine is a **phospholipid**, a class of lipids (fats) that makes up a major part of cell membranes. Synthetic phosphatidylserine was once derived from cows' brains, but due to concerns about mad cow disease, it is now manufactured primarily from soy lecithin.

Until November 2004, the FDA held the position that phosphatidylserine showed no benefit in people with cognitive dysfunction, citing a lack of credible scientific evidence. However, on November 24, 2004, they changed their position in a letter titled, *Letter Updating the Phosphatidylserine and Cognitive Function and Dementia Qualified Health Claim*. The letter acknowledged studies demonstrating the beneficial effects of phosphatidylserine for individuals at risk of dementia and cognitive dysfunction and admitted that there is "credible evidence" for its use (USFDA, 2004).

Senilife®, manufactured by Ceva Animal Health, combines phosphatidylserine with ginkgo biloba, vitamin E, pyridoxine (vitamin B6) and grape skin extract. According to the company's studies, Senilife® improves several signs of CCD, including:

- Decreases sleeping problems.
- Decreases apathy and disorientation.
- Increases playful behavior.
- Increases response to commands.

According to Ceva, dogs began showing improvement within seven days of taking Senilife® (Straus, 2012).

SAMe (s-adenosylmethionine)

As you'll recall, DNA methylation as an important epigenetic signaling tool for normal gene expression. *SAMe is the brain's major methyl donor* and is responsible for forming a variety of compounds, including proteins, nuerotransmitters, phospholipids, glutathione, myelin, coenzyme q10, carnitine, and creatine (Brogan, 2013; Messonnier, n.d.).

SAMe also improves neuron membrane fluidity and increases levels of serotonin and dopamine metabolites (Messonnier, n.d.).

In several human studies, reduced SAMe concentrations were detected in the brains of patients with Alzheimer's disease, indicating that a methyl group deficiency in the central nervous system may play a part in causing the disease (Bottiglieri, 2002). Supplementation with SAMe has also been shown to effectively reduce the symptoms of depression in people—and might even be as beneficial as some prescription antidepressants (WebMD, 2013).

Novifit®, a SAMe supplement manufactured by Virbac Animal Health, has undergone testing in senior dogs with signs of CCD. Novifit showed favorable results beginning after just one month of testing on client-owned dogs, including:

- A 44% reduction in problem behaviors, including a reduction in house soiling, after both four and eight weeks (compared to 24% in the placebo group).

- Marked improvement in activity and playfulness.

- Significant increase in awareness.

- Decreased sleep problems.

- Decreased disorientation and confusion.

(Straus, 2012)

A separate study on laboratory dogs supplemented with Novifit® showed improvement in cognitive processes, including attention and problem solving (Straus, 2012).

Denosyl®, manufactured by Nutramax Laboratories, is another SAMe product marketed to support liver and brain health. See the Resources section for purchasing information on these products.

SAMe works in conjunction with the methyl donors folate and vitamin B12, so supplementing with a B-complex vitamin is also advised.

People with bipolar disorder, migraine headaches, Parkinson's disease and active bleeding, as well as those on prescription antidepressants, should not take SAMe. While the contraindications in dogs are not known, similar precautions should be followed. We advise starting with a very low dose and monitoring your dog for adverse effects, which in people have been noted to include anxiety, restlessness, insomnia and mania (Messonnier, n.d.; WebMD, 2013).

Berries

A moment ago we talked about the benefits of antioxidants on the cognitive health of senior dogs; anthocyanins, the phytochemical compounds that give *berries* their pigment, are a rich source of antioxidants. Anthocyanins can protect against—and even reverse—declines in cognitive function due to age-related oxidative stress (Joseph, 1999; Lila, 2004; Mercola, 2012).

Anthocyanins are credited with:

- Enhancing memory.

- Helping prevent age-related declines in neural function.

- Modulating cognitive and motor function.

(Lila, 2004)

Gluten impairs brain health

Here's even more reason to remove gluten from you senior dog's diet: gluten sensitivity in people has been linked with impairment of brain function, including learning disabilities, ADHD and memory problems. Gluten sensitivity may even manifest *exclusively* as a neurological disease, without any GI symptoms (Perlmutter, n.d.).

The link between gluten sensitivity and impairment of brain function makes perfect sense, according to David Perlmutter, MD, FACN, ABIHM, a board certified neurologist and fellow of the American College of Nutrition as well as the author of *Grain Brain: The Surprising Truth about Wheat, Carbs, and Sugar—Your Brain's Silent Killers*. Perlmutter points out that the body's antibody response to gliadin, a protein in gluten, results in elevated levels of inflammatory cytokines that are present in Alzheimer's disease and other neurological conditions, such as Parkinson's, multiple sclerosis and autism (Perlmutter, n.d.).

In 2006, researchers from the Mayo Clinic found an association between patients with both Celiac Disease and progressive cognitive impairment, further supporting the link between the damaging effects of gluten and impaired brain health (Hu, 2006).

The last thing your aging dog needs is a cascade of brain-related inflammation. For this and many other reasons we've previously discussed, we advise removing gluten from your dog's diet.

Before we move on to the next chapter, we'd like to point out an important non-nutritional aspect of canine cognitive health—mental stimulation. Just as with humans, dogs "use it or lose it" when it comes to their cognitive ability. And, while your canine companion can't pick up the latest *New York Times* crossword puzzle, he can engage in a variety of mentally challenging "dog brain games." Don't for a second believe the old adage, "you can't teach an old dog new tricks." It's not true! Old dogs are wonderful students and most love to learn. There are lots of great books and articles with fun tricks you can teach your dog, which will not only help keep his brain young, but will also add a new dimension to your relationship and deepen the bond the two of you share. There are also a wide variety of mentally challenging games for your dog to play while you're away. Check out the Resources section for manufacturers and retailers of these products.

Success!

Functional ingredients reverse cognitive decline

Fifi was an older spayed female Yorkshire Terrier. After years of providing ideal companionship, her behavior started to change noticeably when she was about 12 years old. This change continued to the point where Fifi turned into an overly anxious and nervous pet. She became hyper-excitable when anyone visited her home, barking continuously and becoming obnoxious. Her distraught guardians took Fifi to her veterinarian for a checkup, thinking that perhaps she had suffered a stroke or was becoming blind or deaf. After a thorough examination and lab workup failed to identify any reason for this progressive behavioral change, Fifi was diagnosed with CCD.

The question then became whether Fifi's CCD should be treated immediately with drugs such as Anipryl® (selegiline; L-deprenyl; an MAOI) or whether nutritional therapy should first be tried. It was ultimately decided to first try nutritional therapy. Fifi was given a commercial grain-free diet to which extra vitamins B, E and C, along with **blueberries**, were added. Additional supplements included L-carnitine and alpha-lipoic acid. Lavender aromatherapy was also used around the home for its calming effect. Within 60 days of changing her diet, Fifi calmed down, stopped her frantic licking, barking and pacing, recognized family members and friends more easily and even became more agile!

Takeaway Points

- Dogs are thought to be the first animals to be domesticated, around 15,000 years ago. But even though our canine companions often understand us better than our human ones, dogs are not "furry people." They live in a "foreign culture" (the human culture) and must understand a foreign language (human language).

- Sometimes, dogs exhibit behaviors that are "undesirable" to humans, such as excessive barking, running away and house soiling. Sadly, millions of dogs each year are relinquished to shelters and euthanized due to behavioral issues.

- While nutrition is rarely considered as a possible contributing factor to canine behavioral issues, we need to start taking a closer look at this relationship. Evidence shows that dietary components do affect the behavior of both humans and animals.

- High-GI carbs can cause similar mood swings in dogs as they can in people, resulting in hyperactivity and lack of focus that then "crashes" into sluggishness, moodiness and irritability.

- Impaired glucose metabolism caused by sugary foods could also promote brain starvation, leading to memory problems such as Alzheimer's disease, which is very similar to Canine Cognitive Disorder (CCD) in dogs.

- High-glycemic foods can also lead to hunger-related behavioral problems. Since simple carbohydrates digest and absorb quickly (hence the rapid rise and fall in blood sugar concentrations), dogs feel hungry again quickly, which can result in hunger-related behavioral problems.

- Tryptophan and tyrosine are amino acids that act as precursors to neurotransmitters, which play an important role in regulating everything from heartbeat and digestion to mood and behavior.

- Dogs can suffer from a canine version of Alzheimer's disease, called Canine Cognitive Dysfunction (CCD) or Cognitive Dysfunction Syndrome (CDS).

- Senior and geriatric dogs often display impaired learning and memory, disorientation, a reduced ability to interact socially, house soiling, destructive behaviors, lethargy and disturbances in sleep patterns.

- Free radicals, molecules that cause oxidation of cells, have been identified as a major cause of aging, including reduced memory capacity. The brain is extremely vulnerable to oxidation.

- Left unprotected, oxidation in the brain can cause damage and even death of neurons, resulting in a decline in cognitive function.

- A diet rich in antioxidants can help counteract the effects of free radicals on the brain.

- Nutrients shown to improve cognitive function in senior dogs are: vitamins E and C (antioxidants); alpha-lipoic acid; L-carnitine; *milk thistle*; phosphatidyl-serine; SAMe (s-adenosylmethionine); medium-chain triglycerides (e.g., *coconut oil*); *omega-3 fatty acids* (EPA and DHA) and *berries*.

- Gluten impairs brain health, and gluten sensitivity may even manifest exclusively as a neurological disease, without any GI symptoms.

- The body's antibody response to gliadin, a protein in gluten, results in elevated levels of inflammatory cytokines that are present in Alzheimer's disease and other neurological conditions.

- Just as with people, dogs "use it or lose it" when it comes to their cognitive ability. Mental stimulation, such as challenging "brain games" for your dog to play with you and by himself, are important to keep his brain in tip-top shape.

Chapter 11

A Nutrigenomics Approach to Other Common Canine Health Issues

---

You've discovered that functional nutrients wield the power not only to prevent disease, but also to diminish and even *reverse* some of the most serious health conditions. One of the many miracles of life is that cells constantly repair, re-grow and renew, so we have the opportunity to "start fresh" with the environmental messages we send them via the epigenome. This means that even if your dog currently suffers from one or more health issues, you can change his destiny by nourishing him at the cellular level.

The following flow chart illustrates the relationship between nutrition and chronic illness. While we have simplified the chart by using liver, kidney, bowel and skin disorders as examples, the concept applies to all chronic health conditions. The key is to lay a solid nutritional foundation with the basal diet (described in Chapters 4 and 5) and then to incorporate the appropriate functional nutrients based on your dog's specific health concerns.

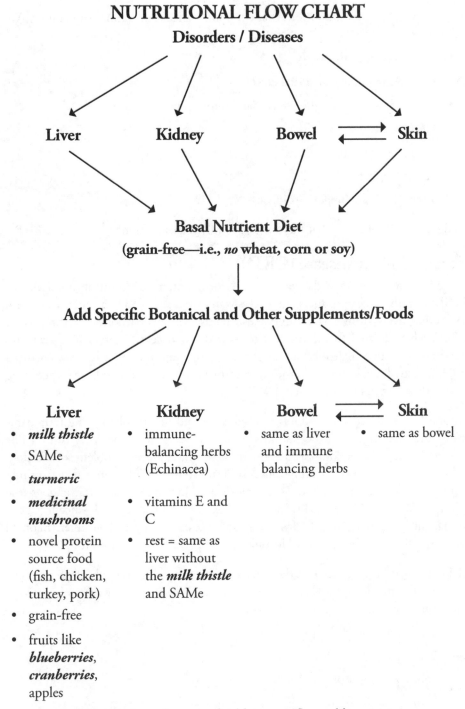

NUTRITIONAL FLOW CHART
Disorders / Diseases

Liver Kidney Bowel Skin

Basal Nutrient Diet
(grain-free—i.e., *no* wheat, corn or soy)

Add Specific Botanical and Other Supplements/Foods

Liver	Kidney	Bowel	Skin
• **milk thistle**	• immune-balancing herbs (Echinacea)	• same as liver and immune balancing herbs	• same as bowel
• SAMe			
• **turmeric**	• vitamins E and C		
• **medicinal mushrooms**			
• novel protein source food (fish, chicken, turkey, pork)	• rest = same as liver without the **milk thistle** and SAMe		
• grain-free			
• fruits like **blueberries**, **cranberries**, apples			

Flow diagram of common health issues influenced by nutrition

In this chapter, you'll learn about functional nutrients that benefit the disorders listed above in the flow chart (refer back to Chapter 6 for the discussion on skin disorders), as well as other chronic conditions that commonly affect our canine companions. We will discuss:

- Chronic kidney disease (CKD)
- Diabetes mellitus (sugar diabetes)
- Gastrointestinal tract disease (Inflammatory Bowel Disease)
- Heart disease
- Liver disease (hepatopathy)
- Seizures/epilepsy
- Thyroid disease (hypothyroidism)

Read on to find solutions that fit your dog's individual situation.

Chronic kidney disease (CKD)

The kidneys are bean-shaped organs that perform a number of critical functions, including filtering waste products and excess water from the blood and removing them via the bladder as urine. The kidneys also release several hormones: erythropoietin (EPO), which is vital to the production of red blood cells; renin, which regulates blood pressure; and calcitriol, the bioactive form of vitamin D, which as we discussed earlier is actually a steroidal hormone that plays an important role in influencing thousands of different genes (NKUDIC, 2012).

Chronic kidney disease, or CKD, is a progressive condition involving long-term damage to the kidneys over a few months to several years, resulting in an irreversible decrease in kidney function. CKD is the most common kidney problem seen in dogs and cats and is one of the leading causes of death in dogs. Although it is seven times more likely to affect cats than dogs, diagnosis of kidney disease in geriatric dogs rose almost 22% from 2007 to 2011. Early diagnosis of CKD is essential, since it is both permanent and progressive; if left unmanaged, it can become a silent killer (Banfield Pet Hospital, 2012; Banfield Pet Hospital, 2013; Brown, 2013; Howard, 2012).

CKD can be difficult to spot in the early stages because dogs initially show no clinical signs. The first symptoms are typically increased thirst (polydipsia) and increased urination (polyuria). Other signs include:

- Bad breath
- Inactivity
- Poor coat condition
- Reduced appetite
- Vomiting
- Weight loss

(Brown, 2013)

CKD can result from any condition that damages the kidneys over time, including:

- Abnormal protein deposits in the kidneys (amyloidosis).
- Bacterial infections, such as leptospirosis.
- Chronic high blood pressure (hypertension).
- Chronic urinary tract infections.
- **Glomerulonephritis**, an inflammatory condition causing dysfunction of the glomeruli (networks of capillaries in the kidneys that help filter blood into the urine).
- Kidney stones.
- Toxins, such as antifreeze.
- Tumors.

(Brown, 2013)

Older dogs and certain genetically predisposed breeds, such as the Basenji, English Cocker Spaniel and English Springer Spaniel are at greatest risk (Brown, 2013).

Obesity and CKD

Obesity is a risk factor for CKD independent of the fact that obesity leads to diabetes and hypertension, both of which are major contributors to kidney disease. Researchers are still studying the exact method by which obesity leads to CKD; it could be because obesity creates inflammation, **lipotoxicity** (accumulation of excess lipids in non-adipose tissues, which leads to cell dysfunction or cell death) and **hemodynamic** (circulatory) effects, as well as through other mechanisms (Schaffer, 2003; Wahba & Mak, 2007).

Beware of kibble

Eating those dry nuggets of kibble can stress your dog's kidneys because kibble contains only about 6% to 10% moisture, versus 70% or more moisture in fresh meats. A dog's body must use a significant amount of water just to move kibble through his GI tract during digestion. Dry foods are also typically high in carbohydrates, which can cause inflammation in the kidneys (note that canned foods can also contain a significant amount of carbs). If your dog has kidney failure, your veterinarian might recommend a dry "kidney diet." We typically advise against these diets, since they can actually aggravate the problem by contributing to dehydration while simultaneously adding too many carbohydrates (more on this below) (Case et al., 2011).

Dietary management of CKD

Contrary to the belief of some "experts," kidney sparing diets should *not* be low in protein, except for dogs in moderate to severe kidney failure, where excessive protein creates toxic nitrogen-based by-products that the damaged kidneys cannot filter. Most dogs already consume diets that are low in protein. Not only are low-moisture, high-carbohydrate dry diets bad for dogs with kidney issues for the reasons listed above, they also short-change the dog of his required high quality protein. Sick dogs still need to eat species-appropriate foods; the kidney's workload will not decrease by offering less protein than what's required to support a healthy body (Case et al., 2011).

Omega-3 fatty acids and CKD

EPA and DHA *omega-3 fatty acids* are beneficial in supporting kidney health and managing kidney problems. Research with people has found that long-term use (two years) of fish oil can slow the loss of kidney function in high-risk patients with IgA nephropathy, a form of glomerulonephritis (see bulleted list above). Fish oil also appears to reduce the amount of protein in the urine of people with diabetes-related kidney disease (MedlinePlus, 2012).

Omega-3s are also shown to directly benefit dogs with kidney disease. One study of 18 adult mixed-breed dogs found that while supplementation with omega-6 fatty acids accelerated the decline of kidney function in the early stages of the disease, supplementation with *omega-3s* had a protective effect (Brown et al., 2000).

Kidney cleansing diet

The following diet is designed for dogs with kidney dysfunction:

Ingredients

- White and/or brown rice OR white potato
- White fish (or sardines, pork or duck)

If using rice, cook according to package directions. If using potato, cook until tender (e.g., bake in skin or remove skin, cut into pieces and boil or steam). Remove skins and lightly mash.

Bake, broil or steam the fish until thoroughly cooked throughout, or drain if using canned sardines. If using pork or duck, cook well throughout.

Combine the rice or potato with the protein (fish, pork or duck) at a ratio of 2/3 rice or potato and 1/3 protein. Season with mixed Italian herbs or parsley.

Later, when your dog has begun feeling better, you can gradually add in finely chopped, lightly cooked (e.g., steamed) vegetables such as carrots, zucchini, yellow squash, spinach, kale and green beans as well as one scrambled egg per meal, if your dog tolerates these foods.

Supplements

Add supplements as listed in the sample diet in Chapter 4, including a high quality *probiotic*. Be sure to include an *omega-3 fatty acid* supplement. Adjust supplement doses according to your dog's weight.

Feed three to four small meals per day (or at least two meals per day, if your schedule does not allow for more). The total amount of food given should meet your dog's required daily caloric intake.

Note: Do not use high-mercury fish, such as tuna and swordfish.

Success!

A kidney sparing diet extends Hallie's life

Hallie, a seven-year-old, spayed female Shetland Sheepdog, was a very active agility dog. She competed in regional obedience and agility trials and received annual wellness examinations and laboratory testing. Her owner noticed that she started to become distracted during eventing and that she seemed to have less stamina. A checkup revealed elevated BUN and creatinine levels in her blood and significant proteinuria, all suggesting renal (kidney) disease. Further studies with abdominal ultrasound showed abnormal kidneys, which turned out to be caused by congenital renal dysplasia, unbeknownst to anyone until Hallie hit mid-life. Hallie's veterinary internist placed her on a commercial kidney diet, but she refused to eat it. A home cooked kidney diet was prepared and she thrived on it to the extent that the specialist was amazed at the improvement and wanted the recipe! Hallie continued the diet and lived another three years in generally good health.

Diabetes mellitus (sugar diabetes)

Finding out that your dog has diabetes mellitus can be frightening and confusing. If you've never dealt first-hand with diabetes, you may initially feel overwhelmed at the prospect of administering long-term care. Unfortunately, euthanization is the leading cause of death for diabetic dogs because many owners give up before they even give it a chance. We are here to tell you that caring for a dog with diabetes is very doable, and we urge you to refrain from making any hasty (and irreversible) decisions. One veterinarian we know who treats many dogs with diabetes tells her clients not to even think of the treatment in terms of years—just to make the commitment to give it a try for three months to see how it goes. She's says that advice has never failed! Just like her clients, we're certain that once you learn this new skill of caring for your diabetic dog, it will quickly become second nature. One day you'll wake up and realize that giving your dog his insulin injections is just part of the daily routine, like walking or feeding him—and you'll be glad you didn't do anything rash (Murray, 2012).

Diabetes in dogs increasing

Diabetes is on the rise in both dogs and people. In fact, diabetes in dogs has doubled within the past five years (Banfield Pet Hospital, 2013). Traditionally, canine diabetes has not been considered a lifestyle disease, as it is with people (and cats), because dogs typically only get the Type 1 form.

Type 1 diabetes, formerly known as juvenile diabetes in humans, occurs when beta-cells in the pancreas fail to make insulin (remember that insulin is the hormone responsible for controlling blood glucose levels). Insulin enables glucose to travel from the bloodstream into the cells, where it is used as energy. Without insulin, glucose can't enter the cells and instead accumulates to dangerous levels in the blood and urine. Type 1 diabetes is not considered to be a lifestyle-related disease.

Type 2 diabetes, also known as insulin resistance, occurs when the pancreas produces insulin, but the body cannot properly utilize it. Type 2 diabetes is also known as adult onset diabetes because it occurs later in life and is associated with lifestyle factors such as diet and obesity.

But here's the interesting part. Even though canine diabetes typically results from a problem producing insulin, which occurs in Type 1, dogs do not develop diabetes as youngsters. Just like Type 2 diabetes in humans, diabetes in dogs occurs later in life. So, even though it is identified as Type 1 because it relates to insulin production rather than insulin resistance, *diabetes in dogs is still an adult onset disease influenced by diet and lifestyle* (Becker, 2013).

Obesity and high-GI carbs: leading contributors to diabetes

You're probably not surprised to learn that the two leading lifestyle causes of diabetes in people are obesity and consumption of high-GI carbohydrates. But here's something interesting that you likely didn't know. While failure of the beta cells in the pancreas to make insulin is typically viewed as irreversible, a 2011 study in people showed that *caloric restriction alone can reverse both beta cell failure and insulin resistance within just one week*. The authors concluded that diabetes is "a potentially reversible condition and not one that is inevitably progressive." (Lim et al., 2011, pp. 2513).

Obesity in dogs is known to cause insulin resistance, a hallmark of diabetes (Swanson, 2007), but a 2012 study of 35 obese dogs in England found that *20% also had metabolic syndrome*. This is an amazing finding, since metabolic syndrome is a condition typically associated with obese humans, not dogs, and can wreak havoc on multiple systems including the nervous system, muscles, pancreas, kidneys, heart, immune system and liver (see below). In people, metabolic syndrome is closely tied to insulin resistance and Type 2 diabetes (Bugianesi et al., 2005). The obese dogs in the study also showed increased blood insulin levels, indicating additional stress on the pancreas to control blood glucose levels. As with the research in people just mentioned, *when these dogs lost weight, their metabolic issues improved* (University of Liverpool, 2012).

The appearance of metabolic syndrome in dogs further proves that our canine companions are succumbing to human lifestyle diseases and that drastic nutritional intervention is necessary to halt and reverse this trend.

It's recently been proposed that insulin resistance could actually be an inflammatory disorder caused by pro-inflammatory cytokines produced by adipose tissue (Bugianesi et al., 2005). Whatever the underlying mechanism, it's clear that obesity is bad news for your dog—as it relates to diabetes and every other chronic health condition.

We've already discussed in detail how to optimize your dog's weight and carbohydrate consumption, so we won't repeat ourselves here. Simply refer back to earlier discussions for complete information, and take heart in knowing that you can make a significant impact on your diabetic dog's health simply by getting him lean and cutting his intake of unhealthy carbohydrates.

DNA methylation: a new risk factor for Type 1 diabetes?

Even though Type 1 diabetes in people has traditionally been classified as a genetic—and not a lifestyle—disease, more recent research is discovering that epigenetic factors, such as DNA methylation, also contribute. One interesting study analyzed genome-wide DNA methylation profiles in identical twins, where one twin had Type 1 diabetes and one did not (which in itself is interesting, considering that if Type 1 diabetes were strictly genetic, identical twins, which are born with the same genomes, should either both have or not have it). The study showed that the diabetic twins had 132 different DNA sites where methylation significantly correlated with the diabetic state, whereas the non-diabetic twins did not have these variations. Some of these aberrant methylation profiles were identified *before* the twins were even diagnosed with the disease, suggesting that DNA methylation is a potentially important risk factor for Type 1 diabetes (Rakyan et al., 2011). This is just one more reason to serve your diabetic dog lots of foods that promote optimum DNA methylation, such as *curcumin* and folate-rich foods (see Chapter 9).

US FDA approves first insulin pen for dogs and cats

Another recent advancement makes caring for your diabetic dog even easier. If you find drawing insulin using a vial and syringe difficult or time-consuming, VetPen from Merck Animal Health could be your solution. The first insulin injection pen manufactured specifically for use in diabetic dogs and cats, VetPen received approval in March 2014 by the U.S. Food and Drug Administration (FDA). The refillable device, which resembles a thick ballpoint pen, exclusively holds Merck's Vetsulin® (porcine insulin zinc suspension) cartridges. Simply turn a dial to select the prescribed dose, insert VetPen's needle through your dog's skin and push the release button, holding in place for five seconds to deliver the insulin.

The refillable pen comes in two sizes:

- The small pen, designed for more accurate dosing of smaller units, dispenses 0.5—8 units (IU) of insulin per dose and allows for dosing increments of 0.5 IU.

- The large pen dispenses 1—16 IU of insulin per dose, with increments of 1 IU.

Dogs allergic to pork products should not use Vetsulin®. For more information, visit www.vetsulin.com.

Gene therapy: a future cure for canine diabetes?

As we write this book, exciting developments are taking place in diabetes research, which might enable people and dogs to say goodbye to insulin needles forever. Researchers from the Universitat Autonoma de Barcelona in Spain have used gene therapy to successfully regulate Type 1 diabetes in dogs for more than four years, without the side effects of hypoglycemia or other risks associated with conventional treatments. The study was published in the May 2013 issue of the journal *Diabetes* (American Diabetes Association, 2013).

In a single treatment session, the researchers injected five diabetic laboratory Beagles with glucokinase and insulin, two genes that are critical in maintaining normal blood glucose levels. The researchers "infected" cells in the dogs' skeletal muscle with the two genes using a vector, or vehicle for DNA transmission, consisting of a non-pathogenic virus. Since skeletal muscle cells do not divide, the genes could be injected just one time and remain undisturbed for years to carry out their job of maintaining normal blood glucose levels (American Diabetes Association, 2013).

After fine-tuning the procedure in companion dogs, the researchers plan to move on to testing on human patients (American Diabetes Association, 2013).

We will be watching the progress closely, and hope to see gene therapy available for canine and human diabetes patients in the not-too-distant future. Imagine regulating your dog's diabetes with just one simple treatment!

Gastrointestinal tract disease (Inflammatory Bowel Disease)

As the name implies, Inflammatory Bowel Disease (IBD) involves inflammation of the GI tract; it is also one more example of the damage caused by a leaky gut. As you'll recall, when the gut's mucosal barrier is compromised, substances can pass through the intestinal wall and into the bloodstream (Woodruff Health Sciences Center, 2012). The body sends white blood cells to attack the foreign invaders, which leads to intestinal inflammation—and, not surprisingly, to IBD (Robinson & Reeves, 2013). Please refer back to Chapter 3 and remove any ingredients that can cause leaky gut from your dog's diet.

As we discussed in Chapter 6, there is a strong link between the IgA/IgM antibody response that occurs as a result of food intolerances/sensitivities and leaky gut syndrome. If you suspect that your dog has IBD, we advise using NutriScan to identify which specific foods are causing the problem so that you can eliminate them from his diet. It is nearly impossible to effectively treat your dog's IBD if he continues to consume antigenic foods that promote GI inflammation and perpetuate the disease.

Dietary modifications for dogs with IBD

The ideal diet for dogs with IBD is:

- Highly digestible: to provide bowel rest, decrease the amount of antigenic dietary protein in the lower small intestine, reduce the amount of potentially harmful bacteria in the bowel and reduce **osmotic diarrhea**, which occurs when the GI tract cannot properly break down and absorb the substance ingested, causing the ingredient to pass too quickly through the digestive system. When this occurs, the dog cannot properly absorb the nutrients from the food or liquid, and the waste products don't have time to come together, resulting in loose and watery stools.

- Gluten-free: to prevent the GI inflammatory response and leaky gut caused by eating gluten.

- Hypoallergenic: to reduce the potential for food sensitivities that result in GI inflammation.

- Lactose-free: to reduce the inflammatory response to lactose.

- Low fat: IBD can disrupt fat digestion and absorption, and poorly absorbed fats worsen diarrhea.

(Guilford & Matz, 2003; Weil, 2013).

Soluble fiber also helps to treat diarrhea associated with IBD. Soluble fiber, a type of indigestible carbohydrate, absorbs water and turns to gel during digestion, slowing the digestive process.

Good sources of soluble fiber include:

- Apples
- Barley
- Beans
- Beet pulp
- Carrots
- Chicory
- Green beans
- Jerusalem artichokes (sunchokes)
- Lentils
- Oats (choose gluten-free)
- Peas
- Psyllium
- Pumpkin
- Sweet potatoes

(Straus, 2012)

Prebiotics: fiber that feeds beneficial bacteria in the intestines

Soluble fiber can also act as a prebiotic. Prebiotics are indigestible carbohydrates (i.e., fiber) that act as food for **probiotics** and stimulate the growth and/or activity of beneficial bacteria in the colon. Unlike **probiotics**, prebiotics are not live organisms. Prebiotics are *soluble* fiber that passes intact through the small intestine to the large intestine, where it acts as food for the good bacteria in the colon. The most common prebiotics, fructooligosaccharides (FOS), are highly fermentable by numerous species of bifidobacteria, a type of bacteria associated with gut health, as well as by some other types of beneficial microflora (Swanson et al., 2002). Inulin is a prebiotic similar to FOS. Prebiotics are found in foods such as Jerusalem artichokes, asparagus, bananas, chicory root and whole grains.

Mannan-oligosaccharides (MOS) are another type of indigestible carbohydrates that promote GI health. MOS are composed of the sugars glucose and mannose, and are normally obtained from the yeast cell walls of *Saccharomyces cerevisiae*. Like FOS, MOS influence immune function by stimulating local body defenses and increasing nutrient digestibility, as well as improving and protecting the health of the large bowel (Swanson et al., 2002; Yamka et al., 2006).

Some specific benefits of prebiotics include:

- Boost the immune system by assisting in the growth of good bacteria (remember that the gut contains the largest immune organ in the body).
- Help prevent diarrhea by keeping bad bacteria in the gut under control.
- Help prevent disease by aiding the immune system.
- Improve digestion.
- Improve nutrient absorption, especially of minerals.

(Straus, 2012)

Prebiotics are best given with **probiotics**, since they work in tandem. Foods and supplements that contain prebiotics and **probiotics** together are called synbiotics. Fermented dairy products, such as yogurt and kefir, are considered synbiotic (opt for fermented dairy products made from sheep or goat's milk, not cows). When purchasing yogurt or kefir, be sure the product states that it contains live or active cultures; remember, **probiotics** must be live to do their job.

Many commercial **probiotic** supplements also include prebiotics. Use caution if you plan to give your dog a fiber supplement as a source of prebiotics, as an excessive amount of soluble fiber can lead to gas and loose stools. Start with a low dose and gradually increase the amount. Reduce or discontinue if you notice adverse signs such as gas or diarrhea (Straus, 2012).

We also suggest avoiding highly fermentable fiber sources, such as citrus pectin, guar gum and lactulose, which can cause gas or bloating.

Note that *insoluble* fiber (e.g., cellulose), also known as roughage, has a laxative effect by speeding intestinal transit time and can reduce mineral absorption. Insoluble fiber is not fermentable by the beneficial bacteria in the colon and so is not considered a prebiotic (Straus, 2012).

Probiotics: essential for the health of your dog's GI tract

As we discussed earlier, the trillions of beneficial bacteria that inhabit the gut are important for a variety of important functions, including regulating digestion, producing and metabolizing vitamins and other trace nutrients, maintaining the integrity of the gut lining, fighting off bad bacteria such as *E. coli* and other pathogens and protecting the body from infection.

When the balance of good and bad bacteria goes awry, humans and animals can experience a whole host of digestive disturbances, including bloating, constipation or diarrhea, as well as abdominal cramping, surface erosions and ulcers. Reversing your dog's GI symptoms and returning his gut to optimum health could be as simple as adding a high quality *probiotic* supplement to his diet.

GI cleansing diet

The following GI cleansing diet is suitable for dogs with IBD. Note that this diet can also serve as a liver cleansing diet.

Ingredients

- White potato
- Sweet potato
- White fish (such as cod, halibut, sole, haddock, tilapia). You can substitute baked chicken or pork if your dog won't eat fish.

Cook the potatoes until tender (e.g., bake in skin or remove skin, cut into pieces and boil or steam). Remove skins and lightly mash. Combine cooked potatoes in a ratio of 50/50 (half white potato and half sweet potato).

Bake, broil or steam the fish until thoroughly cooked throughout. **Note:** Do not use high-mercury fish, such as tuna and swordfish.

Combine the potato mixture with the cooked fish at a proportion of 2/3 potato mixture with 1/3 fish. Season with mixed Italian herbs or parsley.

Later, when your dog has begun feeling better, you can gradually add in finely chopped, lightly cooked (e.g., steamed) vegetables such as carrots, zucchini, yellow squash, spinach, kale and green beans as well as one scrambled egg per meal, if your dog tolerates these foods.

Supplements
Add supplements as listed in the sample diet in Chapter 4, including a high quality *probiotic*. Be sure to include an *omega-3 fatty acid* supplement to reduce inflammation. Adjust supplement doses according to your dog's weight.

Feed three to four small meals per day (or at least two meals per day, if your schedule does not allow for more). The total amount of food given should meet your dog's required daily caloric intake.

Since dogs with IBD also tend to suffer from excessive loss of potassium as well as both water-soluble and fat-soluble vitamins, we also recommend discussing with your veterinarian the possibility of supplementing these nutrients in amounts up to double the recommended daily allowance (Guilford & Matz, 2003).

Once your dog is following an anti-inflammatory diet that allows the bowel to heal, he can lead a normal life, likely without the need for medications.

Success!

An anti-inflammatory diet reverses GI distress
Delilah, a three-year-old spayed female American Staffordshire Terrier, was diagnosed with IBD on biopsy. She had been on steroids and antibiotics for chronic diarrhea and periodic vomiting for much of her adult life. Her diet was changed to an anti-inflammatory diet, and all corn and wheat were removed from her food and treats. Initially, Delilah's guardians lightly cooked (at 250 degrees for 10 to 15 minutes) a commercially prepared boneless raw food diet. (Note: Be sure to never cook a raw food containing bones.) After significant improvement, the food was fed raw. The diet was supplemented with *coconut oil* and *probiotics*. Delilah was slowly weaned off all steroids and antibiotics and never had any more gastrointestinal issues.

Heart disease
We all know that dogs are fun-loving animals with big hearts, but canine heart disease is no laughing matter. Unfortunately, according to the American Veterinary Medical Association, one in 10 dogs suffers from some form of heart disease. Fortunately, more than 50 years of research into the treatment of human cardiovascular disease has uncovered nutritional therapies that can also benefit dogs, including slowing the progression of the disease, minimizing prescription medications, improving quality of life and, in some instances, even curing the condition (Devi & Jani, 2009; Dove, 2001; Li et al., 2013).

Canine heart disease refers to a number of conditions involving dysfunction of the heart. Many of these conditions can benefit from nutritional therapies, including:

- Diseases of the heart valves (mitral regurgitation and valvular disease).
- Diseases of the heart ventricles (primary diastolic dysfunction).

- Diseases of the heart muscle tissue (cardiac hypertrophy, dilated and restrictive cardiomyopathy, congestive heart failure).

- Diseases resulting from abnormal electrical activity (cardiac arrhythmias, atrial fibrillation).

- Injury from **ischemia** (restricted blood supply to the tissues, causing a lack of oxygen and nutrients) and **reperfusion** (tissue damage caused when blood supply returns to the tissue after ischemia, creating a condition in which the restoration of circulation results in inflammation and oxidative damage).

- Non-fatal heart attacks.

(Chu et al., 2005; Dove, 2001; Li et al., 2013)

Here are some of the most well researched nutrients to benefit your dog's heart health:

Coenzyme Q10 (CoQ10)

- Found in almost every cell in the body and is critical for a number of functions, including energy production.

- Antioxidant that can neutralize damaging free radicals implicated in a number of diseases, including degenerative heart disease.

- May provide enhanced antioxidant protection, help slow the progression of canine heart disease and improve overall heart health.

Dose: 100 to 400 mg daily.
(Devi, 2009; Dove, 2001)

L-Carnitine

- Amino acid used by the body to turn fat into energy.

- In several breeds, a deficiency results in the development of **cardiomyopathy** (deterioration in the function of the heart muscle).

- Typically used in combination with taurine, has been shown to improve outcome of dogs with congestive heart disease.

Dose: 500 to 1,500 mg daily.
(Dove, 2001)

Magnesium

- Mineral important to healthy functioning of the heart.

- Properties include **antiarrhythmic** (alleviates abnormal heart rhythms) and **antithrombotic** (reduces blood clots) activities.

- Deficiencies can cause conditions such as hypertension, coronary artery disease, congestive heart failure and cardiac arrhythmias.

- Deficiencies may correlate to the development of mitral valve prolapse in dogs. (Devi, 2009; Dove, 2001)

Omega-3 fatty acids

- Benefits include antiarrhythmic, anti-inflammatory, **hypotensive** (promotes low blood pressure) and **antivasopressor** (lowers blood pressure) properties.

- Decrease the production of inflammatory cytokines interleukin-1 (IL-1) and tumor necrosis factor (TNF) in dogs with congestive heart failure (CHF). Inflammatory cytokines are a major cause of **cardiac cachexia** (loss of weight and lean body mass). Reduced IL-1 is correlated with increased survival in dogs with CHF.

- May prevent fatal arrhythmias in dogs with CHF.

- Low plasma concentrations of EPA and DHA are associated with heart failure in dogs.

(Devi, 2009; Dove, 2001)

See Chapter 4 for dosing.

Taurine

- An amino acid found in relatively high concentrations in heart tissue.

- Even though dogs' bodies are thought to make adequate amounts of taurine and it is not considered required in the diet, taurine deficiency is linked with dilated cardiomyopathy (DM) in several breeds, including Cocker Spaniels, Doberman Pinchers, English Setters, Golden Retrievers, Labrador Retriever, Portuguese Water Dogs and Saint Bernards.

- One study showed that taurine supplementation at 100 mg per kilogram of body weight daily over the course of a month improved the condition of dogs with congestive heart failure.

Dose: 500 to 1,500 mg daily.
(Devi, 2009; Dove, 2001)

Vitamin D

- Plays an important role in cardiac function.

- In people, evidence indicates that vitamin D deficiency is associated with the development of congestive heart failure (CHF); a recent study conducted at Cornell University's College of Veterinary Medicine showed that vitamin D might play a similar role in dogs.

- The study of 82 companion dogs compared blood levels of vitamin D in dogs with CHF to healthy dogs.

- The researchers found that the dogs with CHF had lower blood levels of vitamin D than the healthy dogs. Low blood levels of vitamin D were also associated with poor survival rates in the dogs.

- The researchers concluded that improving vitamin D levels in some dogs with CHF might prove beneficial without causing toxicity.

- As previously discussed, consult with your veterinarian regarding appropriate levels of vitamin D supplementation to avoid toxicity.

(Becker, 2014; Kraus et al; 2014)

Vitamin E

- Protects the **myocardium** (the muscular tissue of the heart) from damage brought about by free radicals.

- Lower plasma concentrations of vitamin E correlates with increased incidence and severity of heart disease in dogs.

Dose: 200 to 500 IUs daily.
(Dove, 2001)

Dogs with heart disease also require sufficient amounts of calories and protein to manage cardiac cachexia. When dogs don't take in enough calories to meet their nutritional requirements, the body will utilize protein, resulting in loss of lean body mass. If your dog suffers from **anorexia** (loss of appetite) due to the side effects of medications, try using a little raw honey or maple syrup to increase his food's palatability (Devi, 2009).

We recommend discussing nutritional therapies for canine heart disease with your veterinarian, as specific recommendations and dosages will vary based on your dog's age, breed and individual medical condition (Dove, 2001).

Success!

Dietary changes get to the heart of the matter

Satan, a six-year-old, neutered male Doberman Pinscher, was admitted for what appeared to be shortness of breath on exertion and puffiness of both forelimbs. His weight had ballooned to more than 95 pounds due to his reluctance to exercise. Satan was seen by a veterinary cardiologist and was found to have dilated cardiomyopathy (DCM), which is not uncommon in this breed. Development of DCM is believed to be caused by many factors and could involve nutritional, familial and infectious agents. The mode of inheritance has not been determined in the Doberman Pinscher, but a strong male predisposition in affected breeds like the Great Dane suggests a sex chromosome (X-linked) mode of inheritance (O'Grady, 2002; O'Sullivan et al., 2011).

Satan was fed a diet containing the supplements and nutrients discussed above. He was also treated with a diuretic (furosemide = Lasix®) to help remove the excess fluid that had accumulated in the tissues; an ACE (angiotensin-converting enzyme) inhibitor (enalapril = Vasotec®) to slow the progression of heart failure; and pimobendan (Vetmedin®) to dilate the blood vessels and help make the heart muscle contract more efficiently. At the time of this writing, Satan's cardiac disease has been stable for 11 months and his weight, energy and coat condition are much improved.

Liver disease (hepatopathy)

The liver is a complex organ involved in almost every biochemical process essential to life, such as:

- Filters toxins such as drugs, chemicals, bacteria and excess ammonia (a by-product of protein metabolism) from the blood.
- Metabolizes fats, carbohydrates and proteins.
- Processes raw materials.
- Removes waste.
- Rids the blood of old or damaged red blood cells.
- Stores, activates and degrades vitamins.
- Stores **glycogen** (the storage form of glucose) for energy.
- Synthesizes proteins essential to normal blood clotting.
- Produces bile to aid in digestion.

(Smith, 2009)

Liver cells, called **hepatocytes**, go through thousands of chemical reactions every second in order to efficiently carry out their jobs. As you can imagine, when the liver becomes diseased and can't function properly, serious problems can result (Smith, 2009).

Typical signs of liver disease include:

- Anorexia (lack of appetite)
- Diarrhea
- Increased thirst
- Increased urination
- Lethargy
- Jaundice
- Orange urine
- Seizures (severe cases)
- Vomiting

(Messonnier, 2007)

Diagnosing liver disease can be difficult because the liver is intimately connected with so many of the body's systems and signs of liver disease are often non-specific. Another problem stems from the fact that the liver is able to continue functioning even when up to 80% of the organ is diseased; this means that by the time a diagnosis is made, the damage could be too severe to treat. The good news is that liver cells have an amazing ability to regenerate (more than any other organ). So, with diligence in catching damage in a timely manner and initiating proper treatment, a complete recovery is possible (Smith, 2009).

Unless liver damage results from an identified toxin that can be treated or a condition in which surgery is warranted, conventional therapy is often limited. This means that complementary therapies, such as dietary modification and the addition of functional nutrients, can be your most important ally in optimizing the health of your dog's liver (Messonnier, 2007).

Here are our recommendations to bolster the health of your dog's liver:

Eliminate toxins

As the primary organ responsible for removing toxins from the blood, imagine the stress the liver endures when it must deal with filtering chemicals, pesticides, heavy metals, medications, anesthetic agents and all the other impurities that we've previously discussed at length and that are so common in today's processed foods.

One example illustrating the link between commercial pet foods and liver disease in dogs involves a skyrocketing incidence of the disease in Labrador Retrievers that has occurred since the mid-to-late 1990s. After examining copper concentrations in the dogs' livers (a sign that correlates with liver disease), researchers concluded that these illnesses were likely caused by an increased amount of copper in their diets. Interestingly, this was the same time that AAFCO recommended that dog food manufacturers discontinue using cupric oxide as a source of supplemental copper and instead switch to more bioavailable forms, such as cupric sulfate or other chelated forms (Johnston et al., 2013). Although the researchers could not prove definitively that the copper in the commercial pet foods resulted in the higher incidences of liver disease, they concluded that, "We believe that the amount of copper in many commercial dog foods is excessive and that Labrador Retrievers, because of their popularity as family pets, may be functioning as sentinels for trends in hepatic [liver] copper concentrations in the general pet dog population" (Johnston et al., 2013, p. 378).

A wide array of prescription and non-prescription drugs used to treat dogs can also damage the liver, including:

- Anthelmintics (worming medication)
- Glucocorticoids (corticosteroids, such as cortisone)
- Ketaconazole (fungal treatment)
- Parasiticides (to rid the body of parasites)
- Phenobarbital (seizure/epilepsy medication)

- Rimadyl (arthritis treatment)
- Thiacetarsamide (heartworm treatment)
- Tylenol (acetaminophen)

(Smith, 2009)

Be sure to discuss the use of any medications with your veterinarian and eliminate dietary and environmental toxins. This includes foregoing vaccinations (assuming your dog has already received his complete puppy vaccines), which can stress and damage the liver and the immune system.

Beware of this liver damaging imitation "vitamin"

While natural vitamin K can help prevent bleeding disorders associated with certain liver diseases (Smith, 2009), *never* give Vitamin K3, or Menadione Sodium Bisulfate (which may also be listed as Menadione Dimethyl-Pyrimidinol Bisulfate, Menadione Dimethyl-Pyrimidinol Bisulfite, Menadione Sodium Bisulfate Complex, Menadione Sodium Bisulfite or Menadione Sodium Bisulfite Complex) to a dog with liver problems (or *any* dog, in our opinion!). As we discussed in Chapter 3, Menadione is a synthetic form of vitamin K that is toxic to liver cells and causes a number of other health problems. Please note that synthetic vitamin K1 (phytonadione), sold as Mephyton® and AquaMephyton® by Merck, is safe and effective for use in people and animals.

Your dog doesn't drink alcohol, but he can still get fatty liver disease

Fatty liver disease, also called hepatic lipidosis, used to be primarily associated with excessive alcohol intake, something that our dogs don't have to worry about! But that's not so anymore. Obesity, which contributes to just about every chronic disease, is now the leading cause of fatty liver disease in people. Non-alcoholic fatty liver disease (NAFLD), which occurs when more than 5% of liver cells have abnormally high concentrations of fat, is predicted to become the most common cause of primary liver cancer and liver transplantation in people by 2025 (Walker, 2013).

Dogs can also get fatty liver disease, either as a primary disease or secondary to other conditions. In the section on diabetes, we discussed obesity's link with metabolic syndrome, insulin resistance and diabetes—conditions that are leading risk factors for NAFLD (Bugianesi et al., 2005; Walker, 2013). In people, obesity has been shown to increase the risk of elevated liver enzymes, fatty liver, **cirrhosis** (end stage liver disease) and even **hepatocellular carcinoma** (liver cancer) (Marchesini et al., 2008).

Fatty liver disease is a serious condition that can cause build-up of toxins inside the body and generalized liver failure. If fat-laden cells in the liver rupture, high amounts of fat can rapidly release into the bloodstream, obstructing the arteries (VetInfo, 2012).

Symptoms of fatty liver disease in dogs include:

- Loss of appetite.

- Rapid weight loss.

- Jaundice (yellow pigment typical for liver diseases in the ears, eyes, gums).

- Vomiting.

- Salivating abundantly.

- Diarrhea or constipation.

- Depression.

(VetInfo, 2012)

Controlling risk factors for fatty liver disease—including obesity-related conditions such as metabolic syndrome, insulin resistance and diabetes—is crucial to optimizing the health of your dog's liver. This is one more reason why your dog should shed those excess pounds.

Milk thistle: the most researched plant for the treatment of liver disease

Several pharmacological studies have demonstrated *milk thistle's* silymarin benefits to the liver, including:

- Anti-fibrotic.

- Anti-inflammatory.

- Antioxidant (milk thistle is more potent than vitamin E).

- Stimulates protein biosynthesis and liver regeneration.

- Possesses immuno-modulation activity.

(Abenavoli et al., 2010; Messonnier, 2007)

Silymarin's anti-inflammatory and immune-modulating activities work across multiple cell structures and pathways, most notably inhibiting the formation of pro-inflammatory leukotrienes. Silymarin also displaces toxins trying to bind to the liver and stimulates the production of new liver cells to replace damaged cells.

Moreover, silymarin increases levels of **glutathione**, a super antioxidant that plays a critical role in liver detoxification and in protecting the liver from oxidative stress. Glutathione is the body's most powerful antioxidant and maximizes the activity of all other antioxidants; it is critical for immune function, detoxification, controlling inflammation, protecting cells and detoxification in the liver. But glutathione doesn't absorb well from the digestive system into the bloodstream, so supplementing with it directly is typically ineffective. Therefore, it's important to consume nutrients, such as silymarin, that boost the body's own production of gluathione (Abenavoli et al., 2010; Hyman, 2010; Mercola & Hofmekler, 2010; Messonnier, 2007).

In rats, silymarin has been found to stimulate the synthesis of DNA where part of the liver has been removed. This increases protein synthesis, which is necessary for repairing and regenerating damaged liver cells and restoring normal liver function (Abenavoli et al., 2010).

In Chapter 8, we discussed an example of a DNA microarray heat map depicting the gene expression levels of arthritic dogs before and after herbal treatment with *Andrographis paniculata* (King of bitters) and **curcumin**. Here we discuss results for dogs with liver disease before and after treatment with milk thistle (silymarin). The heat map illustrating the "molecular dietary signature" for dogs treated 28 days with this botanical extract to cleanse the liver can be found at www.nutriscan.org. The heat map depicts the expression levels of the genes that encode (transmit the genetic information) for normal, healthy dogs of genotype D1 or D2 and for unhealthy dogs severely (D1) and mildly (D2) affected with liver disease. The heat map profile compares the results both before and after administration of silymarin for 28 days. Gene expression levels ranged from negative (green bands) to positive (red bands). The horizontal line (from -3 to +3) indicates the graded intensity of the values.

The results show the severely affected D1 dogs that had only red (positive) gene expression(in the far two left-hand columns) before the herbal treatment became completely "cleansed" with only green (negative) gene expression (in the center two columns) after taking silymarin for 28 days. Remarkable!

The response to the silymarin in the dogs mildly affected with liver disease was less impressive, which is to be expected because their liver pathology was less severe (with some green and red bands).

As we pointed out in Chapter 9, studies also show that silymarin exerts cancer-protective benefits, an important factor since liver disease can lead to primary liver cancer (Walker, 2013).

Dose: 200 mg given 2 to 3 times a day. A form of silymarin bound to phosphatidylcholine has been shown to have greater bioavailability than unbound silymarin. The standard dosage of the bound form is 100 to 200 mg given twice daily (Messonnier, 2007).

N-acetylcysteine (NAC) increases glutathione production

As with **milk thistle**, supplementation of NAC can help prevent liver damage by increasing levels of glutathione in the liver cells. NAC exerts further benefits on glutathione production when given in combination with alpha-lipoic acid (Perricone, 2010).

SAMe

Metabolism of SAMe and its precursor, the essential amino acid methionine, are necessary for production of glutathione in the liver. Individuals with liver disease lack the enzyme capacity to properly metabolize methionine into SAMe, however, which results in a deficiency in SAMe and a decline in gluthatione. Experimental studies and clinical trials show that taking oral SAMe can increase glutathione levels in red blood cells and liver tissue. SAMe is also essential to proper methylation in the liver (Bottiglieri, 2002; Lieber, 2002).

Spirulina

You already learned about the powerful antioxidant and anti-inflammatory effects of phycocyanin (C-PC) from *spirulina*. C-PC also exhibits a protective effect on the liver, likely through its ability to scavenge free radicals, as well as via other mechanisms. In one study, a single dose of C-PC significantly reduced toxin-induced liver injury in rats (Vadiraja et al., 1998).

Branched chain amino acids: new hope for managing cirrhosis

A new study at the time of this writing demonstrates that long-term oral supplementation with branched chain amino acids (BCAA) prolonged survival in rats with liver cirrhosis. The researchers concluded that BCAA (comprised of the essential amino acids leucine, isoleucine and valine) likely reduced oxidative stress on the rats' livers by reducing iron accumulation, reducing the effect of fibrosis and improving glucose metabolism in the livers. BCAA also decreased frequency and development of liver cancer. Supplemental BCAA is also used to improve malnutrition in patients with liver cirrhosis (Iwasa et al., 2013). Cirrhosis in dogs occurs as the end stage of chronic, non-infectious hepatitis, especially in breeds prone to copper storage disease, such as Bedlington Terriers, Doberman Pinschers, Cocker Spaniels, West Highland White Terriers and Standard Poodles.

Liver disease and protein: it's no time to go raw

Dogs in many situations thrive eating a raw food diet, but liver disease is not one of them. Raw meat can contain bacteria such as *Salmonella* and *E.coli,* which will likely pass through a healthy animal without causing harm. However, since the liver is responsible for filtering bacteria, dogs with liver disease are at increased risk of food-borne infection. In addition, red meat is high in **aromatic amino acids** (phenylalanine, tyrosine and tryptophan), which dogs with liver disease do not tolerate well. Instead, a diet rich in proteins derived from dairy products (preferably from goat and sheep sources), which contain predominantly branched chain amino acids (see above), is recommended over meat-based sources. Studies show that dogs with liver disease live longer and have less severe clinical signs when fed dairy-based protein diets than diets containing meat-based proteins (Messonnier, 2007).

Optimum nutrition promotes optimum liver health

Dogs with liver disease should eat a fresh, wholesome diet packed with easily digestible, anti-inflammatory nutrients that nourish the liver cells, promote detoxification and support health and healing. Most dogs with liver disease require normal amounts of protein to repair tissue and muscle, prevent muscle wasting and to perform all of the other essential functions previously discussed (dogs with encephalopathy are an exception and require a protein-restricted diet).

However, when the liver is damaged, it can't efficiently process protein and there is the danger that urea and ammonia, toxic byproducts of protein metabolism, can build up and affect the brain. To reduce the buildup of toxic waste, be sure to feed a protein source of high biological value, such as the dairy-based proteins high in branched-chain amino acids we mentioned a moment ago or the white fish we use in our GI and liver cleansing diet (see section above for gastrointestinal tract disease). Avoid commercial diets, which often contain poor quality proteins of low bioavailability. Commercial foods may also contain chemicals, hormones, antibiotics, salt, artificial colors and flavors, excess amounts of copper and vitamin A and even mycotoxins—all of which can further damage an already struggling liver (Messonnier, 2007).

Dogs with liver disease also need highly digestible, simple carbohydrates to supply energy—but again, avoid the high-GI carbs we've warned against throughout the book. White or preferably brown rice and potatoes are good options, as are vegetable sources that provide important nutrients and supply fiber to help remove toxins from the system (Messonnier, 2007).

Since many dogs with liver disease refuse to eat, we suggest feeding several smaller meals per day.

Since the signs of liver disease typically don't come to light until the advanced stage, we strongly advise bi-annual serum chemistry panels that include testing for all liver enzymes as part of a complete wellness workup. If these levels are more than slightly elevated, a urine bile acid or a pre- and post-bile acid can detect liver damage. Dogs with known liver disease should be tested every three to four months (Canine Epilepsy Guardian Angels, 2011). And, as always, if your dog refuses to eat or seems "not quite right," be sure to seek immediate veterinary attention.

Success!

A liver cleansing diet reverses congenital liver disease
Candy, a three-year-old, six-pound spayed female Mi-Ki (a toy breed combining Papillon, Japanese Chin and Maltese) was found to have significantly elevated liver enzyme levels compatible with a liver shunt or hepatic microvascular dysplasia (MVD). These types of anatomical congenital liver defects are not uncommon in the toy breeds that make up this new popular hybrid. Candy's ALT (alanine aminotransferase, a liver cell-specific enzyme) level was more than 800 IU/dL, with the normal range being 12-118 IU/dL. She was given *milk thistle* and SAMe to cleanse the liver, along with a special gluten-free liver cleansing homemade diet. Candy's ALT level dropped to 158 IU/dL, however she discontinued the supplements, as they appeared to upset her stomach. She remained on the diet, and six months later, Candy's ALT level was 47 IU/dL. She was healthy once again!

Success!

A liver cleansing diet helps Rottie mix's behavioral issues
Thor, a four-year-old Rottie/Lab mix with chronically elevated liver enzymes, was treated with a combination of diet change and supplements. Thor also had fear aggression from a young age. He had been eating a commercially prepared, high carbohydrate, kibble diet that contained both corn and wheat. After a complete blood

workup, radiographs, ultrasound and examination, the cause of the liver enzyme elevation was still undetermined.

Thor's diet was changed to a modified liver detox diet (1:1 ratio of fish to potato). His guardians cooked white fish and salmon, adding sweet potatoes and white potatoes with an occasional addition of cottage cheese or organic chicken. They added a multi vitamin and bone meal daily. The diet was also supplemented with **omega-3 fatty acids** from fish oil along with **milk thistle**, turmeric (**curcumin**) and Denosyl® (see Resources section under CCD supplements). Supplements for the fear aggression were discussed, but because of the unknown situation in the liver, the decision was made to focus solely on the liver issue for the short term.

As Thor's liver enzymes improved, his guardians noticed a marked change in his behavior. He became gentler, friendlier and was less easily frightened. After two months on the liver detox diet, Thor's enzymes had normalized. His guardians switched him to a commercially prepared raw food and his behavior never returned to his previous agitated, aggressive state.

Success!

Dachshund scores with a liver cleansing diet

Hooper, a 10.5-pound, 12-year-old miniature Dachshund, began experiencing seizures as a younger dog. The seizures had been well controlled on a gluten-free diet. However, when they increased, he started taking a low dose of phenobarbital. About a year before, Hooper had suffered a bout of pancreatitis and began having very bad gastrointestinal signs, including irregular bowel movements, gas accumulation, persistent diarrhea and occasional episodes of explosive, liquid diarrhea. Despite therapy, extensive testing and a change in Hooper's diet, the diarrhea persisted to the point where his serum albumin (a protein made by the liver) level became quite low from loss of protein through the feces. His weight dropped to 7.5 pounds.

Hooper's coat color and texture also changed: it became lifeless and he experienced some hair loss, especially on his ears. Several gluten-free diets with novel protein sources were tried, as well as home cooked foods, but with no progress. At this point, Hooper's guardian contacted author (WJD) for more advice. The decision was made to treat him with tylocine (Tylan® powder), famotidine (Pepcid®-AC) and budesonide (Entocort®, a steroid with effects limited to the bowel) rather than with prednisone, which has known side effects. Hooper was also placed on the author's homemade liver cleansing diet, fed in four smaller meals per day. He loved the diet and his bowel issues resolved. However, he remained constantly hungry and whining, and he failed to gain any weight back. Melatonin was added at 1.5 mg daily to try and curb his whining.

The whining essentially stopped and his medications were gradually tapered down over a two-month period, except for the tylocine, which was continued on a daily basis. Hooper's local veterinarian was so impressed that another six dogs with liver and bowel issues were started on the diet—and all have improved remarkably!

As of this writing, Hooper continues to do amazingly well: he eats the fish-based liver cleansing diet (twice daily now) plus takes the tylocine and a small amount of ***coconut oil*** (¼ teaspoon) with breakfast and dinner, as well as fish oil with breakfast. He is bathed with Murphy Oil Soap, the lemon-scented vegetable oil cleaner for wood floors, to control any dry seborrhea. His hair has grown back and is as smooth as velvet, with the colors now vividly black and brown. His behavior has also returned to normal and he once again loves to cuddle. At 12 years old, Hooper acts like he is three. Best of all, his weight is back to an ideal 10.5 pounds!

Seizures/epilepsy

Seizures are the most common neurological disorder in dogs (Wong, 2013). Witnessing a beloved dog in the throes of a seizure is terrifying; the fear that he will injure himself, that he shouldn't be left alone or that his quality of life will suffer so much that you will be forced to make a dire decision regarding his future are all enough to cause feelings of helplessness and constant stress in even the most resilient dog parent. But the good news is that seizures do not necessarily get worse over time, and there are proactive steps you can take to help reduce both their intensity and frequency (Canine Epilepsy Guardian Angels, 2011).

Minimizing the total number of seizures and decreasing their frequency is critical, since it's theorized that every time the brain has a seizure, it "learns" how to have the next seizure. This phenomenon is called "kindling," and essentially it means that the more seizures a dog has, the more likely it is he will continue to have them. It is a vicious cycle that becomes harder to break with each episode (Canine Epilepsy Guardian Angels, 2011).

Seizures result from abnormal bursts of electrical activity in the brain. There are three main types:

- **Extracranial** are caused by outside factors that affect the brain, such as a poison or low blood sugar. Diagnosis is made via blood and urine tests.

- **Intracranial**, or **structural**, result when there is something wrong inside of the brain, such as a brain tumor. These are more worrisome and are diagnosed via MRI and spinal tap.

- **Idiopathic**, which are the most common type, result from a functional problem in the brain in which the neurons over-fire, causing the brain to become excessively excitable. Idiopathic seizures typically appear in dogs between one and fiver years of age and most commonly affect Cocker Spaniels, Labrador Retrievers and German Shepherds, although any breed can suffer from them.

(Wong, 2013)

Specific causes of seizures include:

- Brain tumors

- Certain medications

- Environmental toxins
- Fever
- Food toxins
- **Hypoxia** (inadequate levels of oxygen in the blood or tissues)
- Infection
- Inflammation
- Inherited structural problems in the skull or brain (e.g., **Syringomyelia**, a disorder in which a cyst forms in the spinal cord, damaging the spinal cord and injuring nerve fibers that carry information from the brain to the extremities. This is especially prevalent in Cavalier King Charles Spaniels.)
- Liver problems
- Low blood sugar
- Meningitis
- Metabolic diseases (e.g., diabetes mellitus, thyroid disease)
- Parasites
- Sinus or ear infections
- Strokes or clots
- Stress
- Systemic diseases (e.g., kidney or liver failure)
- Tick-borne diseases
- Traumatic injuries
- Vaccinosis (adverse effects of vaccines)
- Viruses (e.g., distemper, rabies)

(Canine Epilepsy Guardian Angels, 2011; Wong, 2013)

Be aware of the following signs that indicate your dog is having a seizure:

- Falling over onto side
- Convulsions
- Loss of consciousness
- Salivation
- Stiffening and paddling motion of the legs
- Uncontrolled urination and/or defecation
- Vocalization

(Wong, 2013)

While you can't stop a seizure once it's started, there are steps you can take to help reduce the severity and frequency. Here are our recommendations:

Eliminate environmental toxins

Resistance to all disease involves an optimally functioning immune system, which can be damaged by environmental and food toxins. Many of the toxins we've discussed throughout the book have also been linked to neurological issues.

Vaccines are linked to seizures. Distemper, parvovirus, rabies and, presumably, other vaccines have been linked with **polyneuropathy**, a nerve disease that involves inflammation of several nerves. Symptoms of polyneuropathy include **muscular atrophy** (wasting away of the muscle), the inhibition or interruption of neuronal control of tissue and organ function, **muscular excitation** (stimulation of muscle fibers), **incoordination** (poor muscle control or coordination), weakness, and seizures. In addition, MLV (modified live virus) vaccines are associated with the development of temporary seizures in both puppies and adult dogs who are members of susceptible breeds or crossbreeds (Dodds, 2001).

Certain flea and tick treatments are bad news for dogs with seizures. As we mentioned in Chapter 9, spot-on flea and tick control products continue to stir concern regarding their safety. In particular, products containing organophosphates and carbamates pose severe health risks and should not be used on pets. Organophosphates are neurotoxins that kill insects by interfering with the transmission of nerve signals in their brains and nervous systems. Like organophosphates, carbamates are toxic to the brain and nervous system. If the product label lists atropine as an antidote to poisoning, the product most likely contains carbamates.

Spot-on flea and tick products containing pyrethroids have gained popularity over the last decade, as they are considered to be less acutely toxic to birds and mammals than organophosphates and carbamates. However, these insecticides carry their own potential toxicity risks. Pyrethrins are botanical insecticides derived from certain species of chrysanthemums. They work by penetrating the nerve system and causing paralysis and eventual death of the target pests and have been linked with dizziness, headache, nausea, muscle twitching, reduced energy, changes in awareness, convulsions, loss of consciousness, hyperexcitability, tremors, profuse salivation and seizures in companion animals. Other flea and tick control products that are contraindicated for dogs prone to seizures are those containing spinosad (Comfortis®, Trifexis®) or afoxolaner (NexGard™).

Check the thyroid

Low thyroid function, known as hypothyroidism (more below), can precipitate or aggravate existing seizure disorders. While the exact mechanism of how this works is unknown, it may relate to the important role thyroid hormones play in cellular metabolism of the central nervous system. In some cases, simply giving a hypothyroid dog the appropriate levels of thyroid medication reduces the severity and frequency of the seizures, and may even stop them altogether. If your dog has seizures, it's important that he has a full 6-panel thyroid test involving TotalT4, FreeT4, TotalT3, FreeT3, Canine Thyroglobulin Autoantibodies (TgAA) and T3 Autoantibody (T3AA)/T4 Autoantibody (T4AA). Since many veterinarians do not understand how to properly test for canine hypothyroidism, the condition often goes undiagnosed or misdiagnosed, and the dog unfortunately suffers unnecessarily. For this reason, it's critical to carry out the testing at a lab specializing in interpreting hypothyroidism in dogs, such as the author WJD's Hemolife diagnostics lab (http://hemopet.com/hemolife/thyroid-testing.html). For more information on canine hypothyroidism, the most common endocrine disorder in dogs, please refer to our book, *The Canine Thyroid Epidemic*.

Avoid these dietary ingredients

Dogs prone to seizures should not eat the following:

Foods that promote inflammation. Inflammation affects every organ in the body, including the brain, so it probably comes as no surprise that inflammation can cause seizures. Dogs prone to seizures should not consume any potentially inflammatory ingredients, including foods that trigger allergies or intolerances/sensitivities, such as chemical additives, wheat, corn, soy, beef or cow's milk products—but remember that it can also include any food that causes a problem for your individual dog. If your dog has seizures, we advise testing him with NutriScan to identify any problematic ingredients. In particular, never give products containing gluten to dogs with seizures, since gluten is specifically linked with neurological disorders, including epilepsy (Hyman, 2013).

Foods that cause fluctuations in blood sugar. Sugars can disrupt the body's equilibrium or homeostasis, possibly leading to seizures (Wilson, 2013). Avoid giving your dog the sugary, hi-glycemic carbohydrates we've been talking about throughout the book.

Foods containing glutamate and aspartate. Glutamate and aspartate are two very excitatory non-essential amino acids (Stafstrom, 2004; Wilson, 2013). Foods high in these amino acids include: grains, especially wheat, barley and oats; all cow's milk products (opt instead for goat's milk, which is much lower); beans, especially soy, pinto, lima, black, navy and lentils; nuts, especially peanuts, cashews and pistachios; seeds, including sunflower and pumpkin; any food sweetened with aspartame, such as NutraSweet and Equal; rabbit; turkey; and monosodium glutamate (MSG), a glutamine salt. MSG is used in many prepared foods and can appear on pet food labels under a number of pseudonyms, including "hydrolyzed vegetable protein," "soy protein extract" and "textured vegetable protein" (Wilson, 2013).

Rosemary and oregano. Rosemary is commonly added as an antioxidant and anti-inflammatory to commercial pet foods. While it's likely fine for most dogs, it is a neurotoxin that can promote seizures in vulnerable dogs. Oregano is also a powerful neurotoxin and should not be fed to epileptics.

Vitamin/mineral deficiencies and seizures

Many vitamins and minerals are important for normal functioning of the nervous system. Deficiencies in the minerals calcium, magnesium and sodium, for example, can affect electrical activity of brain cells and result in seizures (Schachter, 2006). Calcium and magnesium, as well as zinc, are also referred to as sedative minerals because they are calming for the nervous system (Wilson, 2013). Antioxidant vitamins (A, C and E) help boost the immune system and fight inflammation.

Perhaps the most important vitamins to protect against seizures are the B vitamins, as we'll discuss next.

DNA Methylation: an explanation for the "kindling" effect?

A minute ago you read about kindling, whereby the more seizures an individual has, the more he will tend to have. Recently, scientists have uncovered a possible reason for this phenomenon; not surprisingly, it lies in epigenetics.

We've already discussed the important epigenetic role of DNA methylation on gene expression; now, scientists are recognizing that DNA methylation also regulates processes that lead to neurologic disorders. A recent "methylation hypothesis" suggests that seizures themselves induce epigenetic modification of **chromatin** (the combination of DNA and proteins that make up the contents of a cell's nucleus) in a manner that aggravates an existing epileptic condition (Kobow, 2011). This means that, quite literally, seizures "teach" cells how to have more seizures and that we can interrupt this genomic "lesson" by reducing the frequency of attacks. This hypothesis certainly provides a plausible explanation for the kindling effect since, as we know, everything that happens in our bodies originates at the cellular level.

Since vitamin B-12 and folate promote optimum functioning of the methylation cycle, deficiencies can lead to seizures. Deficiency in biotin, another B-vitamin that modulates chromatin regulation, can also cause epilepsy. In people, a rare inherited form of seizures known as pyridoxine-dependent epilepsy results from mutations in the *ALDH7A1* gene, which leads to impairment of normal vitamin B-6 function. Pyridoxine is involved in the breakdown of amino acids and the production neurotransmitters, chemicals that transmit signals in the brain. Pyridoxine-dependent epilepsy does not respond to traditional medical therapy and is treated with high daily doses of pyroxidine (National Library of Medicine, 2013).

Consuming a diet rich in B vitamins may help lower the susceptibility to seizures through their epigenetic ability to regulate gene expression (Foti & Roskams, 2011).

Omega-3 fatty acids: too important to ignore

Research on the effects of *omega-3 fatty acids* and epilepsy are still in the early stages, however we believe that this important nutrient makes perfect sense to help combat seizures. *Omega-3s* contain potent anti-inflammatory properties, and inflammatory mediators are increased in epileptic patients. *Omega-3s* also increase seizure thresholds, promote optimal brain development and modulate neuronal excitability (Stafstrom, 2004; Yuen et al., 2005).

Ketogenic diet: proven effective for people, but not for dogs

A ketogenic diet contains high amounts of fat, low carbohydrates and moderate protein. Under normal circumstances, glucose broken down from carbohydrates is the primary form of dietary energy. By severely limiting carbohydrates (and thus glucose), the ketogenic diet mimics a constant state of starvation, forcing the body to burn fat for energy. The diet gets its name because the fat is converted to ketones that are utilized as energy in place of carbohydrates. Ketogenic diets are often used in people who do not respond to seizure medications, especially children. While it's uncertain why they work, about two-thirds of people on a ketogenic diet show significant improvement. But the diet can cause serious health problems, including GI tract upset, hyperlipidemia, renal calculi, stunted growth and pancreatitis (Carr, 2013). Ketogenic diets have never been proven effective—or safe—in dogs (Thomas, 2011.)

In a 2005 study, researchers compared the effects of a ketogenic diet containing 57% crude fat, 5.8% NFE (carbohydrates) and 28% crude protein to a control diet containing 16% crude fat, 25% crude protein and 54% NFE (carbohydrates) in dogs diagnosed with idiopathic seizures. The objective of the study was to determine if the ketogenic diet resulted in a significant reduction in seizure frequency. The dogs were all receiving phenobarbital and/or potassium bromide and had experienced at least three seizures in the three months prior to the study. All of the dogs were fed the control diet for a monitoring period of three to six months while their seizure frequency was established. Dogs who had suffered five or more seizures during that time were randomly divided into two groups; one group continued to receive the control diet, while the other group received the ketogenic diet. The dogs were evaluated at 0, 0.5, three and six months. Of the 12 dogs who completed the trial, there was no difference in seizure frequency between the group fed the ketogenic diet and the control diet (Carr, 2013; Coates, 2013).

The fact that dogs can naturally tolerate longer periods without eating likely accounts for their lack of response to the ketogenic diet. A high fight/low carbohydrate diet apparently just does not create the same biochemical changes in our canine companions as it does in people (Coates, 2013).

Moreover, ketogenic diets may create adverse health effects in dogs. Pancreatitis, or inflammation of the pancreas, is a serious condition that often results from an excess of dietary fat. Due to a lack of proven efficacy and safety, we do not recommend a ketogenic diet for dogs with seizures.

Could your dog's seizures originate in his gut?

You're now aware of the importance of gut health and that a compromised GI system can lead to a whole host of medical conditions. But did you know that imbalances in intestinal flora can also produce seizures? The condition is known as "abdominal epilepsy," and it occurs due to the gut-brain connection. Abdominal epilepsy occurs when an unhealthy microbial environment in the gut creates toxins that cross into the brain. In addition, sections of the intestine known as Peyer's Patches—where the gut connects with the lymphatic system—are closely associated with nerve bundles and fibers directly connected with the brain, so intestinal irritation may result in seizures via this pathway. Many veterinarians misdiagnose—and thus mistreat—this type of seizure because rather than looking in the gut, they only look at the patient "from the neck up." If your dog suffers from seizures in combination with ulcerative colitis, manic itching or GI trouble (e.g., constipation and/or diarrhea) he may have abdominal epilepsy.

Gelatin: a friend to your dog's brain

Gelatin, a potent anti-inflammatory and brain protective food, is an important supplement for dogs with epilepsy (as well as those with arthritis and hip dysplasia). The primary amino acid in gelatin is glycine, which is known to protect against seizures and brain damage (Canine Epilepsy Guardian Angels, 2011).

You can incorporate plain, unflavored gelatin into your dog's diet in many ways. Try sprinkling it on his food or making treats out of it. However, *never* use Jell-O or other gelatins intended for dessert, as they contain sweeteners (either sugar or artificial) that can potentially worsen the seizure condition (and don't forget that the artificial sweetener Xylitol is toxic to dogs).

Dose: (give twice a day, added to food)

- 10 to 25 lbs: 1 ½ tsp (teaspoons)
- 25 to 50 lbs: 3 tsp
- 50 to 75 lbs: 6 tsp
- 75 to 100 or more: 3 tablespoons

Gelatin dog treats

This simple recipe for gelatin treats is provided courtesy of Joanne Carson, PhD, founder of The Epi Guardian Angels. They are like Gummy Bears for dogs!

Ingredients

- ½ cup of unflavored gelatin

- ½ cup of cold, flavored liquid (such as broth)
- 1 ½ cup of boiling liquid (either water or broth)

Put ½ cup of gelatin in a 1-quart bowl. Add ½ cup of the cold liquid and let stand one minute to soften. Pour 1 ½ cups of boiling liquid (water or broth) over the softened gelatin, and stir until the gelatin completely dissolves (about five minutes or less). For chewier treats, add more gelatin. Pour the mixture into a 9 x 12 pan and let harden. Cut into 1" by 3" strips or an appropriate size for your dog. Watch him enjoy his healthy treats!

It's estimated that 20% of dogs on phenobarbitol anti-seizure medication develop liver damage (Canine Epilepsy Guardian Angels, 2011). If your dog takes phenobarbital, we advise that you follow the suggestions provided in the liver disease section (above), such as adding **milk thistle** to his diet.

For a wealth of excellent information on canine epilepsy, including detailed commentary by the author, WJD, please visit Canine Epilepsy Guardian Angels at http://www.canine-epilepsy-guardian-angels.com.

Success!

Coal and corn do not mix

Coal, a two-year-old female black Labrador Retriever, experienced seizures every other month. Hoping to avoid treating her with anti-seizure medication, Coal's guardians weaned her over to a prepared raw diet with lamb as the meat source. After discussing the options, an anti-inflammatory diet was chosen as the primary treatment. Coal was also treated with Western herbs (lime blossom, valerian and chamomile) as well as **coconut oil**. The seizures stopped. Six months later, however, Coal experienced another seizure after finding some taco shells in the garbage (made from corn). She had yet another seizure one month later, which her guardians attributed to eating leftover popcorn from a slumber party. Three months later, Coal had another seizure and her guardians remembered that she had licked several plates clean after a dinner that included corn-battered meat and frozen corn. Over the next four years, Coal had only three seizures—all of which were connected to an episode of eating corn! She never required anti-seizure medication.

Thyroid disease (hypothyroidism)

As we brought to light in our book, *The Canine Thyroid Epidemic*, canine thyroid disorder has reached epidemic proportions. Since many veterinarians don't understand how to properly diagnose and treat it, dogs are suffering needlessly from a variety of physical and behavioral symptoms related to this common—and easily manageable—condition. Millions of dogs are surrendered to shelters each year, and even euthanized, due to abnormal behavior. Sadly, many of these falsely labeled "bad dogs" suffer from a simple, easily treatable medical condition.

The thyroid gland is part of the endocrine system, the collection of glands that produces all of the body's hormones. The thyroid gland is located in the upper third of the neck. It is shaped roughly like a butterfly and is about the size of a lima bean (this varies depending on the size of the dog). The thyroid gland produces thyroxine (T4) and triiodothyronine (T3), hormones that control virtually every metabolic and cellular function, including body temperature, resting metabolic rate, heart and respiratory rate and organ and tissue functions.

About 90% of the time, thyroid disorder in dogs manifests as **hypothyroidism** (low thyroid function), as opposed to **hyperthyroidism** (overactive thyroid, which is common in cats). Hypothyroidism occurs when the thyroid gland becomes diseased or destroyed and cannot secret enough thyroxine (T4). Symptoms of hypothyroidism can also occur when the liver fails to properly convert T4 into T3, creating a hormone deficiency in the tissues.

Hypothyroidism in dogs can result in disruption to a variety of critical systems causing many symptoms, including:

- Abnormal behavior: (fear, aggression, anxiety, irritability).
- Blood disorders: (bleeding, anemia, bone marrow failure).
- Cardiac abnormalities: (slow heart rate, cardiac arrhythmia, cardiomyopathy).
- Eye disorders: (corneal lipid deposits, corneal ulceration, dry eye).
- Gastrointestinal and liver disorder: (constipation, diarrhea, vomiting).
- Listlessness, fatigue or just "ain't doing right."
- Metabolic changes: (lethargy, weight gain, mental dullness, cold intolerance, exercise intolerance, mood swings, chronic infections, seizures).
- Neuromuscular (nerve/muscle) problems: (weakness, stiffness, facial paralysis, head tilt, incontinence, drooping eyelids).
- Reproductive disorders: (infertility, absence of heat cycles, silent heats, testicular atrophy).
- Skin diseases: (dry, scaly skin and dandruff, chronic offensive skin odor, hyperpigmentation, rat tail, puppy coat, pyoderma).
- Unexplained weight gain.

Genetic predisposition is the greatest risk factor for thyroid disorder in dogs. About 80% of canine hypothyroidism results from an inherited condition known as autoimmune thyroiditis, in which the body's disease-fighting T-lymphocytes are genetically programmed to destroy its own thyroid gland.

Foods that inhibit thyroid hormone production

Certain foods contain naturally occurring substances that can interfere with the thyroid gland's production of hormone. These substances are called **goitrogens**, which comes from the term **goiter** (an enlargement of the thyroid gland). The most goitrogenic foods are:

Cruciferous vegetables. While we love the many health benefits of cruciferous vegetables, hypothyroid dogs should not eat them because they are rich in naturally occurring compounds called isothiocyanates. These compounds, like the isoflavones in soy, reduce thyroid function by blocking the activity of thyroid peroxidase (TPO), an important thyroid enzyme that helps convert T4 to T3 (Cerundolo et al., 2009).

If your dog suffers from a thyroid problem, avoid feeding him the following vegetables:

- Broccoli
- Brussels Sprouts
- Cabbage
- Casaba
- Cauliflower
- Kale
- Kohlrabi
- Mustard
- Rutabagas
- Radishes
- Turnips

Millet is an ancient grain that has been cultivated for thousands of years. It is a good source of key nutrients such a manganese, phosphorous, tryptophan and magnesium and is rich in insoluble fiber. In dog food, millet is often included in foods traditionally touted as "grain-free," since it is considered a healthier alternative to wheat. Hypothyroid dogs should indulge sparingly in millet, since the hulls and seeds contain small amounts of goitrogens.

Soy. The isoflavones in soy inhibit the effects of thyroid peroxidase, disrupting normal thyroid function (Cerundolo et al., 2009). The prevalence of soy as a source of non-animal based protein in many dog foods helps to explain the increasing incidences of canine hypothyroidism.

Dietary iodine modifies soy's effect on the thyroid gland: a deficiency in iodine increases soy's goitrogenic effects, while iodine supplementation (e.g., kelp in modest amounts) is protective. However, the iodine concentration in today's commercial pet foods is three to five times the stated minimum requirement, which causes more problems because excess iodine is associated with hypothyroidism and autoimmune thyroiditis in dogs (and *hyper*thyroidism in cats).

Gluten is strongly linked to autoimmune thyroiditis

You already know about the relationship between gluten and autoimmune diseases, and autoimmune thyroiditis is no different. Several studies show a strong link between autoimmune thyroiditis in people (both Hashimoto's and Graves' diseases) and gluten intolerance. In fact, researchers suggest that all people with Hashimoto's and Graves' diseases be screened for gluten intolerance, and *vice versa*. Similarly, dogs with IBD should be screened for thyroid dysfunction, and those with thyroid dysfunction should be screened for IBD. This illustrates just how important the connection is between the two conditions.

What explains the connection? It's a case of mistaken identity. The molecular structure of gliadin (which, as you'll recall, is a protein found in gluten) closely resembles that of the thyroid gland. As we already discussed, when gliadin crosses through a compromised gut barrier and enters the bloodstream, the immune system views it as a foreign invader and tags it for destruction. The antibodies to gliadin also cause the body to attack its own thyroid tissue. If your dog has autoimmune thyroid disease and eat foods containing gluten, his immune system will attack the thyroid gland, causing progressive damage leading to clinical signs of hypothyroidism.

This immune response can last up to *six months* each time your dog eats gluten. So, if your dog is gluten intolerant, his diet must be totally gluten-free to prevent immune destruction of the thyroid gland. For this reason, we highly suggest testing your dog with NutriScan to determine whether he suffers from gluten intolerance.

Thyroid boosting nutrients

The following nutrients play an important role in maintaining optimal thyroid function:

Iodine is vital to normal thyroid function, since it is essential to the production of thyroid hormone. Given this, it's understandable that many dog parents supplement the diets of their hypothyroid canines with kelp and other foods rich in iodine in an attempt to help boost the thyroid gland. However, iodine supplementation is extremely tricky, and giving too much can prove harmful. An excess of iodine can negatively affect your dog's thyroid medication, leading to a worsening of the very hypothyroidism that you are trying to treat.

Whether or not you should supplement with iodine depends largely upon your dog's diet. Follow these guidelines to ensure that you do not "overdose" your dog on iodine:

- If you feed your dog cereal-based kibble, do not supplement with sea kelp or other forms of iodine more·than three times per week. These foods are already fortified with high doses of iodine.

- If you feed your dog a home cooked or raw diet, you can supplement with iodine every day, taking care to follow the product guidelines.

Selenium. A link has recently been shown between selenium deficiency and hypo-thyroidism. Selenium as it relates to hypothyroidism is often difficult to spot because blood, but not tissue, levels of thyroid hormones rise in cases of selenium deficiency. This means that although a selenium deficient dog may display clinical signs of hypothyroidism, his blood thyroid levels will appear normal. Synthetic antioxidants still used to preserve some dog foods can impair the bioavailability of selenium (as well as vitamins A and E). To help prevent selenium deficiency, feed a diet preserved naturally with vitamins E and C rather than with synthetic chemical antioxidants. As we mentioned earlier, selenium is the most toxic mineral and is only required in very low doses.

See Chapter 4 for dosing.

Zinc is critical to the function of the entire immune system and plays a key role in more than 300 enzymatic and metabolic processes, including cell replication and the production of thyroid hormones.

See Chapter 4 for dosing.

Success!
Dietary changes promote a healthy thyroid
Bounty, a five-year-old intact male American Cocker Spaniel, was diagnosed with chronic skin disease, infertility and poor coat quality. After more than two years of steroid and antibiotic therapy, which provided only temporary relief of his skin and coat condition, Bounty was diagnosed with thyroid dysfunction due to an underlying heritable autoimmune thyroiditis (common in American Cocker Spaniels). In an attempt to address the thyroid and skin conditions, he was mistakenly prescribed a soy-based veterinary diet with additional daily kelp supplementation (remember that soy is a goitrogen, which can aggravate thyroid disorders). While Bounty's skin and coat improved rapidly, the improvement only lasted about four months; after that time, the original problems returned and his skin became dry and scaly. During this period, his testicles also became shrunken and he produced little sperm (not that he should ever be used for breeding, given his heritable thyroid condition!). He was placed on thyroid medication given twice daily.

Bounty's case was then referred to the author, WJD, who fortified the underlying nutritional imbalance created by the soy-based diet with extra iodine. His diet was then switched to a grain-free whitefish and potato diet without kelp supplement, while the thyroid medication was continued. Bounty responded dramatically: even his testicles regained their normal mass. His sperm production returned after another six months, at which time he was neutered. Bounty now remains healthy eating a dehydrated raw diet consisting of alternating animal protein sources.

Epigenetics and chronic disease: you have the power to optimize your dog's health

When a beloved dog suffers from a serious health condition, we don't want to sit idly by on the sidelines; we want to get in the game and help. The good news is that now you can. Maybe right now you feel confused and helpless—especially if conventional medical therapies have failed to achieve satisfactory results and trusted professionals seem to have run out of answers. But just because the "experts" don't have the answers, doesn't mean those answers don't exist. All too often, authorities are unwilling to acknowledge the possibility that solutions exist outside of their knowledge base. Fortunately, you no longer have to accept that limited mind-set.

You now know that you have more influence over your dog's health than you ever imagined—even when it comes to the most serious conditions. The epigenome plays a powerful role in regulating gene expression, and it is highly responsive to environmental messages, such as diet. Moreover, cells are remarkable machines, capable of an astounding ability to repair, regenerate and renew (Lavebratt, Almgrem & Ekström, 2012). By applying the information you've read in Part III to your dog's individual health concerns, you can support his cells in their quest to achieve optimum physiological balance.

Please don't give up hope on your canine buddy. Just because he is battling an illness today, doesn't mean he can't shine with optimal health soon.

Takeaway Points

- Even though dogs typically suffer from Type 1 diabetes, which stems from a problem with insulin production rather than insulin resistance, diabetes in dogs is still an adult onset disease that can be influenced by diet and lifestyle.

- The two leading lifestyle causes of diabetes are obesity and consumption of high-GI carbohydrates.

- You can make a significant impact on your diabetic dog's health simply by getting him lean and cutting back on his intake of unhealthy carbohydrates.

- DNA methylation is a potentially important risk factor for Type 1 diabetes, so it's important to feed your dog foods that promote optimum DNA methylation, such as **curcumin** and foods rich in folate.

- Chronic kidney disease, or CKD, is a progressive condition involving long-term damage to the kidneys over a few months to several years. CKD is one of the leading causes of death in dogs.

- Early diagnosis of CKD is essential, since it is both permanent and progressive; if left unmanaged, it can become a silent killer.

- Obesity is a risk factor for CKD independent of the fact that obesity leads to diabetes and hypertension, both of which are major contributors to kidney disease. Researchers are still studying the exact method by which obesity leads to CKD.

- Kibble can stress a dog's kidneys because it contains only about 6% to 10% moisture, versus 70% or more moisture in fresh meats. This means that a dog's body must use a significant amount of water just to move kibble through his GI tract during digestion. Dry foods are also typically high in carbohydrates, which can cause inflammation in the kidneys.

- We typically advise against dry kidney diets, which are low in moisture and high in carbohydrates, since they can actually aggravate the problem by contributing to dehydration while simultaneously adding too many carbohydrates.

- Kidney sparing diets should *not* be low in protein, except for dogs in moderate to severe kidney failure, where excessive protein creates toxic nitrogen-based by-products that damaged kidneys cannot filter.

- **Omega-3 fatty acids** from marine sources such as fish oil are beneficial in supporting kidney health and managing kidney problems.

- Inflammatory Bowel Disease (IBD) is one more example of how a leaky gut can wreak havoc on the GI tract. Fortunately, nutritional modification can manage and even reverse signs of IBD.

- It's especially important for dogs with IBD to eat as pure and "clean" a diet as possible. Be sure to refer back to earlier chapters and remove any potentially reactive ingredients, such as foods containing chemical preservatives, flavors and colors, as well as the most commonly antigenic foods (beef, corn, cow's milk, eggs, soy, wheat and other gluten-containing foods).

- The ideal diet for dogs with IBD is: highly digestible; gluten-free; hypoallergenic; lactose free; and low fat.

- Prebiotics are non-digestible food ingredients that selectively stimulate the growth and/or activity of one or more strains of beneficial bacteria in the large intestines, thereby benefiting the host.

- Both prebiotics and *probiotics* support healthy gut microflora and are beneficial for dogs with IBD.

- *Omega-3 fatty acids* support a healthy digestive tract by reducing inflammation.

- According to the American Veterinary Medical Association, one in 10 dogs suffers from some form of heart disease.

- Canine heart disease refers to a number of acquired conditions involving dysfunction of the heart. Nutritional therapies can benefit many of these conditions, including slowing the progression of the disease, minimizing prescription medications, improving quality of life and, in some instances, even curing the condition.

- Some of the most well researched nutrients to benefit your dog's heart health include: coenzyme Q10 (CoQ10); L-carnitine; magnesium; *omega-3 fatty acids*; taurine; and vitamin E.

- Dogs with heart disease also require sufficient amounts of calories and protein to manage cardiac cachexia.

- The liver is a complex organ involved in almost every biochemical process that is essential to life. Consequently, when it becomes diseased and can't function properly, serious problems can result.

- Fortunately, the liver has an amazing capacity to regenerate itself.

- Unless liver damage results from an identified toxin that can be treated or a condition in which surgery is warranted, conventional therapy is often limited. Complementary therapies, such as dietary modification and the addition of functional nutrients, can be your most important ally in optimizing the health of your dog's liver.

- Steps to promote a healthy liver include: eliminate food and environmental toxins; never give your dog vitamin K3; and keep your dog trim to avoid obesity-related risk factors.

- Functional nutrients for liver disease include: *milk thistle*, n-acetylcysteine, SAMe, *spirulina* and branched chain amino acids.

- While raw meat diets benefit many dogs, they are not recommended for dogs with liver disease due to possible bacterial contamination and high levels of aromatic amino acids. Instead, a diet rich in protein derived from dairy products (preferably from goat and sheep sources), containing predominantly branched chain amino acids, is recommended over meat-based sources.

- Dogs with liver disease should eat a fresh, wholesome diet packed with easily digestible, anti-inflammatory nutrients that nourish the liver cells, promote detoxification and support health and healing.

- Avoid commercial diets, which often contain poor quality proteins of low bioavailability and may also contain ingredients that will further damage an already struggling liver.

- If your dog suffers from seizures, minimizing the total number of seizures and decreasing their frequency is critical, since it's theorized that every time the brain has a seizure, it "learns" how to have the next seizure. This phenomenon is called "kindling."

- To reduce the severity and frequency of your dog's seizures: eliminate environmental toxins such as unnecessary vaccines and spot-on flea and tick treatments; check your dog for hypothyroidism; avoid foods that promote inflammation, especially gluten; avoid sugary foods as well as foods containing the non-essential amino acids glutamate and aspartate and the herbs rosemary and oregano; check for vitamin/mineral deficiencies; and supplement with B vitamins and *omega-3 fatty acids*.

- While ketogenic diets (those containing high amounts of fat, low carbohydrates and moderate protein) are proven effective for epileptic people (especially children), the same results have not been demonstrated in dogs. In addition, ketogenic diets are risky for dogs, as they may lead to pancreatitis due to the high fat content.

- We do not recommend ketogenic diets as a form of treatment for canine seizures.

- A condition known as "abdominal epilepsy" occurs when imbalances in intestinal flora result in seizures. If your dog suffers from seizures in combination with ulcerative colitis, manic itching or GI trouble (e.g., constipation and/or diarrhea), he may have abdominal epilepsy.

- Gelatin is an important supplement for dogs with epilepsy. The primary amino acid in gelatin is glycine, which is known to protect against seizures and brain damage.

- Hypothyroidism in dogs has reached epidemic proportions.

- Hypothyroidism occurs when the thyroid gland becomes diseased or destroyed and cannot secret enough thyroxine (T4). Symptoms of hypothyroidism can also occur when the liver fails to properly convert T4 into T3, creating a hormone deficiency in the tissues.

- Genetic predisposition is the greatest risk factor for thyroid disorder in dogs. About 80% of canine hypothyroidism results from an inherited condition known as autoimmune thyroiditis, in which the body's disease-fighting T-lymphocytes are genetically programmed to destroy its own thyroid gland.

- Certain foods contain naturally occurring substances that can interfere with the thyroid gland's production of hormone. These substances are called goitrogens, which comes from the term goiter (an enlargement of the thyroid gland). The most goitrogenic foods are: cruciferous vegetables; millet; soy; and gluten.

- Nutrients that help optimize function of the thyroid gland include iodine (when appropriate), selenium and zinc.

Part IV

Living the
Nutrigenomics Lifestyle

Chapter 12

Getting Real with Your Dog's Food

As we noted in the Introduction, this book is not an all-or-nothing, take-it-or-leave-it instruction manual. In an ideal world, we would all have the time and resources to create delectable and functional meals for our dogs, day-in and day-out. But in today's hectic society, many of us barely have the time to prepare wholesome meals for ourselves! Not to worry. In this chapter, you'll learn how to significantly improve the health benefits of your dog's diet, regardless of whether that diet is based on kibble, home prepared meals or anything in between.

While we'll rate the major types of canine diets according to how they *generally* stack up to the principles of nutrigenomics, please bear in mind that there are a wide range of qualities available within each category. For example, while canned food is typically healthier than kibble (we'll tell you why in a moment), you can certainly purchase a high quality kibble (e.g., free of grains, by-products and chemical preservatives) that is more in keeping with a functional diet than a poor quality wet food. Moreover, even though we rate raw diets as most beneficial, we don't recommend that you purchase a commercial raw diet from an inexperienced small producer with little to no knowledge of dog food formulation or adherence to raw sanitation protocols.

We would also like you to know that it's okay if you can't feed your dog an optimum diet every day. We'd like to be able to say that we eat only healthy, functional foods, but the reality is that's not the case. As we stressed in Chapter 4, it isn't necessary to balance every single meal or to serve your dog only meals teeming with functional ingredients. It's about doing your best and coming out ahead in the long run. For example, you might be able to prepare your dog's meals a few times a week, but on the other days your schedule necessitates that you have a quicker option on hand. No problem!

Perhaps feeding your dog kibble is the most logical choice for your situation. Please don't stress about that, either. The bottom line is that even small dietary changes can translate into huge health benefits. Simply opting for a more nutrigenomics-friendly kibble can eliminate food intolerances/sensitivities, remove harmful chemicals from your dog's diet and reduce the assault on his GI and immune systems. Toss in some functional foods and suddenly you have dramatically improved the dietary messages to his epigenome—while still feeding the same category of food.

Let's take a look at the most popular canine diets—raw, homemade, kibble, canned, dehydrated and freeze-dried—and discuss how you can optimize each for optimal gene expression benefits.

Raw diets

Have you ever wondered why the topic of raw diets generates such passionate opinions, regardless of which side people are on? Maybe it's because so many well-intentioned mainstream veterinarians are vehemently opposed to feeding raw. These professionals have been warned against raw diets since veterinary school by—guess who?—nutrition spokespeople who represent large commercial pet food producers! Suitably fearful, they pass this fear along to their clients. Some of these veterinarians even refuse to treat dogs who consume raw meats. While these practitioners no doubt mean well, they likely haven't considered that the companies propagating this fear typically don't produce raw diets; they are the same pet food companies with bags and cans of food stacked ready for sale on veterinary clinic shelves (including, likely, their own).

Because of the controversy surrounding feeding raw, it's important for consumers to have the facts, rather than rely on hype or misinformation, before making a decision (Olson, 2010). The following information on raw diets is adapted from our book, *The Canine Thyroid Epidemic*:

Some like it raw

A raw canine diet consists of animal meat, organ meats (such as the liver, kidney and heart), some bone, and small amounts of vegetation given in their raw, uncooked state. A major advantage of raw food is that the nutrients—such as amino acids, vitamins, minerals, prebiotics, probiotics, and enzymes—have not been altered or destroyed by the heat of cooking. Keeping the food in its whole, "pristine" form also makes it much more readily bioavailable, providing our pets with more easily assimilated nutrition per serving than processed foods.

Raw food may also pose much less risk of allergic reaction than its cooked counterparts. In saliva studies of allergic people, researchers found that there was a five times greater allergenic reaction to the exact same food when eaten processed versus in its raw, unaltered form (Vojdani, 2009). This makes sense, since cooking food breaks down its cellular integrity and exposes **neo-antigens** (new antigens) that were not there in the original raw form.

If we extrapolate these findings to our canine companions, we can surmise that commercially prepared kibble or canned foods—both of which are cooked at high temperatures—may also be exposing neo-antigens created through the heating process. While still nutritious, these foods could pose a higher risk of a dietary intolerance or immune reaction, especially for animals with already compromised immune systems.

Many people are afraid to feed their pets a raw diet, which is understandable considering the mixed information available on raw food. Even the majority of traditional veterinarians still warn their clients against feeding raw, citing concerns that their patients will become ill from possible bacteria and parasites in raw meats. This fear, although well meaning, does not take into account the physiological differences between people and dogs, which make them far less prone to illness resulting from contamination. There are several reasons why dogs tolerate raw meats far better than people do, including:

- Dogs have shorter digestive tracts than humans. This lessens the potential of parasites or bacteria causing problems as food passes through.

- The stomach acid of dogs on raw diets is very low, generally between a pH of 1 and 2. These strong acids, which are necessary to break down the proteins in the raw meats, make it much less likely that bacteria will survive in a healthy dog's gut than in a human's, which operates with a stomach pH of around 5.

- Veterinarians do not take into account that salmonella occurs naturally in the digestive tracts of many dogs, regardless of their diet. Even so, these dogs do not become sick.

In addition, freezing meats for at least three weeks kills most parasites. This is a benefit of feeding a frozen prepared raw diet, since these diets are properly frozen to ensure the elimination of parasites. Those buying fresh meat can simply freeze it themselves before feeding it to their dogs.

If you're feeding your dog a raw diet, remember to follow all of the same common sense precautions you would use when cooking raw meat for yourself or your family. This includes thoroughly washing your hands as well as all surfaces, plates and utensils that come into contact with the raw meat.

Although raw meats, when properly handled and fed, have numerous health benefits for our canine companions, dogs should never be fed raw fish. Fish from certain areas can contain parasitic cysts or **flukes** (flat worm parasites), particularly around the liver. If a dog ingests fish infested with these parasites, he can become very ill. Home freezers typically do not reach temperatures low enough to kill the parasites in fish. And since the origin of fish is often questionable, it is best to avoid feeding any raw fish to your pet.

The good news is that you don't need a degree in canine nutrition to successfully feed your dog a raw diet. Today there are many reputable commercial producers of prepared raw diets. These come packaged in a variety of forms to suite any preference—from frozen patties to nuggets and chubs—and they already contain the proper balance of meats, vegetables, herbs, vitamins and minerals. All you have to do is remember to defrost your dog's daily portion in the refrigerator and he will be all set with a nutritionally balanced raw meal.

Some reputable producers of commercial raw canine diets include:

- Answers Pet Food
- Aunt Jeni's
- Bravo
- Darwin's Natural
- Fresh is Best
- Nature's Menu
- Nature's Variety
- Oma's Pride
- Pepperdogz
- Primal
- Raw Advantage
- Stella and Chewy's
- Steve's Real Food
- Vital Essentials

If you choose to formulate your dog's raw diet yourself rather than purchasing from a commercial source, we suggest that you work with a credentialed canine nutritionist or holistic veterinarian to ensure that your dog receives the proper balance of nutrients properly tailored for his individual needs.

It's also important to understand that the "normal" values for some of the standard diagnostic lab tests do not apply to raw-fed dogs. Studies by author WJD and Dr. Susan Wynn found that dogs fed raw meats have higher red blood cell and blood urea nitrogen (BUN) levels than dogs fed cereal-based food. The dogs fed raw meats also showed statistically higher hemoglobin, MCH, MCV, MCHC, total protein, albumin, BUN/creatinine ratio, sodium, osmolality and magnesium. These same dogs displayed lower values for total leukocyte, neutrophil and lymphocyte counts, as well as phosphorous and glucose.

Many veterinarians, however, do not understand the normal variation of lab tests for raw-fed dogs and misinterpret the findings to mean that the dog is ill. Practitioners have been known to send dog guardians into a panic by warning them that a raw diet is destroying their dog's kidneys, because the BUN is 35 and the normal range ends at 30. The poor person, who doesn't understand that dogs fed raw diets exhibit naturally higher BUN levels, thinks that she is killing her beloved companion! The lesson here is that laboratories have developed their normal ranges based on dogs fed cereal grain foods. The normal ranges for many of these tests simply do not apply for healthy dogs fed raw diets, and the interpretation of laboratory results for these dogs should take these differences into account.

Although raw diets represent the most nutritionally bio-available and natural diet for dogs, there are times when dogs should not be fed raw animal proteins. Dogs with bowel problems such as gastroenteritis, which might include bouts of vomiting, diarrhea, constipation or all of the above, should not be fed a raw diet during flare-ups. When the bowel is not moving at its normal rate, there is increased risk for bacteria present in raw meat to incubate and multiply in the bowel pockets and then to enter the bile duct and damage the liver. This is very serious and can be fatal. As long as the raw food does not contain bones, you can lightly cook it during times of illness (never cook the bones as they can become brittle and splinter, causing a choking hazard). Once your dog recovers, simply transition him back to his raw diet. Alternately, you can keep a high quality grain-free kibble or canned food on hand for these times.

As you can see, raw diets adhere to the principles of nutrigenomics for several reasons:

- The nutrients in raw foods are generally more bioavailable than in cooked foods. A 2012 study found that the digestibility of raw meat is far greater than the typical digestibility of kibble (Beloshapka et al., 2012). The digestibility of a food is critical, since even the most nutritious food can't send positive messages to the cells if the body can't efficiently absorb its nutrients.

- Raw foods contain high quality amino acids.

- Raw foods are typically free of chemical additives (be sure to seek out a high quality manufacturer to ensure this).

- Research shows that the risk of allergenic reactions to raw foods is far less than to processed foods (Vojdani, 2009). No matter how nutritionally sound a food appears, if it triggers an allergic reaction or other type of immune response, it won't create optimum cellular health and gene expression.

The raw food controversy continues

In summer 2012, the American Veterinary Medical Association (AVMA) and the American Animal Hospital Association (AAHA) passed position statements opposing feeding dogs and cats raw protein diets that have not first undergone a process to eliminate pathogens, such as cooking, pasteurization or irradiation. Prior to this time, neither organization had taken an official position on the matter.

The AVMA and AAHA cited scientific evidence that raw meats, poultry, fish, eggs and dairy might contain harmful pathogenic organisms, including *Salmonella spp., Campylobacter spp., Clostridium spp., Escherichia coli, Listeria monocytogenes* and *enterotoxigenic Staphylococcus aureus.*

The AVMA and AAHA's primary concern is the potential for raw-fed dogs to shed (excrete) pathogens such as *Salmonella* in their feces. These organizations reason that if pathogens are shed into the environment, such as homes, parks and other public places, it's possible for people to encounter them and become ill.

But these organizations fail to recognize that *Salmonella is a fact of life in dogs' digestive tracts—as is the potential for Salmonella shedding—whether or not they are fed raw protein diets.* A 1975 study published by Morse and Duncan showed that more than 20% of dogs in any given population might be infected with *Salmonella.* And, the textbook *Small Animal Clinical Nutrition* (Hand et al., 2000), estimates that 36% of healthy dogs carry *Salmonella* in their intestinal tracts. *Both of these sources reflect numbers from kibble-fed animals, not dogs fed raw diets.*

A 2007 Canadian study showed that 30% of raw-fed dogs shed *Salmonella* at any given time. However, the 16 dogs in this study were fed raw meat *deliberately contaminated with Salmonella. Yet, none of the dogs became ill, despite eating the Salmonella-laced food.* Moreover, only seven of the dogs shed *Salmonella* in their feces (Finley et al., 2007).

Many respected holistic veterinarians, including the author, WJD, have witnessed first-hand the health and vigor of dogs and cats fed raw diets: these animals just "shine" in all respects. While these observations are shared by a growing number of animal health care professionals as well as experienced dog (and cat) fanciers, they could be considered as merely anecdotal. Perhaps so, but we consider them *experiential* findings based on years of observations by many dedicated professionals in the holistic veterinary field. We believe, therefore, that to criticize *all* raw diets on the basis that they are inherently harmful is misleading and conveys an inflexible message.

Some members of the veterinary community even believe that the FDA's Center for Veterinary Medicine, which regulates all pet foods, allows commercially produced raw foods to contain some level of *Salmonella. This is false.*

Whereas the United States Department of Agriculture (USDA) allows a certain threshold of *Salmonella* in meat sold for human consumption, *the FDA's Center for Veterinary Medicine mandates a zero-tolerance policy of Salmonella for all commercially produced pet foods, not just cooked products.*

And, as anyone who follows pet food recalls knows, commercially produced kibbled products and treats are sadly recalled on a regular basis due to contamination with *Salmonella*, as well as with *E. coli (Campylobacter* is also of concern).

Steps to eliminate pathogens in raw food

The largest producers of commercial raw pet foods, which at the time of this writing accounted for about 75% of all commercial raw pet food sold in the United States, incorporate what is termed a "kill-step" into their production process to eliminate pathogens while creating the least impact on the food's enzymes, proteins and other nutrients. One such method involves high pressure processing (HPP), which works by using intense pressure rather than heat to kill the pathogens including *E. coli, Salmonella* and *Listeria*. HPP also kills yeasts and molds.

Since HPP does not use heat, the nutritional integrity of the raw product remains intact, including its flavor, color and texture. Moreover, the finished product remains raw. HPP, therefore, creates a "pathogen-free" raw meat product.

The top raw food manufacturers also test each batch of food before releasing it into the marketplace, and the products must test negative for pathogens before they go out. Any raw food manufacturer that releases food with *Salmonella* in the product is not abiding by the FDA's regulatory guidelines.

That said, there are many mom and pop producers of commercial raw pet foods, and these companies may not abide by "safe raw" standards. So, prior to feeding your pet any raw food, be sure to contact the manufacturer and ask what steps they take to ensure your pet's food is free of *Salmonella* and other potentially dangerous pathogens.

What about the safety of home-prepared raw diets?

As we mentioned above, the USDA allows meat sold for human consumption to contain some pathogens. So, why don't people become ill from grocery store meat more often? The answer is likely because most people cook their meat, thereby killing the pathogens. However, when you feed this same meat to your dog in a raw state, no safeguard has been taken to ensure destruction of harmful organisms. If your dog is healthy, it's unlikely he will suffer any ill effects. However, the likelihood of human contact with potentially harmful pathogens may be increased compared with exposure from commercial raw diets manufactured using a pathogen kill step such as HPP. Dogs with compromised immune systems may also be at greater risk of experiencing illness related to food-borne pathogens from meat purchased at the grocery store.

The bottom line

At the time of this writing, the American Holistic Veterinary Medical Association (AHVMA) crafted the following statement regarding raw diets:

> *The feeding of a diet that includes raw meat is a complex subject, encompassing more than the possibility of bacterial contamination. Many have seen benefits in cats and dogs fed raw meat, and there is published research to support these observations. There is a need for personal considerations in any choice of feeding practices, including this one. Careful review and significant discussion need to occur among those who have seen the benefits of this practice as well as those who have cited the downside of including raw meat as part of the diet for companion animals, before making a blanket statement about any diet choice.*

As the AHVMA states, *published research supports the health benefits of a raw food diet for dogs.* For this reason, along with the many reasons discussed above, we believe that, when fed correctly, a raw diet offers dogs optimal nutrition aligned with the principles of nutrigenomics.

There are, as we previously discussed, common-sense precautions that should be exercised when feeding raw foods:

- Practice impeccable hygiene. Thoroughly wash your hands with hot, soapy water and disinfect all surfaces, plates, utensils, bowls and anything else that has come into contact with the raw meat.

- Never feed your dog raw meats (or any meats, for that matter) that are not fit for human consumption. If you wouldn't feel safe eating it, why should you give it to your dog?

- Never feed raw meats to dogs suffering from gastrointestinal disorders or liver disease.

- Never feed raw fish to dogs.

- Avoid feeding raw eggs, especially to very young, old or ill dogs. Raw egg whites contain enzyme inhibitors that can disrupt digestion and cause gastrointestinal upset.

- Avoid feeding raw foods in households with babies or young children who may be prone to touching contaminated surface areas.

- Never let any unfinished portion sit in your dog's bowl for longer than 10 to 15 minutes, as it will become a natural breeding ground for harmful organisms.

- Exercise extra caution in feeding raw foods in multiple-dog households, where feeding time may be messier.

Kibble/dry diets

Dry food, or kibble, represents the most highly processed form of commercial pet food. Kibble typically combines many ingredients that are cooked via a process called "extrusion." Extrusion involves the use of an extruder machine, which mixes all of the ingredients together into dough, then cooks it at temperatures ranging from 80 to 200 degrees Celcius (176 to 392 degrees Fahrenheit) (Case et al., 2011). At the end of the cooking process, the extruder forms and cuts the dough into the desired shape and size, resulting in the dry nuggets you pour into your dog's bowl.

Unfortunately, many commercial manufacturers of kibble rely on inferior ingredients, such as wheat, corn and soy, which immediately decrease the food's ability to send healthy messages to the cells. Kibble also requires starch to bind it together. As we've previously discussed, subsisting on high-glycemic starches day-in and day-out does not send messages of vibrant health to the epigenome. In our opinion, kibble is the least nutrigenomics-friendly choice to feed your dog. The fact is that no food can ever be more nutritious than the individual ingredients that make up the finished product, no matter how pretty the pictures or catchy the marketing slogan on the bag. Since many ingredients in the typical commercial kibble may cause a reactive response or cellular damage when eaten *individually*, just imagine the effect when several are combined.

In addition, the extrusion process adversely affects the quality of the food in several ways. The high temperatures used release even more antigenic (reactive) sites on the foods' molecules (cooked foods have been found to cause more allergenic reactions than raw foods, as we previously mentioned), which alter the body's immune surveillance and recognition responses. Extrusion also kills valuable enzymes and ***probiotics***, which are vital to a healthy digestive tract and immune system. In addition, kibble contains only 6% to 10% moisture and 90% or more dry matter (DM) (Case et al., 2011). Removing most of the water actually *concentrates* the reactive molecules. Then, to top it off (literally), kibble is often sprayed with all sorts of chemical flavor enhancers, colors and preservatives.

Even companies that begin with "premium" ingredients alter them to a point where the finished product is often unrecognizable by a dog's body. The dog's immune system views these ingredients as foreign invaders, setting off a cascade of immune responses that typically manifest as chronic itchy skin and GI problems associated with food intolerances/sensitivities.

For these reasons, we do not advocate feeding kibble as the staple of your dog's diet. If you're able to include even some home-cooked, raw, freeze-dried, dehydrated or canned food, we recommend that you do so. However, if kibble is your only, or your primary, option, you can still take important steps to select the best nutrition possible in this category.

Pet food labels can be misleading and difficult to decipher, so if you feed kibble, you'll need to learn the language well enough to ensure that your chosen brand provides the best quality dry food you can buy. Check out Appendix B for the low-down on deciphering pet food labels as well as these "do's" and "don'ts":

- **Do** ensure that the first ingredients listed are from high quality animal proteins (from a specific named source as per the fourth bullet point) and not from inferior quality, grain-based sources.

- **Do** select novel proteins such as venison, goat, bison, duck or rabbit to minimize the risk of food intolerances.

- **Don't** purchase products containing by-products.

- **Do** opt for products containing specific named protein sources, such as lamb, duck or venison rather than unidentified "animal" proteins or generic sources, such as "poultry" or "meat."

- **Do** choose products containing natural preservatives such as vitamins C and E, green tea polyphenols or rosemary (unless your dog is prone to seizures) rather than chemical preservatives such as BHA, BHT or ethoxyquin.

- **Don't** select foods with artificial colors or flavors.

- **Do** look for foods containing fresh sources of fruits and vegetables.

- **Do** opt for a grain-free/gluten-free food, especially if your dog has shown signs of food intolerances/sensitivities, such as itchy skin or GI disorders.

- **Do** select organic-based products whenever possible.

- **Do** look for dry foods with the least amount of ingredients on the bag. As with human food, the longer the ingredient list, the least "natural" the food tends to be.

When evaluating dog foods, it's important to realize that all ingredients must be listed in descending order of weight, and that these weights include the water content of the ingredient. This complicates matters when comparing ingredients with different moisture contents. The following excerpt from the FDA provides an excellent example of the importance of comparing ingredients on a dry matter (DM) basis:

> One pet food may list "meat" as its first ingredient, and "corn" as the second ingredient. The manufacturer doesn't hesitate to point out that its competitor lists "corn" first ("meat meal" is second), suggesting the competitor's product has less animal-source protein than its own. However, meat is very high in moisture (approximately 75% water). On the other hand, water and fat are removed from meat meal, so it is only 10% moisture (what's left is mostly protein and minerals). If we could compare both products on a dry matter basis (mathematically "remove" the water from both ingredients), one could see that the second product had more animal-source protein from meat meal than the first product had from meat, even though the ingredient list suggests otherwise. That is not to say that the second

product has more "meat" than the first, or in fact, any meat at all. Meat meal is
not meat per se, since most of the fat and water have been removed by rendering
(US FDA, 2010).

In Appendix B, we'll show you how to mathematically "remove" the water content of ingredients, converting them to a DM basis. This is especially important when comparing kibble with canned food or fresh meat, which contain vastly more moisture.

Note also the FDA's statement that, "meat meal is not meat per se." Advocates of meat meals point out that it is a necessary source of protein in dry foods, since it provides far more protein by weight than fresh meat. On the other hand, there is the potential for meat meals to originate from dubious and unsavory sources. Yes, meat meals pack a larger protein punch than fresh meat when used in kibble, but at what potential cost to our dogs' health at a cellular level?

Rather than choosing kibble containing meat meals, we suggest pumping up the protein content by adding some fresh, free-range animal protein from novel sources such as venison, bison or rabbit, or mixing in some high quality canned food. Just be sure to adjust down the volume of kibble to compensate for the extra calories.

If you still prefer to feed your dog a food containing meat meal, we urge you to follow these "do's" and "don'ts" to help ensure that the meal originates from a high quality animal source.

- **Do** be sure the meal lists a specific named source, such as "lamb meal," rather than generic "meat meal" or "poultry meal." Unspecified sources are too vague to feel confident about the meal's origin or quality.

- **Don't** choose meals that have the word "by-product" before them, such as "beef by-product meal," "chicken by-product meal," etc.

- **Do** contact the manufacturer and ask where they obtain the meat used to make their meals. If the manufacturer refuses to disclose the origin of the animals used, we urge you to avoid the product.

Once you've narrowed your kibble search to a few brands (or even picked one that you think is best) based on the above criteria, there is one more important step left before making your final decision. Call the manufacturer and ask some straightforward questions:

- Where do they source their ingredients? Sadly, as of this writing, many pet food recalls involve ingredients originating from China, and therefore we strongly advise against purchasing from any company that sources any of its ingredients from China. (Note: Some trace supplements used today only come from China, so check to see if your dog's food contains any of these ingredients.)

- Where is the manufacturing facility located? Again, pass on any products manufactured in China.

- Is the product manufactured in the company's own facility, or is it outsourced? The company will ideally manufacture the product in its own facility rather than outsourcing the process to another company that manufactures and private labels for several brands. In cases where the manufacturing process is outsourced, the company you purchase from is removed from the day-to-day oversight and, in our opinion, is less able to guarantee the final product's quality and safety.

"Kick up your kibble" with functional foods

Top-dressing your kibble with some of the functional foods we've discussed throughout the book is a great way to incorporate the concepts of nutrigenomics into a kibble-based diet. Top-dressing simply means to add additional ingredients on top of the kibble. Try incorporating some fresh meat, as well as fresh fruits, vegetables, eggs, sardines, goat or sheep's milk cheese or any other functional ingredients we have discussed. Imagine your dog's surprise—and delight—when he digs into his bowl and experiences the unexpected taste and aroma of fresh *blueberries*, steamed carrots, goat's milk cheddar or other wholesome, delicious ingredient buried like a treasure inside his kibble. Again, just be sure to compensate for the extra calories by reducing the amount of kibble. You don't want to end up with a fat dog!

Canned/wet diets

Canned/wet foods are more closely aligned than kibble with the principles of nutrigenomics for several reasons:

- Canned/wet foods tend to cause fewer food intolerances/sensitivities than kibble. One reason is that each can contains about 75% to 80% water, which dilutes antigens in the food.

- Canned foods contain significantly more protein on a DM basis than kibble.

- The meats contained in cans are less processed and thus tend to be closer to their natural state than those found in kibble.

- Because canned foods are pressure sterilized and sealed, the contents are naturally protected from rancidity, so manufacturers don't need to add potentially harmful chemical preservatives.

- Canned foods are typically free of artificial colors and flavors, making them more "natural" than kibbles that do contain these ingredients.

But dogs that eat canned foods are still at an increased risk of food intolerances/sensitivities compared to those who eat a non-reactive homemade or raw diet. Several reactive ingredients such as wheat, corn and soy may be combined into one can. And although it's not necessary to add chemical preservatives to canned foods, each can is sterilized once the food is added. As discussed above, processing increases the food's antigenic qualities, which can trigger an immune reaction and subsequent skin and/or GI issues associated with food intolerances/sensitivities.

If you feed canned food to your dog, check out the "do's" and "don'ts" listed in the kibble section, as many will apply to you. To boost the nutritional quality, you may also incorporate fresh, wholesome foods such as fresh fruits, lightly steamed vegetables, organic meats and eggs and sheep or goat milk products to the canned diet. Just be sure that you appropriately adjust the quantity of the canned food so that you don't overfeed calories.

Homemade diets

You've already read about the ins and outs of the basal diet in Chapters 4 and 5, so we won't repeat ourselves here. To sum up, home-prepared diets offer several advantages, including:

- You know exactly what your dog is eating.
- You control the quality of the ingredients.
- You can offer fresh, wholesome ingredients to support optimum cellular health.
- Homemade diets are minimally processed and thus provide superior nutritional benefits to kibble or canned foods.
- Homemade diets benefit dogs with food intolerances/sensitivities, as you can adjust the protein and carbohydrate sources accordingly to avoid reactive ingredients.
- You can rotate ingredients for variety. You wouldn't want to eat the same food every day, so why should your dog?
- You can prepare large batches of the diet and freeze them in single-serve quantities to increase the convenience.
- You don't have to worry that the next pet food recall will include your dog's brand.

Be sure to purchase the purest (i.e., organic, pasture-raised, antibiotic and hormone-free, etc.) and freshest meats, dairy, fruits and vegetables your budget allows and to follow our Three Keys discussed in Chapter 4 to obtain nutritional balance over time. To recap, these are:

- **Variety**: To obtain nutritional balance, you *must* include all necessary food groups, including red meat, poultry (including fat), fish, eggs, organ meats (e.g., liver from beef, chicken, lamb, pork or bison), dairy (sheep and goat), fruits and vegetables (Straus, 2013).
- **Nutrient-dense**: Select fresh, wholesome foods packed with antioxidants, phytonutrients, essential fatty acids and high quality amino acids we discuss throughout the book.
- **Whole foods**: This means *real* food, including fresh meats, fish, eggs, dairy, fruits and vegetables—*not* rendered meals, by-products and synthetic chemicals.

Also, don't forget to supplement with added calcium and other nutrients to meet your dog's individual needs.

Dehydrated and freeze-dried

Dehydrated and freeze-dried products begin with raw, fresh ingredients such as meats, fruits, vegetables and herbs. The water content of the raw foods is then removed, resulting in a shelf-stable product that, when combined with water, rehydrates to closely resemble its original form. The major advantages of dehydrated and freeze-dried diets are:

- They're more convenient than homemade (just add water to rehydrate).
- They're as close to the dog's archetypal diet as possible without feeding raw.
- No chemicals are used in the dehydration or freeze-drying process.
- The brands we researched as of this writing were all free of byproducts, meat meals, artificial colors, flavors, preservatives and other potentially harmful chemicals.
- Several of the products use organic fruits and vegetables and pasture-raised meats.

While both dehydration and freeze-drying involve the removal of moisture, the processes used differ considerably.

Dehydration

Dehydration uses warm air to slowly evaporate a food's water content. Dehydrated foods include everyday products such as dried raisins, figs, dates, powdered soup mixes and beef jerky. One of the biggest misconceptions is that dehydrated food is raw, but this is only true if the air temperature used is below 118 degrees Fahrenheit, which research shows is the point at which a food's nutritional value becomes compromised.

We found that the temperatures used by manufacturers of dehydrated products varied (among those that listed temperatures). One company states on its Web site that fruits and vegetables are dehydrated at 104 degrees Fahrenheit, however meat and fish are steamed prior to dehydration at a temperature of 140 to 165 degrees Fahrenheit. The only way to know for certain the dehydration temperature used is to call the company.

A benefit of dehydration is that it diminishes the growth of pathogens such as bacteria, yeasts and molds without adding chemicals, since pathogens need water to grow. However, typically only about 90% to 95% of the water is removed during the dehydration process, so growth of bacteria is not completely avoided.

Freeze-drying

Freeze-drying removes a food's water content without using heat. Freeze-dried foods are first flash-frozen, then placed in a special pressurized chamber. Drastically decreasing the pressure and increasing the temperature inside the chamber, while still keeping it below the freezing point, changes the ice in the frozen product directly from a solid to a gas, bypassing the liquid stage. This occurs over a period of several hours or days, until the product is virtually completely dried, with just a tiny amount of water remaining (Harris 2002).

Since freeze-drying maintains the nutrient composition of the raw ingredient, freeze-dried foods are perfect for people who want to feed their dogs raw, but who want a more convenient option than defrosting and handling raw frozen meat. Be aware that safe handling practices should still be followed, however, since freeze-dried meats are raw.

A major benefit of dehydrated and freeze-dried products is that functional ingredients such as specialized herbs and botanicals can easily be incorporated into the food with the benefit of minimal processing. We look forward to the day (which we predict is not far away) that manufacturers of dehydrated and freeze-dried foods will use functional ingredients to further optimize the nutrient content of their products.

Some reputable producers of dehydrated and freeze-dried foods include:

- Addiction Foods
- Bravo
- Champion Petfoods (Orijen)
- DNA Pet Food
- Dr. Harvey's
- Fresh is Best
- Grandma Lucy's
- Nature's Menu
- Nature's Variety
- NRG USA
- Only Natural Pet
- Primal Pet Foods
- Stella & Chewy's
- Sojo's
- The Honest Kitchen
- Vital Essentials
- ZiwiPeak

(Kerns, 2014)

Takeaway Points

- No matter what type of diet you feed your dog, you can make choices that significantly improve the food's health benefits based on the principles of nutrigenomics.

- Fear of raw foods has been passed on from nutrition spokespeople from large commercial pet food manufacturers to veterinarians, who then pass that fear along to their clients.

- The reality is that raw foods are in keeping with the principles of nutrigenomics for several reasons, including increased bioavailability of nutrients, high quality amino acids, typically no chemical additives and lesser propensity to cause food allergies.

- The large raw food manufacturers use a "kill step" to eliminate harmful pathogens from their foods, creating a "safe raw" product.

- Following safe handling protocols will help prevent against potential cross-contamination of harmful bacteria between your dog's raw food and other members of your household.

- Kibble is the most highly processed form of commercial dog food. It is also the most likely food to cause intolerances/sensitivities because it contains many potentially antigenic ingredients condensed into each nugget. We advise against feeding kibble as the only, or primary, source of your dog's diet.

- If you must feed kibble on a regular basis, please follow our "do's" and "don'ts" guidelines to help ensure you purchase a product containing maximum health benefits within this category.

- Try incorporating some fresh, wholesome ingredients, such as fresh meats, fruits and vegetables, into your dog's kibble to pump up the nutritional content—as well as to add taste and variety to his diet.

- Canned/wet foods are more closely aligned than kibble with the principles of nutrigenomics, however dogs that eat canned foods are still at increased risk of food intolerances/sensitivities compared to those who eat a non-reactive homemade or raw diet.

- If you feed canned food to your dog, check out the "do's" and "don'ts" listed in the kibble section, as many of them will apply to you.

- Home-prepared diets are superior to canned and kibble for several reasons, including freshness, quality and the ability to control the ingredients. The key is to purchase the freshest meats, dairy, fruits and vegetables your budget allows (preferably organic), to follow our Three Keys and to add necessary supplementation to create wholesome meals that are balanced over time.

- Always supplement home-prepared diets with added calcium and other essential nutrients.

- Dehydrated and freeze-dried products begin with raw, fresh ingredients such as meats, fruits, vegetables and herbs. The water content of the raw foods is then removed, resulting in a shelf-stable product that, when combined with water, rehydrates to closely resemble its original form.

- Dehydration uses warm air to slowly evaporate a food's water contented, so dehydrated foods are not raw.

- Freeze-drying removes a food's water content without the use of heat, so freeze-dried foods are raw foods that retain the original nutrient composition.

Chapter 13

Putting it all Together

"It's all in the genes." We introduced that saying back in Chapter 1. You'll remember it as the rallying cry of individuals who would rather surrender their health to their DNA than take control and reap the rewards associated with positive dietary changes. Back then, maybe you even believed it or used it yourself to excuse poor nutritional choices. But here's the ironic part. After hundreds of pages of cutting-edge nutrition information based on the emerging science of nutrigenomics, we've come full circle: it *is* "all in the genes." Only, we now realize just how empowering that statement is when viewed through the lens of nutrigenomics. It means that, when we nourish our bodies with nutritional ingredients that send positive messages to the epigenome, the epigenome in turn rewards us by instructing our genes to express for optimum health. What a beautiful, symbiotic relationship between our environment and our cells!

So, how do you put all the information in this book together and start using it right away to benefit your dog? Just follow these four simple steps:

Step 1: Conduct a pantry raid

If you feed your dog a commercial, mass-market pet food and want to continue to do so, we suggest you grab the bag or can from your pantry and scrutinize the label with a fresh eye. Here are some important clues that your dog's commercial food is sending messages of disease and destruction to his epigenome:

- Does the food contain artificial colors, preservatives, flavor enhancers or other chemicals?

- Does the food rely on inferior quality proteins, such as corn, wheat or soy that can cause inflammation, leaky gut and other health issues?

- Does the food contain by-products?

- Does the food contain "meals" from unnamed animal sources (e.g., "meat meal") rather than from named sources such as "lamb meal," "chicken meal," etc.?

- Does the food contain antigenic ingredients likely to cause a food intolerance/sensitivity? Unless you confirm your dog's individual food intolerance/sensitivity issues via NutriScan (Chapter 6), we advise keeping the most common antigens out of his bowl. Remember that, for most dogs, the foods known to cause the strongest reactions are beef, corn, dairy, wheat (and other glutens) and soy.

Remember also that just because your dog's food meets the criteria for "complete and balanced" as defined by AAFCO does not necessarily mean that it promotes optimum cellular health. Again, don't be afraid to call the manufacturer and ask some direct questions. Your dog is depending on you!

Step 2: Formulate your basal diet

Preparing a healthy, balanced homemade diet is not as difficult as mass-market, commercial pet food manufacturers (and many veterinary professionals) would like you to believe. The secret is to combine functional proteins, fats and low-glycemic carbohydrates along with phytonutrient rich fruits and vegetables in accordance with our Three Keys.

Remember that when preparing your own food, you don't strive to make each meal "complete and balanced." Instead, you take care to create a balanced, healthy diet over the course of several days or weeks. The same holds true for your canine companion. Think about the bigger picture rather than stressing over balancing each meal.

That being said, even properly constructed home-prepared diets *do* require some supplementation to ensure your dog receives all the essential nutrients. In Chapter 4, we detailed the vitamins and minerals that typically come up short in home-prepared diets. (Your dog will *absolutely* require added calcium.) See the Resources section for information on where you can purchase high quality supplements to round out your home-prepared basal diet. And, remember to select supplements made from whole food sources rather than synthetic ingredients whenever possible.

Stocking the canine functional kitchen

We suggest keeping the following items on hand so you can create a balanced, functional meal for your dog at a moment's notice:

In the pantry:

- Cans of wild Alaskan salmon (Be sure it says "Wild Alaskan" on the can or it could be farm-raised.)

- Cans of sardines

- **Coconut oil** (organic, virgin, cold-pressed)

- Gluten-free oatmeal (great for breakfast with **blueberries**!)

- Healthy, grain-free treats (See Resources section for online sellers.)

- **Raw honey** (not for puppies)

In the refrigerator:

- Fresh fruits (e.g., apples, **blueberries**, cantaloupe, pears, watermelon) (*not* strawberries)

- Fresh vegetables (e.g., carrots, sweet potatoes, broccoli, leafy greens)

- Organic, pasture-raised eggs

- Organic goat or sheep's dairy (e.g., milk, cheese, yogurt)

- Pasture-raised, novel meat sources (e.g., bison, buffalo, turkey, venison) and organ meats (e.g., chicken liver, beef liver). We suggest storing a variety in the freezer in single-serve portions and defrosting on an as-needed basis for freshness.*

In the freezer:

Same as above in fridge section, but in larger quantity. Store in freezer and remove as needed to refrigerator:

- Pasture-raised, novel meat sources (e.g., bison, buffalo, turkey, venison) and organ meats (e.g., chicken liver, beef liver)*

- Bags of organic frozen **berries** (*not* strawberries)

- Bags of organic frozen vegetables (e.g., butternut squash, broccoli; kale)

*If you feed a commercial raw frozen diet, substitute with your desired brand.

Step 3: Take it to the next level

By now, you have either chosen the best commercial food possible based on the principles of nutrigenomics or created a balanced home-prepared basal diet. Now, it's time to take it to the next level by adding in specific functional ingredients based on your dog's individual needs. Factors you'll want to consider are his:

- Age
- Lifestyle
- Activity level
- Current health concerns
- Cognitive issues

You've probably already highlighted, circled, checked off, bookmarked or made other notes as you've been reading along. All you have to do is revisit these sections and prioritize the nutrients you want to start with based on your dog's most immediate needs.

Be sure to do this slowly to avoid "shocking" your dog's system. Remember that even functional nutrients are foreign to your dog's intestinal flora and should be incorporated cautiously. This is especially true if he's eaten the same commercial diet for months or years. We suggest beginning your new dietary regimen with the addition of a high quality ***probiotic***. As you'll remember, health begins in the gut, and ***probiotics*** provide the beneficial bacteria necessary to optimize gut health as well as to help smoothly assimilate new ingredients.

We suggest a high quality ***omega-3 fatty acid*** in the form of EPA and DHA from low-mercury fish or other marine source as the second functional nutrient to add to your dog's diet. As we've repeatedly pointed out, the potent anti-inflammatory properties of ***omega-3s*** make them a powerful ally in the fight against chronic, inflammation-based health conditions.

Just by adding ***probiotics*** and ***omega-3s*** to your dog's diet, you will create massive positive change to your dog's cells and enable all other functional ingredients to perform their jobs even better.

Step 4: Invest in the test

Remember that food intolerances/sensitivities appear in the saliva long before they manifest in physical disorders such as skin and GI issues. Even though your dog might appear fine on the outside now, he could still harbor a latent, or pre-clinical, food intolerance/sensitivity that will one day appear out of nowhere to wreak havoc on his physical and emotional well being.

Cost is likely a determining factor in whether you will choose to test your dog with NutriScan. While most of us keep a sharp eye on our wallets, there are times when saving money up front results in much larger expenditures down the road. This, we believe, is such a time.

A small investment in saliva-based food intolerance/sensitivity testing costs considerably less than the investment of purchasing inappropriate foods, veterinary visits and medications—all of which would be unnecessary by simply eliminating the offending ingredient(s) from your dog's diet. Not to mention the mental and emotional cost of watching your dog suffer—and the poor health he needlessly endures.

Refer back to Chapter 6 for a refresher on NutriScan food intolerance/sensitivity testing and its benefits for your dog.

Okay. You've got the information. You've got a plan. You're all set to rock your dog's world by applying the principles of nutrigenomics. Certainly, this must be the end of the story (and the book). Not quite. In Chapter 14, you'll learn strategies and tactics to "Stay the Course" in the midst of resistance from well-meaning (but misguided) friends and, yes, even some veterinary professionals.

Takeaway Points

- As we discussed in Chapter 1, "It's all in the genes." With the knowledge you now have about nutrigenomics and functional foods, you understand how empowering this phrase really is!

- Just follow our simple four-step plan to immediately get your dog on the road to optimum health.

  o Step 1: Conduct a Pantry Raid. If you feed your dog a commercial, mass-market pet food, scrutinize the label with a fresh eye to ensure it does not contain any ingredients that can send unhealthy messages to his cells.

  o Step 2: If you choose to feed your dog a home-prepared diet, follow our Three Keys (variety, nutrient-dense, whole foods) to ensure he receives a proper balance of nutrients over time. Be sure to also include a high quality calcium supplement and other nutrients listed in Chapter 4.

  o Step 3: Take it to the next level by adding in specific functional ingredients based on your dog's individual needs, such as his age, lifestyle, activity level, current health concerns and/or cognitive issues.

  o Step 4: Check out NutriScan saliva-based food intolerance/sensitivity testing to be sure you eliminate any reactive ingredients from your dog's diet.

- Stock your pantry, fridge and freezer with a variety of foods based on the principles of nutrigenomics so that you always have nourishing ingredients on hand.

Chapter 14

Stay the Course

Congratulations! You now have the knowledge to optimize your dog's health using functional nutrition based on the principles of nutrigenomics. We're so happy that you can help your canine companion live a long, vibrant life free of the chronic diseases that are afflicting our beloved companion animals in increasing—and in some cases even skyrocketing—numbers. We're also excited for your dog, because he's about to experience a culinary transformation that will both tantalize his taste buds and promote vibrant health!

But remember that eating for optimum cellular health and gene expression is not a diet fad; it is a way of life. With that in mind, here are a just few parting words to help you "stay the course."

Don't be intimidated by the "experts"

It happens all too often when we visit our own doctors. We've done our homework on a particular health matter, gathered lots of pertinent information and formulated insightful questions and suggestions. We enter our doctor's office eager to speak with her and discuss the information, confident that she'll bring an open-minded attitude to the table and be willing to engage in a mutually respectful exchange of ideas. And then we are shocked that not only is she *unwilling* to enter into a discussion with us—she is actually resistant to what we have to say on behalf of our own health!

This dismissal of our input regarding our own well being is not limited to medical doctors. It also occurs all too frequently in the veterinary community. Many professionals are so convinced that their ways are best (ways that are sometimes outmoded) that they are unwilling to listen to new ideas—especially from lay people. While we find most veterinarians are quite sincere in their dedication to providing the best care for their patients, veterinary nutrition education is sorely lacking. As you'll recall from earlier, most of the nutrition information veterinarians receive originates from the major pet food manufacturers—*the same companies producing the prescription diets that are sold in veterinary clinics.*

Veterinarians likely don't realize that by limiting their clients' choices in this manner, they may actually be doing a disservice to their patients. We believe that the only way for veterinary professionals to provide truly unbiased, cutting-edge nutritional advice is to remove the financial incentive to steer their clients towards the one or two brands of canned or kibble food that they sell in their clinics. We hope that one day, veterinarians will break out of this limited model and instead form relationships with local pet food distributors (much like retail stores do), enabling them to provide a large variety of choices to meet their patients' individual needs.

The information you've learned throughout this book is backed by the latest science, so trust it and stay resolved that when it comes to your dog's diet, *you* are now the most capable person to direct the course.

If your veterinarian doesn't respect your choices, we urge you to find one who does and who will partner with you in creating optimum health for your dog. The connection between nutrition and chronic disease in companion animals has long been underrated. As the exciting fields of epigenomics and nutrigenomics teach us, we are all closely intertwined with our environments. The foods we eat and the lifestyle choices we make exert measurable effects on gene expression and cellular health, and in turn can determine whether we will thrive or suffer from chronic disease and preventable decay. Let's not rob our dogs of their birthright of vibrant health because we don't want to "make waves" with our veterinarian—or with the commercial pet food industry.

Create a plan that fits your lifestyle

For a nutritional plan to work, it must be sustainable on a consistent basis over the long term. This means that it must be practical for your lifestyle and budget. If cost is a consideration, remember that a healthy dog will require far fewer trips to the veterinarian and far fewer medications to "manage" his chronic illnesses. Feed your dog an optimum diet and he'll repay you with vibrant health that will more than save you money in the long run.

Everybody has a different degree of time and financial resources available to dedicate to their dog's dietary regimen (it's hard enough to find time for our own!). We're not asking that your life revolve around your dog's mealtimes, or that they create an added burden in what we're certain is an already full schedule. Embracing the principles of nutrigenomics is not an "all or nothing" endeavor. The beauty of this information is that you can apply it at whatever level you choose and your dog will benefit. The key is to keep it realistic and doable so that you stick with it.

Watch your dog's health blossom!

As you remove ingredients that can sabotage your dog's health and replace them with fresh, wholesome nutrients that send positive messages to his epigenome, you'll likely notice that astonishing improvements appear rather quickly. His eyes may look clearer and his coat shinier. His persistent scratching may suddenly vanish. He may shed those previously hard-to-lose pounds. He'll also likely become spryer, more alert and generally happier. We suggest that you keep a canine health journal (described in detail in *The Canine Thyroid Epidemic*) to track his progress on the new diet. A canine health journal will enable you to correlate positive changes in your dog's health to nutritional modifications. It will also allow you to identify foods that might impede his achieving optimal health and to remove them from his diet (assuming that you choose not to test him for food intolerances/sensitivities).

Your canine companion can't stroll down the pet store aisle, log onto a holistic pet care Web site or open the pantry door and whip up his own dinner, but if he could do any of these things, we're certain he'd choose foods that nourish his body. Dogs in the wild know exactly what prey to select to provide "complete and balanced" nourishment; they don't need to have it scientifically formulated by a pet food manufacturer and pre-packaged in bags or cans.

As you prepare your dog's meals, remember that *you* are his health care advocate. The information you've gained from this book can literally mean the difference between sickness and health for your beloved canine companion. It can mean the difference between a life riddled with chronic illness—along with the uncomfortable associated symptoms—or a vibrant, long life full of kisses, long walks, cuddles and tail wags. Which life do you think your dog would choose if he had his say? Which one do you choose for him?

Apply the knowledge in this book, trust your instincts and every bite of food your dog happily munches will lead him further along the path to true, vibrant, optimum health—the kind of health that originates at the deepest cellular level. He might even bring you along for the ride!

Bon appetite!

Takeaway Points

- Congratulations! You now have the knowledge to optimize your dog's health using functional nutrition based on the principles of nutrigenomics.

- As you move forward with your dog's new diet, be prepared for resistance from friends, family and even some veterinary professionals.

- While these individuals no doubt mean well, they are basing their opinions on incorrect, outdated or even biased information—not on the latest scientific findings.

- Trust what you've learned in this book and stand up for your dog's health.

- Seek out partners in your dog's health care who are open-minded and respectful of your knowledge and opinions.

- Create a nutritional plan for your dog that fits your budget and lifestyle, so that you can maintain it throughout his life.

- Remember that a healthy dog requires fewer veterinary and related medical expenses than a chronically ill dog.

- You can optimize your dog's diet and improve his health at whatever level is appropriate for your situation.

- As you apply the principles of nutrigenomics, watch your dog's health blossom!

Post Script

A Dog Nipping at Our Heels

Writing this book was a bit like running a marathon with a dog nipping at our heels (to use an apt analogy). We had to run (or in this case, write) as fast as we could just to keep a step ahead of all the new information constantly chasing us. The process took much longer than expected because every time we thought we had finished, we would discover a new research study with important ramifications for the health of dogs, and we just *had* to include it!

But one of the realities about the science of nutrigenomics is that, if we waited to include every new study that emerged, this book would not now be in your hands. Researchers are constantly uncovering new information regarding the effects of diet on the epigenome and gene expression.

So, while we have made every attempt to include what we feel is the most relevant and up-to-date information at the time of this writing, unless we frantically insert new pages as copies roll off the presses (or whatever books do these days), we must resign ourselves to the fact that we can't possibly cover everything. And that's what's so exciting.

As we put the final touches on this book, we are confident that there are discoveries yet to be made that we can't possibly envision right now—discoveries that will further empower all of us to use the wonderful ingredients nature has graced us with to create optimum health in our dogs—and ourselves—at the cellular level.

And who knows? Perhaps there might even be a sequel in it for us. Stay tuned.

Appendix A
Digging Deeper

Chapter 1

⤙ A brief history of epigenetics

The concept of epigenetics is not new. Conrad H. Waddington, a developmental biologist, coined the term back in 1942. Later, it came to refer to changes in gene expression that do not involve alternations in the DNA sequence (Esteller, 2008; Hardy & Tollefsbol, 2011).

In 2009, nearly a decade after scientists from the Human Genome Project mapped the first human genome, scientists from the Salk Institute in La Jolla, California, decoded and mapped the first epigenome, giving us incredible insight into the chemical signals that control gene expression (Sample, 2009; The University of Utah, 2014).

We now know that epigenetic tags on some genes actually have a "memory" that not only follows us through our lives, but is passed on to future generations. These are called "imprinted genes" and it means that your healthy—or unhealthy—lifestyle choices can directly impact the health of your children and grandchildren (The University of Utah, 2014).

⤙ The epigenome: a tale of two twins

Let's say that Judy and Jody are identical twins. Since they developed from a single **zygote** (fertilized egg cell), they have the exact same genome at birth and, of course, the exact same phenotype. This means that as they age, Judy and Jody should experience the same level of health, suffer from the same diseases, live to the same age (assuming, Heaven forbid, that one doesn't get into a terrible accident) and generally inhabit bodies that look and behave the same.

But let's say that you knew Judy and Jody when they were adorable, and identical-looking, 10 year olds. Now, you've just run into them both again after having not seen them for 50 years. You're shocked, because at 60 years old, Judy looks fit and trim, with the clear, smooth complexion of a woman 20 years younger (and, no, she hasn't had plastic surgery). Moreover, you're very impressed when she tells you that she has just finished a three-mile run.

As you study them, you become confused because Jody, who's standing next to Judy, appears much shorter than her sister. In fact, she's hunched over, and she reveals to you that indeed she suffers from chronic back problems. Jody's skin is also wrinkled and haggard looking. What on earth is going on, you wonder? How could these "identical" twins look so different?

You learn that while in college, Judy became a "health nut," eating lots of fresh fruits and vegetables and exercising regularly—a way of life that she still practices. She also does yoga and meditates to center herself and manage the stress of her busy career.

Jody, on the other hand, tended to reach for pizza and fries rather than apples and bananas while studying—a habit that she has also carried with her throughout her life. She also has a busy career, and she barely even has time to sit down and have a proper meal. In fact, she pretty much dines at the drive-through every night. She's also really stressed out, and took up cigarette smoking about 20 years ago, which she insists helps to "calm her nerves."

Given the vastly different lifestyle choices Judy and Jody have made over the course of most of their lives, is it any wonder that over time their phenotypes have diverged? Not at all, when you understand that environmental factors, such as diet, stress and smoking, affect the epigenetic tags that control gene expression (Sample, 2009; The University of Utah, 2014).

Epigenetics: the difference between queen bees and worker bees

There is perhaps no better example of the epigenetic effects of diet on phenotype than the honeybee. All honeybee larvae start out genetically identical, and there is just one factor that determines whether a bee will develop the phenotype of a lowly "worker bee" or rise to "queen bee" phenotype superstardom—whether or not she dines exclusively on a diet of *royal jelly* (see Chapter 2), a protein-rich substance secreted from glands on the heads of worker bees (Choi & Friso, 2010; The University of Utah, 2014). Scientists discovered that royal jelly works its magic on the honeybee epigenome by silencing the Dnmt3 gene, which affects the bees' genome. When the Dnmt3 gene is active in the bee larvae, it epigenetically silences the genes that are a necessary to develop into a queen, so the bees remain as worker bees. But when the bees eat *royal jelly*, it turns off the Dnmt3 gene, enabling the "queen genes" to become activated (The University of Utah, 2014).

That's an important advantage when you consider that the life span of the average worker bee is a paltry four to nine months during the winter and only about six weeks during the high-producing summer months. A queen bee, on the other hand, can live for three to five years, laying about 2,000 eggs per day (Back Yard Beekeepers Association, n,d.; Puotinen, 2007).

What is inflammation?

World-renowned anti-aging dermatologist, Nicholas Perricone, MD, describes the normal inflammatory response as a seven-step process:

1. A pathogen enters the cell.

2. The blood vessels widen, increasing blood flow.

3. The blood vessels become more permeable (able to take in more fluid).

4. Fluid enters into the tissue, causing it to swell.

5. White blood cells enter the tissue from the blood vessels.

6. The white blood cells destroy the pathogen (the invader).

7. Having done their job, the tissues repair themselves.
(Perricone, 2012)

In this capacity, acute inflammation plays an important role in the body's defense and healing processes. Little or no long-term damage occurs, since at the end of the cycle (once the body has destroyed the pathogen), the tissue or organ experiencing the inflammation repairs itself and returns to its normal, healthy, pre-inflammatory state (Punchard, Whelan & Adcock, 2004). A disruption of this normal cycle, however, leads to chronic inflammation and a variety of health problems.

Chapter 2
USDA National Organic Program (NOP) definition of organic

Organic food is produced by farmers who emphasize the use of renewable resources and the conservation of soil and water to enhance environmental quality for future generations. Organic meat, poultry, eggs, and dairy products come from animals that are given no antibiotics or growth hormones. Organic food is produced without using most conventional pesticides; fertilizers made with synthetic ingredients or sewage sludge; bioengineering; or ionizing radiation. Before a product can be labeled "organic," a government-approved certifier inspects the farm where the food is grown to make sure the farmer is following all the rules necessary to meet USDA organic standards. Companies that handle or process organic food before it gets to your local supermarket or restaurant must be certified, too (USDA, 2014).

Chapter 3

✂ Phytoestrogens in soy activate estrogen-dependent breast cancer genes

Numerous studies have been conducted on the relationship between the soy isoflavone genistein and estrogen-dependent breast cancer. A data review of research focusing on the effects of dietary genistein on the growth of estrogen-dependent mammary tumors showed that genistein enhances the proliferation of estrogen-dependent human breast cancer tumor growth both *in vitro* and *in vivo*. Dietary genistein has also been shown to stimulate mammary tumor growth in rodents, while withdrawal of genistein resulted in tumor regression. Dietary genistein was found to activate the expression of the estrogen-target genes pS2, progesterone receptor and cyclin D1, which correlated with the growth of estrogen-dependent tumors (Helferich, Andrade & Hoagland, 2008). Genistein in soy exerts an additional disturbing effect on cancerous gene expression when combined, as it often is, with glyphosate in the popular weed killer Roundup (see below).

✂ More on BPA

Researchers have found that feeding BPA to pregnant yellow agouti mice decreased methylation of the developing fetuses' agouti gene, resulting in the birth of more unhealthy babies than normal. But when pregnant yellow agouti mice were fed methyl-rich foods, their babies were mainly brown and healthy; the methyl-rich foods actually reversed the negative epigenomic effects of the BPA (The University of Utah, 2014).

As of this writing, consumers are on their own to protect themselves and their pets from BPA exposure. Although some companies claim to use BPA-free cans, the issue is complex, confusing and even misleading. Some companies claim that only their small cans (3 oz and 5.5 oz) are BPA-free, but that their large cans contain BPA, while others claim that all of their cans are BPA-free.

Even companies that claim to use BPA-free cans may in fact use one of BPA's close chemical relatives, such as bisphenol A diglycidyl ether (abbreviated as BADGE or DGEBA), bisphenol F, bishphenol F diglycidyl ether (BFDGE) or bisphenol sulfonate (bisphenol S) (Kerns, 2012). The only way to ensure your dog does not ingest BPA—or any of its potentially hazardous relatives—is to stop buying canned dog foods.

✂ More on the dangers of glyphosates and GMOs

A new study at the time of this writing revealed even more disturbing information regarding glyphosate's effect on gene expression. The study showed that "low and environmentally relevant concentrations of glyphosate possessed estrogenic activity" and specifically that glyphosate exerted "proliferative effects" in human hormone-dependent breast cancer, T47D cells. The study also found an additive estrogenic effect when glyphosate was combined with genistein (the phytoestrogen in soybeans discussed above). This is particularly concerning, since we just pointed out that soybeans are among the crops most widely sprayed with herbicides (Ji, 2013; Thongprakaisang et al., 2013).

GM crops and the dramatically increased use of herbicides are far from helping us win the war on weeds; 21 types of weeds have evolved to become resistant to glyphosate. Reminiscent of a horror movie, these new weeds, called "superweeds," occupy more than 14 million acres where GM soy, corn and cotton crops grow. In response, the chemical companies are creating new genetically engineered seeds that tolerate even stronger herbicides (EWG, 2013).

Moreover, the Food and Drug Administration (FDA), which is responsible for ensuring the safety of the nation's food supply, does not use its own experts to determine whether a GM food is safe. Instead, it turns to biotechnology companies to decide whether new GM crops that *they* create are "not materially different in any respect relevant to food safety" (EWG, 2013). Over the last decade, the chemical industry has spent more than a billion dollars ($572 million) on campaign contributions and lobbying, with one of its primary goals to prevent mandatory labeling of GM foods (EWG, 2013).

But that's not all. At the time of this writing, there are petitions pending for federal approval of three new genetically engineered foods that transgress into even more disturbing areas of the food supply and raise additional concerns over long-term health ramifications to humans and animals:

- **Genetically engineered fish**: If scary movies about giant killer fish are your thing, you'll love the idea of genetically engineered salmon! These new superfish would produce growth hormones year-round rather than seasonally, causing them to grow at twice their normal size, while reducing their levels of ***omega-3 fatty acids*** (EWG, 2013).

- **Genetically engineered fruit**: Hate brown spots on your apples? Then you'll love genetically engineered, non-browning apples. A Canadian company is awaiting approval from the U.S. Department of Agriculture (USDA) to sell "Arctic" apples, which are genetically modified with extra copies of genes the apple already possesses. The genes make polyphenol oxidase, an enzyme that creates the chemical reaction that results in browning. Adding additional copies of the gene switches off the apple's production of the enzyme and—*voilà*—no more browning (Charles, 2014). The downside? It's unknown what price we'll pay for perfect-looking apples, since no one knows the changes in nutritional quality or safety the altered genes will produce (EWG, 2013).

- **Genetically engineered "2, 4-D" crops:** As we mentioned a minute ago, increased use of herbicides has led to "superweeds" that have evolved to become even more resistant to Roundup (glyphosate). In response, Dow is seeking approval of genetically engineered crops that are resistant to an older, high-risk herbicide (EWG, 2013). Talk about stepping backwards!

Neither GMOs already in the food supply nor new ones proposed for market have been subjected to independent safety testing or clinical trials to determine their long-term health effects (EWG, 2013).

Chapter 6

✂ More about DNA microarrays courtesy of the National Human Genome Research Institute

DNA microarray technology is a developing technology used to study the expression of many genes at once. It involves placing thousands of gene sequences in known locations on a glass slide called a gene chip. A sample containing DNA or RNA is placed in contact with the gene chip. Complementary base pairing between the sample and the gene sequences on the chip produces light that is measured. Areas on the chip producing light identify genes that are expressed in the sample.

Although all of the cells in the human body contain identical genetic material, the same genes are not active in every cell. Studying which genes are active and which are inactive in different cell types helps scientists to understand both how these cells function normally and how they are affected when various genes do not perform properly. In the past, scientists have only been able to conduct these genetic analyses on a few genes at once. With the development of DNA microarray technology, however, scientists can now examine how active thousands of genes are at any given time.

Microarray technology will help researchers to learn more about many different diseases, including heart disease, mental illness and infectious diseases, to name only a few. One intense area of microarray research at the National Institutes of Health (NIH) is the study of cancer. In the past, scientists have classified different types of cancers based on the organs in which the tumors develop. With the help of microarray technology, however, they will be able to further classify these types of cancers based on the patterns of gene activity in the tumor cells. Researchers will then be able to design treatment strategies targeted directly to each specific type of cancer. Additionally, by examining the differences in gene activity between untreated and treated tumor cells—for example those that are radiated or oxygen-starved—scientists will understand exactly how different therapies affect tumors and be able to develop more effective treatments.

DNA microarrays are created by robotic machines that arrange minuscule amounts of hundreds or thousands of gene sequences on a single microscope slide. Researchers have a database of over 40,000 gene sequences that they can use for this purpose. When a gene is activated, cellular machinery begins to copy certain segments of that gene. The resulting product is known as messenger RNA (mRNA), which is the body's template for creating proteins. The mRNA produced by the cell is complementary, and therefore will bind to the original portion of the DNA strand from which it was copied.

To determine which genes are turned on and which are turned off in a given cell, a researcher must first collect the messenger RNA molecules present in that cell. The researcher then labels each mRNA molecule by using a reverse transcriptase enzyme (RT) that generates a complementary cDNA to the mRNA. During that process fluorescent nucleotides are attached to the cDNA. The tumor and the normal samples are labeled with different fluorescent dyes. Next, the researcher places the labeled cDNAs onto a DNA microarray slide. The labeled cDNAs that represent mRNAs in the cell will then hybridize—or bind—to their synthetic complementary DNAs attached on the microarray slide, leaving its fluorescent tag. A researcher must then use a special scanner to measure the fluorescent intensity for each spot/areas on the microarray slide.

If a particular gene is very active, it produces many molecules of messenger RNA, thus, more labeled cDNAs, which hybridize to the DNA on the microarray slide and generate a very bright fluorescent area. Genes that are somewhat less active produce fewer mRNAs, thus, less labeled cDNAs, which results in dimmer fluorescent spots. If there is no fluorescence, none of the messenger molecules have hybridized to the DNA, indicating that the gene is inactive. Researchers frequently use this technique to examine the activity of various genes at different times. When co-hybridizing tumor samples (red dye) and normal sample (green dye) together, they will compete for the synthetic complementary DNAs on the microarray slide. As a result, if the spot is red, this means that that specific gene is more expressed in tumor than in normal (up-regulated in cancer). If a spot is green, it means that that gene is more expressed in the normal tissue (down-regulated in cancer). If a spot is yellow that means that that specific gene is equally expressed in normal and tumor (NHGRI, 2014).

Chapter 7
Studies linking obesity and gene expression

Study 1
This 2013 study originated from the University of Minnesota and was reported at the American Heart Association's Epidemiology and Prevention/Nutrition, Physical Activity and Metabolism meeting. The genome-wide study of 2,873 patients measured the association between Body Mass Index (BMI) and DNA methylation, which is critical to healthy gene expression. After adjusting for other confounding factors, the researchers identified evidence of an association between BMI and DNA methylation on about 20 regions across 11 autosomes (pairs of chromosomes other than sex chromosomes) (Demerath et al., 2013; Fiore, 2013). Since humans have 22 pairs of autosomes, this means that half were affected by obesity.

Study 2
In 2010, researchers Xiaoling Wang, PhD, study researcher and genetic epidemiologist at the Georgia Prevention Institute, Medical College of Georgia along with Paul W. Franks, PhD and Charlotte Ling, PhD, both of the Skane University Hospital,

Lund University in Malmo, Sweden, conducted a genome-wide methylation analysis of seven obese and seven lean children ages 14 to 18 years. They then replicated the study in six genes among 46 obese and 46 lean participants ages 14 to 30 years. The results of both studies found associated methylation changes in two genes—*UBA-SH3A* and *TRIM3*—with dysfunction of the immune system (Endocrine Today, 2011; Franks & Ling, 2010).

Study 3
A 2013 study linked the methylation of another gene associated with inflammation, LY86, with obesity. The findings showed that LY86 was consistently and highly methylated in obese people. The author concluded that environmental factors such as consumption of high fat foods may increase methylation of LY86, leading to obesity as well as obesity-related disease (Medical College of Georgia, 2013).

Chapter 8
✑ Details on the science behind gene expression and arthritis. Gene expression changes leading to the up-regulation of inflammatory markers associated with osteoarthritis (OA)

At elevated levels, the omega-6 fatty acid Arachidonic acid (AA) initiates the production of **eicosanoids**, "signaling molecules" that include prostaglandins E (PGE2), thromboxanes and leukotrienes B4 (LTB4) that serve as important cellular mediators of inflammation in diseases such as OA (Calder, 2006; Laflamme, 2004; Laflamme, 2012; Waldron, 2004). Prostaglandins are found in many tissues and act as local messenger molecules, while the other messengers come from blood platelets (thromboxanes) and leukocytes/white blood cells (leukotrienes). The body metabolizes AA into these inflammatory mediators via two enzymatic pathways—the COX [cyclooxygenase-1 (COX-1) and cyclooxygenase-2 (COX-2)] and the LOX [5-lipoxygenase (5-LOX)] pathways. Prostaglandin PGE2, produced via the COX pathway, causes degradation of cartilage glycoproteins, inhibits the rebuilding of collagen and these glycoproteins, stimulates pain receptors and promotes further inflammation (Laflamme, 2004; Laflamme, 2012; Waldron, 2004). Produced via the LOX pathway, LTB4 initiates oxidative stress, up-regulates the inflammatory cascade and causes breakdown of cell membranes, thus resulting in creation of even more pro-inflammatory AA and increased expression of LOX and COX -2 pathways (Primus Pharmaceuticals, 2013).

How EPA and DHA break the inflammatory cycle of OA
As discussed above, Arachidonic acid (AA) in cell membranes initiates the production of pro-inflammatory "signaling molecules," such as PGE2, thromboxanes and leukotrienes B4 (LTB4) that serve as important cellular mediators of inflammation in diseases such as OA. Increasing dietary intake of EPA and DHA increases the proportion of these *omega-3 fatty acids* in cell membranes, replacing part of the AA. Less AA in turn decreases the production of PGE2, LTB4 and other pro-inflammatory eicosanoids. One human study showed that consuming six grams of DHA in the

form of fish oil per day decreased production of pro-inflammatory PGE2 by 60% and LTB4 by 75%. At the same time, EPA can produce its own eicosanoids, such as PGE3 and LTB5, which have a slightly different structure than those produced by AA and are considered anti-inflammatory (Calder, 2006; Laflamme, 2004; Laflamme, 2012; Middleton & Hannah, 2004; Waldron, 2004).

In addition to replacing pro-inflammatory AA in cells, EPA and DHA can also regulate gene expression to suppress the production of pro-inflammatory cytokines such as interleukin-1β (IL-1β) and (TNF- α), which have long-term damaging effects on bone and cartilage. IL-1β stimulates production of PGE2 and both IL-1β and TNF-α activate MMPs, the enzymes responsible for cartilage degradation (Middleton & Hannah, 2004; Waldron, 2004).

✺ Summary of a study supporting the importance of diets containing a high *omega-3* to omega-6 fatty acid ratio for dogs with OA

In 2010, 18 privately owned veterinary clinics performed a randomized, double blind clinical trial of 127 client-owned dogs with OA in one or more joints. Over a six-month period, the dogs were randomly selected to consume either a typical commercial pet food (the "control" diet) or a test food containing a 31-fold increase in total *omega-3 fatty acid* content and a 34-fold decrease in omega-6 to *omega-3* ratio (compared with the control food). The objective of the study was to determine whether food containing a high concentration of *omega-3 fatty acids* derived from fish and a low omega-6 to *omega-3 fatty acid* ratio affected the clinical signs of OA in dogs. The dogs' conditions were assessed based on a questionnaire completed by the owners about their dog's arthritic condition, a physical examination by investigators and blood work performed at the beginning of the study and at six, 12 and 24 weeks.

Based on reports from owners, the dogs that ate the test food showed a significant improvement in their ability to rise from a resting position and to play at six weeks, as well as an improved ability to walk at 12 and 24 weeks, compared with dogs in the control group. Serum concentrations of total *omega-3 fatty acids* were also significantly higher and serum concentrations of Arachidonic acid (omega-6) were significantly lower at six, 12, and 24 weeks in dogs fed the test food. The researchers concluded that a diet high in *omega-3 fatty acids* derived from fish oil and low in omega-6 fatty acids improved the clinical signs of arthritis in dogs with OA (Roush et al., 2010).

Chapter 9

✺ A few brief examples of human and animal studies supporting the anti-cancer benefits of *spirulina*

Example 1

In one study, phycocyanin significantly inhibited the growth of human leukemia K562 cells in a dose-dependent manner (Liu et al., 2000; Messonnier, 2006). In

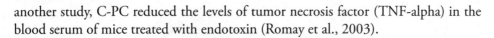
another study, C-PC reduced the levels of tumor necrosis factor (TNF-alpha) in the blood serum of mice treated with endotoxin (Romay et al., 2003).

Example 2

In a double-blind study, tobacco chewers who took one gram of *spirulina* per day for one year showed a 45% remission of oral precancerous lesions (leukoplakia), compared to 7% in the placebo group (University of Maryland Medical Center, 2011; Wolf, 2009).

Example 3

In *in vitro* and *in vivo* studies, *spirulina* has been shown to boost the immune system by increasing the production of bone marrow stem cells, macrophages, T-cells, B-cells and natural killer cells; improve GI health by boosting the production of *probiotics* in the gut; protect against allergic reactions by blocking the release of histamines; and protect against infections and viruses such as herpes, HIV and influenza (University of Maryland Medical Center, 2011; Wolf, 2009).

Appendix B

Reading Pet Food Labels

If you've ever felt that reading a pet food label was like trying to understand the secret language of a club to which you did not belong, you're not alone. But you don't need a magic decoder ring to figure out what's inside a bag or can of dog food; you just need to learn the "secret language" used by manufacturers. Once you know their language, you can read anything written in it. In this chapter, we are going to teach you that language.

When we refer to the "label," we mean the information contained on the *back panel* of the product. As we pointed out earlier, mass market commercial pet food manufacturers are so adept at painting idyllic pictures of "freshness," "wholesomeness" and "healthfulness" on the fronts of their packages that you half expect sunshine to pour out when you open them. So, we're going to forget the marketing hype and get to the nutritional facts, which are contained on the *back*.

Manufacturer's contact information

Companies must provide their name and mailing address, but are not required to include a telephone number. When reading a label, pay close attention to the exact wording, as there is a big difference between "manufactured by…" and "manufactured for…" If the statement "manufactured for…" or "distributed by…" precedes the company name, this tells you that the food was made by an outside source (US FDA, 2010). Although the name on the label indicates the "responsible" party, once manufacturing is outsourced, the company loses its ability to maintain strict oversight on quality control. In the past, many pet food recalls have involved brands that were outsourced and traced back to one manufacturer.

Nutritional adequacy

Nutritional adequacy statements indicate whether a product is "complete and balanced" according to AAFCO guidelines, as well as for which life stage it's intended. A product labeled for "all life stages," for example, indicates that according to AAFCO guidelines it is nutritionally adequate to support the needs of all dogs, including growing puppies, pregnant or lactating bitches and adults in a maintenance stage. Mass-market commercial pet food manufacturers are increasing their offerings of foods intended for specific purposes, such as specific medical conditions. Manufacturers of such foods should indicate their nutritional adequacy for these conditions, as well as whether such foods are "complete and balanced" (Fascetti & Delaney, 2012; US FDA, 2010).

Products claiming to be "complete and balanced" must verify these claims in one of two ways:

- The food must be formulated to meet specified nutrient levels as established by AAFCO. Products formulated via this method should include the words, "(Name of product) is formulated to meet the nutritional levels established by the AAFCO (Dog/Cat) Food Nutrient Profiles" (US FDA, 2010).

- The product is tested using an AAFCO Feeding Trial Protocol. In this case, a group of dogs have been fed the product (or "lead" member of a "family" of products) based on strict controls and have been monitored to ensure the product provides adequate nutrition. Products formulated in this manner should bear the statement, "Animal feeding tests using AAFCO procedures substantiate that (name of product) provides complete and balanced nutrition" (Fascetti & Delaney, 2012; US FDA, 2010).

Foods that do not meet these requirements for "complete and balanced" must be labeled "intended for intermittent or supplemental feeding only" or otherwise clearly indicate that they are for use as a treat, snack or supplement (Fascetti & Delaney, 2012; US FDA, 2010).

Ingredients

Ingredients must be listed in descending order according to their weight, with the ingredient weighing the most listed at the top. This can be deceiving, however, because ingredient weights are listed on an "as fed" basis, which includes the original water content prior to any cooking or drying. To accurately compare the nutritional value of two foods we must mathematically "remove" the water content and convert the ingredients to a "dry matter" (DM) basis. Let's take another look at the FDA statement we previously discussed in Chapter 12:

> One pet food may list "meat" as its first ingredient, and "corn" as the second ingredient. The manufacturer doesn't hesitate to point out that its competitor lists "corn" first ("meat meal" is second), suggesting the competitor's product has less animal-source protein than its own. However, meat is very high in moisture (approximately 75% water). On the other hand, water and fat are removed from meat meal, so it is only 10% moisture (what's left is mostly protein and minerals). If we could compare both products on a dry matter basis (mathematically "remove"

the water from both ingredients), one could see that the second product had more animal-source protein from meat meal than the first product had from meat, even though the ingredient list suggests otherwise. That is not to say that the second product has more "meat" than the first, or in fact, any meat at all. Meat meal is not meat per se, since most of the fat and water have been removed by rendering (US FDA, 2010).

The product that lists "meat" first and "corn" second is misleading, as the FDA points out, because the weight of meat is approximately 75% water. Since corn contains very little water in its weight, in reality a product that lists meat first and corn second actually contains *more* corn than meat when the ingredients are converted to a DM basis.

The manufacturer that listed "corn" as the second ingredient could also have used a strategy called "ingredient splitting" or "fractioning" to make it appear as if their product contains less corn. In this case, the ingredient "corn" could be listed according to its various components, including ground corn, corn meal, corn bran and corn gluten. By "splitting" the corn this way and listing each component separately, no individual corn product would weigh enough to appear high on the list of ingredients (Fascetti & Delaney, 2012; Segal, 2008). We urge you to pay close attention to such tactics, as they can make a significant difference in the quality of your dog's food.

Since we've already covered the issue of "by products" at length, we will not repeat that information here. Refer to our earlier discussions for our views on these ingredients.

Guaranteed analysis

A pet food's guaranteed analysis must contain the following:

- Minimum percentage of crude protein.
- Minimum percentage of crude fat.
- Maximum percentage of crude fiber.
- Maximum percentage of moisture.

(US FDA, 2010; Fascetti & Delaney, 2012)

The word "crude" refers to how the nutrient was measured (crude protein is based on nitrogen analysis, while crude fat is measured by ether extract); it does not mean that the nutrient is inferior (Segal, 2008).

Manufacturers are not required to list the amount of "ash," which refers to the food's mineral content, nor are they required to list carbohydrates; however, these nutrients are sometimes included, along with others (Fascetti & Delaney, 2012; US FDA, 2010).

Bear in mind that "minimum" and "maximum" levels listed don't necessarily match the actual amount contained in the food, so if your dog has a medical condition that requires specific nutrient levels, be sure to contact the company and ask for the "average" level of that nutrient (Fascetti & Delaney, 2012).

Feeding directions

The feeding directions indicate the manufacturer's recommended daily intake, usually expressed by X cups or X cans per amount of the dog's body weight. Since these recommendations typically overestimate the amount you should feed, use them only as a general guideline and refer to the information in Chapter 7 to keep your dog at his ideal weight and body composition. Remember, however, that dogs who are nursing or in the late stage of pregnancy should eat *ad libitum* (as much as they desire).

Calorie content

Currently, AAFCO does not require pet food companies to list the calorie content of their foods on their labels; manufacturers provide calorie information on a strictly volunteer basis. This can provide a challenge to people who wish to keep track of the amount of calories they feed their dogs each day. After all, one of the most basic ways people count calories for themselves is to check package labels. It's unfortunate that many mass-market commercial pet food companies fail to provide us with that same basic information for our companion animals—especially when calorie content can vary so greatly between brands or between different products within the same brand.

Manufacturers that do provide calorie information must express it in terms of "kilocalories per kilogram," or kcal/kg. Remember that kilocalories are the same as Calories on human food labels. A kilogram equals 2.2 pounds. Along with stating "kilocalories per kilogram," manufacturers can express caloric information in terms of "kilocalories per cup" or "kilocalories per can." These units are typically easier to understand because they more closely resemble the manner in which we evaluate the calorie content of our own foods (US FDA, 2010).

If a label does list calories, it will reflect an "as fed basis" (just like the guaranteed analysis), so you will need to factor in the water content. This can provide a challenge when attempting to compare the calorie or nutrient contents of dried versus wet foods. To roughly compare the calorie content of a canned and a dry food, multiply the calories listed on the canned food by four (US FDA, 2010).

Converting as fed basis to dry matter (DM) basis

Fortunately, it's not difficult to mathematically remove the water content from dog food products so that we can accurately compare their nutrient values. Here's how to do it:

Step 1

Subtract the percent of the food's moisture content from 100 to determine the dry matter. For example, a kibble containing 8% moisture will contain 92% DM.

Step 2

To determine the amount of protein on a DM basis, take the crude protein listed under the Guaranteed Analysis on the food's label and divide that number by the

DM number you determined in Step 1. If the food lists a guaranteed analysis of 30% protein, for example, calculate 30 divided by 92, which equals 33%. In this example, the food contains 33% protein on a DM basis. You can use this same formula to determine the DM amount of fat and other nutrients.

Step 3

Let's compare the protein content of this kibble with the protein content of a canned food containing 75% moisture, which contains 25% dry matter (100 – 75 = 25). According to the label's Guaranteed Analysis, this food contains 10% protein on an "as fed" basis.

To convert the protein value to a "dry matter" basis, divide the 10% protein by the food's 25% DM, which equals 40% protein.

We just learned that the canned food contains more protein per pound on a DM basis than the kibble (40% compared to 33%), even though at first glance the kibble appears to have much more protein. This example illustrates the importance of converting nutrient values from an "as fed" to a "dry matter" basis when comparing foods. Otherwise, you simply cannot compare "apples to apples."

We prefer feeding fresh, wholesome foods rather than commercially processed products whenever possible. But if you do give your dog kibble or canned, knowing what's in the food by understanding what's on the label can help to optimize your dog's health by feeding him more in keeping with the principles of nutrigenomics.

Resources

We hope you enjoyed reading *Canine Nutrigenomics: The New Science of Feeding Your Dog for Optimum Health* as much as we enjoyed writing it. Most importantly, we hope that you put the information in this book to work so that your dog can express true, vibrant health from the cellular level and the two of you can revel in many blissful years together. To further help you toward this goal, this section contains a list of manufacturers and retail sources where you can find the products listed in the book. We have also suggested some informative reading material to help you in all aspects of caring for your canine companion, as well as provided information on how to contact the authors for canine nutrition consulting and food intolerance/sensitivity testing.

Further reading

Books
Most of the books listed here can be purchased on Amazon.com, Barnesandnoble.com and Dogwise.com.

Pet food industry
Not Fit for a Dog!: The Truth About Manufactured Dog and Cat Food, Michael W. Fox, Elizabeth Hodgkins & Marion E. Smart, Quill Driver Books, 2009.

The Truth About Pet Foods, R. L. Wysong, Inquiry Press, 2002.

Healthcare and nutrition books
Applied Veterinary Clinical Nutrition, Andrea J. Fascetti & Sean J. Delaney, Wiley Blackwell, 2012.

Earl Mindell's Nutrition & Health for Dogs, Earl Mindell & Elizabeth Renaghan, Prima Publishing, 1998.

Emerging Therapies: Using Herbs and Nutraceutical Supplements for Small Animals, Susan G. Wynn, AAHA Press, 1999.

How to Have a Healthier Dog: The Benefits of Vitamins and Minerals for Your Dog's Life Cycles, Wendell O. Zucker & Martin Belfield, Doubleday, 1991.

Manual of Natural Veterinary Medicine: Science and tradition, Susan G. Wynn, Mosby, 2003.

Nutrition, Health & Disease, Gary Price Todd, Donning Company Publishers, 1985.

Natures Benefit for Pets: Unifying Human and Pet Nutraceutical Technology, Stephen Holt & Dean R. Bader, Wellness Publishing, 2001.

Small Animal Clinical Nutrition (4th ed.), Michael S. Hand, Craig D. Thatcher, Rebecca L. Remillard, Phillip Roudebush & Bruce J. Novotny, Mark Morris Institute, 2000.

Small Animal Clinical Nutrition (5th ed.), Michael S. Hand, Craig D. Thatcher, Rebecca L. Remillard, Phillip Roudebush & Bruce J. Novotny, Mark Morris Institute, 2010.

The Canine Thyroid Epidemic: Answers You Need for Your Dog, W. Jean Dodds, DVM & Diana R. Laverdure, Dogwise Publishing, 2011.

The Healthy Pet Manual: A Guide to the Prevention and Treatment of Cancer, Deborah Straw, Healing Arts Press, 2005.

The Holistic Dog Book: Canine Care for the 21st Century, Denise Flaim, Howell Book House, 2003.

The Holistic Guide for a Healthy Dog, Wendy Volhard & Kerry Brown, Howell Book House, 1995.

The Natural Dog: A Complete Guide for Caring Owners, Mary L. Brennan & Norma Eckroate, Plume /Penquin Books, 1994.

The Natural Vets Guide to Preventing and Treating Cancer in Dogs, Shawn Messonnier, New World Library, 2006.

The New Holistic Way for Dogs & Cats: The Stress-Health Connection, Paul McCutcheon & Susan Weinstein, Celestial Arts, 2010.

The Pet Lover's Guide to Natural Healing for Dogs and Cats, Barbara Fougère, Elsevier Saunders, 2006.

The Royal Treatment: A Natural Approach to Wildly Healthy Pets, Barbara Royal, DVM, Atria/Emily Bestler Books, 2013.

Veterinary World Herb Handbook: A Practical Guide for Effective Herbal Pet Care, Geoff D'Arcy, Wellbeing Publications, 2001.

Homemade diet books

Back to Basics: Whole Foods for Healthy Dogs (Volume 1), Susan Lauten, PhD & Joseph A. Lascola, Preneur Press, 2011.

Canine Nutrition and Choosing the Best Food for Your Breed of Dog, William D. Cusick, Adele Publishing, 1990.

Dr. Becker's Real Food for Healthy Dogs and Cats: Simple Homemade Food, Beth Taylor & Karen Shaw Becker, DVM, Natural Pet Productions, 2013.

Dr. Khalsa's Natural Dog. A Holistic Guide for Healthier Dogs, Deva Khalsa, BowTie Press, 2009.

Give Your Dog a Bone, Dr. Ian Billinghurst, Self-published, 1993.

K9 Kitchen—Your Dog's Diet: The Truth Behind the Hype, Monical Segal, Doggie Diner Inc., 2002.

Natural Nutrition for Dogs and Cats, Kymythy Schultze, Hay House, 1998.

Not Fit for a Dog!: The Truth about Manufactured Dog and Cat Food, Michael W. Fox, Elisabeth Hodgkins & Marion E. Smart, Quill Driver Books, 2009.

Optimal Nutrition. Raw and Cooked Canine Diets: The Next Level, Monica Segal, Doggie Diner Inc., 2007.

Raw and Natural Nutrition for Dogs: The Definitive Guide to Homemade Meals, Lew Olson, North Atlantic Books, 2010.

The Truth about Pet Foods, R. L. Wyson, Inquiry Press, 2002.

Training/behavior

The Loved Dog: The Playful, Non-Aggressive Way to Teach Your Dog Good Behavior, Tamar Geller, Gallery Books, 2007.

30 Days to a Well-Mannered Dog: The Loved Dog Method, Tamar Geller, Gallery Books, 2010.

Magazines

Animal Wellness, www.animalwellnessmagazine.com

Dog Fancy, www.dog-channel.com

Dogs USA, www.dog-channel.com

Natural Dog, www.dog-channel.com

Puppies USA, www.dog-channel.com

Ready, Set, Rescue, www.dog-channel.com

Rescue Me, www.dog-channel.com

The Bark, www.thebark.com

Whole Dog Journal, www.whole-dog-journal.com

Canine food intolerance/sensitivity testing

NutriScan (saliva food intolerance testing), www.nutriscan.org

Hemopet (animal blood bank, greyhound rescue/adoption, full-service veterinary diagnostic laboratory), 714-891-2022, www.hemopet.org

Canine nutrition consulting

Diana R. Laverdure, MS (2015) www.petfooddiva.com

Supplements

Behavior/Canine Cognitive Dysfunction

Animal Health Options (ProQuiet®), 800-845-8849, www.animalhealthoptions.com

Ceva Animal Health (Senilife®), 800-999-0297, www.ceva.us/

MVP Laboratories (Cholodin®), 800- 856-4648, www.mvplabs.com

Nutramax Labs (Denosyl® SAMe), 888-886-6442, www.nutramaxlabs.com

Quincy Animal Health (Neutricks®), 877-681-4321, www.neutricks.com

Vet's Best (Comfort Calm), 800-272-6336, www.vetsbest.com

Virbac Animal Health (Novifit® NoviSAMe®), 800-338-3659, www.virbacvet.com

Calcium

Animal Essentials Natural Seaweed Calcium, (888) 551-0416, www.animalessentials.com

Curcumin

CurcuVET® (Thorne Research), 800-228-1966, http://veterinary.thorne.com/

Liver Support

Hepatosupport, 800-792-2222 , www.rxvitamins.com

Denamarin, Nutramax Labs, 888-886-6442, www.nutramaxlabs.com

Medicinal mushrooms

I'm-Yunity®, 866-932-9993, www.imyunity.com

Organic Pet Superfood, 303-956-0045, http://shop.bixbipet.com/collections/super-food

Omega fish oils

Nordic Naturals (omega oil supplements), www.nordicnaturals.com

Vitamins/minerals

Balance It, https://secure.balanceit.com

Rx Dog Essentials, 800-792-2222, www.rxvitamins.com

The Missing Link, 800-774-7387, www.missinglinkproducts.com

Vetri-Science Canine Plus, 1.800.882.9993, www.vetriscience.com

Innate Response Balanced Minerals, 800-634-6342, www.innateresponse.com

Weight loss

K-9 Slim Down™ and K-9 Slim Down Plus™ (Pet Naturals of Vermont), 888-340-1995, www.petnaturals.com

Other sources of high quality supplements

Animal Apawthecary, 877-595-5276, www.naturalpetwarehouse.com

Nature's Farmacy, 800-733-4981, www.naturesfarmacy.com

Pet Naturals of Vermont, 800-340-1995, www.petnaturals.com

Rx Vitamins for Pets, 800-792-2222, www.rxvitamins.com

Standard Process, 800-558-8740, www.standardprocess.com

Thorne Veterinary, 800-228-1966, www.thorneveterinary.com

VetriScience, 800-882-9993, www.vetriscience.com

Raw and freeze-dried dog foods

Answers Pet Food, 800-431-8480, www.answerspetfood.com

Aunt Jeni's Home Made, 301-702-0123, www.auntjeni.com

Bravo, 866-922-9222, www.bravorawdiet.com

Darwin's Natural Pet Products, 877-738-6325, www.darwinspet.com

Grandma Lucy's, 800-906-LUCY (5829), www.grandmalucys.com

Nature's Variety, 888-519-7387, www.naturesvariety.com

Primal Pet Foods, 866-566-4652, www.primalpetfoods.com

Stella and Chewys, 888-477-8977, www.stellaandchewys.com

The Honest Kitchen, 866-437-9729, www.thehonestkitchen.com

ZiwiPeak, 877-464-9494, www.ziwipeak.com

Fresh Prepared Meals

Just Food For Dogs, 866-726-9509, www.justfoodfordogs.com

Freeze-dried veggie "pre-mixes"

Dr. Harvey's, 866-362-4123, www.drharveys.com

Sojos, 888-867-6567, www.sojos.com

The Honest Kitchen, 866-437-9729, www.thehonestkitchen.com

Retail web sites

You can find many of the items listed in this book, including foods, supplements, and herbs, as well as mentally stimulating games and toys, at the following retail Web sites:

Chewy.com (foods; treats, vitamins and supplements; holistic remedies, grooming; toys; supplies), 800-67-CHEWY, www.chewy.com

Front Porch Pets (maker of Sam's Yams, U.S. made sweet potato chews and other grain-free sweet potato-based dog treats), 800-922-2968, www.frontporchpets.com

Only Natural Pet Store (foods; treats; vitamins and supplements; holistic remedies; natural care products; toys; supplies), 888.937.6677, www.onlynaturalpet.com

The Hungry Puppy (Web site of New Jersey-based retail store. Stocks over 18,000 different products for pets), 888-564-3787, www.thehungrypuppy.com

References

Introduction

Broad Institute. (2014). *Dog Genome Project*. Retrieved from https://www.broadin-stitute.org/mammals/dog.

Dodds, W. J. (2014). Epigenetics: programming for health and longevity. *Journal of the American Holistic Veterinary Medical Association*. 36 (winter issue).

Dodds, W. J. (2014)(a). Functional foods: the new paradigm based on nutrigenom-ics. *Journal of the American Holistic Veterinary Medical Association*. 36: 26-35 (summer issue).

Elliot, R. & Ong, T.J. (2002). Science, medicine, and the future: Nutritional ge-nomics. *British Medical Journal*, 324,1438-1442.

Fekete, S.G. & Brown, D.L. (2007). Veterinary aspects and perspectives of nutrig-enomics: A critical review. *Acta Veterinaria Hungarica*, 55(2), 229-239.

Lee, J.J. (2013, May 14). Dog and Human Genomes Evolved Together. *National Geographic Daily News*. Retrieved from http://news.nationalgeographic.com/news/2013/13/130514-dogs-domestication-humans-genome-science/?rptregcta=reg_free_np&rptregcampaign=20131016_rw_membership_n1p_us_se_w#.

National Human Genome Research Institute (NHGRI). (2011). *A Brief Guide to Genomics: DNA, Genes and Genomes*. Retrieved from http://www.genome.gov/18016863.

National Human Genome Research Institute (NHGRI). (2012). *An Overview of the Human Genome Project: What was the Human Genome Project?*. Retrieved from http://www.genome.gov/12011238.

National Human Genome Research Institute (NHGRI). (2012a). *Epigenomics*. Retrieved from http://www.genome.gov/27532724.

Sample, I. (2009, October 14). Scientists Decode Human Genome's Instruction Manual. *The Guardian*. Retrieved from http://www.guardian.co.uk.

Starr, A. (2011). T*he canine genome: Instruction manual.* American Kennel Club Health Foundation. Retrieved from http://www.akcchf.org/news-events/library/articles/canine-genome-instruction.html.

Swanson, K.S., Schook, L.B. & Fahey, G.C. (2003). Nutritional genomics: Implications for companion animals. *Journal of Nutrition*,133(10), 3033-3040.

The University of Utah. (2014). *Epigenetics*. Retrieved from http://learn.genetics.utah.edu/content/epigenetics/.

Wang, G, Zhai, W, Yang, H, Fan, R, Cao, X, Zhong, L, Wang, L et al. (2013, May 14). The genomics of selection in dogs and the parallel evolution between dogs and humans. *Nature Communications*. doi:10.1038/ncomms2814.

Chapter 1

Beynen, A.C. & Legerstee, E. (2010). Influence of dietary beta-1,3/1,6- glucans on clinical signs of canine osteoarthritis in a double-blind, placebo-controlled trial. *American Journal of Animal and Veterinary Science*, 5(2), 97-101.

Choi, S.W. & Friso, S. (2010). Epigenetics: A new bridge between nutrition and health. *Advances in Nutrition*, 1, 8-16. doi: 10.3945/ an.110.1004.

Daniel H. (2002). Genomics and proteomics: importance for the future of nutrition research. *British Journal of Nutrition*, vol. 87, pp. S305-S311.

Dodds, W. J. (2014). Epigenet.ics: programming for health and longevity. *Journal of the American Holistic Veterinary Medical Association*. 36 (winter issue).

Dodds, W. J. (2014)(a). Functional foods: the new paradigm based on nutrigenomics. *Journal of the American Holistic Veterinary Medical Association*. 36: 26-35 (summer issue).

Elliot, R. & Ong, T.J. (2002). Science, medicine, and the future: Nutritional genomics. *British Medical Journal*, 324,1438-1442.

Epigenetics Project Blog. (2012). Genetic risk, Our choice, May 16, 2012. Retrieved from https://georgefebish.wordpress.com/tag/nutrigenomics.

Essa, M.M. & Memon, M.A. (2013). *Food as Medicine*. New York: Nova Biological.

German J B, Roberts M A, Fay L, Watkins SM. (2002). Metabolomics and individual metabolic assessment: the next great challenge for nutrition. *Journal of Nutrition*, vol. 132, pp. 2486-2487.

Hardy, T.M. & Tollefsbol, T.O. (2011). Epigenetic diet: Impact on the epigenome and cancer. *Epigenomics*, 3(4), 503-518. doi:10.2217/epi.11.71.

Hyman, M. (2011, February 8). *Maximizing methylation: The Key to Healthy Aging* [Web log post]. Retrieved from http://drhyman.com/blog/2011/02/08/maximizing-methylation-the-key-to-healthy-aging-2/.

Kaput, J. & Rodriguez, R.L. (2006). *Nutritional Genomics: Discovering the Path to Personalized Nutrition*. Somerset, NJ: John Wiley & Sons.

National Human Genome Research Institute (NHGRI). (2011). *A Brief Guide to Genomics: DNA, Genes and Genomes*. Retrieved from http://www.genome.gov/18016863.

National Human Genome Research Institute (NHGRI). (2012). *An Overview of the Human Genome Project: What was the Human Genome Project?*. Retrieved from http://www.genome.gov/12011238.

National Human Genome Research Institute (NHGRI). (2012a). *Epigenomics*. Retrieved from http://www.genome.gov/27532724.

Ostrander, E.A. and Wayne, W.K. (2005). The canine genome. *Genome Research*, *15*(12), 1706-1716.

Ostrander, E.A. (2012). Both ends of the leash: The human links to good dogs with bad genes. *New England Journal of Medicine*, 367, 636-646.

Perricone, N. (2010). *Forever Young: The Science of Nutrigenomics for Glowing, Wrinkle-free Skin and Radiant Health at Every Age*. New York: Atria Books.

Phillips, T. (2008). The role of methylation in gene expression. *Nature Education*, 1(1). Retrieved from http://www.nature.com/scitable/topicpage/the-role-of-methylation-in-gene-expression-1070.

Punchard, N.A., Whelan, C.J. & Adcock, I. (2004, September 27). The Journal of Inflammation. *Journal of Inflammation*, 1(1):1.

Ricci, R., Granato. A., Vascellari, M., Boscarato, M., Palagiano, C., Andrighetto, I.,...Mutinelli, F. (2013). Identification of undeclared sources of animal origin in canine dry foods used in dietary elimination trials. *Journal of Animal Physiology and Animal Nutrition*, 97, 32-28.

Science Daily. (2007, November 1). *Domestic Cat Genome Sequenced* [Media release]. Retrieved from http://www.sciencedaily.com/releases/2007/10/071031172826.htm.

Silverman, J. (2008). *What have we Learned from the Human Genome Project?*. Retrieved from http://science.howstuffworks.com/life/genetic/human-genome-project-results.htm.

Starr, A. (2011). *The canine genome: Instruction manual.* American Kennel Club Health Foundation. Retrieved from http://www.akcchf.org/news-events/library/articles/canine-genome-instruction.html.

Stein, L.D. (2004). End of the beginning. *Nature*, 431(7011), 915-916.

Swanson, K.S., Schook, L.B. & Fahey, G.C. (2003). Nutritional genomics: Implications for companion animals. *Journal of Nutrition*, 133(10), 3033-3040.

The Epigenome NoE. (n.d.). *You are What you Eat.* Retrieved from http://epigenome.eu/en/2,48,872.

The University of Utah. (2014). *Epigenetics.* Retrieved from http://learn.genetics.utah.edu/content/epigenetics/.

Chapter 2

Agency for Toxic Substances & Disease Registry (ATSDR). *n-Hexane.* (2011, March 3). Retrieved from USA.gov, http://www.atsdr.cdc.gov/substances/toxsubstance.asp?toxid=68.

Axelsson, E, Ratnakumar, A, Arendt, MJ, Maqbool, K, Webster, MT, Perloski, M, Liberg, O, Arnemo, JM, Hedhammar, A & Lindblad-Toh, K. (2013, January 23). The genomic signature of dog domestication reveals adaptation to a starch-rich diet. *Nature* 495, 360–364 (2013, March 21). doi:10.1038/nature11837.

Bauer, J.E. (2001). Evaluation of nutraceuticals, dietary supplements, and functional food ingredients for companion animals. *Journal of the American Veterinary Medical Association*, 218, 1755-1760.

Case, L.P., Daristotle, L., Hayek, M., Rausch, M.F. (2011). *Canine and Feline Nutrition: A Resource For Companion Animal Professionals.* (3rd ed.). Maryland Heights, MO: Mosby Elsevier.

Castaldo, S. & Capasso, F. (2002). Propolis, an old remedy used in modern medicine. *Fitoterapia*, 73(1), S1-S6.

Drewnowski, A. & Gomez-Carneros, C. (2000). Bitter taste, phytonutrients, and the consumer: A review. *The American Journal of Clinical Nutrition*, 72 (6), 1424-1435.

Egan, S. (2013, July 31). *Making the Case for Eating Fruit* [Web log post]. Retrieved from http://well.blogs.nytimes.com/2013/07/31/making-the-case-for-eating-fruit/?_r=0.

Environmental Working Group (EWG). (2012). *Frequently asked Questions about Produce and Pesticides.* Retrieved from http://www.ewg.org/foodnews/faq.php.

Environmental Working Group (EWG). (2014). *Executive Summary: EWG's Shopper's Guide to Pesticides in Produce*™. Retrieved from http://www.ewg.org/foodnews/summary.php.

Fekete, S.G. & Brown, D.L. (2007). Veterinary aspects and perspectives of nutrigenomics: A critical review. *Acta Veterinaria Hungarica*, 55 (2), 229–239.

Hill, R.C. (1998). The nutritional requirements of exercising dogs. *The Journal of Nutrition*, 128 (12), 2686S-2690S.

Ji, S. (2014, May 23). Amazing food science discovery: Edible plants 'talk' to animal cells, promote healing. *GreenMedInfo*. Retrieved from http://www.greenmedinfo.com/blog/amazing-food-science-discovery-edible-plants-talk-animal-cells-promote-healing.

Kaput, J. & Rodriguez, R.L. (2006). *Nutritional Genomics: Discovering the Path to Personalized Nutrition*. Somerset, NJ: John Wiley & Sons.

Kealy, R.D. (1999). Protein in life stage nutrition– factors influencing lean body mass in aging dogs. *Compendium on Continuing Education for the Practicing Veterinarian*, 21, 34-37.

Knueven, D. (2014, April 29). [personal correspondence].

Linus Pauling Institute. (2013). *Micronutrient Information Center*. Retrieved from http://lpi.oregonstate.edu.

Lu, C., Toepel, K., Irish, R., Fenske, R.A., Barr, D.B., Bravo, R. (2006). Organic diets significantly lower children's dietary exposure to organophosphorus pesticides. Environmental Health Perspectives, 114(2), 260-3.

Lu, C., Barr, D.B., Pearson, M.A., Waller, L.A. (2008). Dietary intake and its contribution to longitudinal organophosphorus pesticide exposure in urban/suburban children. *Environmental Health Perspectives*, 116(4), 537-42.

Mercola, J. (2006). *The Healing Properties of Raw Honey*. Retrieved from http://articles.mercola.com/sites/articles/archive/2006/12/19/the-healing-properties-of-honey.aspx.

Mercola, J. (2009). *This Bee Product has Enormous Benefits for Your Health*. Retrieved from http://articles.mercola.com/sites/articles/archive/2009/11/17/This-Bee-Product-Has-Enormous-Benefits-for-Your-Health.aspx.

Mercola, J. (2011). *Fresh evidence…Could 1 Teaspoon Per Day Tame Your Allergy Problems?*. Retrieved from http://articles.mercola.com/sites/articles/archive/2011/05/27/can-eating-local-honey-cure-allergies.aspx.

Mu J., Zhuang, X., Wang, Q., Jiang, H., Deng, Z.B., Wang, B…Zhang HG. (2014, May 19). Interspecies communication between plant and mouse gut Host cells through edible plant derived exosome-like nanoparticles. *Molecular Nutrition & Food Research*. doi: 10.1002/mnfr.201300729. [Epub ahead of print] PubMed PMID: 24842810.

National Library of Medicine. (2013). *What are Proteins and what do they Do?* Retrieved from http://ghr.nlm.nih.gov/handbook/howgeneswork/protein.

New York University (NYU) School of Medicine. (n.d.). *Calcium Oxalate*. Retrieved from https://files.nyu.edu/rabenr01/public/calcium%20oxalate.htm.

Organic.org. (2013). *Frequently asked questions*. Retrieved from http://www.organic.org/home/faq.

Oxalosis and Hyperoxaluria Foundation. (2008). *The Oxalate Content of Food*. Retrieved from http://ohf.org/diet.html.

PetMD. (2013). *The Power of Protein*. Retrieved from http://www.petmd.com/dog/slideshows/nutrition-center/the-power-of-protein.

Puotinen, C.J. (2007). *Bee Products have a Special Meaning for Dogs*. Retrieved from http://www.whole-dog-journal.com/issues/10_9/features/Bee-Honey-Products-Help-Canines_15967-1.html.

Puotinen, C.J. & Straus, M. (2010). *Preventing Bladder & Kidney Stones in Dogs*. Retrieved from http://www.whole-dog-journal.com/issues/13_5/features/Dogs-With-Kidney-Stones_16222-1.html.

Ramadan, M.F. & Al-Ghamdi, A. (2012). Bioactive compounds and health-promoting properties of royal jelly: A review. *Journal of Functional Foods*, 4(1), 39-52.

Saarinen, K., Jantunen, J. & Haahtela, T. (2011). Birch pollen honey for birch pollen allergy—A randomized controlled pilot study. *International Archives of Allergy and Immunology*, 155,160–166. doi: 10.1159/000319821.

Sforcin, J.M. & Bankova, V. (2011). Propolis: Is there a potential for the development of new drugs? *Journal of Ethnopharmacology*, 133(2), 253-260.

U.S. Food and Drug Administration (USFDA). (2005). *Phytonutrient FAQs*. Retrieved from http://www.ars.usda.gov/aboutus/docs.htm?docid=4142.

WebMD. (2014). *Types of Fats—Topic Overview*. Retrieved from http://www.webmd.com/food-recipes/tc/types-of-fats-topic-overview.

Wolf, D. (2009). *Superfoods: The Food and Medicine of the Future*. Berkeley, CA: North Atlantic Books.

Chapter 3

Allred, C.D., Allred, K.F., Ju, Y.H., Virant, S.M. & Helferich, W.G. (2001). Soy diets containing varying amounts of genistein stimulate growth of estrogen-dependent (MCF-7) tumors in a dose-dependent manner. *Cancer Res*, 61(13), 5045-50.

Becker, G.S. (2004). *Animal Rendering, Economics and Policy*. Retrieved from http://nationalaglawcenter.org/wp-content/uploads/assets/crs/RS21771.pdf.

Boermans, H.J. & Leung, M.K. (2007). Mycotoxins and the pet food industry: Toxological evidence and risk assessment. *International Journal of Food Microbiology*, 119 (2007), 95–102.

Cerundolo, R., Court, M.H., Hao, Q. & Michel, K.E. (2004). Identification and concentration of soy phytoestrogens in commercial dog foods. *American Journal of Veterinary Research*, 65(5), 592-596.

Cerundolo, R., Michel, K.E., Court, M.H., Shrestha, B., Refsal, K.R., Oliver, J.W.,… Shofer, F.S. (2009). Effects of dietary soy isoflavones on health, steroidogenesis, and thyroid gland function in dogs. *American Journal of Veterinary Research*, 70(3), 353-360.

Dodds, W.J. (2013). *NutriScan data*. Retrieved from www.nutriscan.org.

Environmental Working Group (EWG). (2009, June 26). *Dog Food Contaminated with Levels of Fluoride above EPA's Legal Limit for Humans*. Retrieved from http://www.ewg.org/.

Environmental Working Group (EWG). (2012). *EWG Farm Subsidies*. Retrieved from http://farm.ewg.org/.

Environmental Working Group (EWG). (2013, March). *We have the Right to Know about our Food*. Retrieved from http://static.ewg.org/reports/2012/gmolandingpage/pdfs/we_have_the_right%20to_know.pdf.

Environmental Working Group. (2013)(a). *Executive Summary: EWG's Shopper's Guide to Pesticides in Produce™*. Retrieved from http://www.ewg.org/foodnews/summary.php.

Fallon, S. & Enig, M.G. (2000). *Cinderella's Dark Side*. Retrieved from http://www.mercola.com/article/soy/avoid_soy3.htm.

Fahey, G.C. (n.d.). *Soybean Use: Companion Animals*. Retrieved from http://www.soymeal.org/FactSheets/domesticpets.pdf.

Ferrara, D. (2010). *Potassium Bisulphate as a Food Preservative*. Retrieved from http://www.livestrong.com/article/308673-potassium-bisulphate-as-a-food-preservative/.

Fort, P., Moses, N., Fasano, M., Goldberg, T. & Lifshitz, F. (1990). Breast and soy-formula feedings in early infancy and the prevalence of autoimmune thyroid disease in children. *Journal of the American College of Nutrition*, 9(2), 164-167.

Gallo, A.C. (2013, June 18). *Three-month Update on GMO Labeling*. Retrieved from http://www.wholefoodsmarket.com/tags/gmos.

Gram, D & Rathke, L. (2014, April 24). Vermont Lawmakers Pass GMO Labeling Bill; Governor Expected to Sign. *Huffington Post*. Retrieved from http://www.huffingtonpost.com/2014/04/24/vermont-lawmakers-pass-gmo-labeling-bill_n_5203569.html.

Hyman, M. (2012). *How Hidden Food Sensitivities Make You Fat*. Retrieved from http://drhyman.com/blog/2012/02/22/how-hidden-food-sensitivities-make-you-fat/.

Hyman, M. (2013). *Gluten: What You don't Know Might Kill You*. Retrieved from http://drhyman.com/blog/2011/03/17/gluten-what-you-dont-know-might-kill-you/.

Hyman, M. (2013)(a). *Three Hidden Ways Wheat Makes You Fat*. Retrieved from http://drhyman.com/blog/2012/02/13/three-hidden-ways-wheat-makes-you-fat/.

Jamadar-Shroff, V., Papich, M.G. & Suter, S.E. (2009). Soy-derived isoflavones inhibit the growth of canine lymphoid cell lines. *Clinical Cancer Research*, 15(4), 1269-1276.

Ji, S. (2013, June 13). *Glyphosate (Roundup) Carcinogenic in the Parts per Trillion Range* [Web log post]. Retrieved from http://www.greenmedinfo.com/blog/breaking-glyphosate-roundup-carcinogenic-parts-trillion-range?utm_source=www.GreenMedInfo.com&utm_campaign=e624913b6e-Greenmedinfo&utm_medium=email&utm_term=0_193c8492fb-e624913b6e-86768346.

Markovich, J.E., Heinze, C.R., & Freeman, L.M. (2013). Timely topics in nutrition: Thiamine deficiency in dogs and cats. *Journal of the American Veterinary Medical Association*, 243(5), 649-656.

Mount Sinai Medical Center. (2013). Soy-based compound may reduce tumor cell proliferation in colorectal cancer. *ScienceDaily*. Retrieved from http://www.sciencedaily.com/releases/2013/04/130411194031.htm.

Kerns, N. (2012). Canned controversy: Consumers are demanding BPA-free cans, but industry isn't ready with an alternative. *Whole Dog Journal*, 15(5), 4-5.

Kressler, C. (2012). *RHR: Pioneering Researcher Alessio Fasano M.D. on Gluten, Autoimmunity & Leaky Gut*. Retrieved from http://chriskresser.com/pioneering-researcher-alessio-fasano-m-d-on-gluten-autoimmunity-leaky-gut.

National Corn Growers Association. (2013). *2012 Facts and Figures in New World of Corn*. Retrieved from http://www.ncga.com/news-and-resources/news-stories/article/2013/03/-2012-facts-and-figures-in-new-world-of-corn.

PetfoodIndustry.com. (2013, August 23). *Petfoods with Plant-derived Proteins may Contain more Mycotoxins, Researcher says* [Press release]. Retrieved from http://www.petfoodindustry.com/48909.html.

Perricone, N. (2010). *Forever Young: The Science of Nutrigenomics for Glowing, Wrinkle-free Skin and Radiant Health at Every Age*. New York: Atria Books.

Renter, E. (2013). *Target to Remove GMOs from Major Food Brand*. Retrieved from http://naturalsociety.com/target-to-remove-gmos-from-major-food-brand/.

Robinson, L.E. & Reeves, S. (2013). *Review of sIgA's Major Role as a First Line of Immune Defense and New Indications Regarding Inflammation and Gut Health*. Retrieved from http://www.embriahealth.com.

Roudebush, P. (1993). Pet food additives. *Journal of the American Veterinary Medical Association*, 203, 1667-1970.

Sapkota, A.R., Lefferts, L.Y., McKenzie, S. & Walker, P. (2007). What do we feed to food-production animals? A review of animal feed ingredients and their potential impacts on human health. *Environmental Health Perspectives*, 115(5), 663–670. doi: 10.1289/ehp.9760.

Sisson, M. (2013). The Lowdown on Lectins [Web log post]. Retrieved from http://www.marksdailyapple.com/lectins/#axzz2ZEGf7fPq.

The Association of American Feed Control Officials (AAFCO). (n.d.). *Definition of Food & Drugs*. Retrieved from http://petfood.aafco.org/DefinitionofFoodDrugs.aspx.

The Dog Food Project. (2012). *Menadione (Vitamin K3)* [Web log post]. Retrieved from http://www.dogfoodproject.com/index.php?page=menadione.

Thongprakaisang, S., Thiantanawat, A., Rangkadilok, N., Suriyo, T., & Satayavivad, J. (2013). Glyphosate induces human breast cancer cells growth via estrogen receptors. *Food and Chemical Toxicology*, 59, 129-36. doi:pii: S0278-6915(13)00363-3.

University of Illinois College of Agricultural, Consumer and Environmental Sciences. (2013). Soy and Tomato may be Effective in Preventing Prostate Cancer. *ScienceDaily*. Retrieved from http://www.sciencedaily.com/releases/2013/05/130508114307.htm.

U.S. Food and Drug Administration (USFDA). (1997). *CVM Update: FDA Requests that Ethoxyquin Levels be Reduced in Dog Foods.* Retrieved from http://www.fda.gov/animalveterinary/newsevents/cvmupdates/ucm127828.htm.

U.S. Food and Drug Administration (USFDA). (2009). FDA 101: *Animal Feed.* Retrieved from http://www.fda.gov/ForConsumers/ConsumerUpdates/ucm164473.htm.

U.S. Food and Drug Administration (USFDA). (2010). *Pet Food Labels-General.* Retrieved from http://www.fda.gov/animalveterinary/resourcesforyou/ucm047113.htm.

U.S. Food and Drug Administration (USFDA). (2012). *FDA Continues to Study BPA* [Media release]. Retrieved from http://www.fda.gov/ForConsumers/ConsumerUpdates/ucm297954.htm.

Voiland, A. (2007). *Health Reasons to Cut Back on Corn Consumption.* Retrieved from http://www.usnews.com/news/50-ways-to-improve-your-life/articles/2007/12/17/health-reasons-to-cut-back-on-corn-consumption.

Williams, K. (2012, October 26). *A Tale of Two Corns* [Web log post]. Retrieved from http://nefb.wordpress.com/2012/10/26/whats-the-difference-between-field-corn-and-sweet-corn/.

Woodford, K. (2009). *The Devil in the Milk.* White River Junction, VT: Chelsea Green Publishing.

World Health Organization (WHO). (2013). *Food, Genetically Modified.* Retrieved from http://www.who.int/topics/food_genetically_modified/en/.

Yamka, R.M., Harmon, D.L., Schoenherr, W.D., Khoo, C., Gross, K.L., Davidson, S.J. & Joshi, D.K. (2006). In vivo measurement of flatulence and nutrient digestibility in dogs fed poultry by-product meal, conventional soybean meal and low-oligosaccharide low-phytate soybean meal. *American Journal of Veterinary Research,* 67, 88-94.

Zhang, Y., Li, Q., Chen, H. (2013). DNA methylation and histone modification of Wnt genes by genistein during colon cancer development. *Carcinogenesis* . doi: 10.1093/carcin/bgt129 ; published online April 18, 2013. Retrieved from ACES, 2013; Aug 5, 2013.

Chapter 4

Becker, K. (2014). *Vitamin D: Don't Let Your Dog Overdose on this Popular Human Nutrient.* Retrieved from http://healthypets.mercola.com/sites/healthypets/archive/2014/05/09/dog-vitamin-d-levels.aspx?e_cid=20140509Z1_PetsNL_

art_1&utm_source=petnl&utm_medium=email&utm_content=art1&utm_
campaign=20140509Z1&et_cid=DM44226&et_rid=515307302.

Case, L.P., Daristotle, L., Hayek, M. & Rausch, M.F. (2011). *Canine and Feline Nutrition: A Resource For Companion Animal Professionals.* (3rd ed.). Maryland Heights, MO: Mosby Elsevier.

Frantz, N.Z., Yamka, R.M., Friesen, K.G., Gao, X. & Al-Murrani, S. (2008). Identification of genes differences between geriatric dogs with early indications of kidney disease compared to geriatric dogs without kidney disease. *The FASEB Journal*, 22, 442.2.

Han, S.N., Adolfsson, O., Lee, C-K., Prolla, T.A., Ordovas, J., Meydani, S.N. (2006). Age and vitamin E-induced changes in gene expression profiles of T cells. *Journal of Immunology*, 177(9), 6052-6061.

Haladová, E., Mojžišová, J., Smrčo, P., Ondrejková, A., Vojtek B. & Hipíková V. (2009). The effect of ß (1,3/1,6)D-glucan on selected non-specific and specific immunological parameters in dogs after vaccination. *Folia Veterinaria*, 53, 43-46.

Haladová, E., Mojžišová, J., Smrčo, P., Ondrejková, A.,Vojtek, B., Prokeš, M. & Petrovová, E. (2011). Immunomodulatory effect of glucan on specific and nonspecific immunity after vaccination in puppies. *Acta Veterinaria Hungarica*, 59, 77-86.

Hofve, J. (2013). *Why Switch Food?* Retrieved from http://www.onlynaturalpet.com/knowledgeBase/knowledgebasedetail.aspx?articleid=111&SubjectId=13253&SubjectName=Food+&click=77140&utm_source=eps&utm_medium=email&utm_campaign=epm-111613-wkly-why-switch-foods-p-r.

Institute of Neuroscience. (2011). *Research Interests.* Retrieved from http://www.ion.ac.cn/laboratories/int.asp?id=67.

McDonald, P., Edwards, R.A., Greenhalgh, J.F.D., Morgan, C.A., Sinclair, L.A. & Wilkinson, R.G. (2011). *Animal Nutrition* (7th ed.). Harlow, England: Pearson Education Limited.

MedlinePlus. (2013). *Vitamin D.* Retrieved from http://www.nlm.nih.gov/medlineplus/druginfo/natural/929.html.

Mercola, J. (2010). *Is this the New Silver Bullet for Cancer?* Retrieved from http://articles.mercola.com/sites/articles/archive/2010/03/11/is-vitamin-d-the-silver-bullet-for-cancer.aspx.

National Institutes of Health (NIH). (2011). *Dietary Supplement Fact Sheet: Vitamin D.* Retrieved from http://ods.od.nih.gov/factsheets/VitaminD-HealthProfessional/.

National Research Council of the National Academy of Sciences (NRC). (2006). *Nutrient Requirements of Dogs and Cats*. Washington, DC: NRC Press.

PetMD. (2013). *Excess Calcium in the Blood in Dogs*. Retrieved from http://www.petmd.com/dog/conditions/endocrine/c_multi_hypercalcemia#.

Segal, M. (2007). The Senior Canine. In *Optimal Nutrition- Raw and Cooked Canine Diets: The Next Level* (pp. 175-181). Toronto, Canada: Doggie Diner, Inc.

Sheffy, B.E., Williams , A.J., Zimmer, J.F. & Ryan, G.D. (1985). Nutrition and metabolism of the geriatric dog. *The Cornell Veterinarian*, 75(2), 324-347.

Stockman, J., Fascetti, A.J., Kass, P.H. & Larsen, J.A. (2013). Evaluation of recipes of home-prepared maintenance diets for dogs. *Journal of the American Veterinary Medical Association*, 242(11), 1500-5. doi: 10.2460/javma.242.11.1500.

Straus, M. (2007). *Introduction to Homemade Diets for Dogs*. Retrieved from http://dogaware.com/articles/wdjhomemade1.html#vegetarian.

Straus, M. (2011). *Crash Course on Calcium*. Retrieved from http://dogaware.com/articles/dwcalcium.html.

Straus, M. (2013). Dishing on diets: Veterinary nutritionists conclude that only they can properly formulate a homemade diet. *Whole Dog Journal*, 16 (9), 3-5.

Stuyven, E., Verdonck, F., Van Hoek, I., Daminet, S., Duchateau, L., Remon, J. P., ... Cox, E. (2010). Oral administration of ß-1,3/1,6-glucan to dogs temporally changes total and antigen-specific IgA and IgM. *Clinical & Vaccine Immunology*, 17(2), 281-285.

VetInfo. (2012). *The Benefits of Liver for Dogs*. Retrieved from http://www.vetinfo.com/the-benefits-of-liver-for-dogs.html#b.

Wannemacher Jr., R.W., McCoy, J.R. (1966). Determination of optimal dietary protein requirements of young and old dogs. *Journal of Nutrition*, 88(1), 66-74.

Zicker, S.C., Jewell, D.E., Yamka, R.M. & Milgram, N.W. (2012). Evaluation of cognitive learning, memory, psychomotor, immunologic, and retinal functions in healthy puppies fed foods fortified with docosahexaenoic acid-rich fish oil from 8 to 52 weeks of age. *Journal of the American Veterinary Medical Association*, 241, 583-594.

Chapter 5

Blasa, S.E., Booles, D.B. & Burger, I.H. (1989). Is carbohydrate essential for pregnancy and lactation in dogs? In *Waltham Symposium No. 7: Nutrition of the dog and cat* (pp. 229-242). New York: Cambridge University Press.

Case, L.P., Daristotle, L., Hayek, M. & Rausch, M.F. (2011). *Canine and Feline Nutrition: A Resource for Companion Animal Professionals* (3rd ed.). Maryland Heights, MO: Mosby Elsevier.

Coffman, M. (n.d.). *Feeding the High-performance Bird Dog.* Retrieved from http://www.wec.ufl.edu/floridaquail/Documents/FEEDING%20THE%20HIGH%20PERFORMANCE%20BIRD%20DOG.pdf.

Fascetti, A.J. & Delaney, S.G. (2012). *Applied Veterinary Clinical Nutrition.* West Sussex, United Kingdom: Wiley Blackwell.

Gillette, R.L. (1999). *Feeding the Canine Athlete for Optimal Performance.* Retrieved from http://www.sportsvet.com/Art3.html.

Hand, M.S., Thatcher, C., Remillard, R.I, Roudebush, P. & Lewis, L.D. (2000). *Small Animal Clinical Nutrition* (4th ed.). Topeka, KS: MMI.

Hand, M.S., Thatcher, C., Remillard, R.I., Roudebush, P. & Novotny, B.J. (2010). *Small Animal Clinical Nutrition* (5th ed.). Topeka, KS: MMI.

Heffernan, A. (2012). *All about Your Metabolic Energy Systems.* Retrieved from http://experiencelife.com/article/all-about-your-metabolic-energy-systems/.

Hill, R.C. (1998). The nutritional requirements of exercising dogs. *The Journal of Nutrition,* 128 (12), 2686S-2690S.

Lauten, S. & Lascola, J.A. (2011). *Back to Basics: Whole Foods for Healthy Dogs* (Volume 1). Charleston, SC: Preneur Press.

McNamara, J.T. (2006). *Principles of Companion Animal Nutrition.* Upper Saddle River, NJ: Pearson Education, Inc.

Merck Veterinary Manual. (2011). *Puerperal Hypocalcemia in Small Animals.* Retrieved from http://www.merckmanuals.com/vet/metabolic_disorders/disorders_of_calcium_metabolism/puerperal_hypocalcemia_in_small_animals.html.

National Research Council of the National Academies. (2006). *Nutrient Requirements of Dogs and Cats.* Washington, DC: The National Academies Press.

Schenck, P. (2010). *Home-Prepared Dog & Cat Diets* (2nd ed.). Ames, IA: Wiley-Blackwell.

Segal, M. (2007). Ally's pregnancy. In *Optimal Nutrition- Raw and Cooked Canine Diets: The Next Level.* Toronto, Canada: Doggie Diner, Inc.

Piercy, R.J., Hinchcliff, K.W., Morley, P.S., Disilvestro, R.A., Reinhart, G.A., Nelson, S.L., ... Morrie Craig, A. (2001). Association between vitamin E and enhanced athletic performance in sled dogs. *Medicine & Science in Sports & Exercise*, 33(5), 826-833.

Wills, J.M. & Simpson, K.W. (1994). *The Waltham Book of Clinical Nutrition of the Dog and Cat*. Tarrytown, NY: Pergamon Press/ Elsevier.

Chapter 6

Buchanan, B.B. & Frick, O.L. (2002). The dog as a model for food allergy. *Annals of the New York Academy of Sciences*, 964, 173-183.

Cave, N.J. & Marks, S.L. (2004). Evaluation of the immunogenicity of dietary proteins in cats and the influence of the canning process. *American Journal of Veterinary Research*, 65, 1427-1433.

Challacombe, S.J. (1987). The induction of secretory IgA responses. In *Food Allergy and Intolerance*. Eastborne, England: W. B. Sanders.

Day, M.J. (2005). The canine model of dietary hypersensitivity. *Proceedings of the Nutrition Society*, 64, 458-464.

Dodds, W. J. (2014). Food intolerance: Diagnostic testing & dietary management. *Journal of the American Holistic Veterinary Medical Association*, 36: 36-42 (summer issue).

Fekete, S.G. & Brown, D.L. (2007). Veterinary aspects and perspectives of nutrigenomics: A critical review. *Acta Veterinaria Hungarica*, 55(2), 229-239.

Foster, A.P., Knowles, T.G., Hotson-Moore, A., Cousins, P.D., Day, M.J. & Hall, E.J. (2003). Serum IgE and IgG responses to food antigens in normal and atopic dogs, and dogs with gastrointestinal disease. *Veterinary Immunology and Immunopathology*, 92, 113-124.

Jeffers, J.G., Shanley, K.J. & Meyer, E.K. (1991). Diagnostic testing of dogs for food hypersensitivity. *Journal of the American Veterinary Medical Association*, 198, 245-250.

Kiyono, H., Kweon, M.N., Hiroi, T. & Takahashi, I. (2001). The mucosal immune system: From specialized immune defense to inflammation and allergy. *Acta Odontologica Scandinavica*, 59, 145-153.

Kraft, S. C, Rothbert, R. M, Kramer, C. M. (1967). Gastric output and circulating anti-BSA in adults. *Clinical and Experimental Immunology*, 2:321-326.

Lee, Y.H. & Wong, D.T. (2009). Saliva: An emerging biofluid for early detection of disease. *American Journal of Dentistry*, 22, 421-428.

Miller, C.S., Foley, J.D., Bailey, A.L., Campbell, C.L., Humphries, R.L., Christodoulides, N., … McDevitt, J.T. (2010). Current developments in salivary diagnostics. *Biomarker Medicine*, 4, 171-189.

Ricci, R., Granato. A., Vascellari, M., Boscarato, M., Palagiano, C., Andrighetto, I.,…Mutinelli, F. (2013). Identification of undeclared sources of animal origin in canine dry foods used in dietary elimination trials. *Journal of Animal Physiology and Animal Nutrition*, 97, 32-28.

Rinkinen, M., Teppo, A.M., Harmoinen, J. & Westermark, E. (2003). Relationship between canine mucosal and serum immunoglobulin A (IgA) concentrations: Serum IgA does not assess duodenal secretory IgA. *Microbiology and Immunology*, 47, 155-159.

Robinson, L.E. & Reeves, S. (2013). *Review of sIgA's major role as a first line of immune defense and new indications regarding inflammation and gut health*. Retrieved from http://www.embriahealth.com.

Swanson, K.S., Schook, L.B. & Fahey, G.C. (2003). Nutritional genomics: Implications for companion animals. *Journal of Nutrition*, 133(10), 3033-3040.

Vojdani, A. (2009). Detection of IgE, IgG, IgA and IgM antibodies against raw and processed food antigens. *Nutrition and Metabolism*, 6(22), 1-15.

Chapter 7

Allard, J.S., Perez, E., Zou, S. & de Cabo, R. (2009). Dietary activators of Sirt1. *Molecular & Cellular Endocrinology*, 299(1), 58-63.

Association for Pet Obesity Prevention. (2013). *2012 National Pet Obesity Survey Results*. Retrieved from http://www.petobesityprevention.com/2012-national-pet-obesity-survey-results/.

Banfield Pet Hospital. (2012). *State of Pet Health 2012 Report*. Retrieved from www.stateofpethealth.com.

Bartges, J. (2013, May 29). Personal correspondence.

Brand-Miller, J.C., Holt, S.H., Pawlak, D.B. & McMillan, J. (2002). Glycemic index and obesity. *American Journal of Clinical Nutrition*, 76(1), 281S-285S.

Byers, C.G., Wilson, C.C., Stephens, M.B., Goodie, J., Netting, F.E. & Olsen, C. (2011, April). Obesity in Dogs, Part 1: Exploring the Causes and Consequences of Canine Obesity. *DVM 360Magazine*. Retrieved from http://veterinarymedicine.dvm360.com/vetmed/Nutrition/Exploring-the-causes-and-consequences-of-canine-ob/ArticleStandard/Article/detail/715423.

Byers, C.G., Wilson, C.C., Stephens, M.B., Goodie, J., Netting, F.E. & Olsen, C. (2011, April)(a). Obesity in dogs, part 2: Treating Excess Weight with a Multiple Modality Approach. *DVM 360Magazine*. Retrieved from http://veterinarymedicine. dvm360.com/vetmed/Nutrition/Treating-excess-weight-with-a-multimodality-approa/ArticleStandard/Article/detail/715431.

Celleno, L., Tolaini, M.V., D'Amore, A., Perricone, N.V. & Preuss, H.G.(2007). A dietary supplement containing standardized Phaseolus vulgaris extract influences body composition of overweight men and women. *International Journal of Medical Sciences*, 4(1), 45-52.

Demerath, E.W., Guan, W., Pankow, J.S., Grove, M.L., North, K.E., Fornage, M., … Boerwinkle, E.A. (2013). Genome-wide methylation study of body mass index (BMI) in African American adults: preliminary data from the ARIC study. *Circulation*, 127, A052.

Dotinga, R. (2013). *Gene Variants may Play Role in Obesity*. Retrieved from http://www.14news.com/story/22612476/gene-variants-may-play-role-in-obesity.

Eisele, I.S., Wood, I.J., German, A.J., Hunter, L.J. & Trayhurn, P. (2005). Adipokine gene expression in dog adipose tissues and dog white adipocytes differentiated in primary culture. *Hormone and Metabolic Research*, 37(8), 474-481.

Endocrine Today. (2011). Fat Linked to DNA Methylation may Help Explain Obesity-related Diseases. *Endocrine Today*. Retrieved from http://www.healio.com/endocrinology/obesity/news/print/endocrine-today/%7Bf0484521-8015-4f71-a5dd-383d0236a57d%7D/fat-linked-to-dna-methylation-may-help-explain-obesity-related-diseases.

Fiore, K. (2013). *Obesity tied to DNA regulation*. Retrieved from http://www.medpagetoday.com/Genetics/GeneralGenetics/38082.

Franks, P.W. & Ling, C. (2010). Epigenetics and obesity: The devil is in the details. *BMC Medicine*, 8, 88. doi:10.1186/1741-7015-8-88.

German, A.J. (2006). The growing problem of obesity in dogs and cats. *Journal of Nutrition*, 136(7), 1940S-1946S.

Harvard School of Public Health (HSPH). (2013). *Genes are not Destiny*. Retrieved from http://www.hsph.harvard.edu/obesity-prevention-source/obesity-causes/genes-and-obesity/.

Howard, B. (2012). *Banfield Sees Bump in Fat Pets. DVM360*, 43(6), 1-43. Retrieved from http://veterinarynews.dvm360.com/dvm/Veterinary+news/Banfield-sees-bump-in-obese-and-overweight-pets/ArticleStandard/Article/detail/775267.

Hyman, M. (2012). *How Hidden Food Sensitivities Make You Fat*. Retrieved from http://drhyman.com/blog/2012/02/22/how-hidden-food-sensitivities-make-you-fat/.

Hyman, M. (2013). *Three Hidden Ways Wheat Makes You Fat*. Retrieved from http://drhyman.com/blog/2012/02/13/three-hidden-ways-wheat-makes-you-fat/.

Kealy, R.D., Lawler, D.F., Ballam, J.M., Mantz, S.L., Biery, D.N., Greeley, E.H., ... Stowe, H.D. (2002). Effects of diet restriction on life span and age-related changes in dogs. *Journal of the American Veterinary Medical Association*, 220(9), 1315-1320.

Kilpeläinen, T.O., Qi, L., Brage, S., Sharp, S.J., Sonestedt, E., Demerath, E., ... Loos, R.J.F. (2011). Physical activity attenuates the influence of FTO variants on obesity risk: A meta-analysis of 218,166 adults and 19,268 children. *PLoS Medicine*, 8(11), e1001116. doi:10.1371/journal.pmed.1001116.

Lawler, D.F. Evans, R.H., Larson, B.T., Spitznagel, E.L., Ellersieck, M.R. & Kealy, R.D. (2005). Influence of lifetime food restriction on causes, time, and predictors of death in dogs. *Journal of the American Veterinary Medical Association*, 226(3), 225-231.

Lawler, D.F., Larson, B.T., Ballam, J.M., Smith, G.K., Biery, D.N., Evans, R.H., ... Kealy, R.D. (2007). Diet restriction and ageing in the dog: Major observations over two decades. *British Journal of Nutrition*, 98, 1–13, 497-503.

Lavebratt, C., Almgren, M. & Ekström, T.J. (2012). Review: Epigenetic regulation in obesity. *International Journal of Obesity*, 36, 757-765. doi:10.1038/ijo.2011.178.

Lefebvre, S.L., Yang, M., Wang, M., Elliott, D.A., Buff, P.R. & Lund, E.M. (2013). Effect of age at gonadectomy on the probability of dogs becoming overweight. *Journal of the American Veterinary Medical Association*, 243(2), 236-243.

Li, W. (2010). *Can we Eat to Starve Cancer?* [Video]. Retrieved from http://www.youtube.com/watch?v=B9bDZ5-zPtY.

Medical College of Georgia at Georgia Regents University. (2013, March 21). Scientists Identify Gene that is Consistently Altered in Obese Individuals. *ScienceDaily*. Retrieved from http://www.sciencedaily.com /releases/2013/03/130321133114.htm.

Mercola.com. (2012). *This New Drug Appears to Cause Cancer Cells to Self-destruct*. Retrieved from http://articles.mercola.com/sites/articles/archive/2012/08/04/dca-and-turmeric-on-cancer.aspx.

Norris, S. (2013). You are what you eat-nutrigenomics and obesity. *Veterinary Nursing Journal*, 28(6), 190-191. doi/:10.1111/vnj.2013.28.issue-6/issuetoc.

Perricone, N. (2010). *Forever Young: The Science of Nutrigenomics for Glowing, Wrinkle-free Skin and Radiant Health at Every Age*. New York: Atria Books.

Roudebush, P., Schoenherr, W.D. & Delaney, S.J. (2008). Timely topics in nutrition: An evidence-based review of the use of nutraceuticals and dietary supplementation for the management of obese and overweight pets. *Journal of the American Veterinary Medical Association*, 232, 1646-1655.

Sjøgren, K. (2013). *Seven New Genetic Causes of Obesity Identified*. Retrieved from http://sciencenordic.com/seven-new-genetic-causes-obesity-identified.

Swanson, K.S. (2007). *Using nutritional genomics to study canine obesity and diabetes*. Retrieved from http://en.engormix.com.

Veerman, J.L. (2011). On the futility of screening for genes that make you fat. *PloS Medicine*, 8(11), e1001114. Doi:10.1371/journal.pmed.1001114.

Ward, E. (2007). *Weight Reduction in Dogs- General Information*. Retrieved from http://www.petobesityprevention.com/wp-content/uploads/2010/05/Weight_Reduction_in_Dogs_General_Information.pdf.

Yamka, R.M., Frantz, N.Z. & Friesen, K.G. (2007). Effects of 3 canine weight loss foods on body composition and obesity markers. *International Journal of Applied Research in Veterinary Medicine*, 5(3), 125-132.

Yamka, R.M., Friesen, K.G., Gao, X. & Al-Murrani, S. (2007). Identification of genes related to obesity in dogs. *The FASEB Journal*, 21, 28.4.

Chapter 8

Adams, C. (2013). *Ginger Treats Osteoarthritis with Topical Application*. Retrieved from http://www.greenmedinfo.com/blog/ginger-treats-osteoarthritis-topical-application.

Banfield Pet Hospital. (2012). *State of Pet Health 2012 Report*. Retrieved from www.stateofpethealth.com.

Bensimoun, C. (2013). Brain food. *Animal Wellness*, 15(1), 32-36.

Beynen, A.C. & Legerstee, E. (2010). Influence of dietary beta-1,3/1,6- glucans on clinical signs of canine osteoarthritis in a double-blind, placebo-controlled trial. *American Journal of Animal and Veterinary Science*, 5(2), 97-101.

Boileau, C., Martel-Pelletier, J., Caron, J., Msika, P., Guillou, G.B., Baudouin, C. & Pelletier, J.P. (2009). Protective effects of total fraction of avocado/soybean unsaponifiables on the structural changes in experimental dog osteoarthritis: Inhibition of nitric oxide synthase and matrix metalloproteinase-13. *Arthritis Research & Therapy*, 11(2), R41.

Bren, L. (2006, September-October). Pain drugs for dogs: Be an informed pet owner. *FDA Consumer Magazine*, p.7.

Deckelbaum, R.J., Worgall, T.S. & Teo, S. (2006). N-3 fatty acids and gene expression. *American Journal of Clinical Nutrition*, 83(6), S1520-S1525.

Dodds, W.J. & Lassin, A.J. (2013). *Reduce Inflammation, Improve Detoxification, and Promote Repair* [Web log post]. Retrieved from www.hemopet.org.

Evert, A. (2013). *Vitamin A*. Retrieved from http://www.nlm.nih.gov/medlineplus/ency/article/002400.htm.

Fritsch, D., Allen, T.A., Dodd, C.E., Jewell, D.E., Sixby, K.A., Leventhal, P.S., … Hahn, K.A. (2010). A multi-center study of the effect of a therapeutic food supplemented with fish oil omega-3 fatty acids on the carprofen dosage in dogs with osteoarthritis. *Journal of the American Veterinary Medical Association*, 236(5), 535-539.

Gosslau, A., Jao, D.L., Huang, M-T., Ho, C-T., Evans, D., Rawson, N.E. & Chen, K.Y. (2011). Effects of black tea polyphenol theaflavin -2 on apoptotic and inflammatory pathways *in vitro* and *in vivo*. *Molecular Nutrition & Food Research*, 55(5)198-208.

Howard, B. (2012). *Banfield Sees Bump in Fat Pets*. DVM360, 43(6), 1-43. Retrieved from http://veterinarynews.dvm360.com/dvm/Veterinary+news/Banfield-sees-bump-in-obese-and-overweight-pets/ArticleStandard/Article/detail/775267.

Huskisson, E.C. (2008). Glucosamine and chondroitin for osteoarthritis. *Journal of International Medical Research*, 36(6), 1161-1179.

Koonce, R.C. & Braverman, J.T. (2013). Obesity and osteoarthritis: More than just wear and tear. *Journal of the American Academy of Orthopaedic Surgeons*, 21(3), 161-9. Doi: 10.5435/JAAOS-21-03-161.

Middleton, R.P. & Hannah, S.S. (2010). Osteoarthritis and its origins: Disease development at the cellular and molecular level. *Nestle Purina Clinical Edge*, 6-9.

Moreau, M., Dupuis, J., Bonneau, N.H. & Lécuyer, M. (2004). Clinical evaluation of a powder of quality elk velvet antler for the treatment of osteoarthrosis in dog. *The Canadian Veterinary Journal*, 45, 133–139.

Laflamme, D.P. (2004). Osteoarthritis and diet: Joined at the hip. *Nestle Purina Clinical Edge*, 10-12.

Laflamme, D.P. (2012). Nutritional care for aging cats and dogs. *Veterinary Clinics of North America: Small Animal Practice*, 42(4), 769-791.

Lippiello, L., Nardo, J.V., Harlan, R. & Chiou, T. (2008). Metabolic effects of avocado/soy unsaponifiables on articular chondroyctes. *Evidence-Based Complementary and Alternative Medicine*, 5(2), 191–197. Doi: 10.1093/ecam/nem132.

Linus Pauling Institute. (2013). *The Bioavailability of Different Forms of Vitamin C (Ascorbic Acid)*. Retrieved from http://lpi.oregonstate.edu/infocenter/vitamins/vitaminC/vitCform.html.

Logar, D.B., Komadina, R., Prezelj, J., Ostanek, B., Trošt, Z. & Marc, J. (2007). Expression of bone resorption genes in osteoarthritis and in osteoporosis. *Journal of Bone and Mineral Metabolism*, 25(4), 219-225.

Messonnier, S. (2006). *The Natural Vet's Guide to Preventing and Treating Cancer in Dogs*. Novato, CA: New World Library.

Moreau, M., Troncy, E., Del Castillo, J.R., Bédard, C., Gauvin, D. & Lussier, B. (2012). Effects of feeding a high omega-3 fatty acids diet in dogs with naturally occurring osteoarthritis. *Journal of Animal Physiology and Animal Nutrition*, 97(5), 830–837. Doi: 10.1111/j.1439-0396.2012.01325.x.

Pollack, P. (2013). *Is there a Systemic Link between Obesity and OA?*. Retrieved from http://www.aaos.org/news/aaosnow/mar13/clinical10.asp.

Pollard, B., Guilford, W.G., Ankenbauer-Perkins, K.L. & Hedderley, D. (2006). Clinical efficacy and tolerance of an extract of green-lipped mussel (Perna canaliculus) in dogs presumptively diagnosed with degenerative joint disease. *New Zealand Veterinary Journal*, 54(3), 114-118.

Puotinen, C.J. (2010). Alternatives to canine surgery. *Whole Dog Journal*, 13(2), 13-23.

Reddy, C.M., Bhat, V.B., Kiranmai, G., Reddy, M.N., Reddanna, P. & Madyastha, K.M. (2000). Selective inhibition of cyclooxygenase-2 by C-phycocyanin, a biliprotein from Spirulina platensis. *Biochemical and Biophysical Research Communications*, 277, 599–603.

Rialland, P., Bichot, S., Lussier, B., Moreau, M., Beaudry, F., del Castillo, J.R., … Troncy, E. (2013). Effect of a diet enriched with green-lipped mussel on pain behavior and functioning in dogs with clinical osteoarthritis. *Canadian Journal of Veterinary Research*, 77(1), 66–74.

Romay, C.H., González, R., Ledón, N., Remirez, D. & Rimbau, V. (2003). C-phycocyanin: A biliprotein with antioxidant, anti-inflammatory and neuroprotective effects. *Current Protein and Peptide Science*, 4(3), 207-216.

Roush, J.K., Dodd, C.E., Fritsch, D.A., Allen, T.A., Jewell, D.E., Schoenherr, W.D.,… Hahn, K.A. (2010). A multi-center veterinary practice assessment of the effects of omega-3 fatty acids on osteoarthritis in dogs. *Journal of the American Veterinary Medical Association*, 236(1), 59-66.

Roush, J.K., Cross, A.R., Renberg, W.C., Dodd, C.E., Sixby, K.A., Fritsch, D.A.,…
Hahn, K.A. (2010)(a). Effects of dietary supplementation with fish oil omega-3 fatty
acids on weight-bearing dogs with osteoarthritis. *Journal of the American Veterinary
Medical Association*, 236(1), 67-73.

Sanchez, C., Deberg, M.A., Bellahcène, A., Castronovo, V., Msika, P., Delcour,
J.P.,… Henrotin, Y.E. (2008). Phenotypic characterization of osteoblasts from the
sclerotic zones of osteoarthritic subchondral bone. *Arthritis and Rheumatism*, 58(2),
442-55. Doi: 10.1002/art.23159.

Sanghi, D., Avasthi, S., Srivastava, R.N., Singh, A. (2009). Nutritional factors and
osteoarthritis: A review article. *Internet Journal of Medical Update*, 4(1), 42-53.

Shanmuganayagam, D., Beahm, M.R., Osman, H.E., Krueger, C.G., Reed, J.D.
& Folts, J.D. (2002). Grape seed and grape skin extracts elicit a greater antiplatelet
effect when used in combination than when used individually in dogs and humans.
Journal of Nutrition, 132, 3592-3598.

Straus, M. (2007). Canine arthritis treatment: Many effective tools can help in the
fight against canine arthritis. *Whole Dog Journal*, 10(3).

Straus, M. (2013). Dishing on diets: Veterinary nutritionists conclude that only they
can properly formulate a homemade diet. *Whole Dog Journal*, 16(9), 3-5.

Therkleson, T. (2013). Topical ginger treatment with a compress or patch for
osteoarthritis symptoms. *Journal of Holistic Nursing*. [Epub ahead of print] PMID:
24305660.

University of Maryland Medical Center (UMMC). (2011). *S-adenosylmethionine*.
Retrieved from http://umm.edu/health/medical/altmed/supplement/sadenosylme-
thionine.

University of Maryland Medical Center (UMMC). (2011)(a). *Spirulina- Overview*.
Retrieved from http://www.umm.edu/altmed/articles/spirulina-000327.htm.

VCA Animal Hospitals. (n.d.). *Glycosamionoglycans*. Retrieved from http://www.
vcahospitals.com/main/pet-health-information/article/animal-health/glycosamino-
glycans-gags/468.

Waldron, M. (2004). The role of fatty acids on the management of osteoarthritis.
Nestle Purina Clinical Edge, 14-16.

Wolf, D. (2009). *Superfoods: The Food and Medicine of the Future*. Berkeley, CA:
North Atlantic Books.

Zhang, R., Fang, H., Chen,Y., Shen, J., Lu, H., Zeng, C.,… Zhao, Q. (2012). Gene
expression analyses of subchondral bone in early experimental osteoarthritis by microarray. *PloS ONE*, 7(2), e32356. Doi:10.1371/journal.pone.0032356

Chapter 9

Adams, L.S., Kanaya, N., Phung, S., Liu, Z. & Chen, S. (2011). Whole blueberry powder modulates the growth and metastasis of MDA-MB-231 triple negative breast tumors in nude mice1-3. *Journal of Nutrition*, 141(10). Doi: 10.3945/jn.111.140178.

Anand, P., Kunnumakara, A.B., Sundaram, C., Harikumar, K.B., Tharakan, S.T., Lai, O.S.,… Aggarwal, B.B. (2008). Cancer is a preventable disease that requires major lifestyle changes. *Pharmaceutical Research*, 25(9), 2097–2116. Doi: 10.1007/s11095-008-9661-9.

Armstrong, S. (2013). Foods as medicine. *Animal Wellness*, 15(1), 18-21.

Ayman, E.I., Abuzinadah, O.A., Baeshen, N.A. & Rahmy, T.R. (2012). Differential control of growth, apoptotic activity, and gene expression in human breast cancer cells by extracts derived from medicinal herbs *Zingiber officinale. Journal of Biomedicine and Biotechnology,* 2012. Doi: 10.1155/2012/614356.

Basu, A., Du, M., Leyva, M.J., Sanchez, K., Betts, N.M., Wu, M.,… Lyons, T.J. (2010). Blueberries decrease cardiovascular risk factors in obese men and women with metabolic syndrome. *Journal of Nutrition,* 140(9), 1582-1587.

Becker, K. (2013). *PBDE: Are You Exposing Your Pet to this Thyroid Ravager?* Retrieved from http//: healthypets.mercola.com/sites/healthypets/archive/2013/10/25/pbde-exposure-aspx.

Bottiglieri, T. (2002). S-Adenosyl-L-methionine (SAMe): From the bench to the bedside—molecular basis of a pleiotrophic molecule. *The American Journal of Clinical Nutrition*, 76(5), 1151S-1157S.

Broad Institute. (2013). *Oncogene.* Retrieved from http://www.broadinstitute.org/education/glossary/oncogene.

Brown, D.C. (2013, December 6). [Personal correspondence].

Brown, D.C. & Reetz, J. (2012). Single agent polysaccharopeptide delays metastases and improves survival in naturally occurring hemangiosarcoma. *Evidence-Based Complementary and Alternative Medicine.* Doi:10.1155/2012/384301.

Davis, C.D., Uthus, E.O. (2004). DNA methylation, cancer susceptibility, and nutrient interactions. *Experimental Biology and Medicine (Maywood).* 229(10), 988-995.

Divisi, D., Di Tommaso, S., Salvemini, S., Garramone, M. & Crisci, R. (2006). Diet and cancer. *Acta Bio Medica,* 77, 118-123.

Dodds, W.J. (2001). Vaccination protocols for dogs predisposed to vaccine reactions. *Journal of the American Animal Hospital Association*, 38, 1-4.

Donaldson, M. (2004). Nutrition and cancer: A review of the evidence for an anticancer diet. *Nutrition of Journal*, 3(19). Doi:10.1186/1475-2891-3-19.

Drake, V.J. (2009). *Carotenoids*. Retrieved from http://lpi.oregonstate.edu/infocenter/phytochemicals/carotenoids/.

Ehrlich, S.D. (2011). *Milk Thistle*. Retrieved from http://umm.edu/health/medical/altmed/herb/milk-thistle.

Environmental Working Group. (2007). *7 Ways to Reduce Your Exposure to PBDE Flame Retardants*. Retrieved from http://www.ewg.org/enviroblog/2007/09/7-ways-reduce-your-exposure-pbde-flame-retardants.

Environmental Working Group. (2009). *Dog Food Comparison Shows High Fluoride Levels*. Retrieved from http://www.ewg.org/research/dog-food-comparison-shows-high-fluoride-levels.

Environmental Working Group. (2009)(a). *Dog Food Comparison Shows High Fluoride Levels: Fluoride and osteosarcoma*. Retrieved from http://www.ewg.org/research/dog-food-comparison-shows-high-fluoride-levels/fluoride-and-osteosarcoma.

Environmental Working Group. (2009)(b). *Dog Food Contaminated with Levels of Fluoride above EPA's Legal Limit for Humans*. Retrieved from http://www.ewg.org/.

Esteller, M. (2008). Epigenetics in cancer. *New England Journal of Medicine*, 358, 1148-1159. Doi: 10.1056/NEJMra072067.

Food and Agriculture Organization of the United Nations & World Health Organization (FAO/WHO). (2001, October 1-4). *Health and Nutritional Properties of Probiotics in Food Including Powder Milk with Live Lactic Acid Bacteria* [Report of a joint FAO/WHO expert consultation]. Retrieved from http://www.who.int/foodsafety/publications/fs_management/en/probiotics.pdf.

Fougère, B. (2012). Herbs for cancer [Newsletter]. *Holistic Veterinary Society of the New Zealand Veterinary Association*.

Gantar, M., Dhandayuthapani, S. & Rathinavelu, A. (2012). Phycocyanin induces apoptosis and enhances the effect of topotecan on prostate cell line LNCaP. *Journal of Medicinal Food*, 15(12), 1091-1095. Doi: 10.1089/jmf.2012.0123.

Gilmore, T. (n.d.). *NF-kB Transcription Factors*. Retrieved from http://www.bu.edu/nf-kb/.

Glickman, L.T., Schofer, F.S., McKee, L.J., Reif, J.S. & Goldschmidt, M.H. (1989). Epidemiologic study of insecticide exposures, obesity, and risk of bladder cancer in household dogs. *Journal of Toxicology and Environmental Health, 28*, 407–414.

Glickman, L.T., Raghavan, M., Knapp, D.W., Bonney, P.L. & Dawson, M.H. (2004). Herbicide exposure and the risk of transitional cell carcinoma of the urinary bladder in Scottish Terriers. *Journal of the American Veterinary Medical Association, 224*(8), 1290-1297.

Hardy, T.M. & Tollefsbol, T.O. (2011). Epigenetic diet: Impact on the epigenome and cancer. *Epigenomics, 3*(4), 503-518. Doi:10.2217/epi.11.71.

Heinze, C.R., Gomez, F.C. & Freeman, L.M. (2012). Timely topics in nutrition: Assessment of commercial diets and recipes for home-prepared diets recommended for dogs with cancer. *Journal of the American Veterinary Medical Association, 241*, 1453-1460.

Howell, A.B. (2012). Health benefits of cranberries—it's not just about UTIs anymore! *Dietitians in Integrative & functional Medicine, 14*(3), 49-51.

Hyman, M. (2011, February 8). *Maximizing Methylation: The Key to Healthy Aging* [Web log post]. Retrieved from http://drhyman.com/blog/2011/02/08/maximizing-methylation-the-key-to-healthy-aging-2/.

Hyman, M. (2012). *How Hidden Food Sensitivies Make You Fat*. Retrieved from http://drhyman.com/blog/2012/02/22/how-hidden-food-sensitivies-make-you-fat/.

Hyman, M. (2013). *Three Hidden Ways Wheat Makes You Fat*. Retrieved from http://drhyman.com/blog/2012/02/13/three-hidden-ways-wheat-makes-you-fat/.

Kressler, C. (2012). *RHR: Pioneering Researcher Alessio Fasano M.D. on Gluten, Autoimmunity & Leaky Gut*. Retrieved from http://chriskresser.com/pioneering-research-er-alessio-fasano-m-d-on-gluten-autoimmunity-leaky-gut.

Krikorian, R., Shidler, M.D., Nash, T.A., Kalt, W., Vinqvist-tymchuk, M.R., Shukitt-hale, B. & Joseph, J.A. (2010). Blueberry supplementation improves memory in older adults. *Journal of Agricultural and Food Chemistry, 58*(7), 3996-4000.

Lawenda, B.D. (2013) *Is there any other Anti-cancer Botanical Compound as Exciting as Curcumin?* Retrieved from http://www.integrativeoncology-essentials.com/2013/03/is-there-any-other-anti-cancer-botanical-compound-as-exciting-as-curcumin/.

Li, W. (2010). *Can we Eat to Starve Cancer?* [Video]. Retrieved from http://www.youtube.com/watch?v=B9bDZ5-zPtY.

Lila, M.A. (2004). Anthocyanins and human health: An in vitro investigative approach. *Journal of Biomedical Biotechnology*, 2004(5), 306–313.

Link, A., Balaguer, F., Shen, Y., Lozano, J.J., Leung, H.C., Boland, C.R. & Goel, A. (2013). Curcumin modulates DNA methylation in colorectal cancer cells. *PLoS One*, 8(2), e57709. doi: 10.1371/journal.pone.0057709.

Magee, E. (2007). *The Super-veggies: Cruciferous Vegetables*. Retrieved from http://www.webmd.com/food-recipes/features/super-veggies-cruciferous-vegetables.

Mason, S. (2013). *UCLA Researchers Find Link between Intestinal Bacteria and White Blood Cell Cancer*. Retrieved from http://newsroom.ucla.edu/portal/ucla/ucla-researchers-find-link-between-245945.aspx.

MedlinePlus. (2013). *Vitamin D*. Retrieved from http://www.nlm.nih.gov/medlineplus/druginfo/natural/929.html.

Mercola, J. (2010). *Is this the New Silver Bullet for Cancer?* Retrieved from http://articles.mercola.com/sites/articles/archive/2010/03/11/is-vitamin-d-the-silver-bullet-for-cancer.aspx.

Mercola.com. (2012). *This New Drug Appears to Cause Cancer Cells to Self-destruct*. Retrieved from http://articles.mercola.com/sites/articles/archive/2012/08/04/dca-and-turmeric-on-cancer.aspx.

Messonnier, S. (2006). *The Natural Vet's Guide to Preventing and Treating Cancer in Dogs*. Novato, CA: New World Library.

Nahleh, Z., Bhattie, N.S. & Mal, M. (2011). How to reduce your cancer risk: Mechanisms and myths. *International Journal of General Medicine*, 4, 277-287. doi: 10.2147/IJGM.S18657.

Narayanapillai, S., Agarwal, C., Deep, G. & Agarwal, R. (2013). Silibinin inhibits ultraviolet B radiation-induced DNA-damage and apoptosis by enhancing interleukin-12 expression in JB6 cells and SKH-1 hairless mouse skin. *Molecular Carcinogenesis*. doi: 10.1002/mc.22000.

Neto, C.C. (2011). Cranberries: Ripe for more cancer research. *Journal of the Science of Food and Agriculture*, 91(13), 2303-2307.

Oates, L. (2009). Medicinal mushrooms. *CM: The Journal of Complementary Medicine*, 8(3), 44-48.

Pons, L. (2006). *Pterostilbene's Healthy Potential: Berry Compound may Inhibit Breast Cancer and Heart Disease*. Retrieved from http://www.ars.usda.gov/is/AR/archive/nov06/health1106.htm.

Raghavan, M., Knapp, D.W., Dawson, M.H., Bonney, P.L. & Glickman, L.T. (2004). Topical flea and tick pesticides and the risk of transitional cell carcinoma of the urinary bladder in Scottish Terriers. *Journal of the American Veterinary Medical Association*, 225(3), 389-394.

Raghavan, M., Knapp, D.W., Bonney, P.L., Dawson, M.H. & Glickman, L.T. (2005). Evaluation of the effect of dietary vegetable consumption on reducing risk of transitional cell carcinoma of the urinary bladder in Scottish Terriers. *Journal of the American Veterinary Medical Association*, 227(1), 94-100.

Reddy, C.M., Bhat, V.B., Kiranmai, G., Reddy, M.N., Reddanna, P. & Madyastha, K.M. (2000). Selective inhibition of cyclooxygenase-2 by C-phycocyanin, a biliprotein from Spirulina platensis. *Biochemical and Biophysical Research Communications*, 277, 599–603.

Robinson, N.G. (2008). *Why the Buzz about Turmeric?*. Retrieved from http://csu-vets.colostate.edu/pain/Articlespdf/TheBuzzAboutTurmeric.pdf.

Romay, C.H., González, R., Ledón, N., Remirez, D. & Rimbau, V. (2003). C-phycocyanin: A biliprotein with antioxidant, anti-inflammatory and neuroprotective effects. *Current Protein and Peptide Science*, 4(3), 207-216.

Serini, S., Fasano, E., Piccioni, E., Cittadini, A.R.M. & Calviello, G. (2012). Apoptosis as a mechanism involved in the anticancer effect of dietary n-3 polyunsaturated fatty acids. In *Novel Apoptotic Regulators in Carcinogenesis*. Dordrecht, Netherlands: Springer Science+Business Media.

Smith, J.E., Rowan, N.J. & Sullivan, R. (2002). Medicinal mushrooms: A rapidly developing area of biotechnology for cancer therapy and other bioactivities. *Biotechnology Letters*, 24(22), 1839-1845.

Tizard I. & Ni, Y. (1998). Use of serologic testing to assess immune status of companion animals. *Journal of the American Veterinary Medical Association*, 213, 54-60.

Tremayne, J. (2010). Using supplements to fight cancer. *Veterinary Practice News*, 22(7).

Twark, L. & Dodds, W.J. (2000). Clinical application of serum parvovirus and distemper virus antibody titers for determining revaccination strategies in healthy dogs. *Journal of the American Veterinary Medical Association*, 217(10), 1021-1024.

Tyagi, A., Agarwal, C., Dwyer-Nield, L.D., Singh, R.P., Malkinson, A.M. & Agarwal, R. (2011). Silibinin modulates TNF-α and IFN-γ mediated signaling to regulate COX2 and iNOS expression in tumorigenic mouse lung epithelial LM2 cells. *Molecular Carcinogenesis*. doi: 10.1002/mc.20851.

Tyagi, A., Singh, A., Bhardwaj, P., Sahu, S., Yadav, A.P. & Kori, M.L. (2012). Punicalagins-A large polyphenol compounds found in pomegranates: A therapeutic review. *Academic Journal of Plant Sciences*, 5 (2), 45-49.

University of Colorado Denver. (2011). Milk thistle extract stops lung cancer in mice, study shows. *ScienceDaily*. Retrieved from http://www.sciencedaily.com / releases/2011/11/111115145236.htm.

University of Colorado Denver. (2013). Silibinin, found in milk thistle, protects against UV-induced skin cancer. *ScienceDaily*. Retrieved from http://www.science-daily.com /releases/2013/01/130130143636.htm.

Venier, M. & Hites, R.A. (2011). Flame retardants in the serum of pet dogs and in their food. *Environmental Sciences and Technology*, 45(10), 4602-4608. doi: 10.1021/es1043529.

Wasser, S.P. (2011). Current findings, future trends, and unsolved problems in studies of medicinal mushrooms. *Applied Microbiology and Biotechnology*, 89(5), 1323-1332. doi:10.1007/s00253-010-3067-4.

WebMD. (2012). *Vitamins and Supplements Lifestyle Guide: Vitamin B-12 (Cobalamin)*. Retrieved from http://www.webmd.com/vitamins-and-supplements/lifestyle-guide-11/supplement-guide-vitamin-b12.

Weese, J.S. & Arroyo, L. (2003). Bacteriological evaluation of dog and cat diets that claim to contain probiotics. *Canadian Veterinary Journal*, 44(3), 212–215.

Wein, H. (2012). *Understanding Insulin Sensitivity and Diabetes*. Retrieved from http://www.nih.gov/researchmatters/april2012/04092012insulin.htm.

Wilken, R., Veena, M.S., Marilene, B., Wang, M.B. & Srivatsan, E.S. (2011). Curcumin: A review of anti-cancer properties and therapeutic activity in head and neck squamous cell carcinoma. *Molecular Cancer*, 10(12). doi:10.1186/1476-4598-10-12.

Wilson-Robles, H. (2013). *Second-hand Smoke and Your Pet* [Web log post]. Retrieved from http://vetmed.tamu.edu/news/pet-talk/second-hand-smoke-and-your-pet#.UgqtgRaAElI.

Wynn, S. & Fougère, B. (2006). *Veterinary Herbal Medicine*. St. Louis, MO: Mosby Elsevier.

Ziech, D., Franco, R., Pappa, A., Malamou-Mitsi, V., Georgakila, S., Georgakilas, A.G. & Panayiotidis, M.I. (2010). The role of epigenetics in environmental and occupational carcinogenesis. *Chemico-Biological Interactions*, 188(2), 340-9. doi: 10.1016/j.cbi.2010.06.012.

Chapter 10

Aldrich, G. (2009). Nutrition-behavior link hard to quantify. *Feedstuffs*, 81(26), 10.

Bensimoun, C. (2013). Brain food. *Animal Wellness*, 15(1), 32-36.

Boler, B.V. (2011). *Nutrition and Canine Behavior: How do Proteins, Lipids, Carbohydrates and Antioxidants in an Animal's Diet Affect Aggression, Stress and Cognition?*. Retrieved from http://www.petfoodindustry.com/NutritionBehavior.html.

Bosch, G., Beerda, B., Hendriks, W.H., van der Poel, A.F.B. & Verstegen, M.W.A. (2007). Impact of nutrition on canine behavior: current status and possible mechanisms. *Nutrition Research Reviews*, 20, 180–194.

Bottiglieri, T. (2002). S-Adenosyl-L-methionine (SAMe): From the bench to the bedside—molecular basis of a pleiotrophic molecule. *The American Journal of Clinical Nutrition*, 76(5), 1151S-1157S.

Brogan, K. (2013). *Methylwho? Why You Should Know About Methylation*. Retrieved from http://www.greenmedinfo.com/blog/methylwho-why-you-should-know-about-methylation?utm_source=www.GreenMedInfo.com&utm_campaign=f3dd2bd89f-Greenmedinfo&utm_medium=email&utm_term=0_193c8492fb-f3d-d2bd89f-86768346.

Cotman, C.W., Head, E., Muggenburg, B.A., Zicker, S.S. & Milgram, N.W. (2002). Brain aging in the canine: a diet enriched in antioxidants reduces cognitive dysfunction. *Neurobiology of Aging*, 23, 809–818.

DeNapoli, J.S., Dodman, N.H., Shuster, L., Rand, W.M. & Gross, K.L. (2000). Effect of dietary protein content and tryptophan supplementation on dominance aggression, territorial aggression, and hyperactivity in dogs. *Journal of the American Veterinary Medical Association*, 217, 504-508.

Dodman, N.H., Reisner, I., Shuster, L., Rand, W., Luescher, U.A., Robinson, I. & Houpt, K.A. (1996). Effect of dietary protein on behavior in dogs. *Journal of the American Veterinary Medical Association*, 208, 376-379.

Durham University. (2012). Modern dog breeds genetically disconnected from ancient ancestors. *ScienceDaily*. Retrieved from http://www.sciencedaily.com/releases/2012/05/120521163845.htm.

Head, E., Rofina, J. & Zicker, S. (2008). Oxidative stress, aging and central nervous system disease in the canine model of human brain aging. *Veterinary Clinics of North America: Small Animal Practice*, 38(1), 167-178.

Hu, W.T., Murray, J.A., Greenaway, M.C., Parisi, J.E. & Josephs, K.A. (2006). Cognitive impairment and celiac disease. Archives of *Neurology (now JAMA Neurology)*, 63(10), 1440-1446. doi:10.1001/archneur.63.10.1440.

Jensen, P. (2009). *The Ethology of Domestic Animals* (2nd e.d.). Cambridge, MA: CAB International.

Joseph, J.A., Shukitt-Hale, B., Denisova, N.A., Bielinski, D., Martin, A., McEwen, J.J. & Bickford, P.C. (1999). Reversals of age-related declines in neuronal signal transduction, cognitive, and motor behavioral deficits with blueberry, spinach, or strawberry dietary supplementation. *Journal of Neuroscience*, 19(18). 8114-21.

Laflamme, D.P. (2012). Nutritional care for aging cats and dogs. *Veterinary Clinics of North America: Small Animal Practice*, 42(4), 769-791.

Landsberg, G.M., DePorter, T. & Araujo, J.A. (2011). Clinical signs and management of anxiety, sleeplessness, and cognitive dysfunction in the senior pet. *Veterinary Clinics of North America: Small Animal Practice*, 41, 565-590.

Lila, M.A. (2004). Anthocyanins and human health: An in vitro investigative approach. *Journal of Biomedical Biotechnology*, 2004(5), 306–313.

Lu, P, Mamiya, T., Lu, L.L., Mouri, A., Zou, L.B., Nagai, T.,…Nabeshima, T. (2009). Silibinin prevents amyloid β peptide-induced memory impairment and oxidative stress in mice. *British Journal of Pharmacology*, 157(7), 1270-1277.

Manteca , X. (2011). Nutrition and behavior in senior dogs. *Topics in Companion Animal Medicine*, 26(1), 33-36.

Mercola, J. (2012). *A Daily 900 mg Dose of this Fat Helped Reverse Memory Loss*. Retrieved from http://articles.mercola.com/sites/articles/archive/2012/02/06/without-krill-oil-your-brain-could-degenerate.aspx.

Messonnier, S. (n.d.). Cognitive disorder: SAMe and choline are two well-studied therapies that can help treat this common condition in geriatric dogs and cats. *Integrative Veterinary Care Journal*, issue V214. Retrieved from http://www.ivcjournal.com/articles/cognitive-disorder/.

Milgram, N.W., Zicker, S.C., Head, E., Muggenburg, BA., Murphey, H., Ikeda-Douglas, C.J. & Cotman, C.W. (2002). Dietary enrichment counteracts age-associated cognitive dysfunction in canines. *Neurobiology of Aging*, 23(5), 737-745.

Murata, N., Murakami, K., Ozawa,Y., Kinoshita, N., Irie, K., Shirasawa, T. & Shimizu, T. (2010). Silymarin attenuated the amyloid β plaque burden and improved behavioral abnormalities in an Alzheimer's disease mouse model. *Bioscience, Biotechnology, and Biochemistry*, 74(11), 2299-2306.

Paige, C. (2007). *The Good Behavior Book for Dogs: The Most Annoying Dog Behaviors…Solved!* Beverly, MA: Quarry Books.

Pan, Y., Larson, B., Araujo, J.A., Lau, W., de Rivera, C., Santana, R.,… Milgram, N.W. (2010). Dietary supplementation with medium-chain TAG has long-lasting cognition-enhancing effects in aged dogs. *British Journal of Nutrition*, 103(12), 1746-1754.

Perlmutter, D. (n.d.). *New Study Links Gluten Sensitivity to Brain Failure* [Web log post]. Retrieved from http://www.vanguardneurologist.com/new-study-links-gluten-sensitivity-to-brain-failure/.

Straus, M. (2012). Senior supplements: These neutraceuticals may offer hope for treating canine cognitive dysfunction. *Whole Dog Journal*, 15(11).

U.S Food and Drug Administration (USFDA). (2004). *Letter Updating the Phosphatidylserine and Cognitive Function and Dementia Qualified Health Claim* [Public letter]. Retrieved from http://www.fda.gov/food/ingredientspackaginglabeling/labelingnutrition/ucm072993.htm.

WebMD. (2013). *SAMe*. Retrieved from http://www.webmd.com/vitamins-supplements/ingredientmono-786-SAMe.aspx?activeIngredientId=786&activeIngredientName=SAMe.

Wolf, D. (2009). *Superfoods: The Food and Medicine of the Future*. Berkeley, CA: North Atlantic Books.

Yurko-Mauro, K., McCarthy, D., Rom, D., Nelson, E.B., Ryan, A.S., Blackwell, A.,… Stedman, M. (2010). Beneficial effects of docosahexaenoic acid on cognition in age-related cognitive decline. *Alzheimer's & Dementia: The Journal of the Alzheimer's Association*, 6(6), 456-64. doi: 10.1016/j.jalz.2010.01.013.

Zicker, S.C., Jewell, D.E., Yamka, R.M. & Milgram, N.W. (2012). Evaluation of cognitive learning, memory, psychomotor, immunologic, and retinal functions in healthy puppies fed foods fortified with docosahexaenoic acid-rich fish oil from 8 to 52 weeks of age. *Journal of the American Veterinary Medical Association*, 241(5), 583-94. doi: 10.2460/javma.241.5.583.

Chapter 11

Abenavoli, L., Capasso, R., Milic, N. & Capasso, F. (2010). Milk thistle in liver diseases: Past, present, future. *Phytotherapy Research*, 24, 1423–1432. doi: 10.1002/ptr.3207.

American Diabetes Association. (2013). *Gene Therapy Used in Dogs to Treat Type 1 Diabetes*. Retrieved from http://www.diabetes.org/for-media/2013/gene-therapy-used-in-dogs-to-treat-type1-diabetes.html.

Banfield Pet Hospital. (2013). *State of Pet Health 2013 Report*. Retrieved from http://www.stateofpethealth.com.

Becker, K. (2013). *A Single Treatment Cures Diabetes- How to Protect Your Pet Now*. Retrieved from http://healthypets.mercola.com/sites/healthypets/archive/2013/03/27/dog-diabetes-treatment.aspx.

Becker, K. (2014). *Vitamin D: Don't Let Your Dog Overdose on this Popular Human Nutrient*. Retrieved from http://healthypets.mercola.com/sites/healthypets/archive/2014/05/09/dog-vitamin-d-levels.aspx?e_cid=20140509Z1_PetsNL_art_1&utm_source=petnl&utm_medium=email&utm_content=art1&utm_campaign=20140509Z1&et_cid=DM44226&et_rid=515307302.

Bottiglieri, T. (2002). S-Adenosyl-L-methionine (SAMe): From the bench to the bedside—molecular basis of a pleiotrophic molecule. *The American Journal of Clinical Nutrition*, 76(5), 1151S-1157S.

Brown, S.A., Brown, C.A., Crowell, W.A., Barsanti, J.A., Kang, C.W., Allen, T., Cowell, C & Finco, D.R. (2000). Effects of dietary polyunsaturated fatty acid supplementation in early renal insufficiency in dogs. *Journal of Laboratory and Clinical Medicine*, 135(3), 275–286. http://dx.doi.org/10.1067/mlc.2000.105178.

Brown, D.C. (2013, December 6). [Personal correspondence].

Bugianesi, E., McCullough, A.J. & Marchesini, G. (2005). Insulin resistance: A metabolic pathway to chronic liver disease. *Hepatology*, 42, 987–1000. doi: 10.1002/hep.20920.

Canine Epilepsy Guardian Angels. (2011). *Canine Epilepsy*. Retrieved from http://www.canine-epilepsy-guardian-angels.com/default.htm.

Carr, A. (2013). *Ketogenic Diet, Zonisamide Ease Seizures*. Retrieved from http://www.veterinarypracticenews.com/vet-practice-news-columns/abstract/ketogenic-diet-zonisamide-ease-seizures.aspx.

Case, L.P., Daristotle, L., Hayek, M., Rausch, M.F. (2011). *Canine and Feline Nutrition: A Resource for Companion Animal Professionals*. (3rd ed.). Maryland Heights, MO: Mosby Elsevier.

Cerundolo, R., Michel, K.E., Court, M.H., Shrestha, B., Refsal, K.R., Oliver, J.W.,... Shofer, F.S. (2009). Effects of dietary soy isoflavones on health, steroidogenesis, and thyroid gland function in dogs. *American Journal of Veterinary Research*, 70(3), 353-360.

Chu, L., Zhang, J-X., Norota, I. & Endoh, M. (2005). Differential action of a protein tyrosine kinase inhibitor, genistein, on the positive inotropic effect of endothelin-1 and norepinephrine in canine ventricular myocardium. *British Journal of Pharmacology*, 144, 430-442.

Coates, J. (2013). *Dietary Therapy for Canine Epilepsy?*. Retrieved from http://www.petmd.com/blogs/nutritionnuggets/jcoates/2013/june/dietary-therapy-for-canine-epilepsy-30491#.UsBsfRaAGFJ.

Devi, S. & Jani, R.G. (2009). Review on nutritional management of cardiac disorders in canines. *Veterinary World*, 2(12), 482-485.

Dodds, W.J. (2001). Vaccination protocols for dogs predisposed to vaccine reactions. *Journal of the American Animal Hospital Association*, 38, 1-4.

Dove, S. (2001). Nutritional therapy in the treatment of heart disease in dogs. *Alternative Medicine Review*, 6, S-38-S45.

Foti, S.B. & Roskams, A.J. (2011). A tale of two epiphenomena: The complex interplay of epigenetics and epilepsy. In *Underlying Mechanisms of Epilepsy*. doi: 10.5772/24529.

Guilford, W.G. & Mataz, M.E. (2003). The nutritional management of gastrointestinal disorders in companion animals. *New Zealand Veterinary Journal*, 51(6), 284-291.

Howard, B. (2012). *Banfield Sees Bump in Fat Pets. DVM360,* 43(6), 1-43. Retrieved from http://veterinarynews.dvm360.com/dvm/Veterinary+news/Banfield-sees-bump-in-obese-and-overweight-pets/ArticleStandard/Article/detail/775267.

Hyman, M. (2010). *Glutathione: The Mother of all Anti-oxidants.* Retrieved from http://www.huffingtonpost.com/dr-mark-hyman/glutathione-the-mother-of_b_530494.html.

Hyman, M. (2013). *Gluten: What You don't Know Might Kill You.* Retrieved from http://drhyman.com/blog/2011/03/17/gluten-what-you-dont-know-might-kill-you/.

Iwasa, M., Kobayashi, Y., Mifuji-Moroka, R., Hara, N., Miyachi, H., Sugimoto, R.,... Takei, Y. (2013). Branched-chain amino acid supplementation reduces oxidative stress and prolongs survival in rats with advanced liver cirrhosis. *PLoS ONE*, 8(7), e70309. doi:10.1371/journal.pone.0070309.

Johnston, A.N., Center, S.A., McDonough, S.P., Wakshlag, J.J. & Warner, K.L. (2013). Hepatic copper concentrations in Labrador Retrievers with and without chronic hepatitis: 72 cases (1980–2010). *Journal of the American Veterinary Medical Association*, 242, 372-380.

Kobow, K. & Blümcke, I. (2011). The methylation hypothesis: Do epigenetic chromatin modifications play a role in epileptogenesis? *Epilepsia*, 52, 15–19. doi: 10.1111/j.1528-1167.2011.03145.x.

Kraus, M.S., Rassnick, K.M., Wakshlag J.J., Gelzer, A.R., Waxman A.S., Struble A.M. & Refsal, K. (2014). Relation of vitamin D status to congestive heart failure and cardiovascular events in dogs. *Journal of Veterinary Internal Medicine*, 28(1). 109-15. doi:10.1111/jvim.12239. Epub 2013 Nov 7. PubMed PMID: 24205918.

Lavebratt, C., Almgren, M. & Ekström, T.J. (2012). Review: Epigenetic regulation in obesity. *International Journal of Obesity*, 36, 757-765. doi:10.1038/ijo.2011.178.

Li, G-R., Wang, H-B., Qin, G-W., Jin, M.W., Tang, Q. & Sun, H.Y. (2013). Acaetin, a natural flavone, selectively inhibits human atrial repolarization potassium currents and prevents atrial fibrillation in dogs. *Circulation*, 117, 2449-2457.

Lieber, C.S. (2002). S-adenosyl-L-methionine: Its role in the treatment of liver disorders. *American Journal of Clinical Nutrition*, 76(5), 1183S-7S.

Lim, E.L., Hollingsworth, K.G., Aribisala, B.S., Chen, M.J., Mathers, J.C. & Taylor, R. (2011). Reversal of type 2 diabetes: Normalisation of beta cell function in association with decreased pancreas and liver triacylglycerol. *Diabetologia*, 54(10), 2506–2514. doi: 10.1007/s00125-011-2204-7.

Marchesini, G., Moscatiello, S., Di Domizio, S. & Forlani, G. (2008). Obesity-associated liver disease. *The Journal of Clinical Endocrinology & Metabolism*, 93(11), s74-s80. doi: 10.1210/jc.2008-1399.

MedlinePlus, U.S. National Library of Medicine. (2012). *Fish Oil*. Retrieved from http://www.nlm.nih.gov/medlineplus/druginfo/natural/993.html.

Mercola, J. & Hofmekler, L. (2010). *This ONE Antioxidant Keeps all Other Antioxidants Performing at Peak Levels*. Retrieved from http://articles.mercola.com/sites/articles/archive/2010/04/10/can-you-use-food-to-increase-glutathione-instead-of-supplements.aspx.

Messonnier, S. (2007). *Liver Disease*. Retrieved from http://www.petcarenaturally.com/articles/liver-disease.php.

Murray, L. (2012, August 28). [Personal correspondence].

National Kidney and Urologic Diseases Information Clearinghouse (NKUDIC), National Institute of Diabetes and Digestive and Kidney Diseases (NIDDK), U.S. Department of Health and Human Services. (2012). *The Kidneys and how They Work*. Retrieved from http://kidney.niddk.nih.gov/kudiseases/pubs/yourkidneys/.

National Library of Medicine. (2013). *Pyridoxine-dependent Epilepsy*. Retrieved from http://ghr.nlm.nih.gov/condition/pyridoxine-dependent-epilepsy.

National Research Council of the National Academy of Sciences. (NRC/NAS). (2006). *Nutrient Requirements of Dogs and Cats*. Washington, DC: NRC Press.

O'Grady, M. (2002). *DCM in Doberman Pinchers: Lessons Learned in the First Decade of Study*. ACVIM Abstr.2002; Retrieved from www.DobermanData.com.

O'Sullivan M.L., O'Grady, M.R., Pyle ,W.G. & Dawson, J.F. (2011). Evaluation of 10 genes encoding cardiac proteins in Doberman Pinschers with dilated cardiomyopathy. *American Journal of Veterinary Research*, 72(7), 932-939.

Perricone, N. (2010). *Forever Young: The Science of Nutrigenomics for Glowing, Wrinkle-free Skin and Radiant Health at Every Age*. New York: Atria Books.

Rakyan, V.K., Beyan, H., Down, T.A., Hawa, M.I., Maslau, S., Aden, D.,…Leslie, R.D. (2011). Identification of type 1 diabetes–associated DNA methylation variable positions that precede disease diagnosis. *PLoS Genetics*, 7(9), e1002300. doi:10.1371/journal.pgen.1002300.

Robinson, L.E. & Reeves, S. (2013). *Review of sIgA's Major Role as a First Line of Immune Defense and New Indications Regarding Inflammation and But Health*. Retrieved from http://www.embriahealth.com.

Schachter, S.C. (2006). *Nutritional Deficiencies*. Retrieved from http://www.epilepsy.com/epilepsy/provoke_nutrition.

Schaffer, J.E. (2003). *Lipotoxicity: When tissues overeat*. Current Opinion in Lipidology, 14, 281–287.

Straus, M. (2012). How prebiotics improve your dog's digestion and nutrient absorption: Special ingredients support the friendly bacteria that aid digestive health. *Whole Dog Journal*. Retrieved from http://www.whole-dog-journal.com/issues/15_4/features/Prebiotics-and-Canine-Digestive-Health_20496-1.html.

Smith, L. (2009). *Canine Liver Disease Foundation*. Retrieved from http://canine-liverdiseasefoundation.org/?cat=5.

Stafstrom, C.E. (2004). Dietary approaches to epilepsy treatment: Old and new options on the menu. *Epilepsy Currents*, 4(6), 215–222. doi: 10.1111/j.1535-7597.2004.46001.x.

Swanson, K.S., Grieshop, C.M., Flickinger, E.A., Bauer, L.L., Healy, H.P., Dawson, K.A.,…Fahey Jr., G.C. (2002). Supplemental fructooligosaccharides and mannonoligosaccharides influence immune function, ileal and total tract nutrient digestibilities, microbial populations and concentrations of protein catabolites in the large bowel of dogs. *Journal of Nutrition*, 132(5), 980-989.

Swanson, K.S. (2007). *Using Nutritional Genomics to Study Canine Obesity and Diabetes*. Retrieved from http://en.engormix.com.

Thomas, W.B. (2011). *Does the Ketogenic Diet Work for Dogs?* Retrieved from http://www.canine-epilepsy.com/KetogenicDiet.html.

University of Liverpool. (2012). Obese dogs at risk of health condition experienced by humans. *ScienceDaily*. Retrieved from http://www.sciencedaily.com/releases/2012/10/121031111419.htm.

Vadiraja, B.B., Gaikwad, N.W. & Madyastha, K.M. (1998). Hepatoprotective effect of C-phycocyanin: Protection for carbon tetrachloride and R-(/)-Pulegone-Mediated hepatotoxicty in rats. *Biochemical and Biophysical Research Communications*, 249, 428–431.

VetInfo. (2012). *Fatty Liver Disease in Dogs*. Retrieved from http://www.vetinfo.com/fatty-liver-disease-in-dogs.html#b.

Wahba, I.M. & Mak, R.H. (2007). Obesity and obesity-initiated metabolic syndrome: Mechanistic links to chronic kidney disease. *Clinical Journal of the American Society of Nephrology*, 2, 550-562. doi: 10.2215/CJN.04071206.

Walker, A.K. (2013, July 24). Obesity can lead to liver disease. *The Baltimore Sun*. Retrieved from http://www.baltimoresun.com/.

Weil, A. (2013). *Condition Care Guide: Diarrhea*. Retrieved from http://www.drweil.com/drw/u/ART00344/diarrhea.html.

Wilson, L. (2013). *Epilepsy and Seizures*. Retrieved from http://drlwilson.com/Articles/epilepsy.htm.

Wong, M. (2013, December 4). [Personal correspondence].

Woodruff Health Sciences. (2012). *Immune System Compensates for 'Leaky Gut' in IBD Susceptibility*. Retrieved from http://news.emory.edu/stories/2012/09/immune_system_compensates_for_leaky_gut/index.html.

Yamka, R.M., Harmon, D.L., Schoenherr, W.D., Khoo, C., Gross, K.L., Davidson, S.J. & Joshi, D.K. (2006). In vivo measurement of flatulence and nutrient digestibility in dogs fed poultry by-product meal, conventional soybean meal and low-oligosaccharide low-phytate soybean meal. *American Journal of Veterinary Research*, 67, 88-94.

Yuen, A.W., Sander, J.W., Fluegel, D., Patsalos, P.N., Bell, G.S., Johnson, T. & Koepp, M.J. (2005). Omega-3 fatty acid supplementation in patients with chronic epilepsy: A randomized trial. *Epilepsy Behavior*, 7(2), 253-8.

Chapter 12

Beloshapka, A.N., Duclos, L.M., Vester Boler, B.M. & Swanson, K.S. (2012). Effects of inulin or yeast cell-wall extract on nutrient digestibility, fecal fermentative end-product concentrations, and blood metabolite concentrations in adult dogs fed raw meat-based diets. *American Journal of Veterinary Research*, 73(7), 1016-1023.

Case, L.P., Daristotle, L., Hayek, M. & Rausch, M.F. (2011). *Canine and Feline Nutrition: A Resource for Companion Animal Professionals*. (3rd ed.). Maryland Heights, MO: Mosby Elsevier.

Finley, R., Ribble, C., Aramini, J., Vandermeer, J., Popa, M., Litman, M. & Reid-Smith, R. (2007). The risk of salmonellae shedding by dogs fed Salmonella-contaminated commercial raw food diets. *Canadian Veterinary Journal*, 48(1), 69-75.

Hand, M.S., Thatcher, C., Remillard, R.I, Roudebush, P. & Lewis, L.D. (2000). *Small Animal Clinical Nutrition* (4th ed.). Topeka, KS: MMI.

Harris, T. (2002). *How Freeze-drying Works*. Retrieved from http://science.howstuffworks.com/innovation/edible-innovations/freeze-drying.htm.

Kerns, N. (2014). Dried and true: Meat-rich dehydrated and freeze-dried dog foods have a lot to offer, especially to health-challenged and performance dogs. *Whole Dog Journal*, September, 3-9.

Morse, E.V. & Duncan, M.A. (1975). Canine salmonellosis: Prevalence, epizootiology, signs, and public health significance. *Journal of the American Veterinary Medical Association*, 167(9), 817-820.

Olson, L. (2010, June). *Is a raw diet dangerous?* [Newsletter]. Retrieved from http://www.b-naturals.com/newsletter/is-a-raw-diet-dangerous/.

Straus, M. (2013). Dishing on diets: Veterinary nutritionists conclude that only they can properly formulate a homemade diet. *Whole Dog Journal*, 16 (9), 3-5.

Vojdani, A. (2009). Detection of IgE, IgG, IgA and IgM antibodies against raw and processed food antigens. *Nutrition and Metabolism*, 6, 22-37.

Appendix A

Chapter 1

Back Yard Beekeepers Association. (n.d.). *Facts about Honeybees*. Retrieved from http://www.backyardbeekeepers.com/facts.html.

Choi, S.W. & Friso, S. (2010). Epigenetics: A new bridge between nutrition and health. *Advances in Nutrition*, 1, 8-16. doi: 10.3945/ an.110.1004.

Esteller, M. (2008). Epigenetics in cancer. *New England Journal of Medicine*, 358, 1148-1159. doi: 10.1056/NEJMra072067.

Hardy, T.M. & Tollefsbol, T.O. (2011). Epigenetic diet: Impact on the epigenome and cancer. *Epigenomics*, 3(4), 503-518. doi:10.2217/epi.11.71.

Perricone, N. (2012). *How Chronic Cellular Inflammation Ages Skin* [Web log post]. Retrieved from http://blog.perriconemd.com/how-chronic-cellular-inflammation-ages-skin.

Punchard, N.A., Whelan, C.J. & Adcock, I. (2004, September 27). The Journal of Inflammation. *Journal of Inflammation*, 1(1):1.

Puotinen, C.J. (2007). Bee products have a special meaning for dogs. *Whole Dog Journal*. Retrieved from http://www.whole-dog-journal.com/issues/10_9/features/Bee-Honey-Products-Help-Canines_15967-1.html.

Sample, I. (2009, October 14). Scientists decode human genome's instruction manual. *The Guardian*. Retrieved from http://www.guardian.co.uk.

The University of Utah. (2014). *Epigenetics*. Retrieved from http://learn.genetics.utah.edu/content/epigenetics/.

Chapter 2

United States Department of Agriculture (USDA) (2014). *National Organic Program*. Retrieved from http://www.ams.usda.gov/AMSv1.0/nop.

Chapter 3

Charles, D. (2014, January 8). This GMO apple won't brown: Will that sour the fruit's image?. *The Salt*. Retrieved from http://www.npr.org/blogs/the-salt/2014/01/08/260782518/this-gmo-apple-wont-brown-will-that-sour-the-fruits-image.

Environmental Working Group. (2013, March). *We have the Right to Know about Our Food*. Retrieved from http://static.ewg.org/reports/2012/gmolandingpage/pdfs/we_have_the_right%20to_know.pdf.

Helferich, W.G., Andrade, J.E. & Hoagland, M.S. (2008). Phytoestrogens and breast cancer: A complex story. *Inflammopharmacology*, 16(5), 219-26. doi: 10.1007/s10787-008-8020-0.

Ji, S. (2013). *Glyphosate (Roundup) Carcinogenic in the Parts per Trillion Range*. Retrieved from http://www.greenmedinfo.com/blog/breaking-glyphosate-roundup-carcinogenic-parts-trillion-range?utm_source=www.GreenMedInfo.com&utm_campaign=e624913b6e-Greenmedinfo&utm_medium=email&utm_term=0_193c8492fb-e624913b6e-86768346.

Kerns, N. (2012). Canned controversy: Consumers are demanding BPA-free cans, but industry isn't ready with an alternative. *Whole Dog Journal*, 15(5), 4-5.

The University of Utah. (2014). *Epigenetics*. Retrieved from http://learn.genetics. utah.edu/content/epigenetics/.

Thongprakaisang, S., Thiantanawat, A., Rangkadilok, N., Suriyo, T., & Satayavivad, J. (2013). Glyphosate induces human breast cancer cells growth via estrogen receptors. *Food and Chemical Toxicology*, 59, 129-36. doi:pii: S0278-6915(13)00363-3.

Chapter 6

National Human Genome Research Institute (NHGRI). (2014). Retrieved from https://www.genome.gov.

Chapter 7

Demerath, E.W., Guan, W., Pankow, J.S., Grove, M.L., North, K.E., Fornage, M., … Boerwinkle, E.A. (2013). Genome-wide methylation study of body mass index (BMI) in African American adults: preliminary data from the ARIC study. *Circulation*, 127, A052.

Endocrine Today. (2011). Fat linked to DNA methylation may help explain obesity-related diseases. *Endocrine Today*. Retrieved from http://www.healio.com/ endocrinology/obesity/news/print/endocrine-today/%7Bf0484521-8015-4f71-a5dd-383d0236a57d%7D/fat-linked-to-dna-methylation-may-help-explain-obesity-related-diseases.

Fiore, K. (2013). *Obesity Tied to DNA Regulation*. Retrieved from http://www.med-pagetoday.com/Genetics/GeneralGenetics/38082.

Franks, P.W. & Ling, C. (2010). Epigenetics and obesity: The devil is in the details. *BMC Medicine*, 8, 88. doi:10.1186/1741-7015-8-88.

Medical College of Georgia at Georgia Regents University. (2013, March 21). Scientists identify gene that is consistently altered in obese individuals. *ScienceDaily*. Retrieved from http://www.sciencedaily.com /releases/2013/03/130321133114.htm.

Chapter 8

Calder, P.C. (2006). N–3 polyunsaturated fatty acids, inflammation, and inflammatory diseases. *American Journal of Clinical Nutrition*, 83(6), S1505-S1519.

Laflamme, D.P. (2004). Osteoarthritis and diet: Joined at the hip. *Nestle Purina Clinical Edge*, 10-12.

Laflamme, D.P. (2012). Nutritional care for aging cats and dogs. *Veterinary Clinics of North America: Small Animal Practice*, 42(4), 769-791.

Middleton, R.P. & Hannah, S.S. (2010). Osteoarthritis and its origins: Disease development at the cellular and molecular level. *Nestle Purina Clinical Edge*, 6-9.

Primus Pharmaceuticals. (2013). *Metabolic Processes of OA*. Retrieved from http://www.limbrel.com/hcp-metabolic-processes.php.

Roush, J.K., Dodd, C.E., Fritsch, D.A., Allen, T.A., Jewell, D.E., Schoenherr, W.D.,… Hahn, K.A. (2010). A multi-center veterinary practice assessment of the effects of omega-3 fatty acids on osteoarthritis in dogs. *Journal of the American Veterinary Medical Association*, 236(1), 59-66.

Waldron, M. (2004). The role of fatty acids on the management of osteoarthritis. *Nestle Purina Clinical Edge*, 14-16.

Chapter 9

Liu, Y., Xu, L., Cheng, N., Lin, L. & Zhang, C. (2000). Inhibitory effect of phycocyanin from Spirulina platensis on the growth of human leukemia K562 cells. Journal of Applied. *Phycology*, 12, 125-130.

Messonnier, S. (2006). *The Natural Vet's Guide to Preventing and Treating Cancer in Dogs*. Novato, CA: New World Library.

Romay, C.H., González, R., Ledón, N., Remirez, D. & Rimbau, V. (2003). C-phycocyanin: A biliprotein with antioxidant, anti-inflammatory and neuroprotective effects. *Current Protein and Peptide Science*, 4(3), 207-216.

University of Maryland Medical Center. (2011). *Spirulina—Overview*. Retrieved from http://www.umm.edu/altmed/articles/spirulina-000327.htm.

Wolf, D. (2009). *Superfoods: The Food and Medicine of the Future*. Berkeley, CA: North Atlantic Books.

Appendix B

Fascetti, A.J. & Delaney, S.G. (2012). *Applied Veterinary Clinical Nutrition*. West Sussex, United Kingdom: Wiley Blackwell.

Segal, M. (2008). *Deciphering Dog Food Labels: A Guide to Buying a Better Commercial Food*. Retrieved from www.monicasegal.com.

U.S. Food and Drug Administration. (2010). *Pet Food Labels—General*. Retrieved from http://www.fda.gov/animalveterinary/resourcesforyou/ucm047113.htm.

About the Authors

Dr. W. Jean Dodds

Dr. W. Jean Dodds received the D.V.M. degree with honors in 1964 from the Ontario Veterinary College, University of Toronto. In 1965, she accepted a position with the New York State Health Department in Albany and began comparative studies of animals with inherited and acquired bleeding diseases. Her position there began as a Research Scientist and culminated as Chief, Laboratory of Hematology, Wadsworth Center.

Author W. Jean Dodds, DVM with Issho.

In 1980, Jean also became Executive Director, New York State Council on Human Blood and Transfusion Services. This work continued full-time until 1986, when she moved to Southern California to establish Hemopet, the first nonprofit national blood bank program for animals.

From 1965 to 1986, Jean was a member of many national and international committees on hematology, animal models of human disease, veterinary medicine and laboratory animal science. Dr. Dodds was a grantee of the National Heart, Lung and Blood Institute (NIH) and has more than 150 research publications.

Jean was formerly President of the Scientist's Center for Animal Welfare, Chairman of the Committee on Veterinary Medical Sciences and Vice-Chairman of the Institute of Laboratory Animal Resources, National Academy of Sciences. In 1974, Dr. Dodds was selected as Outstanding Woman Veterinarian of the Year, AVMA Annual Meeting, Denver, Colorado; in 1977 received the Region I Award for Outstanding Service to the Veterinary Profession from the American Animal Hospital Association, Cherry

Hill, New Jersey; in 1978 and 1990 received the Gaines Fido Award as Dogdom's Woman of the Year; and the Award of Merit in 1978 in Recognition of Special Contributions to the Veterinary Profession from the American Animal Hospital Association, Salt Lake City, Utah.

In 1984, Jean was awarded the Centennial Medal from the University of Pennsylvania School of Veterinary Medicine. She was elected a distinguished Practitioner of the National Academy of Practice in Veterinary Medicine in 1987. In 1994, she was given the Holistic Veterinarian of the Year Award from the American Holistic Veterinary Medical Association. She was the editor of *Advances in Veterinary Science and Comparative Medicine* for Academic Press and is an active member of numerous professional societies. She was a member of the National Research Council/BANR Committee on National Needs for Research in Veterinary Science, which released its report in July 2005. She is an inventor and holds numerous patents. She and her husband, Charles Berman, a patent attorney, live in Santa Monica, California.

Dr. Dodds' book, *The Canine Thyroid Epidemic: Answers You Need for Your Dog* (co-authored with Diana R. Laverdure) (Dogwise Publishing, 2011), received the Eukanuba Canine Health Award and the Maxwell Medallion for Best Care/Health Book of 2011 from the Dogwriters Association of America.

Hemopet commenced operations in 1986 and its range of nonprofit services and educational activities include:

- Providing canine blood components, blood bank supplies and related services.
- Adopting retired Greyhound blood donors and companions through Pet Life-Line.
- Contributing to the social needs of the less fortunate in our society by volunteer and interactive programs with the Greyhounds.
- Consulting in clinical pathology through Hemopet/Hemolife, teaching animal health care professionals, companion animal fanciers and pet owners on hematology and blood banking, immunology, endocrinology, nutrition and holistic medicine nationwide and overseas.

Diana R. Laverdure, MS (2015)

Diana R. Laverdure, MS (2015) is an award-winning canine health writer, a nationally recognized expert on dog health and a pet nutrition consultant. She received a Bachelor of Arts degree *magna cum laude* in 1987 from Tufts University in Medford, Massachusetts and a Master of Animal Science degree (2015) from Charles Sturt University in Australia. She has authored more than one hundred articles on dog

Author Diana Laverdure with Chase.

health, which appear in a variety of top national dog magazines, on her award-winning Web site, The Happy Dog Spot (www.the-happy-dog-spot.com) and on her pet nutrition blog, Pet Food Diva (www.petfooddiva.com). Her articles have been nominated for numerous awards from the Dog Writers Association of America (DWAA) and her book, *The Canine Thyroid Epidemic: Answers You Need for Your Dog* (co-authored with Dr. W. Jean Dodds) (Dogwise Publishing, 2011), received the Eukanuba Canine Health Award and the DWAA Maxwell Medallion for Best Care/Health Book of 2011.

Diana strongly believes, as reflected in this book, that many of the chronic health issues suffered by dogs (and cats) today are a result of inappropriate diet and lifestyle choices. As a pet nutrition consultant through her company, Pet Food Diva (www. petfooddiva.com), she provides pet parents with customized nutrition information and individually formulated diets to optimize the health and longevity of their beloved animal companions.

Diana is a staunch advocate of animal rescue and supporter of many rescue organizations serving a wide variety of abused and neglected species. She is blessed by her beloved rescued Belgian Shepherd mix, Chase (14 years old at the time of this writing), who propelled her along her journey of healing and preventing companion animal health issues more than a decade ago. She is also blessed to share her life and home in Delray Beach, Florida, with Dr. Rodney Dunetz, an Acupuncture Physician and Doctor of Oriental Medicine who shares her passion for creating optimum health for people, animals and the planet through compassionate and sustainable living.

Index

Dogwise.com is your source for quality books, ebooks, DVDs, training tools and treats.

We've been selling to the dog fancier for more than 25 years and we carefully screen our products for quality information, safety, durability and FUN! You'll find something for every level of dog enthusiast on our website www.dogwise.com or drop by our store in Wenatchee, Washington.